# The New Managerial Grid®

# The New

Gulf Publishing Company
Book Division
Houston, Texas

# Managerial Grid ®

**Strategic new insights
into a proven system for
increasing organization
productivity and individual
effectiveness—plus a revealing
examination of how your
managerial style
can affect
your mental and
physical health.**

## Robert R. Blake
## Jane Srygley Mouton

# The New Managerial Grid®

Library of Congress
Catalog Card Number 77-84465
ISBN 0-87201-473-8

*Book design by Moira Jon Young*

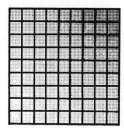 **Preface**

Next to our having clear, purposeful, and human goals that stimulate mutual trust and respect, increasing managerial effectiveness is probably the single most important factor in the improvement of society. Without managerial competence, we stand as victims of the status quo, bureaucracy, and decay. With it there are limitless possibilities of change and development for the strengthening and enrichment of human lives.

Over the past twenty years the Grid and Grid organization development have provided a basic behavioral science framework for thinking, analyzing, sensing, feeling, and reaching toward these possibilities. The value of this formulation is attested to by the close to one million copies of *The Managerial Grid* in print.

Writing this second edition has provided us an opportunity to reexamine and to evaluate the original Grid in the light of twenty-five years experience with it and in comparison with the many variations that have appeared since the original was published.

Changes in this edition are of three kinds. One involves deepening the concepts and skills of personal effectiveness and how to use them in daily management. The second reflects the developments of the past fifteen years in terms of where Grid styles come from. We can now specify with reasonable accuracy the conditions of child rearing that prompt one person to embrace one Grid orientation and another person to approach management from a very different position. These were discussed in the first edition but only briefly.

The third change is concerned with, "so what?" Does it make any difference what Grid style is used to gain production through people? There are three answers, all "Yes." One is with regard to profitability. The 9,9 Grid style is positively correlated with bottom line profitability. A second is in connection with the degree of career success managers experience as a function of Grid style. 9,9-oriented managers enjoy maximum career success. The third answer to the "so what?" question is from a personal health standpoint—the mental and physical health or illness correlates of various extreme Grid styles. We now know the Grid-illness correlations for heart attacks, asthma, ulcers, cancer, and so on in some detail. With knowledge of these correlations between Grid styles and psychosomatic consequences, the stage is set for a major forward movement in mental and physical health.

The preparation of this edition has been the occasion of much joy and gratification. The evidence from this era tells us that the Grid is a sound and basic framework for bringing about a needed integration of thoughts with feelings, aspirations with actions, dreams with realities. Rather than living with the status quo situation, we can change it. Rather than rearing children who are distorted, twisted, or driven, we can bring them up to be open, full, compassionate, and caring adults. Rather than making ourselves ill, we can make ourselves healthy, happy, fulfilled, and contributing.

We adopted one convention and constantly refer to boss, subordinate, colleague, and to him, rather than consistently repeating *he* or *she*, *him* or *her*. Suffice it to say that the book is an outcome of a him/her collaboration of twenty-five years and the reader will recognize that in the text his also means her and that he also means she.

The references are at the end of the book and are grouped by chapter, with the chapter page and line number in the text to which each reference relates. To follow up on some point made, say, on page 14 of Chapter 3, turn to the reference section for Chapter 3 and check the references listed there for page 14.

Robert R. Blake
Jane Srygley Mouton

January 1, 1978

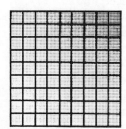

# Contents

## Chapter 1

## Chapter 2

## Chapter 3

## Chapter 4

# Chapter 5

# Chapter 6

# Chapter 7

# Chapter 8

# Chapter 9

# Chapter 10

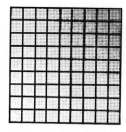

# Assessing Your Own Managerial Style

Open and candid communication is the link between people that permits sound problem solving and decision making. Without them an organization is unlikely to succeed. With them it is able to maximize its use of human resources. The Grid concentrates on what makes person-to-person communication ineffective, what makes it effective, and what to do to change ineffective into effective communication.

## Determining <u>Your</u> Managerial Style

You may find it valuable to assess communications in your own managerial behavior. Rank the paragraphs that follow from most to least typical as a description of your behavior; 5 is most typical, 4 is next most typical, and so on to 1, which is least typical. When you finish ranking the paragraphs, there should be only one of each number from 5 to 1. There can be no ties. Before starting, a word of caution: self-deception is likely to occur when you pick your answers. The deception is caused by the tendency of people to confuse the way they *want* to manage with the way they *do* manage.

How big is the self-deception problem? One indication is that forty-five percent of managers change their self-descriptions when they compare the way they see themselves after completing a one-week Managerial Grid Seminar with how they saw themselves beforehand. These changes will be discussed in Chapter 14.

The first step in accurate self-assessment is to strip away self-deception in order to see your underlying assumptions. Some self-deception is probably unavoidable although it can be reduced by selecting answers based on your *actual* performance as a manager. This is a starting point for improving your managerial effectiveness.

——— A. I accept the decisions of others with indifference. I avoid taking sides by not revealing opinions, attitudes, and ideas. When conflict arises, I try to remain neutral. By remaining uninvolved I rarely get stirred up. My humor is seen as rather pointless. I put out enough to get by.

_____ B. I support decisions which promote good relations. I embrace opinions, attitudes, and ideas of others rather than to push my own. I avoid generating conflict; but, when it does appear, I try to soothe feelings to keep people together. Because of the disapproval tensions can produce, I react in a warm and friendly way. My humor shifts attention away from the serious side. I prefer to support others rather than initiate action.

_____ C. I search for workable, even though not perfect, decisions. When others hold ideas, opinions, or attitudes different from my own, I try to meet them halfway. When conflict arises, I try to find fair solutions that accommodate others. Under tension I feel unsure and anxious about how to meet others' expectations. My humor sells me or my position. I seek to maintain a steady pace.

_____ D. I expect decisions I make to be treated as final. I stand up for my ideas, opinions, and attitudes, even though it sometimes results in stepping on toes. When conflict arises, I try to cut it off or win my position. When things are not going right, I defend, resist, and come back with counter-arguments. My humor is hard-hitting. I drive myself and others.

_____ E. I place high value on sound, creative decisions that result in understanding and agreement. I listen for and seek out ideas, opinions, and attitudes different from my own. I have strong convictions but respond to sounder ideas than my own by changing my mind. When conflict arises, I try to identify reasons for it and seek to resolve underlying causes. When aroused, I contain myself even though my impatience is visible. My humor fits the situation and gives perspective; I retain a sense of humor even under pressure. I exert vigorous effort and others join in.

### Choosing the Elements That Fit You Best

Consider all of the "1" element statements (i.e., A1, B1, C1, D1, and E1) and circle the *one* which best describes your behavior. Follow the same procedure for the "2," "3," "4," "5," and "6" elements.

### Element 1: Decisions

A1. I accept the decisions of others with indifference.
B1. I support decisions which promote good relations.
C1. I search for workable, even though not perfect, decisions.
D1. I expect decisions I make to be treated as final.
E1. I place high value on sound creative decisions that result in understanding and agreement.

## Element 2: Convictions

A2. I avoid taking sides by not revealing opinions, attitudes, and ideas.

B2. I embrace opinions, attitudes, and ideas of others rather than to push my own.

C2. When others hold ideas, opinions, or attitudes different from my own, I try to meet them halfway.

D2. I stand up for my ideas, opinions, and attitudes, even though it sometimes results in stepping on toes.

E2. I listen for and seek out ideas, opinions, and attitudes different from my own. I have strong convictions but respond to ideas sounder than my own by changing my mind.

## Element 3: Conflict

A3. When conflict arises, I try to remain neutral.

B3. I avoid generating conflict; but, when it does appear, I try to soothe feelings to keep people together.

C3. When conflict arises, I try to find fair solutions that accommodate others.

D3. When conflict arises, I try to cut it off or win my position.

E3. When conflict arises, I try to identify reasons for it and seek to resolve underlying causes.

## Element 4: Temper

A4. By remaining uninvolved I rarely get stirred up.

B4. Because of the disapproval tensions can produce, I react in a warm and friendly way.

C4. Under tension I feel unsure and anxious about how to meet others' expectations.

D4. When things are not going right, I defend, resist, and come back with counterarguments.

E4. When aroused, I contain myself even though my impatience is visible.

## Element 5: Humor

A5. My humor is seen as rather pointless.

B5. My humor shifts attention away from the serious side.

C5. My humor sells me or my position.

D5. My humor is hard-hitting.

E5. My humor fits the situation and gives perspective; I retain a sense of humor even under pressure.

**Element 6: Effort**

A6. I put out enough to get by.
B6. I prefer to support others rather than initiate action.
C6. I seek to maintain a steady pace.
D6. I drive myself and others.
E6. I exert vigorous effort and others join in.

We will return to these rankings after reading the next several chapters. Chapter 14 helps you to interpret the rankings you have just completed and to evaluate their implications for your managerial effectiveness. This can aid your understanding of your own assumptions and why others react to you as they do. Also, it can help you to identify alternative ways of managing to gain greater success while simultaneously deepening your sense of satisfaction from work.

## Assumptions Guide Behavior

Whenever a manager approaches a situation, he is not acting according to the objective reality but according to his subjective appraisal of it. The two may be far apart or quite close together. The rankings you have just completed indicate that there are individual differences between managers in the way they approach problems and these differences make each work situation distinctive. However, there are several common themes or sets of assumptions beneath these individual differences. The assumptions one acts on may or may not be based on what have been repeatedly and objectively demonstrated to be sound. Either way, they may have become part of a manager's beliefs or attitudes. Everyone tends to respond to circumstances in the light of his assumptions since these assumptions control our view of our experience. They constitute our personal theory of behavior. They guide our behavior. We act on the premise that assumption $a$ will result in $b$.

For example, a manager who assumes that people are lazy observes several people slacking off. This confirms his theory, so he takes action to push the slackers. They resent it and slow down. The manager's assumption is verified again, and he pushes harder on both the lazy ones and the others as well. A slow-down or sit-down protest confirms his belief that people will do anything to get out of work. The manager never thinks that his assumption $a$, that "people are lazy," may have caused the sit-down process, $b$.

There are many examples of the ways that assumptions control behavior. In different cultures assumptions about illness range from its treatment by magic to cure through scientific medicine. Some cultures operate on the rarely challenged assumption that communism is the one best way to organize the activities of an entire people. The belief in others is that constitutional democracy or limited monarchy is the one best way. Other examples relate to marriage. It is generally held in the western world that monogamy is the ideal way to organize marriage and family life. Some societies favor polygamy, sometimes with the number of wives limited to four. The assumptions held in one culture may be shared by all its members but appear foreign and unreasonable to outsiders. The point is that the assumptions organize our relationships and ways of doing business.

If an assumption we make is also being made by those around us, for all practical purposes it becomes an article of faith, taking on the status of an "absolute." It becomes the basis for action without question or exception. Other possible assumptions are either completely ignored or are tested for validity against the "absolute"; in this way the absolute eliminates courses of action which are inconsistent with it.

Assumptions are formed in childhood through a variety of experiences at home with parents, brothers, and sisters, in school with teachers, in the neighborhood with playmates, and from less personal sources: TV, radio, films, and so on. Not all of these experiences are equally important in forming an individual's dominant assumptions. Parents are probably most important. Brothers and sisters also rate high, then come teachers and other adults.

## Assumptions Can be Changed

How do you change your assumptions if they are so important in controlling your behavior? A first step is to become aware of the assumptions you hold and act on as you work with and through other people.

Sometimes people become dramatically aware of which assumptions control their behavior. We hear people explaining why they did something by saying, "I made the assumption that . . ." or ". . . that assumption didn't pan out." Far more often the assumptions that underlie our conduct are embedded within us but are outside of our awareness. As a result we are sometimes as blind about why we do things as others are baffled in trying to explain our actions from their vantage point. Without new experiences that challenge our assumptions, we could not identify them even if we wanted to. With new experiences and feedback from others as to what assumptions they see behind our actions, change becomes possible. When we become aware of the depth and character of our assumptions, we can analyze them and identify the good and bad consequences of actions based on them. We can consider alternative assumptions that may provide a sounder basis for our actions and practice applying them as we work with other people until they become characteristic of us. A person can change.

### What Are Sound Behavior Assumptions?

It is important to learn the variety of assumptions managers operate on in order to see which ones square with principles of human motivations. The Grid helps you do this. Then you can decide whether the ones that do would better guide your own managerial behavior than the ones you may be operating on now.

The behavioral sciences have helped identify the assumptions that are likely to be most productive and rewarding as the basis for working with and through others and to create the best mental and physical health for those who follow them.

After the assumptions underlying each Grid theory have been learned, we can then answer the question as to which of these theories of management is most closely related to

1. Sound behavioral science principles
2. Positive mental and physical health
3. High quality and quantity of production
4. Strengthened corporate profitability
5. Heightened satisfaction from work

### Summary

The Managerial Grid is useful for helping people identify the assumptions they make as they work with and through others. By using managerial theories to identify one's own assumptions, a person is able to see himself and others more objectively, to communicate with them more clearly, to understand where their differences come from, to see how to change themselves, and to help others toward more productive and rewarding experiences. The more skilled a person becomes in using a sound theory, the more capable he is of reducing frustration, resentment, antagonism, anger, fear, hurt, apathy, indifference, anxiety, and uncertainty and the less likely he is to retaliate, humiliate, to be cruel, or to lie in his effort to manage others. He can shift from these unhappy emotions toward enthusiasm, dedication, and mature responsibility and can enjoy a sense of personal contribution and the rewards of personal fulfillment, which are made possible by excellent managing.

Learning Grid management not only makes people aware of the assumptions under which they operate but also helps them to learn and to embrace scientifically verified principles for effectiveness in production under circumstances that promote mentally healthy behavior.

The next several chapters introduce five sets of managerial theories. The chapters thereafter trace out implications of the 9,9 theory for strengthening individual and corporate effectiveness.

# Chapter 2

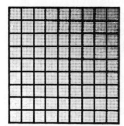

# How Managers Think

To see management in full perspective, it is necessary to examine *what* is being managed. Since management takes place within an organization, attention must be turned first to what organization *is*. Then it will be possible to concentrate on examining the problems and possibilities involved in improving competence in managing it.

## Organization Universals

Several characteristics of organizations seem to be *universal*. They are present, in some degree, regardless of the specific purpose, mission, or line of work of the organization. Effective management of these universals is the condition of efficient production through sound organization.

## Purpose(s)

The first universal is *purpose(s)*. Try to imagine a purposeless organization. Can you picture to yourself an organization that lacks purpose?

Those who have attempted to do so have been unable to identify an organization that does not have a purpose. Admittedly, it is not always easy to identify *what* it is. Furthermore, the purpose for which the organization exists may, or may not, be the same as the one people experience as the basis for joining or remaining in it.

Although more or less specific purposes can be stated for educational, governmental, hospital, military, political, religious and family organizations, it is somewhat easier to describe the purpose of industrial organizations. Organization purpose is expressed in terms of profit. The direct P/L (profit-loss) evaluation of human effort, particularly in government organizations, is not too common. Though P/L statements frequently are unavailable in such institutions, the organization's intention is consistent with profit motivation, that is, to supply service(s) of a given character at the minimum expense. Therefore, for this discussion, the equivalent of profit, that is, the production of *things or services*, will be regarded as the production aim of all organizations—that is, those activities in which people engage toward organization purpose.

For the moment then, production can be accepted as an indication of organization purpose(s). It is to be regarded as a universal of organizations.

## People

Another characteristic of organization is *people*. No organization is without them. It might be said that it would be desirable to eliminate people. Indeed, in some instances it seems wiser to replace people with technological procedures and automated processes, so that human energy is not being wasted in doing work that machine systems can do as well, or even better. But, if a peopleless arrangement were possible to achieve, it is unlikely that the word *organization* would be used to describe it. Other language has already been developed to picture machine operations of production that can be manned by one acting alone. The phrase *automated factory* depicts peopleless operations where organization, as we know it, has been eliminated.

Organization purpose, then, cannot be achieved without people, nor does it exist under circumstances where one person is acting alone. To achieve it, others need to be drawn in. Needing more than one person to achieve a production result is what leads to the condition of organization.

## Power

Power is a third attribute. Some people are bosses. Others are bossed. Some have more power than others. That is the dimension of hierarchy.

The process of achieving organization purpose (the first universal) through the efforts of several people (the second universal) results in some people attaining authority to manage others; that is, to exercise the responsibility for planning, controlling, and directing the activities of others through a hierarchical arrangement (the third universal).

While every organization has a power hierarchy and while many organizations have job descriptions that depict an individual's responsibility under his hierarchical position, the problem of boss-subordinate relations is far more complex than can possibly be pictured by a job description. The foundation for understanding management is in recognizing that a boss's actions are dictated by certain *assumptions* he makes regarding how to manage.

Sometimes management is applied dramatically, as in the case of a boss telling others what he expects of them in no uncertain terms. It also is possible that a person may not act like a boss. For instance he may not hold tight rein on subordinates. In those situations, then, people may not recognize that they are being bossed at all; they have little or no feeling that influence is being exerted on them. Yet the fact is that organizations, by necessity, are hierarchical. No matter how it is utilized, power is seen to be an essential condition of organization.

Other universals of organization play an additional part in understanding managerial behavior. They are not introduced at this time, but one of them, organizational culture and its significance for managerial behavior, is discussed in Chapter 13.

### The Grid

The way the three concerns mesh is represented graphically as the Grid. Production, getting results, is one concern in your mind. A second is for people—your subordinates and colleagues as distinctive individuals. The third is concern for how you use hierarchy to achieve production with and through people. "Concern for" is not a specific term which indicates the amount of actual production or actual behavior toward people. Rather, it indicates the character and strength of assumptions present behind any given managerial style.

#### Concern for Production

Concern for *production, results, bottom line,* or *profits,* for example, may be represented by a key executive's finding new directions for the growth and development of the organization through acquisitions or by launching or expanding innovative research and development. It may be revealed in the scope and quality of policy decisions, the number of creative ideas product development converts into salable items, accounts processed in a collection period, or quality and thoroughness of services provided by a staff organization. Where work is physical, concern for production may take the form of efficiency measurements, work load, the number of units produced, the time required to attain a certain production schedule, or volume of sales. In a hospital, it may be patient load, number of diagnostic tests applied, or length of hospital stay. In a government agency, productivity may be mail delivery time, number of forms processed, or number of union-management conflicts in business brought to successful resolution through federal mediators. Results may be measured in a university by the number of students graduated, faculty, teaching load, research papers published, or graduates in any given year who complete advanced degrees at a later time.

Production, in other words, is whatever an organization hires people to accomplish.

## Concern for People

Since managers exercise leadership with and through people, the assumptions they make about people are important in determining managerial effectiveness. People are people regardless of the context in which the work takes place—industry, government, educational and medical institutions, or the home.

Concern for people is revealed in many different ways. Some managers' concerns are shown in their efforts to ensure that subordinates like them. Others are concerned that subordinates get their jobs done. Accountability for results based upon trust and obedience or sympathy, understanding, and support of another person facing adversity also reflect concern for people. Working conditions, salary structure, fringe benefits, job security, and so on are still other ways concern for people becomes evident. Depending upon the character of concern, subordinates may respond with enthusiasm or resentment, involvement or apathy, innovative or dull thinking, commitment or indifference, and eagerness or resistance to change.

## How These Concerns Interact

These two dimensions are pictured on the Grid in Figure 2-1 as nine-point scales. *1* represents minimum concern. *5* represents intermediate or an average amount of concern. *9* is maximum concern. The other numbers, *2* through *4* and *6* through *8* denote degrees of concern. These numbers signify steps between low and high just as the gauge in an automobile indicates the amount of gasoline from empty to full, rather than specific quantities.

The manner in which these two concerns are linked together by a specific manager defines his use of power. In addition, the character of *concern for* at different Grid positions differs, even though the *degree* may be the same. For example, when high concern for people is coupled with a low concern for production, the people concern expressed, that people be "happy," is far different from that when high concern for people is coupled with a high concern for production, that people be involved in the work and strive enthusiastically to contribute to organization purpose.

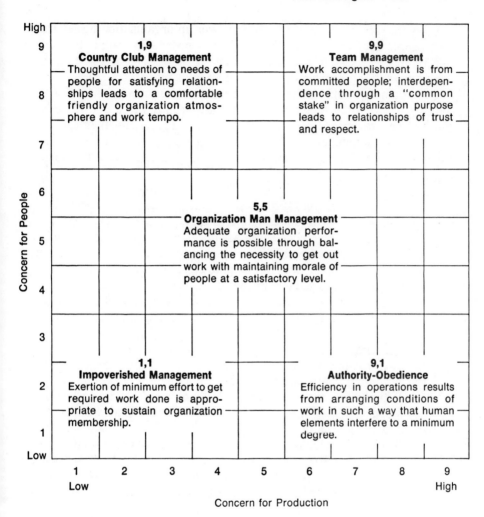

Figure 2-1. *The Managerial Grid* ®

Each theory can be seen as a set of assumptions for using power to link people into production. Each of the theories is found, to some degree, in every kind of organization. The various kinds of assumptions are universal and common throughout various cultures.

The important point is that when a manager confronts a situation in which work is to be accomplished through people, there is a range of alternative ways for him to go about managing. To increase his managerial competence he needs to know them and to be able to select the best course of action for any given situation among a number of possibilities.

*9,1.* In the lower right-hand corner of the Grid a maximum concern (9) for production is combined with a minimum concern (1) for people. A manager acting under these assumptions concentrates on maximizing production by exercising power and authority and achieving control over people through compliance. This is a 9,1 orientation.

*1,9.* The 1,9 leadership style is in the top left corner. Here a minimum concern (1) for production is coupled with a maximum concern (9) for people. Primary attention is placed on promoting good feelings among colleagues and subordinates.

*1,1.* A minimum concern for both production and people is represented by 1,1 in the lower left corner. The 1,1-oriented manager does only the minimum required to remain within the organization.

*5,5.* 5,5 is in the center. This is the "middle of the road" theory or the "go-along-to-get-along" assumptions which are revealed in conformity to the status quo.

*9,9.* Production and people concerns are integrated at a high level in the upper right-hand corner representing the 9,9 style of managing. This is the team approach. It is goal-oriented and seeks to gain results of high quantity and quality through participation, involvement, commitment, and conflict-solving.

**Other Grid Styles**

These five theories encompass the more important differences among managers. A number of additional managerial theories, such as paternalism, the two-hat approach, and so on, may be understood by reference to the Grid. Many mixtures may be pictured as intermediate degrees, such as 9,5 or 5,9, or 8,3, or 4,4. Most of the benefits to be gained from theories at intermediate locations do not seem worth the complexities involved in specifying their characteristics. However, combinations and mixtures of basic theories are described in Chapter 8.

### Factors that Determine Dominant Grid Style

Which managerial style is dominant for any given person in any particular situation is influenced by any one or several sets of conditions.

**Organization.** Managerial behavior frequently is determined by the organization in which the person is employed. When organization rules and requirements are so fixed or rigid as to permit only small variations between managers, the managerial style exhibited may reflect little of a man's personal assumptions and much of his organization beliefs about "the right way to manage."

**Situation.** The situation itself may be the determining or overriding factor dictating which set of managerial assumptions are employed to deal with it. Management of a crisis is likely to be different from management under routine circumstances.

**Values.** The choice of managerial assumption may be based on values or beliefs the manager holds regarding the way to treat people or the way to manage results. Any given set of assumptions can have a personal value attached to them which represents an individual's private conviction concerning the desirability of any managerial style as a dominant one.

**Personality.** The dominant managerial style may, to an important degree, result from deep-rooted personality characteristics which predispose an individual to prefer one approach over another.

**Chance.** A set of managerial assumptions may guide a person's behavior because he has not been confronted with, nor has he discovered in his own experience, that other sets of assumptions about how to manage are available. "Chance," so to speak, has not helped him learn.

It is unreasonable to expect that a Grid style will predict every single feature of managerial behavior for any given individual. Individuals are likely to be aware of their own dominant Grid style but also are able to recognize inconsistencies that do not precisely fit the assumptions of the dominant Grid style. What can be expected is explicit patterns of basic behavior for which the Grid style is an apt description.

### Dominant and Backup Styles

Granted that a manager's Grid style may be consistent over a range of situations, it is also true that managers move from one Grid style to another, sometimes even shifting and adapting Grid styles according to how that person views the situation. How can the concept of a dominant set of assumptions be reconciled with managerial styles that shift and change? One way is through the idea of dominant and backup styles. Not only do most managers have a dominant Grid style, they also have a backup style; sometimes even a third and fourth. A manager's backup style becomes apparent when it is difficult or impossible for him to apply his dominant Grid style. In other words, a backup style is the style a manager reverts to, particularly when under pressure, tension, strain, frustration, or in situations of conflict that cannot be solved in his characteristic way.

Relationships between dominant and backup styles can sometimes be quite easily seen in how parents deal with their children. First we try logic and reason in a 9,9 way, but it doesn't work. Then we get tough and possibly add a touch of ridicule, both 9,1 ways of trying to get the child's attention. Then, since we have created resentment and rejection, we switch over to love and kindness and hope that a 1,9 attitude will bring the child around. Finally, still unable to elicit cooperation, we either return to a 9,1 strategy of threats and punishments or throw our hands up in a 1,1 way and say, "To hell with it."

Any Grid style can be a backup to any other. For example, a 1,9-oriented manager prefers to yield and defer when challenged but may become stubborn and demanding in the manner of a 9,1-oriented manager when the pressure becomes too great. A leader who seeks control and mastery in a 9,1 way may meet continued resistance from subordinates, but when unable to find a way for getting them under control, may shift to a 9,9 teamwork basis of cooperative problem solving. This oscillation can also be observed when a manager works with subordinates in a 9,9 manner in everyday situations, but then switches to a 9,1 orientation when crises arise, taking over and operating without utilizing the resources of those who, in fact, may be best able to contribute to a resolution.

There appear to be few, if any, strong natural or preferred links between any one Grid style as dominant and any other as backup. This great array of dominant-backup combinations is what makes each manager such a unique individual. The point to be emphasized is that managerial styles are *not* fixed. They are not unchanging. They are subject to modification and change through formal instruction or self-training.

### Managerial Facades

Another consideration is that the pure theories—9,1, 1,9, 1,1, 5,5, and 9,9—share a common, basic attribute. They are all authentic. On the other hand, some managerial behavior is dishonest. It can be described as a *facade*. Whether done consciously or not, a managerial facade is a cover for deception, intrigue, trickery or to avoid letting the other person discover his true assumptions. There are facades which project each of the major Grid styles. These are identified, and their uses described as each Grid style is presented.

### Summary

The Grid provides a framework for understanding the assumptions managers make as they compete or cooperate with one another. In each Grid chapter that follows we indicate the positive motivations that a manager may strive for and the negative motivations he seeks to avoid. The consequences of each style in terms of subordinate reactions to them are examined. Numerous experiments also have shown significant correlations between Grid styles practiced throughout an organization, actual productivity achieved, and corporate profitability. These results are discussed in greater detail in Chapter 13.

Consequences for the mental and physical health of the manager himself also are examined. As will be seen, mental and physical health problems are correlated to extremes of a Grid style motivation.

Childhood origins of each Grid style provide a basis for understanding the dynamics of each Grid style.

"Is there one best Grid style or does it depend on the situation?" To answer this question, research on results relating leadership style to career development is discussed, analyzed, and evaluated. They show that " . . . there is one best way to lead." This issue is explored in depth in Chapter 9.

## Chapter 3

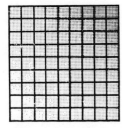

# 9,1

A 9,1-oriented manager strives to be powerful, to control, and to dominate. He is driven to win and to prove himself capable of mastering all, submitting to nothing and no one. Primary emphasis is placed on the importance of willpower. This can lead to an almost inflexible determination to come out on top. When production is high, he feels good, in charge, with little appreciation for what others may have contributed. A 9,1 motto is, "When I have sufficient strength, I can impose my will regardless of resistance or opposition."

Sometimes a 9,1-oriented manager doesn't get the results he counted on. His greatest dread is to falter, to be beaten, to lose control, and to be defeated. When failure does happen, he blames it on others. The 9,1 manager resolves, "Next time I'll watch more closely." The general conclusion from the assumption that "I am the cause of my successes; failure is from the actions of others," is likely to be, "Never depend on them." This also extends to avoiding advice and guidance because accepting assistance, recommendations, or even suggestions indicates that he is not self-sufficient.

Anger is typically experienced as a reaction to the frustration of his will. He focuses on overcoming the outside source that triggered his anger rather than studying the cause of his lack of inner composure in dealing with a problem. Anger is likely to persist and may become more intense, even though the original cause may have been reduced or eliminated. Then the person's surplus of anger and hostility cause him to search for situations where it can be unloaded. Someone with this kind of free-floating anger is usually described as "carrying a chip on his shoulder."

## Boss Behavior

When the organization rewards production and shows little consideration for people, a manager with a 9,1 orientation feels elated because his attitudes are in tune with the purpose of the organization. He is free to drive himself and others in line with the ethic that "results are what count." Whenever a contradiction exists between people and production, it is resolved at the expense of people. This manager thinks about his job and the problems he needs to solve to get production and often awakes with these concerns on his mind. "If you don't look out for yourself, who will? The law of the jungle is what prevails in this dog-eat-dog corporate life. It's survival of the fittest all the way." His determination to overcome obstacles and overpower opposition is seen as headstrong, yet his performance results are likely to be on the plus side, particularly for the short term.

The relationship of a boss to a subordinate is along lines of *authority* and *obedience*. The manager may exercise authority over the smallest details of the activities of subordinates, who are obligated to obedient compliance. Power of hierarchy is not to be questioned. Lines of accountability and responsibility are to be adhered to.

If a subordinate should question a 9,1-oriented boss about how work is to be performed, he might get an answer such as, "These are your instructions. They tell you who, what, where, when, and how. Do them and don't give me any lip. If there's anything I don't like, it's insubordination."

The underlying assumption is that externally imposed direction and control, of necessity, must be applied down through the organization hierarchy. Why? First, people are believed to dislike their work inherently. Therefore, they must be pushed. Second, they are likely to be seen as less than fully capable of organizing their efforts effectively at their own levels of operation. While managers at lower echelons are held responsible for work output, the planning and organizing aspects of their jobs are thought to be done more effectively up the line where perspective, skill, and information are present. Third, to manage otherwise would seem to weaken the structure of established authority and allow "unwilling" subordinates to slack off.

A 9,1 manager views his responsibilities in ways that are distinctive to that orientation.

*Planning:* "I do the planning by setting production quotas and detailing plans to achieve them."

*Organizing:* "I make assignments and tell subordinates what to do, how, when, and with whom."

*Directing:* "I keep in close touch with what's going on to ensure that what I have authorized is being followed."

*Controlling:* "I ensure that schedules are being met and move people along faster if progress permits. I criticize, assign blame for deviations, and impose corrective actions."

*Staffing:* "I get strong people and weed out weak ones. Management development that concentrates on personnel issues may be useful, but on-the-job learning is what counts."

When a boss manages in this way, resentment is more or less inevitable. He comes to expect it. He rationalizes that to get production, one has to give close supervision and step on toes. As a result, people are likely to be critical.

Criticism can be ignored if people are controlled, which is important to the 9,1-oriented manager anyway. It is easier to keep people under control by holding each accountable for his own job. His assumption is that individuals, not groups or teams, are productivity's building blocks.

An office arrangement reflects this one-to-one structure of work relationships. It is a large office accommodating accounts payable and accounts receivable units within an accounting section. There are six accountants in each unit and one supervisor for each unit. The supervisors report to the section manager.

The office is designed so that each accountant works in a frosted-glass cubicle, closed on three sides and open to the front. A five-foot pathway separates the six cubicles of one unit from the six in the other. In front of each of the two sets of six cubicles is another one for the unit supervisors. The unit supervisors' cubicles are closed only on two sides; the fronts and backs are open. Splitting the pathway and at the opposite extreme is the section manager's office. The section manager can see into the cubicles of the two section supervisors. The section supervisors, in turn, can look "upward" toward their boss or "downward" toward their subordinates.

Information flow and work direction is from the manager down to each subordinate, separately. From here the two supervisors carry the work to their subordinates, separately. From their vantage points in the office, the manager and each supervisor are able to visually oversee the work of those for whom each is responsible. The supervisors and the accountants do not know, and are not expected to know, what is happening to the right or left. Decisions or judgments affecting both sections are made at the manager's level. They are passed down the line, individually, to those below him.

A 9,1-oriented manager often concerns himself with the actual design of the work and other arrangements at lower levels. Jobs are defined in terms of operational requirements. People are not expected to contribute ideas to the task; their job is to turn out results. The primary advantage of work simplification and the division of activities into segments, for example, is that judgment and decisions that concern anything more than simple procedures are reduced to a minimum. These arrangements fragment work into mechanical units. People do not need to think.

At higher levels, a similar kind of separation between executives can be achieved through management of, and access to, information. In one company, for example, the president meets with each vice-president separately and frowns on their meeting with one another. He is the central source, the one who knows everything. He does this for several reasons. One is that the president has complete and ultimate control over all decisions and is not subject to criticism by any one subordinate because no one has a sufficiently broad perspective to know the complex considerations that affect the final result. Another is that he avoids creating "generalists" who could go into competition with him. Needless to say, such a president has no replacement and, therefore, is not threatened in that dimension either. When he is removed from his position, for whatever reason—health or any other—the organization is likely to drift, if not crumble.

### Management-by-Objectives

Sometimes referred to as management-by-objectives, management-by-quota is a more apt description of this powerful means of controlling productivity. Quotas usually are set higher than current production. Then, the quota is either met, or it is missed. Thus the quota can become a ceiling. Efforts are made to reach rather than exceed it as a motivational floor. If it is missed, corrective actions are taken to avoid another failure. The quota is simply another means of pushing for production.

Quota has much the same effect as deadline, which is sometimes used for the same purpose—to pressure production. By setting tight deadlines, the 9,1-oriented manager exerts force to achieve results. He might say to a subordinate, "The same job a month ago took two days to complete. Get it done this time in a day and a half." Also used is the "squeeze" play, with a constant deadline. "The committee report last time took four days for ten men; get it done in four days with seven men on this trip."

Quotas and deadlines are more or less acceptable ways of the 9,1-oriented manager to pressure for organization efficiency and gain personal satisfaction from controlling the efforts of others at the same time. When results are not achieved, then coercive means, involving various forms of punishment, can be applied to those not measuring up.

Under management-by-objectives, the 9,1 approach to performance appraisal is, "You let a man know where he stands relative to the quotas that were set, clearly and without qualification." The boss's obligation, in other words, is to thoroughly evaluate those under him and to point out to them the ways in which they are not measuring up. This means the boss concentrates on telling the subordinate what his weaknesses are and what he should do to correct them. After that it is the man's responsibility to shape up.

### Conflict

Conflict arises when one person's thinking contradicts that of another. This usually occurs because colleagues and subordinates have definite feelings about what is right or wrong, good or bad, sound or unsound. A 9,1-oriented approach views conflict as an indication that control is breaking. He reacts by fighting to reestablish his dominion over others. There are many different ways bosses do this, ranging from subtle questions designed to demonstrate to another person that he is wrong to outright suppression of another's point of view.

### Extracting Compliance

These 9,1-oriented assumptions about managing are directed toward eliminating disagreements between a boss and his subordinates before they arise. When subordinates follow directions and comply with instructions, agreement between a manager and his subordinates is automatic. Frequently, in exchange for compliance, a subordinate is paid extremely well. As one subordinate executive remarked, "You have to pay well to get a man to take what I do."

### Offensive Questioning and Defensive Listening

In the ordinary course of person-to-person discussions, 9,1-oriented ways of winning a point can be observed in the manner a manager asks questions as well as how he hears what is being said to him. These are important aspects of communication.

A typical way to take the offensive is to ask a question but not explain the reason the information is wanted. The boss does this because it is a speedy, direct way to get to the point. He is not wasting his own time nor the time of his subordinate. As he sees it, the question is necessary and that is sufficient reason for asking it. The subordinate is put on the defensive when the question implies that it is asked because something is wrong.

On the other hand, when a subordinate speaks, a 9,1-oriented boss is likely to be listening for a threat to his all-important goal of results. If, through such defensive listening, the boss can find errors or omissions, he can launch an attack on those points. Defensive listening has the advantage of keeping the boss alert to the opinions, thoughts, and attitudes being revealed. The disadvantage is that he may not realize what he is really being told. What he hears stimulates his aggressiveness and triggers his own win-lose attitudes.

## Fixed Position Taking

In his efforts to stay in charge, a 9,1-oriented manager is likely to take a position and stick with it. Fixed positions also may occur when a manager who previously may have been characterized as flexible becomes rigid under pressure, operates with tunnel vision, and insists on a course of action that is failing. He is then labeled as stubborn. When opposed, he becomes even more frozen to his position, blind to data that would contradict its validity. At this point, a vicious win-lose cycle that feeds upon itself may occur with the manager becoming more insistent that his is the only course of action. Others become more resistant as they recognize that the essential element of credibility, often referred to as mutual trust, is sacrificed. There is no return when this point has been reached. The tragedy has to be played out; either the 9,1-oriented manager is sacrificed in the name of progress, or progress is abandoned in the name of preserving his fixed position.

## Evaluative, Judgmental Thinking

Whatever else, words are more than vehicles of communication. They can be weapons. A 9,1 orientation leads to evaluative attitudes that result in black-white, good-bad, all-or-none types of thinking where judgments are premised on preestablished criteria. In addition, dogmatic phrases such as *always, never, you can't, you must,* and *you should* are used to box in his adversary. Other verbal put-down tactics include (1) exaggeration, (2) using "marginal" but uncheckable data, (3) quoting authority for one's views, (4) challenging the authority quoted by others, (5) raising one's voice, (6) twisting logic, and (7) dramatics, including threats of physical assault. None of these involve *deliberate* dishonesty. A 9,1-oriented manager is quite certain he has acted with utmost sincerity and personal dedication to the righteousness of his cause.

## Taunts

Taunts also are useful. For example: "How much do you want to bet on whether or not I'm right? C'mon, lay your money down." Even 9,1 humor can be used as a weapon in win-lose banter. It has a sharp prick to it. It is seen as caustic because it is the kind of joke that belittles others by exposing faults and inadequacies, making them look ridiculous.

## Game Playing

A favorite 9,1-oriented manager's game is called "Now I've got you, you S.O.B." This is waiting for something to go wrong and then pouncing on the subordinate who was responsible. He may ferret out unpleasant facts about each of his subordinates and even track down their defects to condemn them. He justifies his effort with the argument that people cannot improve unless they are aware of their shortcomings and take action to correct their own deficiencies.

## Dirty Tricks

An underhanded but often successful way to win, especially over a colleague, is the use of dirty tricks. If colleagues are vying with each other to make a "good showing" to advance to a higher position, each may be as determined to win as the other. What happens next is likely to be a contest where the rules of fair play are no longer obeyed. The aim is to win, not enjoy the game. Acts outside the acceptable realm of managerial behavior may be committed with the ends justifying the means.

## Weakening an Adversary

When a battle is underway, the objective that becomes central is to bring one's adversary to his knees. The opposition may be frustrated, degraded, and made to feel that he has been "had," a total failure. As a result, he may be even *more* ineffective in carrying out his job, but the 9,1-oriented manager has "won."

9,1 tactics include a variety of methods for weakening an adversary in order to shift the balance of power. He can be influenced to doubt his reasons for disagreeing through loud, argumentative remarks. Another weakening maneuver is to put the adversary's opinion under suspicion by attributing it to a bad source. For example, saying, "I've heard our competitor say the same thing a thousand times and look where he is," casts doubt on the legitimacy of the argument.

An approach to attacking an adversary is to cut him down. "You've forgotten how to be honest with yourself." "How could you possibly understand what I'm saying when you don't know what I'm talking about." "Without me, you wouldn't be anything." "The only person you think about is yourself. I'm thinking of what is best for you." "You're just arguing to be disagreeable, your normal personality." Sharp comments are made such as, "That's absolutely ridiculous," "Your logic is all screwed up," "Your facts are wrong," "You can't prove it." These kinds of closed-minded assertions are intended to end the disagreement. Each can be understood as a remark calculated to hurt the other person's self-esteem.

## Leverage

Techniques of *leverage* are disguised tactics to force compliance and can be used to accomplish the same kinds of results achieved by firing. This is possible by creating dilemmas which force the subordinate to submit or face some worse consequence. Typically, a job may be declared no longer necessary. Its occupant is thus made superfluous. Since he cannot be fired, he is offered an equivalent job elsewhere which, for certain reasons (family, etc.), he cannot possibly accept. His only real choice is to resign. That is the use of 9,1 leverage. Leverage strategies are widely used in business, government, and politics to settle differences in favor of the organization or the boss. Though sometimes called "gentle persuasion" or "arm twisting," the thinking behind them is better described as subtle coercion. Regardless of how it is pictured, the attitude stems from 9,1-oriented assumptions. Although the gruffness is eliminated, the effect is the same.

## Ending Disagreement Through Suppression

An ultimate win-lose tactic is to pull rank on a subordinate in order to suppress disagreement. For example, let's say that Bill is boss and John is his subordinate. Bill gives John instructions about something Bill wants him to do. John says, "But boss, it won't work." Bill's first reaction is to say, "It will work. Do it. I am responsible." However, to avoid being abrasive and to let John realize his own mistake Bill says, "Why won't it work?" John goes into an extended explanation. Bill's impatience rises. He says, "You are wrong, but you don't see it. Here is the weakness in your argument." John continues to disagree. At some point Bill becomes angry and says, "Look. I've heard enough. I have told you what I want you to do and how I want it done. I don't want to hear any more. I want you to do it. It's my responsibility if it doesn't work. You're being paid to do what you are told. Do you have any questions?"

The important thing is that Bill has imposed his will on John. Bill may be wrong, but to accept John's point of view would expose him to the risk of failure caused by John's judgment. The further appearance of conflict is prevented as John has no option but to knuckle under. The authority-obedience control formula says, "That's it! That's the way it's going to be!"

A subordinate fighting his boss is one thing, but a 9,1 boss finds it equally intolerable when subordinates are fighting one another. His solution is to "read them the riot act," or "crack their heads together, saying 'either cooperate with one another or you are both washed up.' " In these ways, he puts an end to their productivity-robbing self-indulgence.

Though suppression is often effective in ending open conflict, it fails to get at the core of the problem. It does not detect or remove underlying causes, and the sources of conflict remain.

### Subordinate Reactions

Subordinates react in numerous ways to 9,1-oriented boss behavior. Some feel at ease and apparently submit to domination. However, most subordinates experience tensions that are expressed in ways ranging from oblique resistance to resentment to fighting back.

### Compliance

Few or no problems arise from this managerial approach as long as subordinates see the boss's decisions as good ones. Although the boss manages by edict, there is no disagreement with his demands. Thus a subordinate complies with what he agrees with as best and feels no tension.

Sometimes subordinates comply but privately disagree with their boss. These "yes men" tell him that he is right, regardless of whether he is or not.

Other subordinates comply with 9,1 conditions but limit themselves to implementation of them once they recognize that this is all that is asked. They do not anticipate being involved and are not disappointed when nothing more than obedience is expected. When the implementation demanded of them is dull, subordinates tend to become less and less interested in the work itself and eventually center their attention on private thoughts or engage in discussions on social topics such as sports, politics, or the weather. These activities replace what otherwise would be unbearable boredom in the absence of involvement in the work itself.

### Withdrawal into 1,1

Sometimes a subordinate is resentful because a 9,1-oriented boss makes decisions about the subordinate's work and does not discuss them with him. The action is a *fait accompli*. If the subordinate suppresses his anger at not being consulted and never makes his resentment known, the boss will continue acting this way, constantly angering the subordinate. A "solution" to this untenable circumstance is for the subordinate to retreat into a 1,1 attitude. In his view his ideas are excellent but unappreciated. He justifies his withdrawal by saying to himself, "I'll not help them any more by offering my ideas. Then they'll come to see how really good I am and what they've lost by not using my ideas."

When subordinates withdraw into neutrality and indifference, they do the minimum work required to retain their jobs and income, no more, no less. They avoid being "used" by maintaining a kind of shell that says, "I'm right and the world is wrong." The reaction described here occurs at all levels of organization membership. It appears "obvious" that people who respond in such a 1,1-oriented way are lazy, apathetic, and indifferent. This response is incorrectly interpreted as typical behavior. The more objective observation is that control and mastery deaden those that are subdued.

### Hiding and Forgetting

One way to escape the wrath of a 9,1-oriented manager is to hide actions that the boss sees as undesirable. For example, those who violate practices and procedures, willfully or not, seek to hide their infractions. This creates a need for inspection systems and surveillance strategies calculated to catch the transgressors.

The same thing happens within the communication system as negative information is passed up through each level. For example, information about quality control problems at lower levels is filtered and muted to the point that, when it does reach the top, much of its validity has been lost. However, in this process, subordinate levels are "protected" from aggressive or punitive action from the top, at least in the short term.

Even questions posed by the boss to the subordinate do not get open and straightforward answers because he does not know what the boss is up to. If a subordinate does not know why the boss wants information, the subordinate is likely to resent questions as intrusions and to become more closed, hidden, secluded, and distrustful. He feels defensive. Perhaps the boss will misuse the information, trying to build a case to get rid of him. Everything is screened for possible threats.

"Forgetting" some portion of a frustrating incident is a mental trick that also relieves a subordinate of pressure. 9,1 suspicion creates tension in the subordinate, of which he is sometimes unaware. This occurs whenever a conviction that cannot be dismissed from thought is rejected by the boss. Rather, it is forgotten. This is the emotionally unhealthy mechanism of repression at work. It is another way of hiding unpleasant thoughts and feelings from one's own awareness. We know from many sources that forgotten ideas do not disappear but find their way back into awareness in many disguised ways.

### Going Underground

On the surface, a disgruntled subordinate may bend his knee to authority. However, more often he vindicates his position by going underground. Through this seemingly passive compliance, he may encourage events that can cause the boss's course of action to falter. Unresolved conflicts reappear in disguised ways, such as slowdowns, careless errors, misinterpretation of instructions, and so on. Other disgruntled subordinates come into the subordinate's camp. The arena of conflict is broadened and the boss's position put in greater jeopardy. Low morale leads to antiorganizational activities where many forms of work hindrances appear as a means of discharging resentment. This lowers the quality of cooperation and reduces effective production.

Management-by-quota also suffers from the underground resentment of subordinates who can find innumerable ways to bring production in below quota, again demonstrating that antagonisms are an important factor in lowered productivity.

Thus creative abilities of subordinates are channeled into attempts to thwart the boss and prevent the system from working well. At the least, suggestion systems in a 9,1 environment seem to wither on the vine, and much good grass-roots experience and thinking goes ungarnered. Quicker and more efficient ways of getting sound results are buried. In turn, discovery of ways to work more efficiently are used to the advantage of the individual but in ways that are contrary to organization purpose. Rather than contributing to increased production, he learns to expend less energy in the same amount of time. Efforts by higher management to thwart the creative antiorganization tactics seem always to be countered by even more ingenious and devious blockages. The silent but powerful creative resistance of subordinates to changes designed to promote productivity is a barrier 9,1-oriented management has yet to deal with effectively.

### Fighting Back

A consequence for subordinates of 9,1-oriented management that is complete and continuous is a sense of *powerlessness*. A common reaction is of righteous indignation and a readiness to rebel against the system that dehumanizes but demands. The most extreme form of rebellion is to leave the system; this explains high turnover in 9,1-oriented organizations.

Yet a subordinate may feel that he understands a problem, wants to help solve it, and therefore proposes actions for consideration by his boss. The subordinate does not give up even though the boss disagrees. We know that the boss's strategy is to cut off the conflict, and he attempts to do so. The subordinate sees the boss as overbearing and domineering. He wants to influence the outcome so that he can feel competent and successful. Denial of his desires to participate results in frustration, which in turn produces biological reactions of aggression, and he wants to fight back. He thus becomes angry and defiant.

Open hostility is more or less out of the question, but antagonisms take the form of feelings of dislike, even of rage. These are expressed in a subordinate's finding something wrong whenever an occasion arises as well as in complaining, backbiting, ridicule, and so on. Subordinates may withhold information to prevent a boss from looking good, distort it to cause him to appear inept, and respond in other ways that reveal frustration and aggression but avoid open battles. The more intense the frustration, the more likely a subordinate is to strike back by fair means or foul.

Being powerless is very different from a 1,1 orientation which involves an abandonment of power; a failure to exercise available authority. As a result, a 1,1-oriented subordinate may find the situation unobjectionable, unless it is demanding of him, which is likely. Even then the resentment may go underground and be difficult for even 9,1-oriented managers to recognize.

## Unions

Subordinates who find themselves ignored or offended by arbitrary treatment and who are unable to redress what they regard as injustices or wrongs pursue other, more militant, ways of correcting problems. Given effective leadership, they can achieve through numbers what they are unable to accomplish individually. Recognizing their individual helplessness, workers, foremen, supervisors and professional employees (engineers, etc.) join together to force upon employers the recognition of their common strength. There are many reasons why people join unions, but such a commitment is almost always antiorganizational. This means that the reason for joining the union is to *resist* the organization's attitudes and treatment of its employees. The recent rush toward unionization among white-collar technical workers, school teachers, and government employees indicates that this trend is accelerating.

## Eliminating Your Boss on the Battlefield

The coerced soldier may turn against the leader as in the "fragging" that occurred in Vietnam: the killing of a junior officer by enlisted men under circumstances where the murder could be blamed on an enemy land mine or grenade. Fragging is only a recent example of 9,1-oriented, antiorganizational creativity in the military.

Any one of these reactions, or any combination, may occur in response to a 9,1 boss's orientation. The final impact on subordinate commitment may range from apathetic compliance, to unionization, to retaliation through destructiveness.

Boss behavior has been examined from two angles. One is how a 9,1-oriented boss "sees" subordinates. The other is how subordinates react to being managed in this 9,1 way. What can you do to change if you see yourself managing subordinates in this manner and want to do something about it?

If you are a subordinate and see your boss managing in these ways, then you may actually be managed in a 9,1 way. Thus the question becomes, "What can you do to help your boss manage in a better way if his current approach is in the 9,1 direction?"

There are a number of possibilities, but a discussion of these will be deferred until other Grid styles have been evaluated in greater detail.

## Implications for Mental and Physical Health

The word stress conveys the idea of a system in tension, a natural adjustment when a person's energies are concentrated, say, on solving a problem. Then stress is functional and healthy. The great majority of managers persist in their careers without any adverse consequences that are beyond the strains and stresses associated with everyday living. By comparison, stress-related diseases are illnesses in which the degree and character of stress has become dysfunctional. Whether or not the stress contributes to or prevents problem solving, stress beyond normal limits appears to interact with body processes involving the circulatory, respiratory, digestive, and excretory systems, or the body as a whole in illness-inducing ways. Stress, in other words, is a natural, functional aspect of living. It is only adverse to mental and physical health under special circumstances. Some particular forms taken by stress-induced illness appear to be correlated with a specific Grid style. Thus, for example, it is held that a 9,1-oriented person for whom no success is satisfying, who is angry and hostile towards those on whom he must depend, and who constantly shudders at the risk of failure in his next project, keeps himself under such an undue degree of stress that in time a heart attack may appear.

It is unlikely that any single or specific cause-and effect relationship can be established for most illness conditions. Often a host of factors must come together before an illness develops, or the illness can be "caused" by any one of several factors, possibly in combination. For example, heart attack may be associated with a number of factors, including heredity, cholesterol level, general health and age, as well as Grid orientation.

There also are difficulties of interpretation related to which is cause and which is effect. The interpretations that follow should be regarded as tentative and suggestive of what some of these interrelationships are, rather than as definitive and final. An effort has been made to include only those studies in which it is held that Grid-like behavior is antecedent to the onset of illness.

These relationships are reported in technical studies and clinical descriptions. We have evaluated the extent to which various reports fit one or another Grid style. It is in these terms that conclusions have been reached as to how these "extremes" of Grid style may correlate with a variety of mental and physical health conditions.

The stresses of a 9,1 orientation can build up to a degree that they may have some of the mental and physical health consequences described below.

### "No Time Off"

The 9,1-oriented person feels that any activity not directly enhancing his get-ahead motivation reflects a lazy and irresponsible attitude and is, therefore, unacceptable. For this reason people operating according to more deeply held 9,1 assumptions are likely to have few outside interests, to enjoy little but their work, and to see time off as a waste. They are "workaholics."

Wasting time is a sin, a disregarding of responsibility, and the cause of lost opportunities. The 9,1-oriented person feels uneasy without some definite plan of action which bears the promise of paying off in concrete results. Taken to its extreme, even sleep robs time that should be applied to achievement. This attitude, coupled with tense mental concentration, has been reported to be related to problems of sleeplessness or insomnia.

An exception to the workaholic concentration on work is in competitive pastimes such as tennis and golf. To a 9,1-oriented person this activity is little more than an extension of the same basic attitudes found in work—it offers a new area of win-lose competition.

### Denial of Illness

Illness is likely to be viewed as personal failure, and the biological reality of illness is sometimes ignored. Even medical evidence, such as having a heart attack, is not likely to be convincing, and the person continues to do those things that are deleterious to health and yet give him personal satisfaction.

### Fatigue and Depression

Suppressing the impulse to "attack and destroy," which may be essential to a 9,1-oriented manager's style in large organizations, can be one of the most frustrating and fatiguing parts of seeking to win, dominate, master, and control. The reason is that tensions that would be relieved by attacking must be bound up and lived with. They have no place to go.

Some managers experience failure with a sense of particular dread because it is their equivalent of self-destruction. Failure, in other words, provokes guilt for not having tried harder, for not having been more thorough, or for putting what turned out to be an unjustified trust in others. All of these can cause an individual to feel depressed and to believe that "life isn't worth it." Hostility is central in some depressive reactions. The hostility felt toward others is turned against one's self and the person feels inadequate.

Yet, for most 9,1-oriented managers, this reaction to failure is short-lived. Tomorrow they are ready to fight the next battle.

### "Sick" 9,1

Excessive anger and hostility can produce other deep mental pathology. An individual striking out against others to achieve his goals can come to characteristically respond in this way. Then satisfaction is derived from the striking itself. This satisfaction comes to have its own motivations, not because attacking is necessary to win, but because of the pleasure derived from hurting others. Seeing someone squirm is the layman language to describe it. Sadism is the technical word for it. This can become "sick" 9,1.

Some sadistic 9,1-oriented managers find their way into positions where under "legitimate" business arrangements they can fight no-holds-barred matches. For example, some managers who become responsible for labor relations create an antagonistic relationship where their venom can be released on the union. One way this is done is for the management to create a false polarity between itself and union leaders. The labor leaders respond in a win-lose way without testing for support from their membership. When they in fact get out on a limb, this results in management's elation at their plight. The sadistic pleasure is derived from seeing union officers squirm. The reciprocal of this is that strong unions may pick out some particular company and subject it to punishment for presumed misdeeds, which were in fact unintended.

Thus the ramifications of an extreme 9,1 managerial style are seen to extend far beyond their immediate implications for managing production with and through people. Not only do those who are managed in this manner fight back or retreat, but also the 9,1-oriented manager himself suffers potentially serious harm.

### Distrust and Suspicion

In an extreme 9,1 orientation one frequently observes reactions of distrust that come about in this way: recognizing his own ruthlessness and aware of the antipathy of others and of antiorganizational creativity, the 9,1-oriented manager comes to see in others the same motivations he sees in himself. Thus, an "enemies list" identifies those who are most threatening because, whether real or presumed, it is assumed they can destroy the person they threaten. This is one basis for understanding paranoia.

### Suicide

Suicide is destruction turned against the self. Sometimes it may be understood as a way of escaping from intolerable failure, the most dreaded threat to an extreme 9,1-oriented manager. Other times it may be understood as a way of wreaking vengeance on another. This is so when the suicide is such that the other person is forced to acknowledge, with intense feelings of personal guilt, the attitude, "I made him do it."

### Migraine

Migraine headache is an example of another psychosomatic condition where an extreme 9,1 orientation appears to influence the occurrence of the illness. An extensive study of the "migraine personality" portrays characteristics such as ambitious, successful, perfectionistic, rigid, orderly, cautious, and because he seems emotionally blocked much of the time, he has outbursts of rage or hostility. Others note competitiveness, rigidity and perfectionism as characteristic. However, some investigators who have not corroborated this cluster of characteristics appear to believe that migraine may be an expression of emotional distress of many types.

### 9,1-Related Heart Attack

A basic correlation between an extreme 9,1 managerial orientation and heart attack has been widely reported by medical authorities. In one investigation heart attack victims were characterized by their acquaintances. One hundred fifty San Francisco businessmen identified the habits and characteristics of any friend who had had a heart attack. Seventy percent described them as having "excessive competitive drive in meeting deadlines." One hundred internists responsible for coronary patients indicated that the behavior most frequently found in heart attack victims was "excessive competitive drive in meeting deadlines." From other studies the researchers concluded that in a controlled study in which men whose behavior fits the orientation were compared with others whose behavior did not, the 9,1-oriented men had "seven times as much coronary heart disease . . ., but their diets and exercise habits were almost identical."

The following behavior, which fits the 9,1 pattern, is what has been identified by medical experts Friedman and Rosenman as related to heart attack.

Perhaps no man, at first glance, seems less insecure than the typical Type A [9,1] man. He bristles with confidence and appears to exude lavish amounts of self-assurance and self-conviction. How can we indict a man as being insecure who is always so eager to ask, "What is your problem and how can I help *you?*" a man who is so loath to say, "I have a problem and I need your help"? We do so because we have found, after many years of studying the Type A man, that he either lost or never had any intrinsic "yardstick" by which he can gauge his own fundamental worth to his own satisfaction.

Somewhere in his development process he began to measure the value of his total personality or character by the *number* of his *achievements*. Moreover, these achievements invariably must be those he believes capture the respect and admiration of his peers and superiors. He does not, however, care whether these achievements gain him the love or affection of his fellow man, although he does not particularly care to be disliked.

Having chosen this yardstick, he has committed himself irretrievably to a life course that can never bring him true equanimity. The *number*, not the quality, of his achievements must constantly increase to satiate an appetite that, unchecked by other restraints, ceaselessly increases. Second, he believes that the number of his achievements are always being judged by his peers and subordinates, and since the latter are constantly changing as he ascends in the socioeconomic scale, he feels that the number of his achievements must continue to rise.

Perhaps the prime index of the presence of aggression or hostility in almost all Type A men is the tendency always to compete with or to challenge other people, whether the activity consists of a sporting contest, a game of cards, or a simple discussion. If the aggression has evolved into frank hostility, more often than not one feels, even when talking casually to such men, that there is a note of rancor in their speech. They tend to bristle at points in a conversation where the ordinary person might either laugh self-deprecatingly or pass over the possibly contentious theme.

Similar findings have been reported by other investigators.

## Childhood Origins of 9,1

There are two possible origins of a Grid style. One is heredity. Based on ample behavioral science and biological research, the idea that assumptions and attitudes built up in one generation can be transmitted biologically to another is without foundation.

The other source is environmental, particularly with regard to how parents or adults responsible for the rearing of children use the power vested in them from the standpoint of solving child-rearing problems involving planning, organizing, directing, and controlling. The proposition is that certain Grid styles of child rearing have predictable consequences for the Grid-related behavior of the child as he becomes a teenager and an adult. This hypothesis has led to extensive research and clinical evidence as to which specific patterns of child rearing have what particular effects in terms of predisposing a child in the direction of one Grid style in comparison with another.

A rich and expanding clinical and experimental literature in child psychology and psychiatry attests to the importance of child-rearing practices in shaping individual Grid styles. As might be expected, the patterns to be reported are not simple; yet they are clear and justify serious contemplation by adults as to how their own approaches are likely to be shaping the Grid styles of their children.

Several different approaches to child rearing appear important in forming a 9,1 child pattern. One is that "like begets like": 9,1-oriented parents rear 9,1-oriented children who become 9,1-oriented adults. Another is paternalism. A third is from parental pampering that is incomplete. A fourth stems from childhood experiences of severe deprivation.

From the very beginning, 9,1-oriented parents tend to concentrate their child's attention on performance and achievements. Demands for performance may originate in guilt feelings within the parents themselves, who see anything except hard work as frivolous and unworthy. These anxieties are relieved when they see their child accomplish something through hard work. Then he or she is a worthy son or daughter.

A child can avoid tensions from parental disapproval through compliance. In this way a child's acceptability to parents may increase. Obedience is expected, and, therefore, not rewarded. When children do not obey, the parent's will is challenged. They may disobey but in a way that it is difficult for parents to punish. Dawdling can be seen as a form of passive resistance, which is difficult for parents to punish or to correct because the child has not actively transgressed. He simply has failed to respond in the desired manner.

Outright disobedience is punished. Punishment may be physical or mental: withholding privileges, belittling, ridicule, sarcasm, and so on.

These tend to undermine a child's self-worth. Parents can lower self-worth by constantly demanding more from a child than he is presently able to deliver. Thus, regardless of how his performance is viewed in external or "objective" terms, from a subjective point of view he sees himself a failure. This is not a good, solid basis for the development of self-worth, and later on, he begins to treat others as his parents had treated him.

Parents can induce the same effect through invidious comparisons between their child and others who are performing better, achieving more, or in other ways making themselves appear exceptional. At the same time, parents may be focusing the child's mind on being better than others, doing more than they, reaching higher, and winning. In this manner the compulsion to dominate, control, and master has been strengthened. Thus the child can only see himself as inadequate, not as able—all ingredients of diminished self-worth.

A child who has tried and failed may find these reactions unfair, harsh, and rejecting. They can provoke resentment, which produces more misbehavior, which results in additional punishment. The best prediction is that punitive 9,1-oriented parents create 9,1-oriented children who are hostile and aggressive. A vicious cycle develops in which the child cannot win. Because a child is expected to try even though he or she can only lose, winning, success, and strength take on an exaggerated significance in the child's eyes.

Reinforced by parents' rewards for coming out on top, school is a new battleground for "beating out other students." Many repetitions of success in beating others out, externally rewarded and internally cherished, create a 9,1-oriented value system. Winning over others becomes the game of life.

Parents can also promote a 9,1-oriented child-rearing condition by constantly drawing a child's attention to the fact that others have it better than he does, that poverty is a sin, and that the only point in life is to acquire the skills and the habits of hard work and determination that can overcome deprivation. In this sense, overcoming deprivation becomes equivalent to winning, and acquiring the skills to do so is approximately the same as learning strategies of domination, control, and mastery over others.

Under paternalism, parental control is specific and in detail as to what the child is and is not to do. Even though the child may feel resentment, he complies, and the parents give their positive acceptance and approval, reinforcing the child's efforts to please. Giving affection and approval in exchange for compliance can strongly reinforce the child's desire to meet parental wishes for performance, and in this way a child learns the importance of being competent, of winning and of excelling over others in a closely guided growth experience.

The unexpressed resentment, anger, and hate that result from excessive parental control persist into adulthood and often appear in the form of excessive anger, sometimes converted into hate.

A third source of a 9,1 orientation, particularly as a backup style, comes from parental pampering that has been extensive but not complete. When a parent is overly submissive, the relationship of the child and parent turns upside down. For all practical purposes the child is the boss and the parent the slave. The parent's blind adoration may inflate the child's feelings of significance. When indulgence is complete, everything is provided, and the child needs to demand nothing.

When parents fall short of complete indulgence, a child learns that his persistent demands bring whatever else is lacking and wanted. Parents give in. The pattern is established. The child becomes more demanding, more insistent, more given to temper tantrums. Considering the rights of others becomes extremely difficult. Demanding, in other words, becomes the means for exercising control and mastery over parents. Once the formula is learned, the child applies it to others. This can be seen when an adult's calm approach turns to rage if his wishes are denied. This is a dramatic way of exercising will.

Childhood deprivation may also stimulate a 9,1 orientation. When a child feels "abandoned," if not physically then at least psychologically, the likely consequence is a desperate effort to get the parent's attention. This may be done through "bad behavior," louder and louder protests at feelings of unworthiness. When parents respond and label such behavior as bad, the young person is convinced that he or she is bad and accepts that kind of self-perception. This is one of the paths into delinquency, but, if it is curbed, it can produce an adolescent with a 9,1 orientation, where the youth relies on productivity and achievement to prove himself "good," as an effort to compensate for his earlier feelings of badness.

A young person also may envy others who have things he lacks. Deprivation is equated with weakness. To compensate for what he or she did not have at an earlier time, a person is motivated to strive relentlessly to catch up and get ahead of others. Thus childhood ambitions to overcome deprivation may produce competitive feelings and a desire to reach the top, regardless of the time or effort involved or costs to self or others. One expression of this urge is the desire to acquire possessions, often possible only after achieving the power to control and master others.

Any 9,1-oriented child is likely to have two parents like one of those described above or one "strong" parent and a second one who withdraws from participating in decisions or in guiding the child. When the word "parents" is used in this and other chapters, it is to be understood to cover both of these possibilities.

No matter what the parental attitudes are that lead to a child's learning 9,1 assumptions, anger is a universal property of an individual whose

9,1-oriented control, mastery, and domination motivations are threatened. Anger is preparation for attack. Physical attack on another person is relatively more common between brothers and sisters, on the grade school playground, in high school hallways, between adults at home (the battered wife), between parents and children (the battered child), and in situations where drinking strips away social veneer. Disagreements that lead to anger-based verbal personal attacks and conflict on the other hand are everywhere—in the home, corporation, schools and universities, learned societies, in local, state, and federal governments, and throughout politics.

There are two basic reasons why a dominant 9,1-oriented parent's child-rearing practices may provoke anger reactions by a child. One is tension-reduction. The other is identification with the aggressor.

Anger can be a tension-reducer in this way: although the child's anger may be provoked by parents, it usually cannot be vented on them. It is likely to be taken out on other children who become targets for the frustrated child. By picking on others, the child learns the meaning of power, strength, and mastery. There is experimental evidence that, when frustrated by an adult, young children repeat the same kind of behavior, but on others. One example is the observation that after receiving a scolding or spanking, a child may pick up a doll and scold or spank it. A child learns to do to others what he or she has experienced.

This "displaced" anger, learned in childhood, can be observed both on and off the job. A subordinate disagrees with his boss. Angry but respectful according to his place, the subordinate returns to his own office. He arouses his secretary's anger. She too swallows it with proper respect. On arriving home, she vents her anger on her oldest son. A few minutes later the son is bullying his younger brother. Anyone in a subordinate or less than equal position is a potential candidate, a possible, though innocent, victim of anger and hostility provoked but undischarged in an earlier encounter.

Another cause for anger and hostile feelings is identification with the aggressor. The child sees others discharging their own emotions in aggressive and hostile ways. It stirs him up. Even though the child has not been a target of their aggressive behavior, their reactions are used by the child as a model of what to do to others when angered. Feelings of hostility serve as a trigger, and another person becomes the target for an emotional reaction.

Whichever of these patterns is experienced, a child is less likely to learn how to cooperate with people or how to accomplish results with and through them. When frustrated by others, rather than trying to resolve the problem, the child has learned to react with anger and hostility and in these ways caused his will to prevail.

### Facades

There are a number of facades where a person's actions appear to be motivated by his 9,1-oriented assumptions when other Grid-related attitudes actually are present underneath the surface.

#### Tough Guy

The tough guy appears hard as nails. He rejects the more human or softer aspects of life. This aggressive exercise of arbitrary or coercive power may, in fact, hide 1,9-oriented desires to be liked and accepted. Fear of rejection can be avoided by deliberately doing things that "prove" that rejection is of no importance.

#### Intimidation Dynamics

Another 9,1-oriented facade involves projecting a false image of power and authority. The strategy is to appear stronger than one's adversary when real strength to back up the image may be lacking. Intimidation can be of high value to a facadist in getting what he wants. Though it may be unnecessary, a manager using this strategy flies to meet a business associate to close a deal rather than doing so through the mail or by telephone. For image projection a personal jet is more impressive than commercial flights. Having a business associate come aboard to close the deal in the plane on the ramp is better than meeting in a downtown hotel or office. Bringing along an assistant or secretary to whom details can be entrusted conveys the impression that the person in question is concerned with the proper management of detail but that he himself concentrates his own efforts on the main game. Having legal or other experts readily available adds to the facadist's demonstration of power. Outer trappings such as these are increasingly common at high executive levels and are relied upon to add that additional degree of "persuasion" the facadist is unsure his own competence is sufficient to bring about.

When it comes to disagreement, "principles" may be brought to bear on one's side of the agreement when actually no objective evidence is available that a matter of true principle is involved. This is another way of retaining a win-lose as contrasted with a problem-solving orientation, but making it appear to be of utmost importance because "a matter of principle is involved." On deeper examination, the 9,1 facade-oriented manager's "principle" often turns out to be dogma converted into an "absolute" fueled by self-righteousness.

There are many tricky and deceitful ways of conveying an aura of power and authority. A head waiter, for example, can be used to let associates know why one is late for a business luncheon or dinner engagement when there is no legitimate excuse for tardiness. In this way they gather, incorrectly, impressions of great strength and importance. When the facadist eventually arrives, the conversation is frequently interrupted so that he can answer prearranged telephone calls. The business associates appreciate the significance of the decisions their host is called upon to approve. These kinds of maneuvers can buck up a 5,5-oriented manager and give him the confidence that his natural Grid style inclinations do not give him.

Drawing valid distinctions between straightforward, hard-driving 9,1 and 9,1-oriented facade strategies is important. An individual who wishes to avoid the consequences of becoming a pawn in the facadist game strategies needs to be aware of the difference between coercion and manipulation.

### Implications of 9,1 for Organizations

Many organizations have evolved from an industrial society founded on 9,1 management. Historically, these assumptions are rooted in cultural attitudes toward work and the nature of man, typified in the extreme as baron-serf, master-slave, etc.

The question is how best to achieve organization purpose(s) through people when they are seen to be more or less truculent, unwilling, resistant agents of production. Some experts question, for example, whether 9,1 thinking is not, in fact, "self-fulfilling": "directive leadership creates dependence, submissiveness, and conformity. Subordinates tend to be afraid to exercise initiative. The boss fills in the vacuum with directive leadership. We now have a self-fulfilling prophecy."

This quality of thinking has not yet been seriously challenged by a system that can produce as well or better and not generate some of the secondary side effects already noted. Significant factors such as changing social values, widespread increase in the level of general education, unionization, and the emergence of knowledge industries, have begun to shift management thinking in a different direction than 9,1. Yet, until a theory of management is applied that can do better than 9,1, it is likely that organizations that have a history of 9,1 will not seek more effective alternatives.

What are some of the conditions that promote and maintain 9,1 concepts of management within an organization? One is related to education. Despite educational advantages available today and the general increase in educational level, a large segment of our population still lacks the preparation that would permit them to deal with technical knowledge and judgment. One consequence is that management still finds it necessary to centralize a great degree of planning, directing, and controlling. Technically-trained managers plan; up-from-the-ranks managements supervise implementation, and others execute. Such arrangements foster 9,1 and 1,1.

Economic conditions are still such that large numbers of people are almost wholly dependent for livelihood upon employment. Because of limited skills and as a result of relatively little fluidity in the work market, they are compelled to endure 9,1 close supervision. This is less true today than it was only twenty or thirty years ago but it is still common.

Another factor that promotes 9,1 is keen competition between industrial organizations. There is even greater pressure today for tighter, more efficient controls over organization performance.

All of these make 9,1 a common style of management in a competitive industrial society.

Many of the longer term consequences of a 9,1 orientation already have come to fruition during this generation. One of the greatest of these has been unionization. This is not to say that unionization is a sole result of 9,1 management. But win-lose struggles between unions and managements frequently center on aspects of management that are resisted and resented.

The most general, yet far-reaching, impact of 9,1 is the gradual shift of many people in the direction of 1,1 resignation, boredom, and alienation to organization work.

Lowered productivity is a second axiomatic consequence.

### Summary

Control, mastery, and domination characterize the positive motivations of a 9,1-oriented manager. At the negative end, motivation relates to risk of failure, and such a manager is prepared to take whatever initiative is required to avoid it. Production is the means through which the 9,1-oriented manager reaches achievement. He sees people as obstacles unless compliance is given willingly. A goal of 9,1-oriented management is to exercise power in ways that overcome the adverse impact people can have on production.

A 9,1-oriented person places high value on making decisions that stick or on doing things his own way because it is his way. In terms of convictions, he is ready to stand up for his own ideas, opinions, and attitudes and to press forcefully for their acceptance, even when others are resisting or pushing for their own against him. Once he adopts a conviction, opinion, or attitude, he is likely to cling tenaciously to it. Because he tends to have strong convictions, he is likely to initiate action, to take the ball, run in his own direction, and to drive others to catch up and keep up. Frequently, his momentum builds to such a point that it is difficult for anyone to stop him. The basic attitude is that although he may not always be right, rarely is he in doubt. He is more inclined to misinterpret facts to uphold his own view than to modify his conclusions in line with the objective situation. He is directed from within himself.

From the standpoint of his personal attitudes, he finds little reason to shy away from conflict. Winning for his point of view, even if it results in stepping on toes, is preferable to suffering defeat or in other ways having to admit failure. The characteristic 9,1 approach to conflict is to suppress disagreement. Resistance may stimulate anger and hostility. His temper flares when things are not going according to his wishes. His humor, like his approach to conflict, is hard hitting. It carries a sting.

High productivity may be achieved in the short run by 9,1-oriented management. The evidence, however, is that in the long run the side effects may actually lower production. An extreme 9,1 orientation is reported to have adverse mental and physical consequences for the person who manages this way, including fatigue and depression, suspicion and distrust, sadism, migraine headache, and heart attack.

Child-rearing practices likely to result in 9,1-oriented adults stem from at least four parental approaches: a 9,1 orientation, paternalism, incomplete pampering, and deprivation.

In Chapter 1, the *D* paragraph is the 9,1-oriented manager's self-description. If you avoided self-deception, and in your self-assessment placed a 5 by this paragraph as being most typical of your behavior, this means that you see yourself as managing out of a 9,1 orientation.

# Chapter 4

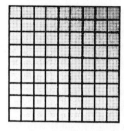

# 1,9

A 1,9-oriented manager believes the attitudes and feelings of subordinates are of utmost importance. When relationships are accepting, he feels emotionally secure. Because of the desire to be liked by them, he is likely to be excessively attentive to what subordinates, colleagues, and bosses think. He seeks their approval by being interested in them, good, kind, and considerate, and above all, responsive to their wishes and desires. When others are pleased and reflect it in their friendly reactions, he feels a oneness with them. For these reasons he cultivates an atmosphere of warmth.

The difference between a healthy need for affection and a 1,9 need is this: someone with a healthy need feels affection for the person from whom he desires it. Reciprocity is characteristic of genuine affection. However, the 1,9-oriented person wants affection and approval from everyone, without regard to whom and whether he feels genuine warmth for them or not.

The other side of the motivation is fear of disapproval. Fear is an intense emotional reaction, and fear of being personally rejected is one of the strongest. A 1,9-oriented manager reacts to others according to his built-in uncertainties rather than to the objective properties of the situation itself. In his efforts to avoid rejection he is likely to be solicitous, acquiescent to others, and malleable.

A basic reaction to fear is flight, but for a 1,9-oriented manager to escape from disapproval and rejection by flight only results in *separation* from those whose acceptance and approval is coveted. Thus his hope of restoring the relationship is to cater to their wishes. He uses ingratiating behavior to increase the likelihood of approval and at the same time to reduce the risk of rejection. The word "deferential" catches a significant aspect of the basic attitude. The manager who fears disapproval feels that it is "better to be safe than sorry." For these reasons some people are spoken of as "being scared of their own shadow" or "always uptight." A 1,9 motivation motto is, "If I am nice to people, they won't hurt me."

He avoids imposing his will on others. He might say, "I would rather lead than push." What he really means is, "I find out what they want or think is okay and help it come true. People should be helped not goaded." This is 1,9 supportive management. However, a person who is 1,9 in his orientation may, in fact, work hard, but he does so to gain approval as contrasted with doing so because of interest in the work itself or because he is committed to organization objectives of production and profit.

A 1,9 orientation spread throughout an organization produces an easy-going, country-club atmosphere where people do what they enjoy at their own pace and with those whom they like. Management may even encourage this ambience because the boss sees subordinates as his most important asset. He goes all out to see that they are satisfied with working conditions and with him. "Subordinates are important. My job is to provide for them and keep their spirits up." Ensuring that people can fit themselves into any situation with comfort, friendliness, and security is the 1,9-oriented manager's desire. The motivations for a 1,9-oriented manager to do so might be said to be hygienic in the sense of preventing dissatisfaction or the likelihood of infecting people with negative attitudes.

## Boss Behavior

When asked to describe his responsibilities, a 1,9-oriented manager may use the same words as one operating under any other style: to plan, organize, direct, control, and staff. However, his administration of these responsibilities is distinctive.

*Planning:* "I suggest assignments and convey my confidence by saying, 'I'm sure you know how to do this and that all will go well.' "

*Organizing:* "Subordinates know what to do and how to coordinate with each other. If they need my suggestions, I'm ready to listen to them and offer whatever help I can."

*Directing:* "I see my subordinates frequently and encourage them to visit. My door is always open. My desire is to get them the things they want without their having to ask. That's the way to encourage people."

*Controlling:* "I rarely need to check on how things are going since my subordinates will try their best. I place emphasis on congratulating each individual for his good efforts. Our discussions usually end by talking about why we did as well as we did and how we can help things to go as smoothly or more so in the future."

*Staffing:* "Even though it's not possible to please everyone, I try to ensure that subordinates are in the jobs they like best and working with those they enjoy."

*Togetherness* is a key concept for a manager who sees his work group as "one big happy family." He is likely to go overboard for "togetherness," not to perform tasks, but for sociability. He feels this can avoid reduction of productivity because one member will help another who is feeling poorly or has fallen behind.

Meetings also are occasions for getting together, but they don't start until "everyone is present," indicating their social importance. When topics are avoided because they might imply work pressure or criticism of a person, meetings continue to be unimportant to organization tasks. Under these conditions people are not antiproduction in the sense of actively resisting, but because of the lack of interest of their manager, they tend to become less and less involved in the work itself.

These concepts may even underlie the design of an office.

In an organization similar in size and level of responsibility to that described in Chapter 3, the manager supervises the work of a unit in a large records section of an old-line, blue-chip insurance company. Fourteen people work in this office, where every door is open. The tradition is that, within broad limits, managers choose their own furniture, create their own desk arrangements, select times for coffee breaks and lunches, etc. Flowers or pot plants sit on several desks. A radio is on another, set to soft music, turned down low in order not to disturb others. It only becomes a center of attention during national or world events. The typical work day passes at a comfortable pace. Crises are muted and fitted into the otherwise untroubled environment.

A coffee maker in a vestibule operates all day. The day begins on a light note as people drift in for coffee and sweets. This is breakfast for many. Around 10 o'clock, pairs and trios take off for a thirty- or forty-minute rest break. The informal rule is "Leave your problems at your desk . . . no serious work discussions during the breaks."

### Management-by-Objectives

Management-by-objectives is attractive to the 1,9-oriented manager but free and unguided discussion is the preferred method for setting objectives. Under this approach, the aim is to help each subordinate establish goals he can embrace. More importantly, self-set and self-managed goals guide the individual's own effort in that he can tell himself what to do. A subordinate who is directing himself is unlikely to have hostile feelings toward his boss.

Performance appraisals are geared to helping people feel appreciated for their past efforts and are rarely correlated to the achievement of objectives. Informal chats with them on personal matters indicate the boss likes them. He treats each subordinate as if he were a hothouse flower, giving as much care and attention as is required to help growth and fulfillment to occur.

## Conflict

A 1,9-oriented manager dreads conflict because it threatens warmth and approval, the main staples in the 1,9 emotional diet. This is what makes conflict seem so devastating. However, if conflict does arise, he tries to get back into a close supportive relationship as quickly as possible.

### Creating a Climate of Pleasantness

A 1,9-oriented manager is characterized by geniality. He seeks to be friendly with his boss, colleagues, associates, and subordinates—everyone. Harmony comes from showering people with kindness, keeping relationships on a first-name basis, being aware of the progress of the children and relatives, showing an active interest in a vacation trip, and so on. Under these conditions people are reluctant to reveal their differences and conflicts, and, because they do not become apparent, the manager lives through another day unmarred by tensions or frustrations.

All of these are reinforced by off-the-cuff chats and counseling with subordinates, which enable a 1,9-oriented manager to be aware of the current state of morale. He pays attention to those who are left out and lonely, seeking to create a climate of approval with compliments and positive reactions to specific requests. Work is enjoyable and life more pleasant with an appreciative pat on the back, a smile, a cup of coffee. This creates an attitude of sharing, a sense of warmth, mutuality, a balm of security. One courts the acceptance and approval of others by extending acceptance and approval to them. Such acts of endorsement promote community and ward off the potentially disgruntled subordinate who might otherwise express unhappiness.

### Letting Others Go First

If one's own thoughts parallel those of others', differences cannot arise. Without differences, there is no need for disagreement. With no disagreement, there is no conflict. One way to stay in agreement is to listen for what others think. Rejection is more likely to result from expressing one's own thoughts first than from responding to others. One reason is that the one who initiates a proposal is subject to criticism if his proposal is challenged, and criticism is a first cousin to outright rejection. Another reason is that if the boss can get others to propose and initiate, he runs no risk of having to impose his will on them. If voluntary proposals are not forthcoming, he urges them to take the lead by asking, "How would you handle this one?"

Sometimes a 1,9-oriented boss must initiate. Before doing so he studies probable reactions based on his intuition and empathy. His senses are fine-tuned, and his ears and eyes pick up impressions and filter them through his 1,9 attitudes to determine whether a suggestion he might make would gain quick acceptance.

A manager might put it this way: "Meetings get people together." Under the guise of consulting with people, meetings are held, not in preference to, but in addition to relating with each subordinate on a one-to-one basis. These free and easy discussions cement good relations and often result in quick and easy group decisions. Many times topics are brought up on which there is already widespread agreement. Points of similarity and agreement are emphasized to promote feelings of unity. These can be discussed until there is no time for controversial issues. Divergent points of view are treated in such a general and abstract way that agreements are reached even though they may have little or no impact on operations. Thus, agreements reached are likely to represent the minimum actions everyone will readily accept.

## Holding Your Tongue When You Disagree

A 1,9-oriented manager avoids saying those most danger-laden words, "I disagree," or, "You're wrong." He is likely to say, but to himself, "I tolerate a lot of things I don't really agree with in the interest of avoiding the frictions that would crop up if I were to ask that these things be changed." He is reluctant to support a point of view when it might be challenged. As a result, possible gains from his own creative thinking are likely to be sacrificed. Issues that are likely to provoke disagreement and to produce tensions are avoided, deferred, and eventually buried.

## Indirect Expressions of Position

There are 1,9 ways of expressing points of view in a noncontroversial manner. A manager may not remain silent but rather may express himself so that he is not taking a fixed position or even making a declarative statement from which he might later have to retreat. For example, instead of saying, "I saw a new model today. I think it's time we changed ours," he would be more apt to say, "Have you noticed how much noise the motors in our machines are making lately?" The latter expresses a point of view but in such an indirect manner that if someone disagrees with it, the point is not directly turned down. Discussion can continue if there is agreement.

### Explaining Away Negatives

A 1,9-oriented manager tries to side-step negative emotions. When others do react angrily or in a hostile manner, he does not respond in kind but lets the matter drop. He tries to explain away the other person's reactions by such phrases as, "He is under terrific pressure," or, "He must be feeling ill." These relieve the 1,9-oriented manager from feeling that he himself is being personally rejected.

Failure of subordinates to respond cooperatively is interpreted as resulting from inconvenience or misunderstanding, not insubordination. Absenteeism is not shirking; it is explained away as sickness or possibly family illness, or even a hangover, but never as contrariness or laziness.

### Apologies and Promises

Sometimes a 1,9-oriented manager gets caught in a situation where differences are unavoidable. For example, disappointing results may be painfully self-evident when a contradiction appears between earlier encouraging reports and actual performance. Then he seeks to reduce the risk of rejection through profuse apologies and promises of "It will never happen again." To relieve his fear of rejection, he may even ask for additional assignments and in this way hope to regain acceptance that has been jeopardized.

### Smothering Differences

In spite of everything, differences are bound to arise, no matter how much diligence may have been applied toward harmony and agreement. Reconciliation through the boss capitulating by saying the issue is not too important and that he really does agree is the most likely step to restore togetherness. The 1,9-oriented manager smooths over discontent by asking people to appreciate how good things are compared to how bad they might be. He hopes to keep morale up by accentuating the positive and eliminating the negative.

### Stifling Creativity

The clash of ideas that sparks creativity is absent under a 1,9-oriented manager. A creative approach is novel. It is different. Differences might result in tensions. Therefore, creative or novel solutions to problems rarely arise. A spark is indistinguishable from antagonism and is something to be smothered so that it does not ignite into active controversy.

## Dampening Pressures

A 1,9-oriented manager often is disturbed by pressures to achieve profit-based goals and objectives because these force him to make demands on others. He believes that pressures only frustrate subordinates and rarely bring about the desired results anyway. On the other hand, increasing profit by reducing expenses, that is, taking away conveniences or privileges, also annoys people. The result is that productivity may be further reduced.

Often pressures from above that must be passed down disturb the possibility of managing in a soft, approval-seeking, and friendly way. The dilemma is that disregarding his own boss's wishes would hurt that relationship and risk rejection from his boss and those higher up. Yet, if he were to pass pressures directly onto them, the 1,9-oriented manager might risk losing his own subordinates' acceptance. One way to deal with this dilemma is to reinterpret production requirements passed down and gently persuade subordinates to work on the problem. He sugar-coats inconveniences with promises or implies favors in return for support. Rather than applying pressure, he coaxes and cajoles in his effort to move subordinates effortlessly in a wanted direction. What might have been an inflexible command thus becomes an apologetic request.

If a problem he considers important enough to pass on down arises, he may explain it a little at a time so that the others do not get upset. A little bit at a time never feels like much whereas putting it all out at once might produce an explosion.

## Forgetting

Forgetfulness is probably more noticeable in 1,9-oriented managers than with other Grid styles. Here is how it may be understood: to gain affection and approval, particularly from someone he may fear, a 1,9-oriented manager accepts a request that he do something when in actuality he resents being asked. He is unable or unwilling to say, "No," yet the resentment bothers him. His mind turns away from the request itself. The result is that he fails to follow through. When this forgetfulness is pointed out, he is excessively contrite. It is partly for such reasons that 1,9-oriented people are sometimes difficult to rely on. They frequently fail to deliver when the task is unpleasant.

## Shading the Truth

The 1,9-oriented manager's inclination is not to give all the facts when asked to explain circumstances that might cause controversy. Passing on bad news might expose him to criticism, so he glosses it over or plays it down. Although he may not actually *lie*, he molds the truth to make it more palatable, sometimes without even being aware of it.

### Subordinate Reactions

Subordinate reactions range from feeling safe and secure within a warm and friendly atmosphere to feeling smothered, stifled, unchallenged, and wanting to escape from it.

### Security

When the human relationships of work sufficiently reinforce a person's desire for approval and diminish his fear of rejection, he finds the 1,9 atmosphere supportive and helpful. When asked about his attitudes a subordinate under a 1,9-oriented boss says, "I would not want to change jobs. I enjoy the people I work with. I couldn't ask for better conditions of comfort and serenity." This kind of person feels secure in a company that satisfies his cravings without imposing demands.

His manager remarked, "Many departments here have a high turnover. We don't. I have been with the company thirty-three years, and most of my people have been with me for years. Commitment is high because of the easy tempo; a low key, accepting atmosphere rather than a pressure-cooker."

### Resentment and Frustration

Many people find challenging work rewarding with stimulation originating in the work itself. When such people are not challenged, frustration arises because, even though they may be paid well, they may feel they are wasting time and making little or no contribution. They become resentful of their manager and contemptuous of his lack of effort in the interest of organization objectives. By giving approval without providing opportunity for genuine accomplishment, a 1,9-oriented manager may provoke frustrations among subordinates that he most devoutly seeks to avoid.

### When Creativity is Stifled

Subordinates who are committed to achievement apply themselves to the tasks at hand, often seeing different and better ways of doing things. Changes that would be required to bring new ways into practice, particularly when they involve several people, are likely to be unsettling and to promote differences and disagreement. Subordinates managed in a 1,9 way learn to withhold creative or original ideas rather than putting them out only to see them smothered. Creativity is stifled and the work situation becomes repetitive, boring, and dull. The unstimulating environment may become intolerable and the creative person seeks other opportunities.

## Ambitious People Leave

Ambitious people who are dedicated to work and want to make a success of things by being productive are unlikely to stay long under a 1,9-oriented manager. They come to realize that their efforts not only are likely to go by unnoticed, but also may be retarded by the boss who subtly "pressures" for less production in order to avoid stirring up others. Because ambitious people are not encouraged, they also are likely to leave rather than abandon their goals of moving forward.

### Implications for Mental and Physical Health

### "Distorted" 1,9

Masochism is the need for punishment, which, after having been received, provides the 1,9-oriented person release from anticipated fear of rejection. Masochism may result when a 1,9 orientation becomes extreme. It can be explained, at least in part, as beginning with intolerable emotions brought about when a 1,9-oriented person *anticipates* rejection. Even though *actual* rejection may not materialize, the fear of it increases in intensity as long as the rejection does not occur. If punishment or pain can be experienced, the exaggerated fear from anticipated rejection may be relieved because, after the episode of suffering has passed, the person expects reacceptance and reassurance such as may have happened in childhood when parents punished him and then he was reaccepted by them. This may explain why some 1,9-oriented people may actually seek painful experiences to reassure themselves.

Furthermore, sadism, the 9,1 distortion introduced earlier, can be coupled symbiotically with masochism, the 1,9 distortion, within a boss-subordinate relationship. The sadistic element of wanting to punish fills the 9,1-oriented manager's need to reject, and the masochistic element of feeling reassured after punishment may satisfy the 1,9-oriented subordinate's need to feel accepted. This coupling can result in the matching of a 9,1 boss and a 1,9 subordinate. Thus, a subordinate might ordinarily be expected to find a 9,1-oriented boss's tirade so objectionable that he would fight back or leave, but a 1,9-oriented subordinate may do neither. He submits, seeming to feel the treatment is his just desert. This pattern can be maintained for years, with nothing to account for it other than the boss's need to release his anger by attacking and the subordinate's need for relief from tension by being punished.

## Hypochondriasis

Another correlation between Grid style and health relates to hypochondriasis. Levinson describes such a typical 1,9-oriented employee:

> ... He is absent from his job an average of a day a week. He is very much concerned about his own health and that of his family. Both are frequently the subject of his conversation. His associates feel that he is given the status, recognition, and consideration due his position. He has been told his work performance is well regarded by his superiors. He demands considerable recognition (love and attention from others), and feels that he does not get enough of it (always *hungry* for love).

> This dependent, self-centered man would prefer to lean on others stronger than he, but that is neither acceptable nor permissible. He feels inadequately loved, so he must love himself and he has little love to give to others. But how can a man gratify his dependent needs and be cared for in our society? By being sick. It is acceptable to have someone else take care of you when you are sick and to be concerned about your health. His doctors will love him if no one else will.

Levinson's explanation is:

> ... the hypochondriac's constant concern with his symptoms provides him with attention, gratifies his dependency needs, and permits him to manipulate his friends and relatives, using his symptoms as an excuse.

Missildine's account of the origins of hypochondriasis reinforces the above:

> Hypochondriasis originates, in most cases, in the fearful attitudes toward disease expressed by parents and heard by a child. The child, helplessly dependent on his all-knowing parents, absorbs and adopts as his own the anxious attitude of his parents, imitating them. It helps him to feel close to them and secure—literally like them, the only adults he knows and his protectors.

Thus it appears that needs for love that are not satisfied by others can result in unrealistic fears for one's own health. These fears in turn provoke the concern of others, and the 1,9-oriented person receives some of the attention he so desperately craves.

## Asthma

Several investigations report that bronchial asthma originates with lack of self-confidence, coupled with a strong feeling of dependence on others for direction, guidance, and approval. An "attack" may be triggered when a person with this orientation faces a situation that provokes his fear of rejection.

## Inflammatory Bowel Disease

Managers who have an extreme 1,9 orientation may be trapped into "intolerable" situations of tension, such as the death of a loved one, the requirement to pull up roots and to accept a transfer, and so on. The inner conflict cannot be resolved and appears to set up a psychobiological connection to a variety of bowel disorders.

The Grid-like style of such persons is described by McMahon *et al* who studied the characteristics of colitis patients in comparison with their healthy brothers or sisters.

Differences between patient and sibling can be viewed in terms of the patient's appearing fixated at the stage of idealizing and complying with parental authority, deriving and maintaining his identity via their approval and protection. In a sense he has an authority problem although not of the kind we associate with the perpetual rebel.

This authority problem is more subtle and difficult to recognize because it does not make waves and gratifies the authority's need to be idealized. The patient, in contrast to his sibling, appears to give up or attenuate his struggle for identity as a psychologically separate, autonomous individual. He is tied to the original source of his gratification and seems to have compromised his autonomy to maintain that tie.

## Hypertension

Hypertension, the "silent" illness also known as high blood pressure, is reported to have origins that can be associated with a dominant Grid style of 1,9 coupled with a strong backup of 9,1. The person suffering this illness is reported to exhibit marked need for affection and approval, coupled with a fear of rejection as demonstrated in the desire to please. However, a seething volcano of anger and hostility lurks submerged just beneath the surface, and the person may be unaware of it.

Alexander points out that persons with hypertension were often "extremely compliant and agreeable and would go out of their way to please their associates." In addition, he draws attention to their inability to express rage coupled with a superficial appearance of being well adjusted and mature.

These two forces, one to seek approval through pleasing, the other to vent frustration by being aggressive, create strong emotional tensions within such a person. It is difficult to reduce these tensions through attack or through other ways of getting them off his chest and out of his system. Unrelieved tensions can reveal their insidious effects on the circulatory system.

## Diabetes

Still another Grid-associated physical illness, involving increase in blood sugar level that triggers the attack, is found in diabetes, as pictured in the following quotation by Dunbar:

> In early childhood, most diabetics develop a strong emotional conflict between resentment of parents and docile submission to them. There is a large proportion of "spoiled" children among them, and a strong jealousy of brothers and sisters. Among the men especially there is a history of domination by the mother with strong ties of affection and dependence.
>
> . . . superficially diabetics seem to get on well with their fellows, but they are bothered by feelings of insecurity in their relations with others so that they tend to alternate between a self-conscious initiative which sends them more than half way to meet people and an inaccessible aloofness which prompts them to withdraw suddenly from friendships. Their strong compulsion to win sympathy often has just the opposite effect.
>
> In their work, they incline to a commendable industry but without much display of initiative. They shrink from responsibility and scatter their energies among a multitude of tasks, often ignoring the important for the trivial. This inability to follow a consistent course of actions prevents them from developing their intelligence and abilities, which are frequently above the average.

This Grid style correlation seems to involve a dominant 1,9 Grid orientation that is extreme, coupled with a strong 1,1 backup style.

### Childhood Origins of 1,9

1,9-oriented children may become 1,9-oriented adults. They are children who are reared to do their parents' bidding in return for love and affection from them. This seems to come about most frequently when one parent, or both, analyze the child so well that they become expert on every detail of what he is thinking and feeling. Thus the parents exercise control over the child, telling him what to do, how to think, and what to feel. Each small step of advice and guidance is easy for the child to follow and accept. Warmth and affection are extended to the child as approval of his dependence on them for direction. The parents' constant helpfulness unwittingly communicates to the child the danger of self-reliance, the importance of ensuring continued help through dependence on them for advice and support, and the warmth and approval that leaning on parents brings.

By comparison, when a child thinks and acts independently or spontaneously, parents feel threatened. They communicate this to the child, saying something like, "If you loved me, you wouldn't do that." This stimulates the child's fear of rejection and inhibits any developing desire to act autonomously. Parents who give love and affection in return for dependence are creating the conditions of a 1,9 orientation.

Punishment that might provoke hostility or anger is likely to be absent. The closest thing to it is likely parents' withholding affection.

Parents of a 1,9-oriented child are, therefore, paternalistic in their approach to child rearing. They exercise strong direction and control, not in a telling or demanding task-oriented way, but in the sense of undermining the child's confidence and independence. The kinds of things the parents of a 1,9-oriented child are likely to say are, "Let me do it for you," "Mother or Daddy knows best," "You're so nice," "You always do what's right (i.e., Right is defined as what I want you do do)." The child learns to fear new, strange, and unfamiliar situations. Life is secure under the umbrella of helpful parents, teachers, and bosses. The child is likely to be accepting and grateful for such control and he continuously rechecks with parents. "Is this good? Is this right? Am I doing what you want? How do you want me to do this?"

Parents employing an approach that produces a 1,9-oriented child usually want him to become an adult-oriented person: loving, kind, gentle, and respectful of them. When a child responds to adults in this way, other adults may compliment the child for being "good." Heard by parents, such compliments by other adults reinforce their own belief that these child-rearing practices are approved of by their neighbors and friends.

Under these conditions of rearing, a child learns to be responsive to all adults in order to gain their acceptance and approval. By comparison, activities with other children are less important. The child has learned to ask, "What must I do to gain adult (later boss) acceptance and approval?" "How must I think or feel?" "How can I be pleasing and in this way avoid rejection?" Thus the child does whatever gains approval, not what promotes self-reliance and independence.

This unpunitive, paternalistic approach is likely to result in 1,9-oriented children, whereas paternalistic parents who punish lack of achievement and disobedience are more likely to rear 9,1-oriented children who resist their control.

A second but probably less frequent childhood origin of 1,9 attitudes is from 9,1 parents who are excessively rejective of their child. Feeling rejected, the child develops stronger and stronger needs for approval, which go unfulfilled. Starved for love, he seems to have an insatiable desire for affection. Any sign of rejection causes hurt and pain, and he reinforces efforts to gain approval, testing each new relationship for what he wants most: to be loved and approved of.

## Facades

Facades that convey personal liking for another in much the same way as a person with a 1,9 orientation are often a cover-up for 9,1 motivations to master, control, and dominate. The manager appears to be reacting from 1,9-oriented assumptions because people feel his actions reflect deep appreciation and affection for them. Since this facadist does not become sentimentally involved with people, he is able to approach them in a warm and friendly manner and to make alliances that he can easily set aside when the occasion demands it for pursuing his personal objectives at the expense of others.

### Praise

A manager with a 1,9-oriented facade builds up people by cleverly using deference and compliments. He is lavish with praise and approbation even when these are unearned, because compliments make people feel important. Someone who has been praised comes to like and admire the individual he received the praise from, and the pleasure derived often makes him think his performance caused him to deserve it. Then the facadist has achieved his purpose because he now can exercise control over the flattered person.

Experts on this facade counsel against "going too far," because flattery can boomerang, and the facadist needs to be careful himself not to be misled by flattery from those he flatters, for he then loses his control over them.

### Criticism

Criticism carries many dangers. As Carnegie said, " . . . even though one feels critical, and criticism is, in fact justified, it should be avoided." Why? He explains in the following quotation:

When dealing with people let us remember that we are not dealing with creatures of logic. We are dealing with creatures of emotions, creatures bristling with prejudices and motivated by pride and vanity ... And criticism is a dangerous spark—a spark that is likely to cause an explosion in the powder keg of pride ...

Criticism is much too volatile for an individual to play with if he wants to create the impression of loving people. Negative reactions can be avoided by not being critical, even when one feels like being so. This is manipulative since the criticism that is withheld might have proved instructive and useful to its recipient. The other person is misled into believing that all is well when it actually is not.

### "Long Toes"

Some people are super-sensitive to rejection, and the 1,9 facadist is aware that offending others may reduce his ability to control them. The individual who is excessively sensitive to being "stepped on" is said to have "long toes."

With such people a facadist goes to any end to create a purely social relationship, apparently for no other purpose than his admiration and personal friendship for them. On closer examination the purpose is to achieve a hidden aim. On a social visit, for example, conversation is primarily directed towards the other person's health, family, vacation plans, etc. Only after the other person feels accepted does the facade builder reveal his true purpose—to ask a favor, to borrow something, or to request needed information which might have been misunderstood or withheld if requested before the personal discussion. Thus, a 1,9-oriented facadist establishes a relationship of warmth and approval of the other person to get what he wants from him.

### "Yes Man"

One way to elicit the favorable notice of a boss is to support his opinions, hiding the fact that one's own personal convictions may differ. The payoff comes when the boss is considering promotions or a replacement. He remembers and rewards those who think "correctly." This means they think as he does. The "yes man" reaction is not motivated by needs for approval, as might be the case were a straightforward 1,9 orientation involved. It is a devious strategy for getting ahead that bypasses consideration of merit but that comes through to the boss as genuine agreement with his positions.

The difference between a 1,9 facade and the genuine 1,9-oriented person is that for the latter the need to be liked is genuine. He is interested in people and needs to be liked by them. The 1,9 facadist wants their warmth and affection and ingratiates himself with them, not for his own feelings of being approved of, but to exploit the other person's readiness to help the facadist.

### Implications of 1,9 for Organizations

There are at least two situations in which the "country club" style may become a company way of life. One is where a company is operating on a cost plus basis or in a situation of such high demand that profits are inevitable. Competition does not force the company to operate effectively. As a result, it becomes unattractive to make efficiency moves because these might spread anxiety among organization members, lead to dissatisfaction, and make leaders appear unappreciative. It is simpler to take the easy way and just let things go as they may.

A second situation occurs in quasi-monopolistic organizations. Such actions as efficiency moves which call for layoffs, tight controls, etc., that would disturb the feelings of people do not need to be taken. These organizations are primarily concerned with maintaining what are believed to be good human relationships.

A dramatic example of 1,9 as an organizational way of life is contained in the following situation: a large manufacturing establishment, up to several years ago, maintained a practice that had been built over the years of employing an extra group of temporary laborers during summer months. This was done to compensate for the absence of regular work force members on vacation. Vacations for permanent organizational members were not scheduled with production objectives in mind. Instead, the organization "picked up the bill" through employing substitutes. The result was that each member of the organization was able to have his vacation exactly when he wanted. A dramatic conclusion from this 1,9 way of life occurred, however. Because its product became hopelessly noncompetitive, the plant shut down. With this luxurious style of management—not facing the problem of involving people in the real issues of production—everyone then had 52 weeks of vacation per year!

Decisions are against efficiency moves, as in the example above. They are motivated by a desire not to disturb people in order to maintain personal security, even though diminishing the productive purpose of the organization. While such decisions seem to favor the development or maintenance of good relationships, such relationships are not sound, in any basic sense. The reason is that, in a profit-motivated economy, those organizations that are alert to economic pressures and business opportunities can and should overtake a "fat and happy" organization. More competitive organizations run them out of business. They are weak, if for no reason other than that they contain the seeds of their own destruction; for example, the closing of the plant just described.

Equally important is the threat they create by bringing about the long-term erosion of free enterprise as a way of economic life.

### Summary

The 1,9-oriented manager places high value on warm and friendly relationships. He remains secure when surrounded by people who give support and appreciation. His natural bent is to anticipate the desires and wishes of others and to do their bidding. He is deferential and eager to please.

To avoid rejection, the 1,9-oriented manager avoids rejecting others— "locking horns" or "crossing them up." This is made possible by accepting the opinions, attitudes, and ideas of others in preference to pushing his own. Therefore, he rarely initiates positive leadership though he actively seeks close contacts and moves to establish bonds of harmony.

He rarely generates conflict, but when it does appear, either between himself and others or between others in his presence, he tries to soothe bad feelings. When those engaged in activities do not react as a 1,9-oriented person needs them to, he reads their reactions as personal repudiation of him and moves to reverse these reactions in whatever ways will restore warmth and approval. This often means acquiescence and reduced self-assertiveness. Thus, a 1,9-oriented person seems to have many friends and few, if any, enemies, but his approach hinders, rather than helps, productivity.

Productivity is unlikely to be high either in the long or short term. It is for this reason that the 1,9 orientation is unlikely to be formed in highly competitive companies and more common under cost plus contracting and in high profit margin and quasi-monopolistic settings.

The mental and physical health consequences of an extreme 1,9 orientation are seen in masochism, hypochondriasis, bowel disorders, asthma, diabetes, and high blood pressure.

Paternalistic parents emphasize the importance of their child being dependent on them. Advice and guidance as to thoughts and feelings that are proper are provided in exchange for giving love and approval to the acquiescent child. He learns to lean on adults (and later, on his bosses), rather than to be self-reliant.

The *B* paragraph in Chapter 1 is the self-description of a 1,9-oriented manager. If you placed a 5 by this paragraph as being most typical of your behavior, you see your managerial style based on 1,9-oriented assumptions.

## Chapter 5

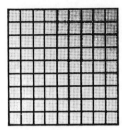

# 1,1

Though he has emotionally resigned and retreated into indifference, the 1,1-oriented manager's motivation is to stay in the system. This means doing enough to preserve his job and to build seniority but without making a contribution that benefits his colleagues or the organization. He expects little and gives little. Although he may appear bored, drifting, and listless, if this does not expose him, he is prepared to put up with the situation as he goes through the motions of being a manager. On the negative side, his motivation is to "hold on" and to avoid sinking into hopelessness and despair.

By being visible yet inconspicuous, he escapes being controversial, having enemies, or getting fired. He is likely to appear somewhat preoccupied, and these attitudes keep others off his back. The degree to which he remains passive, nonresponsive, and uninvolved is governed by the acceptable minimum others are prepared to tolerate. By not becoming emotionally entangled with tasks or people, he avoids coming to grips with his inadequacies and inabilities. This combination of neutrality and physical presence is the key to being able to keep from provoking undue resentment by others because of his noncommitment. His motto is "See no evil, speak no evil, and hear no evil, and you are protected by not being noticed."

How is it possible for an organization to persist in ignoring its "deadwood?" It is in the silent expectations that operate in some organizations to guarantee everyone job security after a few years so that any manager is then safe until retirement. If low productivity exists it is tolerated or ignored. An example is that of a manager, once the president of a subsidiary company, who was promoted to the legal department of the parent organization. The reason given was that legal issues facing the corporation had become more complex, and an executive with legal background and broad business experience to study these matters had become a necessity. For twelve years before his retirement, this executive was seldom seen. He delegated technical problems to subordinates, studied their conclusions, and forwarded their studies as appropriate, often sending them alone to discussions related to the implications of their conclusions. He himself came and went, quietly and unnoticed. His secretary, who rarely did any typing, except for cover letters, saw him relatively infrequently. Incoming and outgoing correspondence and calls were few in the beginning and continued to shrink as executives who needed legal assistance came to contact his juniors directly. His attendance at meetings was regular but more as a listener than as a participant. He had been shelved, and his response to this treatment was a 1,1 reaction. The organization carried his dead weight for years.

A 1,1-oriented individual usually rationalizes his nonproductivity by putting the blame for his situation on something or someone else. For example, "Big government has become so mammoth that nothing can be done about it." He may blame the "onslaught of technology for bringing about a dehumanizing way of life," adding, "I want nothing to do with it." He may point his finger at "the money-crazed corporation where profit is the sole aim," or the "vicious, competitive rat-race for promotion that chews up people." He complains about the "university, which failed to provide me an education pertinent to today's requirements." These rationalizations serve the purpose of justifying indifference, passivity, and a "can't do" spirit and make it unnecessary for him to admit to himself that he is not involved. When others leave him alone, the 1,1-oriented manager is content to treadmill through his tenure. He is an onlooker to his own life.

Sociologists have described behavior that is, in some respects, similar to the 1,1 behavior depicted here. The word used is *anomie*, another way of characterizing the 1,1 adjustment. It pictures that person who has no entity, who is rootless and drifting, and who in his own behavior reveals no direction. The individual managing according to a 1,1 orientation, though, is different in an important aspect. Under anomie, personal behavior has lost any aim except for bare subsistence, with others, like welfare agencies, taking over responsibility for that by providing food and shelter. One does not retain membership of any sort. As an example, a bum in skid row—dirty, ill attired, unshaven, sitting quietly, not communicating with other bums—aptly describes anomic people as rootless, drifting, not trying to influence the environment and, in turn, living in an undemanding environment. Respect for others is absent, but so is self-respect. There is, therefore, an important difference between anomie and 1,1.

The individual's goal in 1,1 is that of maintaining organizational membership and continuity for one's own personal advantages. Yet the manager beats a strategic withdrawal from active participation. In doing so, however, he has maintained the cast and form of acceptable behavior. His withdrawal is hollow. There is a vacuum within him, but exterior trappings remain as they were. He maintains the physical and functional appearances that put his behavior into conformance with that of many others with whom he associates. The organization becomes the means for maintaining a socially acceptable role of citizen by discharging the very minimum of citizenship requirements. Position, status, and pay come from within the organization with minimum effort given in exchange. The difference between anomie and 1,1 stops at this point, because the character of emotional resignation appears to be more or less the same in both situations.

### Situational Dynamics of 1,1

A dominant 1,1 orientation does not always originate at an earlier time. Its origins may be in the adult years and related to the work situation itself.

Consider the individual who does well in grammar school, high school, and in the first years of college. For the next two or three years he becomes an academic vagabond. People say, "He will never amount to anything." Understanding a 1,1 orientation, however, we can appreciate that something may have happened in his sophomore year that caused him to pull back, to cease striving. His academic colleagues might say, "Something threw him for a loop." For the time being he has been thrown from a dominant 9,9, 9,1, 5,5, or 1,9 style into a 1,1 orientation.

After a period he returns to college, picks up where he left off, graduates with flying colors, and enters a career where he also does well. How can we understand this interruption? There are several possible causes. One is that during his vagabond period he was probably avoiding a threat to his private image of himself. Greater maturity provides the capacity for understanding and insight that now permits him to proceed with his career without facing the same personal threat. He is now able to grasp quickly what, as a sophomore, he had been unable to comprehend. Values associated with his sense of personal adequacy, as they may have existed at an earlier time, may have shifted so that now the same performance has a different meaning. No longer does it communicate the same threat. He can now engage in the activity without feeling undue risk. His dominant orientation has shifted again, either back to the original style or to some other, but in either event, he has shifted away from a dominant 1,1 approach.

Another example of the exposure circumstance occurs when a manager gets in over his head. A manager may have an outstanding record, particularly where he has been provided with close supervision.

Because his performance has been excellent, he has been promoted and is now responsible for a section or a unit, where because of very loose supervision his performance is visible to all. Now his personal competence to operate autonomously is exposed, possibly for the first time. At this point he is immobilized, unable to move. As a subordinate operating under precise instructions he was acting in behalf of someone else rather than under his own motivation and inspiration. If he failed, it was not *his* judgment that was in error; he was just operating according to faulty instructions. His internal values are not exposed when acting on behalf of others.When promoted, he is acting on his own behalf, with thinking and judgments exposed at the risk of their being proven inadequate. We can understand how a manager can perform with competence as a subordinate and yet be unable to act under his personal responsibility as a boss.

"Exposure" of 1,1 can be found at all organizational levels, not just instigated at the point of entry into management. Because of unusual qualifications or academic or technical preparation, a manager may be assigned as an assistant, say to a corporation president or some other senior executive. His talent in carrying out assignments is conspicuous. His performance draws attention, and he receives an important line appointment, a young man who arrives at a high position years before his peers. Things go well during the period while he is learning the ropes; that is, while he still is *not* personally responsible. The more he comes to feel greater personal responsibility for decisions and results, the less he is able to initiate. Decisions are postponed until "further studies are completed." When completed, additional unanswered questions that must be explored remain. His decisions are never put to the test. He has become unreachable and unteachable.

Sometimes when action is imperative and direction is not forthcoming, subordinates may act on their own initiative. If these autonomous actions turn out well, they may preserve the manager's reputation for good performance, but the managerial Grid style is still 1,1.

Another case is the boss who has been, at some point in his career, heavily committed but has now withdrawn and is presently managing according to 1,1 assumptions: a case of a backup style becoming dominant. This individual is likely to have been one whose dominant style was 9,1 and who, rather than facing defeat and failure, withdraws from the fight, or caves in from pressures, rationalizing that his contributions are not appreciated. For example, a person may perform quite well up to some age such as forty, forty-five or so. Then he "burns out," losing interest in the job that is empty and has ceased to be challenging, or he feels that he is drained from working too hard and wishes to spend more time with family and friends. The actual causes of burn-out are usually

quite varied. During the early years of his successful performance we
can understand that his dreams of control, mastery, and domination
were far away from what he achieved in his day-by-day performance.
The years have gone by, and now, as a middle manager, he faces middle
age. He is never going to be president. How can he avoid recognizing that
his performance has been inferior to his aspirations? He can maintain
the myth and avoid the risk of self-revelation by "backing off" through
rationalizations of the kind introduced earlier, *i.e.*, "The challenge has
gone out of the job ... I've lost interest ... I want to spend more time
with my family." His dominant style has receded, and a 1,1 orientation
has replaced it.

Still another explanation of how a 1,1 backup orientation may become
dominant has been described in Chapter 3, concerned with 9,1. A 1,1
withdrawal can result when a person can neither fight back nor afford to
leave and seek employment elsewhere. The 1,1 corner is a harbor that
protects him from striving against unfavorable winds.

These are situational origins of 1,1; childhood influences in the 1,1
direction are dealt with later in this chapter.

### Boss Behavior

A 1,1-oriented manager assigns subordinates whatever tasks must be
done and gives them more or less full discretion in completing them.
That this is more abdication than delegation is shown in the following
ways he might view his responsibilities.

*Planning:* "I give broad assignments though I avoid specifying goals or
schedules when possible. Each subordinate fends for himself."

*Organizing:* "If left alone, they carry out assignments, as they know their
own jobs and their capabilities better than anyone else."

*Directing:* "I carry the message from those above to those below. I pass the
story as straight as I can and with as little embroidery or interpretation as
possible."

*Controlling:* "I make the rounds, but I take little on-the-spot action if I can
avoid it. They like it that way. I do, too."

*Staffing:* "You take whomever they give you."

The boss avoids interfering not for the reason that others need the opportunity to be autonomous and to learn from their own efforts, but out
of his own lack of involvement. A remark such as "I don't make decisions, I only work here," communicates a 1,1 sense of withdrawal from
responsibility.

Thus a 1,1 manager occupies his position in only a superficial way. His approach is to do whatever needs to be done to keep from losing his position. He passes like a shadow over the ground, leaving no permanent mark on the organization of which he is a member. Neither does the organization leave its mark on him.

### Management-by-Objectives

The 1,1 approach to management-by-objectives is to cooperate with its requirements. This translates into "going through the motions." If the system calls for each manager discussing goals with subordinates he does so. If it calls for the boss to review these with his own boss, he does so. If it calls for completing paper work, he does so. If it calls for followup with performance appraisal and review, he also does these things. On paper it would appear that management-by-objectives is successful.

Yet the 1,1 approach is "all form, no substance. . . ." The boss has not given his thought and emotion to what it might really be possible for him to accomplish. He has neither encouraged nor discouraged subordinates to think out challenging goals and necessary action steps for reaching them. By doing what the outward requirements expect of him, he "beats the system," though even that is not really what motivates him. It is management-by-default rather than management-by-objectives.

Goals do not exist as ordinarily understood. The reason is that goals are related to concern for production or concern for people. Because of the disinterest in both of these, organizationally related goals are not relevant to a 1,1-oriented manager. Rather, the objective is a self-centered one of personal survival within the system to get the pay and, eventually, retirement benefits. No more. The general attitude is not far away from reactions to the dole of depression days.

Once an employee is in place, his 1,1-oriented manager leaves him alone with the hope that he will do what is necessary. However, if performance appraisals are part of an ongoing formalized management-by-objectives program, they are carried out in a perfunctory manner. If the Personnel Department sends appraisal forms on a periodic basis, they are completed and returned. Little thought goes into the ratings beyond taking care not to rate anyone too high or too low. To do otherwise brings inquiries to him. If an interview is necessary, he asks the subordinates to come to his office, provides a mechanical explanation, and asks him if he has any questions. If required, he asks the subordinate to sign the form. The interview is over if there are no questions.

### Conflict

As with managers operating according to the other Grid styles, he too is faced with boss pressures, dissatisfactions, and unhappy or resentful subordinates who call upon him to act in their behalf. His reactions to such situations range from pseudo-compliance, through neutrality, to physical withdrawal from the situation.

Simply by holding the title of boss, but not acting like one, managers operating from this orientation remain relatively free of involvement and conflict. This is the "ostrich dynamic." Keeping his head buried, he does not have to face problems. He does not see disagreeable situations and frequently they disappear for lack of attention.

### Being Seen but Not Heard

One way to avoid conflict is to be seen but not heard. When unavoidably caught in a group of two or more, a 1,1-oriented manager seldom participates spontaneously in discussions. Neither words nor expressions reveal his thoughts (or lack of them) about what is being said. By not saying anything meaningful, he avoids being provocative and, therefore, being called upon to defend his point of view. Others have no ideas about what is or is not important to him. What makes this kind of silence acceptable is that in the absence of contrary evidence, those around him either fail to notice or believe that silence means agreement or acquiescence.

A grunt is the best reply of all. "Hmm" means more or less "Okay, so what, it's no skin off *my* back." If a 1,1-oriented manager should come straight out with this in words, it might be taken as an affront, a challenge. But "hmm" is a deadener. It leaves the other person with no certain way to respond.

If someone asks, "How are things going?" the answer is "Okay." Further discussion is not encouraged by this kind of answer, yet there is nothing negative about a nice, bland *okay*, particularly when it is not followed up with "How are things with you?" Commenting objectively might start an argument, and arguing is a drag. If X and Y are said to come after Z, well, okay.

Sometimes a 1,1-oriented manager is called upon to do something. If in charge, he ponders, delegating if in trouble, and mumbles or tries to talk his way out of the situation if uninformed. Under these circumstances, inaction is justified by saying, "They wouldn't understand," "There isn't enough time," or "Nobody would pay attention anyway."

At other times, a 1,1-oriented manager cannot help but observe that others are working at cross-purposes. The approach is to ignore them unless the conflict is important enough to pose a threat to his position. He shrugs and hopes that subordinates will not be called to account.

## Message Passing

The 1,1 approach to implementing policies is that of message passing. He moves orders down the line from above so as not to get caught "holding the bag." Also, he faithfully repeats messages from below to his own boss to ensure that he is not pinned as a missing link in the chain. The safest procedure is neither to add to nor to take away from what others have said. By quoting, one passes the message without becoming embroiled in the contents.

The flavor of 1,1 is seen in the example below, where a manager is holding a regularly scheduled meeting for downward communication as a matter of company policy. He has just returned from a weekly staff meeting where changes in procedures, policies, and the like were discussed and where each member was to initiate appropriate changes within his own area of responsibility. In the meeting itself, this manager's behavior appeared commendable. He listened and took notes, both indicators to his own boss of his interest.

As is his usual custom, he calls his five subordinates to his office. When all are seated, he reads the conclusions reached in the staff meeting carefully so that no one can say later that he has not "communicated." After his recitation, he files his dated notes in his desk drawer.

Without looking up, he says, "I'm going to the . . . . Who has the [company car] keys?" As he turns to leave, a subordinate ventures a question concerning how and when a particular change is to be effected.

"They didn't comment on that," is the manager's reply.

Another raises a question about fifteen large boxes of materials in the hallway.

"They said to order them. They didn't say what to do with them when they got here. I mentioned they'd arrived. Let 'em sit." With that he leaves.

This incident describes the 1,1 approach. The "facts" as this manager had heard them from above were carried to his subordinates. When accountability is unavoidable, he does enough to be able to report, "I told them what to do. If they haven't done it, it's because they didn't listen. It's not my problem." When a subordinate does something wrong, he is likely to say, "Oh! *They* are always causing trouble, but so what? What can you do?" He can always place the responsibility elsewhere, on "them," on someone else.

## Camouflaging Uninvolvement

There may be differences between the observable and unobservable behavior of a 1,1-oriented manager. His observable behavior conforms to outer requirements and affords protection by making him unnoticeable.

He is likely to be on time if on-time performance is important, to avoid leaving early, to fit his vacation to the convenience of others, to avoid sick leave whenever possible, and to file required reports promptly. All of these are camouflages that give the appearance of involvement with the deeper objectives of the organization. His mind is not on the work although an expression of mild interest rests lightly on his face.

His behavior is likely to be different when it is not observable by others or subject to their review and likely to reflect the depth of his resignation and indifference. A telephone call is not returned unless explicitly requested. The inquiry that does not demand a response is not answered.

### Procrastination

When someone complains about something or in other ways expresses dissatisfaction, the 1,1-oriented manager either ignores him or implies that the displeasure has been noted. He is likely to down-play any issue and to procrastinate with, "It'll probably work itself out," or "I'll get to that tomorrow." He might suggest "More time is needed to think things over." The way to deal with a disturbing memo is to defer an answer, to file it and "forget" where it was filed, or to pass it to a subordinate to draft an answer. To a query about some past memo, the answer is, "Sorry, I'm not sure I received it."

### Maintaining Neutrality

There are many ways to give the appearance of responding without presenting any views. This is maintaining neutrality in order to be safe.

When asked what other people think or would do, he supplies an infinite variety of neutral answers: "I'm not cut in . . . I haven't heard . . . I don't know . . . I wasn't there." When pressed further, he provides equally adept answers: "It's up to you . . . It's your problem, not mine . . . Whatever you say . . . I'm no expert." He communicates but evades controversy.

Occasionally it is inevitable that a person is asked directly to reveal himself. The 1,1-oriented solution is to speak in vague, abstract, and general terms that reveal little or nothing. Others feel mollified by having been answered, yet the answer has not obligated one to any particular course of action. Whenever the price of agreeing is less than the expense of resisting, saluting is preferable. The standard salute is, "Whatever you say."

## Straddling the Fence

The "straddle the fence" strategy is useful when two points of view exist, each supported by an important faction. The 1,1-oriented manager wishes to offend no one and thus appears to be on both sides at the same time. "Alternative A may be best for the reasons that have been given, but on the other hand, there are strong points on the side of alternative B." Each side in the controversy, furthermore, feels that the manager understands and has a sympathetic appreciation for its point of view. Not quite double talk, straddling the fence permits the straddler to go either way once a final course of action is decided upon.

### Subordinate Reactions

Subordinates managed in a 1,1-oriented way may go all out, or themselves drift into 1,1-oriented reactions, or leave to escape an intolerable situation.

## Going All Out

The subordinate who is eager for "leg room" may find a 1,1-oriented boss ideal, not even recognizing the boss's Grid style for what it is. If the subordinate is self-initiating, the boss's withdrawal is almost unnoticeable. He interprets delegation as approval of his competence, misinterpreting the boss's actions according to his, the subordinate's, own predilections. He charges forward, full steam ahead.

The subordinate may recognize that his immediate boss is deadwood, but if his boss's boss (two levels up) understands the situation and gets pay increases, etc., for the subordinate two levels down, the 1,1 intermediate layer has little or no influence. Then, the subordinate's involvements and commitments can be great. He simply ignores his direct boss, and responds to the boss two levels up who supplies whatever guidance and rewards are essential.

## Leaving

A common response to being managed in a 1,1 way is to recognize the situation for what it is. But that doesn't mean it's acceptable just because it's understandable. A subordinate may find himself offended by this kind of management and leave rather than adjust. Others, recognizing its dead-end qualities, find a way to get out from under it by transferring.

## Into 1,1

A third response is to accept the circumstances as inevitable and to move into the 1,1 corner, receiving a pay check in exchange for the monotony and boredom of it. This is most likely, though, when a person already is headed in a 1,1 direction, and the movement is completed by transferring him from a current assignment into a setting with a 1,1 boss. This movement of people is said to be made necessary because "We can't sacrifice production, but we can't discharge unproductive people either. What are you going to do?" Tolerance for such 1,1 attitudes is built into many organizations, particularly where bureaucratic regulations or union constraints prohibit or severely limit firing.

## 9,1 Reactions to Boss

The 9,1 subordinate reaction may be to maintain a constant attack on his boss in the hope that he will either fight back or leave.

## Inverted 1,1

When situations arise that prevent efficiency moves, for example, 9,1-oriented management action is the opposite of creating 1,1 groups, and sometimes it takes a diabolical form. This results in the "inverted" 1,1 approach, which entails creating an environment that can only be tolerated with a 1,1 attitude. A 9,1-oriented department head may have a surplus of clerical personnel. Ten employees are assigned individual desks within a large office space. All work is withheld, and no one has meaningful activity. Strict discipline ensures that communication does not take place, thus sealing off social outlets. There is no escape. People are powerless to do anything except to accept the situation or to resign. Thus, by creating a 1,1 environment, morale is forced down to such a point that people leave rather than tolerate the loneliness and boredom.

### Implications for Mental and Physical Health

There are significant indications that when 1,1 has become a dominant Grid style in the extreme, it is associated with health problems.

## Premature Death

Prisoner of war camps such as Auschwitz provided some remarkable evidence about the connection between hopelessness, despair, and death. Medical experts, themselves prisoners of war, were in a position to study this relationship firsthand.

According to their studies, prisoners who had given up the hope of escaping or of being freed were found to be more susceptible to a number of diseases than those who persisted in their hope for the future and for being reconnected with loved ones. Beyond that, "simple" death, not traceable to any specific disease, also is reported to have been more common among this kind of 1,1-oriented prisoner.

Another major body of evidence connecting a 1,1 orientation with illness is found in older age where it is maintained that people who "give up" often deteriorate and die with surprising rapidity.

This giving up may also be seen in mandatory retirement which has inverted 1,1 qualities for some people. Retirement that is set by company policy at a certain age, usually at 65, came on the scene in the 1930s and 1940s. Its purposes were to open opportunity to the younger, reduce the risk of senility-encroaching effects, and, coupled with retirement income, free persons who had served the organization to enjoy their remaining active years according to personal choice.

All of these benefits have been realized. Yet it is now coming to be seen that, for some, automatic retirement is not different from "inverted 1,1." Life becomes a vacuum from which there is no escape. It deprives people of what they have been accustomed to doing and creates enforced and unwanted idleness. Alternative activities that might be embraced because they serve no meaningful value to the individual are disregarded.

There are numerous examples of persons who, healthy at 65, are gone at 66 or 67, whereas their colleagues, also retired at 65 but who had anticipated and prepared for retirement, are still going strong.

## Tuberculosis

Tuberculosis is a disease where susceptibility appears to be related to the patient's having come to view his situation in terms of 1,1 hopelessness. Faced with the loss of a significant person, such as the death of a wife or child, he feels he has no reason to live, producing a shift into an extreme 1,1 orientation. This seems to increase his vulnerability. The progress of the disease tends to be rapid, many times leading to a relatively quick death.

## Cancer

Significant evidence implicating an extreme Grid-like 1,1 orientation as one correlation of cancer can be interpreted in the following way. According to LeShan, circumstances seem to be something like this.

The basic emotional pattern of the cancer patient appears, on the basis of my observations, to have three major parts. The first part involves a childhood or adolescence marked by feelings of isolation. There is a sense that intense and meaningful relationships are dangerous and bring pain and rejection. The second part of the pattern is centered upon the period during which a meaningful relationship is discovered, allowing the individual to enjoy a sense of acceptance by others (at least in one particular role) and to find a meaning to his life. The third aspect of the pattern comes to the fore when the loss of that central relationship occurs. Now there is a sense of utter despair, connected to but going beyond the childhood sense of isolation. In this third phase, the conviction that life holds no more hope becomes paramount. And sometime after the onset of the third phase, the first symptoms of cancer are noted. . . .

Perceiving the cosmos as uncaring and unconcerned, the typical cancer victim does not conceive of any meaning beyond the human being and his particular relationships. Yet, at the same time, the individual has the feeling that he has been singled out by fate. No matter what he does, how hard he tries, the course of his life is seen as predetermined, joyless, and doomed. There seems to be little paranoid element in this concept, however. Indeed, it rests in that almost subliminal level of feeling where most of us in the 20th century hold our assumptions about the nature of the universe. Working with these patients, it seemed to me that this concept of personal doom had been fundamental to their belief since childhood. Even in the best moments of their lives, the sense of a predetermined fate remained in the background, a distant but still ominous drum roll.

This emotional orientation is one of bleak hopelessness with regard to ever achieving any meaning in life. When coupled with a catastrophic event, *i.e.*, death of a loved one, children growing up and leaving, loss of job, etc., nothing worthwhile is left. Hope is insufficient for reestablishing a basis of commitment. The stage is set for emotional resignation and a person's resistance to cancer is somehow reduced. LeShan also points out that a 1,1-like orientation was in the background at an earlier time rather than being a new adjustment.

It should be made clear from the outset that this despair was not a result of having contracted cancer. It was rather a fundamental aspect of the patients' emotional makeup, a feeling they had lived with all their lives. To make the point even more strongly, many of the patients specifically expressed the idea that for years they had felt there was no way out of the emotional box they found themselves in short of death itself.

There is no current basis for discriminating why one deeply embedded 1,1-oriented person might be susceptible to cancer and another to tuberculosis.

### Implications of 1,1 for Organizations

There are conditions within organizations that promote the emergence of 1,1 as a dominant style.

A widespread 1,1 reaction is found in work activities where division of labor and task simplification has been carried to the extreme. In situations of monotonous, repetitious, unchallenging work, it has been estimated that as many as one-third of an organizational work force can be apathetic, bored, uninterested, withdrawn, and uninvolved in the job itself. A 1,1 adjustment has occurred.

Technological innovations coupled with either self-imposed or union-imposed restrictions against firing can lead to a 1,1 adjustment. Featherbedding or filling a paper job description that has no functional utility is only likely to emphasize more the personal survival aspects of behavior.

Circumstances of "total" 1,1 organization existence can be envisioned. One is a circumstance where work is "made." An example is the Work Projects Administration during the depression of the 1930s.

It can be found in both industry and government where a person repeatedly has been bypassed for promotions. Rather than looking elsewhere, he adjusts in the work setting by doing as little as possible. He might say, "The work isn't too bad. We like the town. We have a comfortable house. I'm marking time until my retirement. I hope my chair doesn't break down."

The 1,1 style of managing is not the most common. In a competitive economy, a business operated under 1,1 concepts is unable to continue very long. On the other hand, many individuals and organization segments do perform in the 1,1 manner, and survival may be possible for extended periods. This is true especially in production situations that have become bureaucratic in nature, have outlived their usefulness, and where no one is ever fired.

1,1-oriented behavior of managers is "unnatural behavior." Though there are exceptions involving a 1,1 orientation from early childhood, it is many times a situation of personal defeat leading to self-abdication that an individual comes into instead of beginning with. Its presence is really an indication of failure of the individual manager and for the organization as well. It is failure in that he has accepted defeat and has withdrawn to the degree that even criticism no longer carries a sting. It is failure for the organization in that individual productive efforts are not integrated with sound human relationships.

### Childhood Origins of 1,1

There are various childhood origins of a 1,1-oriented Grid style.

A 1,1 orientation may be created by parents who give extremely close supervision, or create an overly coercive situation involving constant criticism and rebuke. In either case the child is left with little or no freedom for the development of initiative or personal discretion. Punishment is immediate whenever the child rebels, bucks, balks, or resists in other ways. His will is broken and he ceases to resist or to fight back. His only option is to escape by withdrawal. He satisfies family demands but protects himself from its pressures and additional pain on a "be seen but not heard" basis. This 9,1-oriented character of child rearing is what "teaches" a person to build a protective wall around himself and to make no more than survival adjustments. This does not mean that anger and hostility toward parents are not experienced; they may be but if so they are concealed to avoid the threat of greater punishment or further loss of love, thus reducing the risk that powerful parents will turn against or even desert him.

A second pattern is where parents may simply be passive, not reacting to the child either in a punitive or a loving way. They may be callously remote. When the parents respond in this neutral manner over extended periods, the child is left more or less isolated. Neglect may be from absence, preoccupation, and poverty, or where the parents have little time for the child, such as when there is divorce or death in the family. The child learns to be by himself and is unstimulated to learn the skills that result from participation. When continued lack of social stimulation coupled with parental neutrality persists over time, the child begins to embrace behavior with a 1,1 flavor—withdrawal, indifference, uninvolvement, and inner emptiness.

Another childhood origin of 1,1 is observed when a child is separated from its parents and placed in a hospital or other residential institution shortly after birth. An initial period of active protest and crying follows this rupture in an established relationship. Then the child tends to become withdrawn and inactive and ceases to make demands, crying only now and then and without observable cause, and appearing to demonstrate increased feelings of hopelessness and sadness. Eventually the despair begins to disappear and to be replaced by shallow reactions that hide withdrawal and a lack of involvement. This pattern of submitting to circumstances without commitment may be one of the important predisposing factors for a dominant or a backup 1,1 orientation among adults.

Still another set of circumstances under which a 1,1 orientation may develop is when parents are in intense conflict with one another and the only escape from the terrifying emotions experienced by the child is total withdrawal. Some children "freeze," immobilized by anguish. They come to react to any conflict situation in these terms, sometimes to the point where it becomes a dominant 1,1 Grid style orientation.

Child-rearing practices can be erratic in a two-hat, 9,1-1,9 way. This origin of 1,1 has been described by Horney.

> ... Or he may have had a parent so erratic in his mood-swings that he gave effusive demonstrative affection at one time and at others could scold or

beat him in a fit of temper without any reason that the child could understand. In short, there was an environment which made explicit and implicit demands for him to fit in this way or that way and threatened to engulf him without sufficient regard for his individuality, not to speak of encouraging his personal growth.

So the child is torn for a longer or shorter time between futile attempts to get affection and interest and resenting the bonds put around him. He solves this early conflict by withdrawing from others. By putting an emotional distance between himself and others, he sets his conflict out of operation. He no longer wants others' affection nor does he want to fight them. Hence he is no longer torn by contradictory feelings toward them and manages to get along with them on a fairly even keel.

Sometimes a 1,1 orientation comes about from overly indulgent parents. They may so idolize their child as to give him a self-image of being perfect in every way: precocious, beautiful, talented, and lovable. Under these circumstances, they are likely to completely pamper him, indulging his every desire, often before one is expressed. As the child enters school, he may be faced with contradictory evidence of his perfection but, if his self-image is strong, this information does not register.

Such evidence may mount, however, and to face up to reality as a young adult can be overwhelming. A way to avoid the necessity of facing up is to stay out of situations that can bring the discrepancy into view. Thus, a young man drops out of college ". . . because it's boring," rather than face the fact that he can't make a straight A record. An interview for a job opening is arranged but not kept, as to put one's availability into competition with others might result in their getting hired, and again demonstrating to the person that others are more perfect than he. For such reasons some people live on the periphery of life, all the while preserving their self-image of perfection.

This helps explain why some managers can perform in an excellent way if carrying out the wishes of others, but who falter, immobilized, when called on for initiative that might reveal inadequacy.

### Facades

A "don't care" attitude may not be indifference at all. It may hide intense concerns one does not wish to reveal. Then 1,1-oriented neutrality may be a facade. It's "never try, never fail" but as a front.

Another 1,1-oriented facade can be seen in the boss who manipulates subordinates into doing more and more by failing to notice or recognize what they are doing. To gain the boss's attention subordinates put out more and more effort which eventually he may acknowledge. The reason is that, if carried on endlessly, this manipulation fails because eventually subordinates turn away and abandon the effort, rationalizing that, no matter how hard they try, they never can please him. At that point the boss steps out of his facade and communicates his appreciation and reinforces their commitment, only to return to the same stance when they have decided it is all worthwhile.

### Summary

The best description of the 1,1 orientation is that it is *nondirection.* The manager who has adopted this orientation is committed neither to mastering the work environment nor to being loved or appreciated by the people in it. His motivation is retreat and resignation but within the system. He goes through the expected motions, frequently following rules of conduct in much the same way as others. Yet he does this, not as a conformist and without responding either positively or negatively, but to avoid being conspicuous or even noticed.

When disagreement arises, he does not take sides. He rarely expresses convictions and does not search out those held by others. He is likely to be described as colorless. While one may not know where he stands, it does not seem to matter. When conflict does arise, he remains neutral and, to the degree possible, out of it. Because of his neutrality, he rarely gets stirred up. If he does express humor, it is likely to be seen by others as rather pointless.

Productivity is likely to sink to the lowest tolerable level, and if it becomes mandatory to increase it, the "solution" is to employ more people or purchase more equipment, thus increasing expense without resolving the basic problem.

Mental and physical health implications point to illnesses that are related to the extremeness of emotional resignation: premature death, tuberculosis, and cancer.

There are several childhood origins of a 1,1 orientation. Parents who are overly directing and coercive may break a child's will so that he withdraws as his only means of adjustment. On the other hand, excessive neglect or unpredictable behavior on the part of parents may also result in a 1,1 orientation as the child does nothing since he is unable to react to consistency.

The 1,1 paragraph description in Chapter 1 is indicated by the letter $A$.

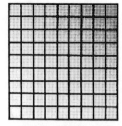

## Chapter 6

# 5,5

The positive motivation of a 5,5-oriented manager is to belong. "I want to look good, to be 'in' with my colleagues." He does this by seeking his sense of direction through finding out what the majority thinks or does and embedding himself within it. Being popular means putting together a package of qualities which are sought after in the human market, including whatever is fashionable in dress, neighborhoods to live in, places to go, books to read, and other forms of social expression. He is likely to develop pleasant manners and to strive to become an interesting conversationalist. His goal is to make many friends, even though not close ones.

A manager who is motivated by membership tends to be superficial in his own convictions. He is cautious to avoid self-exposure. This can be done by taking his cues at any given time from the actions of others. Prevailing opinions are his opinions. What others reject he rejects. Therefore, he is unlikely to have deep ideological commitments, whether political, religious, literary, social, corporate, or otherwise.

He experiences a sense of well-being when evaluated positively by fellow managers. These good feelings may persist even though a person may have just compromised a long-term gain for a short-term convenience, embraced a point of view only because his boss and colleagues did so, withheld a vital piece of information to avoid anticipated ostracism, or winked at a shady practice because "everyone" is doing it. The ability to back and fill, to shift, twist and turn, and yet to stay with the majority is important to a 5,5-oriented person's style. When he achieves this objective, the 5,5-oriented manager feels okay. The motivational motto is, "If I think, look, and act like everyone else, but a little more so, I will be a manager in good standing."

Sometimes the 5,5-oriented manager is unsuccessful and feels unpopular, out of step, and isolated from the group. He experiences shame. Being out of step can lead to ostracism and loss of membership. Viewed from the negative side of his motivation he wants to avoid looking bad and stirring resentment as a minority of one, separated from the mainstream, or to become an object of ridicule even though the position he stands for may, in fact, be a valid one. Risking being put "out" by one's colleagues can result in anxiety, which can build up and become a more or less constant amount for any given individual. Though the anxiety may be apparent to outside observers, the individual may be unaware of it. A key indicator of such free-floating anxiety is being uncertain which way to turn, even in situations where most people have no difficulty in making decisions.

### Boss Behavior

A 5,5 orientation to managing is "responsive" leadership. Many ways of moving forward, always in step with others and never in the lead, typify the approach. It stays within the bounds of what everyone else is doing as the ultimate criterion for appropriateness or pertinence. This amounts to a philosophy of *gradualism,* where change is by improvisation or by trial and error, not by goals-oriented direction or by experiment. The result is not chaotic, nor is it coherent. It is more likely to be conformity-centered and to come out piecemeal and makeshift.

According to this line of thinking, a manager does not *command* or *direct* to get the job done so much as he *motivates* and *communicates.* He avoids exerting formal authority. His approach is to request and to sell in order to get people to want to work.

*Planning:* "I make my plans according to what I know my subordinates will accept and what they will resist. Then I plan for each subordinate according to what he will think is okay."

*Organizing:* "After explaining aims and schedules, I make individual assignments. I double check to make sure my subordinates think what I request is okay. I encourage them to feel free to come back if they don't understand what to do."

*Directing:* "I keep up with each person's performance and review his progress from time to time. If a subordinate is having difficulty, I try to reduce pressure on him by rearranging conditions of work whenever possible."

*Controlling:* "I meet informally to discuss how things are going. I tend to emphasize good points and avoid appearing critical, though I do encourage subordinates to identify their own weak points. My subordinates know I take their thoughts and feelings into account in planning next assignments."

*Staffing:* "I seek people who will fit in."

The boss sees it as important to communicate, to elicit suggestions from subordinates, and to consider their points of view. His goal is to avoid "pushing" beyond what they are ready to agree with. As one manager explained, "I never give an order without testing to see if people are ready to buy it. People are more likely to go along if you let them talk and even gripe a little."

This provides an indication of the 5,5-oriented way of dealing with what he regards as inherent contradictions between production and people needs. Neither set of needs is ignored. He scales production down to what people are prepared to accept. He encourages them to offer suggestions which he uses either to reduce the effort necessary to get a result, to decrease pressure and thereby eliminate frustrations, or to show he listens. This compromising of production, which avoids sacrificing people needs, is a balancing act, giving up some of one to get some of the other. When the boss softens the push for production and considers attitudes and feelings, people accept the situation and are more or less "satisfied." Acceptable production is possible without unduly disturbing people. This orientation assumes that people are practical, that they realize *some* effort is to be exerted on the job. This is the hallmark of a 5,5 approach, which is *not to seek the best position for both production and people* ("that would be too 'ideal' "), but to find the position that is in between both, about halfway.

The 5,5 orientation prefers one-to-one dealings between each subordinate in informal and easy-going, give-and-take discussions. Through touching base with subordinates, he appears to embrace democratic values, which in turn enhance his popularity. However, he is also likely to enjoy group sessions and to rely on group decisions, special committees, or task forces to spread the responsibility for decisions by reaching for agreement of his colleagues or subordinates. He is likely to see his leadership role as that of a catalyst or facilitator, one whose procedural skills help subordinates reach a majority point of view. By giving his okay to what subordinates already approve of, the boss becomes a member; he is "in."

These managerial values may also come to expression in office architecture, as Riesman pictures it.

> It would be interesting to review from this perspective the present trend in America to get rid of private offices and have everybody work 'democratically' in a single accessible and well-lighted room. For many, I would guess, the dual requirement that one be sociable and get the work done has the same consequences that it does in school and college, of leading to censure of those who too obviously like their work, and of anxiety on the part of those who cannot simultaneously orient themselves to the task at hand and to the human network of observers. For others, there must be a reduction in the anxiety of isolated work, and a net gain in friendliness.

Keeping step becomes more important in this kind of open arrangement where what everyone is doing is obvious.

### Management-by-Objectives

The consequence of keeping in tune with others can be seen in the way in which a 5,5-oriented manager goes about management-by-objectives. Regardless of the particular system introduced into an organization, it is unlikely to produce anything very different from what has been typical in the past. Goals are thought of as targets. A target is something at which people aim. As in any contest, failure to hit the bull's-eye exactly in the center is acceptable if the hit is near it, or at least on the target. However, there is more to it than that. Because it is important to keep people with him, the 5,5-oriented manager collaborates with subordinates in setting production targets that he knows they can hit without stretching. A target, in other words, is not a do-or-die quota to be reached on a produce-or-perish basis. Nor is failure to hit the target subject to ridicule or punishment. It is energy enough to keep operations within the acceptable circles surrounding the bull's-eye. He brings the target nearer or draws the circle around the bull's-eye larger so that it is more difficult to fail. Thus, the objectives that are set are watered down to a point where achieving them is little more than mediocrity.

Performance reviews center on how well a subordinate is approaching his personal target or objective. The boss aids the individual to evaluate his own performance. He is likely to take a "sandwich" approach, highlighting strong, then weak points, and then the remainder of his strong points (bread-meat-bread) in such a way as to compensate for discouragement that may be felt over weaknesses. In this way, the score is kept approximately equal but more positive than negative. Even under unfavorable circumstances, a subordinate is likely to come out of a performance review feeling a little better.

### Conflict

The 5,5 approach is based on a persuasive logic. It says, "What person or movement has ever had its exclusive way? Extreme positions promote conflict and are to be avoided. Experience shows, again and again, that steady progress comes from compromise and a willingness to yield some advantages in order to gain others. Democracy, as it has come to be interpreted by many, operates quite well by yielding to the many and mollifying the few."

5,5 conflict runs the gamut from those techniques he relies on to avoid it when imminent to those employed to relieve erupted conflict.

### How Has It Been Done in the Past?

To give a sense of certainty a 5,5-oriented manager often falls back on traditions, long-established practices, or routinized procedures. When he can rely on history, he is relieved of being called to account for his own convictions. When traditions are unavailable, a precedent, even a single one, may be found to solve conflict so that no one loses face or status.

His conformity to the rules gives him the security of being an organization member in good standing. Conflict related to the exercise of independent judgment is avoided and he is operating within the "system" in the safest and most secure way.

## Corporate Protocol

In everyday usage, diplomacy and tact refer to 5,5-oriented kinds of action because they are calculated to avoid conflict by structuring the relationships of people and their interactions according to pre-set but often unstated "rules." Protocol tells people what to do in the absence of their having internal convictions about what would be appropriate and sound. These points of protocol have a great deal to do with the maintenance or enhancement of social position within the hierarchy. Thus, personal self-expression is rejected and replaced by outside "rules" that have no particular function except to let status or hierarchy or seniority prevail over genuineness or competence. Pecking order becomes very important.

## Radar-Scoping

When policies and regulations are ambiguous regarding what course of action to take, the 5,5-oriented manager looks to others for a sense of direction but usually in such a way that hides his own uncertainty. He may tactfully tease "guidance" out of his boss without the boss's recognizing that he is uncertain. Then he can be seen as initiating and exercising responsibility and yet not get himself in a bind by deviating from what his boss thinks best.

An obvious way of avoiding uncertainty and reducing the likelihood of conflict is to look at and to deal with a problem in terms of the other person's needs rather than from one's own perspective. The needs the other person feels may be the real ones or they may be unrelated to the real problem. No matter. If you can help him solve his felt needs, he is satisfied and you are appreciated.

If sources of guidance in one's own company have been exhausted, the question may become, "How would colleagues deal with this kind of a problem in Company X?" Resolution of uncertainty is possible by tapping colleagues in other departments to see what they do under similar circumstances. A phone call to a friend gives the answer. An acceptable method of resolution is established. If criticized, justification is readily at hand.

Opinion polls and related kinds of surveys may also be used to provide a crutch, a source of information that a manager can lean on to make decisions. When a market survey or opinion poll points in a given direction, the manager can embrace that course of action without exposing his own thinking or putting his own judgment "on the line." He can rely on the expertise of the opinion poll without "sticking his neck out." If the decision turns out badly, it was due to "bad" market research.

## Using the Informal System

An informal organization is likely to be most well developed within a 5,5-oriented management. It has its own norms, standards and rules of conduct, its leaders and followers, its conformists and deviants. Its channels of communication—gossip, rumor, and scuttlebutt—are a useful source of information about morale and satisfaction, letting the manager know how people are reacting to corporate moves, such as expansion or layoffs, and union and management tensions. Thus, the informal organization tells much about how people feel by what they are saying.

A 5,5-oriented manager uses it to keep his finger on the organization's pulse. He is seen by influential members in the informal organization as a good guy who comes through when the chips are down and lets people in on what is going on. In this way he can anticipate disturbing antiorganizational trends that may be developing and individual pressure points before they become chronic. As one manager said, "You have to use your sixth sense (i.e., your radar) to know what's going on, that is, to get the signals."

He does far more than monitor the informal organization, however. A trial balloon is one way of using the informal system. Trial balloons ascend when a 5,5-oriented manager is unable to gauge what his coworkers expect and yet is about to be forced to act. Should he make an unpopular decision, he faces the risk of provoking resistance. As a precaution before taking a stand, he puts out signals, anonymously if possible, to see what people might do if a tentative action were to become final. The propriety of the action is assessed in this way before any final decision is made. The 5,5 skill lies in being able to float the balloon without holding the string. Then he has no "investment," he is not accountable for showing bad judgment should the majority view make a tentative suggestion untenable.

He will also input information so that it can circulate, possibly feeding in confidential information on a not-to-be-repeated basis. In this way he is able to counter misguided actions and relieve tensions.

## Implicit Majority Rule

Emphasis on a majority orientation places an equal value on each individual's position and therefore uses social criteria as the model for what is right or valid rather than relying on objective evidence. This kind of measurement-by-plurality, however, can have disastrous effects on valid problem solving.

It is often naively assumed that the validity of ideas and feelings has been demonstrated because a majority share these certain ideas or feelings. The notion of majority agreement as the basis for decision validation may only mean that several people agree on the same faulty assumptions. The greater the conformity pressures the greater the risk of accepting majority agreements as equivalent with objective fact. "Groupthink" is a special case of a 5,5 orientation. Insufficiently sure of themselves or their facts, they prefer to go along and to give their support rather than to dig in, express real convictions, and create opposition to an emerging plan. The plan snowballs and rolls over what few reservations may remain. No one in the situation finds himself "out in left field." Everyone seems together. An agreement is reached. An action is taken. A fiasco results. The Bay of Pigs is said to have come about in this way.

## Tentativeness

Once a person is confronted with an issue on which there are several sides and he is called on to take a position, a 5,5-oriented manager seeks to remain tentative. His reason stems from being cautious in order not to take a position at some point in time which might turn out later on to be seen as wrong. By keeping flexible, he can shift to the popular side without losing face or having others see him as inconsistent and vacillating.

The premium placed on tentativeness for getting workable solutions may result in a contradiction between his own perceptions of himself and how he is seen by others. While a manager may see himself as realistic, shifting his position to reduce conflict, others may see him as lacking character, integrity, and internal strength, not having the courage of his own convictions.

Sometimes, of course, tentativeness is sound. This is particularly so when there is a lack of information or when a situation is changing rapidly and several solutions are possible but no particular one can be chosen based on the best data at hand. By comparison with 5,5 tentativeness, this type is justified by the facts and is part of a reasoned approach rather than a cover-up for uncertainty.

## Compromise

From a 5,5 perspective it is seldom wise to confront conflict directly, even when the evidence is on his side. Someone wins and someone loses. A lot of people do not act as if they know it, but the loser in a fight is a potential enemy when the next disagreement shapes up. Furthermore, many conflicts represent the hot emotions of the moment. Back off. Let the situation cool. Breathing time gives a chance to find middle ground. Frequently, it is possible to take some of one person's ideas and a little of another's and put them together. The solution may not be perfect, but it sells, and everyone feels respected. It is accepted because it contains some of the thinking of each contending faction. To find a basis for pulling the warring parties together, what has to be done is to yield, twist, turn, and bend. But there's nothing bad about appeasing and accommodating. Progress is made by giving something to get something. The final position does not meet the full requirements of either alternative, but it does provide a middle position that people with different views will accept rather than to continue fighting for their own positions. Thus, a whole loaf may be lost, but, on the other hand, no one starves.

There are some situations where the middle situation is the *best* solution, but a 5,5 orientation is not aimed at this position because it is the best one. Rather, the middle ground is sought to *split the difference* in order to get an acceptable resolution. Reservations and doubts that led to the initial differences are likely to remain.

The true goal of managerial competence is to achieve the best result in terms of production through people. The best is rarely defined by something that is in the middle, intermediate, or represents a splitting of differences between divergent points of view. Though the problem is solved, the solution reached may leave deeper-lying problems unresolved.

A distinction is sometimes drawn between compromise when it relates to matters of principle and compromise when it relates to situations of applied decision making. The view is that compromising on operational matters reflects reasonable accommodation. This distinction may be a useful one, but it is clear that principles undergird practices and that managerial practices derive their validity from principles. Thus it is "easy" to enter into compromise on matters of operational practice by simply not considering the underlying principles that may be bent by the operational accommodation.

## "Tailoring" Information

Sometimes a 5,5-oriented manager is "caught" in a situation of conflict where the position he has been responsible for is wrong, but to admit it, he thinks, would cause him to lose popularity.

Bending the truth, half-truths, or white lies all may be useful to affect a face-saving resolution. Over a period of time, however, such distortions are likely to form a patchwork of contradictions, reversals, starts and stops, etc. Yet the 5,5-oriented manager feels that this is the practical or realistic approach to management: one which can get a job done without stirring up too much trouble. This is not conscious manipulation of the sort associated with a facade or outright lying. A 5,5-oriented manager is not likely to realize how he is coloring the understanding of others. If challenged, he might respond by indicating that what he's really doing is what is expected under the circumstances.

## Expediency

When conflict arises the question often is not what is best, but what is politically safe, salable, or workable. Expedient actions are taken, frequently at the expense of a sounder way that might expose differences which need to be resolved.

Expediency has come to have important implications for corporate ethics. A 5,5-oriented manager may feel himself under no particular ethical compulsion beyond, "to do what everybody else is doing." One of the consequences in large, modern, and complex organizations is an erosion of corporate ethics and morality. The reason is that a 5,5 attitude is congenial to the rationalization, "I'm paid to do what is expected of me, not what I might personally think is right or wrong. In this way I demonstrate my integrity as a group member and my loyalty to the organization." This may account for senior executives being involved in payoffs to significant people in key government and corporate positions via intermediaries in return for favored treatment over competitors. It is an important aspect of the Watergate syndrome. The foundation of social equity and justice is undermined when no one is prepared to stand in contradiction to prevailing attitudes that are ethically unsound.

## Separating Those in Disagreement

When two subordinates are in conflict, a 5,5-oriented boss may talk with each one separately. Then he tries to find points on which they can both agree. He suggests his proposal to each one separately. This is likely to result in some basis of agreement that each subordinate can live with, though they may continue to dislike one another. When it does not, other splitting mechanisms may be relied upon.

Physically separating persons who are antagonistic to one another if conflict persists can reduce the incidence of conflict even though it may not resolve basic issues. This can happen, for example, in a large room where a number of people work. The splitting strategy may be no more than suggesting that subordinates in disagreement might find it better to shift their desks to opposite sides of the room. This reduces the tensions between them because they are not close enough to fight. Thus the subordinates are helped, and at least on the surface, the whole situation appears more congenial.

Another way to separate people is to arrange a transfer, preferably for the one who "doesn't fit." An assignment in another location "solves" the problem. Redrawing the organization chart is still another separation tactic. Reporting lines of disagreeing parties are redrawn so they no longer have to report to the same boss. Thus they have no need to maintain mutual relations and the conflict is brought to an end.

Sometimes, however, what the boss's boss wants and what his own subordinates would be willing to go along with are two different things and the solution cannot be had by opting for one or the other. Because of the protocol of hierarchy that says you don't bring three levels together, he becomes a go-between manager, running between his boss and his own subordinates, testing a course of action, first from one side, then from the other. This allows a position to finally emerge through a series of approximations that is more or less acceptable to everyone.

## Subordinate Reactions

Because it is so reasonable, subordinates rarely react to being managed in a 5,5 way in hostile or aggressive terms, with disgust, or by leaving. However, the range of reactions is quite wide.

### Like Begets Like

The prospect is that under a 5,5 orientation subordinates come to think and manage in the same way as they are managed. Because actions are reasonable, in the sense of being accommodating, it is to be expected that boss and subordinates come to move along in a steady-pace way.

### Playing the Status Game

Once immersed in a 5,5-oriented system, a person may enjoy the status game and refine his skills for staying within it, describing his life and work in this fashion: "The company provides every opportunity a person could want. It's an old (or young) and respected company and employs people who are really good. Just say its name and you get consideration. It rewards loyalty and steady service, and that's what I'm giving. There are only five people near my age in my department. I have a better than average chance of becoming the department head or assistant, which isn't too bad either. My wife and I belong to several clubs and we do a lot of entertaining of company friends. I'm popular with the gang. We have a nice home and we should be able to move into a larger one in a few years. Our two kids will have a college education, and later on, I'll get a good retirement. Though I worry now and then, I've got it made—no heart attack for me."

This acceptance of the status quo life with its conventional values, status symbols, and steady progress through seniority, popularity, and reasonableness is a 5,5 response to a 5,5 environment. It is an uncomplicated approach characterized by accommodation and adjustment. The commitment demands no effort beyond staying up with or maybe just a little ahead of the middle of the pack.

Subordinates know that challenge to the status quo is a jarring element. They are, therefore, unprepared to buck the system. If they want to stay, they must abide by the organization's rules. One such rule is always to ask, "What will my boss buy?"; then design a package that is sure to sell. Because of the 5,5 orientation's pervasiveness, anyone who stands out as an organization star runs the risk of provoking envy and promotes uneasiness. His effort to make a contribution is confused with "making waves." The result is that even people who want to try take a "better think twice" attitude. Innovation and creativity that could lead to better solutions to problems tend to be sacrificed.

### "Statistical" 5,5

A manager may seek to fit into a 5,5 organization by being a regular guy to each subordinate on an "everyone is different and unique" approach which appreciates individual differences in comparison with an "everybody fits in" attitude of a straightforward 5,5 approach. This is the "statistical" 5,5-oriented person who may employ all styles in his daily management, doing what is most "acceptable" with each person or in each situation—whether or not it is objectively appropriate to realizing production through people. If a subordinate wants to be left alone, or if the manager doesn't know how to approach him, he is left to fend for himself, as in 1,1. If the subordinate seems to want warm, friendly relations and a supportive atmosphere he is given warmth, support, and friendliness, as in 1,9. If the subordinate wants to knock heads and to argue, as in 9,1, the boss responds with a "tough" attitude. If he seeks to avoid conflict by compromising in a 5,5 way, the boss responds in kind in an accommodating manner, and so on. In other words, the statistical 5,5 manager operates all over the Grid, and his managerial style averages out to be 5,5. Treating various people in varying manners, he behaves in an inconsistent way, and this sometimes is called "being flexible." Yet, he sees little or no contradiction in his actions and is unlikely to be accused of shiftiness. His rationale is that each person is different from all others and that the same situation never repeats itself; therefore, one can't expect to treat all subordinates or situations in a consistent manner. As in straightforward 5,5, the status quo is maintained without anyone having to change. This flexibility is discussed in Chapter 9.

## Drifting into, 1,1

Another subordinate reaction is from those who want to contribute more but find their efforts unrewarded, unappreciated, and even sidetracked. If unprepared to leave the organization for another position, they are likely to drift slowly into 1,1 as their efforts continue to meet resistance and to be rebuffed. They continue to operate within the 5,5 system because they can't afford to leave it but with little or no involvement in their work or in the organization's success.

### Implications for Mental and Physical Health

Mental health implications point to a common correlation between anxiety and self-doubt and a number of mental and physical health consequences.

### "Inferiority Complex"

When someone cautions, "Don't stick your neck out," the underlying intention is to tell a person to get back in line, to "play the game" in a 5,5-oriented manner. The once popular term, "inferiority complex," reflects the reaction of a 5,5-oriented manager who has been caught out of step or exposed in a group setting as a minority of one. The feelings of inferiority are not related to the quality of his thinking, which may be valid. It is related to the feeling of being caught, unable to play the game according to the rules set up by the group.

### "Who am I?"

5,5 popularity motivation has brought a new psychological problem into focus. For some it borders on "sickness," which appears sometimes in the teen years, again in middle life, and a third time soon after retirement. It occurs when a person searches his thinking for real convictions and self-direction and finds he has neither, when he examines his real accomplishments and finds there have been none, when, after retirement, he seeks his real friends and recognizes that his "friends," all business associates, have little or no time for him.

Managers who respond in this way often  report a lack of personal identity, the "Who am I?" dilemma. This comes about when personal beliefs, values, and convictions are constructed out of what others think, rather than from a personal philosophy of life. Thus a person has sacrificed personal identity and ceased being a distinctive individual.

There is no acceptable answer to the question, "Who am I?" because the objective answer in a certain sense is that by having become a part of everyone he is no one in his own right. He is no one because his patterns of living have been adopted from others. When they are gone, as often happens in the teen years; or when others advance more rapidly career-wise and leave him behind, or disappear after his retirement, he is left without his sense of belonging. This loss of identity can be disturbing when it comes into focus and produces a shock of self-recognition.

## Peptic Ulcers

Peptic ulcers, sometimes referred to as the businessman's disease, but actually found among people in all walks of life, is repeatedly traced, on the Grid-emotions side, to anxiety and worry. These are 5,5 kinds of feelings. Though medical experts disagree with one another beyond the critical role of the anxiety and worry factors, one basis of understanding the Grid-to-ulcer correlation is that of a 5,5-oriented person who wants to be popular. He gets caught up in a work situation that demands more of him than he can deliver with confidence. The tensions between wanting to be popular as measured by his acceptability to his colleagues and in terms of what is expected by way of performance produce a constant state of anxiety about being "out." Because he has insufficient skills in doing those things that could relieve the anxiety, the unrelieved anxiety may create the conditions of an ulcer.

### Childhood Origins of 5,5

Parents whose children embrace a 5,5 orientation as a dominant style themselves appear to be more guided by outer expectations than by inner convictions. The social ethic of adjustment based on appropriateness as defined by others places an ultimate value on being in step. This becomes their overriding source of direction in child rearing.

Parents see their child-rearing responsibilities as bringing up a child who is adaptable and socially-centered. They value a child who can fit into the appropriate group, take on popular points of view, who feels "in," and gains satisfaction from belonging.

The 5,5-oriented manager is likely, at one time or another, to have had the characteristics of the All-American boy. He is a person whose

development has proceeded without a major hitch. He identifies successfully, through his parents, with the values, rules, and mores of the community. He accepts them as givens rather than examining them and
evaluating his attitudes toward them in the light of systematic concepts
or his own emerging values.

Two parental guidelines tell the specifics for child-rearing efforts that
lead to this kind of adjustment. The child is continuously reminded that
"others will not like you if you are different, but you will always have
friends and be popular if you do as others do." The child's attention is
constantly focused on getting along with the other children of his age
group. Exaggerated emphasis is likely to be placed on the undesirability
of being left out. This can have a strong anxiety-inducing effect on the
child's orientation while his readiness to accept prevailing norms can
reduce anxiety about his own acceptability.

Anxiety becomes a red flag which says, "The risks of independence
and uniqueness are not worth the loss of feelings of belonging that come
from being liked." Thus, happiness and virtue are equated with popularity, which is itself equated with conformity.

A 5,5-oriented child confides in people of his own generation instead of
his parents; thus peers become dominant in molding a child's reactions.
Parents in turn are reluctant to discuss intimate topics. From a child's
point of view parents are likely to seem preoccupied with their own living, so it appears that the child's own generation knows best. The 5,5-
oriented girl is concerned with how her mother looks and acts with her
and her friends as opposed to how she thinks and feels about things, issues, and people.

This group-centered and "rules-oriented" approach to child rearing
does not result in strong relationships with parents. They are likely to
praise the child for external attributes like being pretty or handsome or
having a good voice rather than to consider the child a thinking, feeling,
and striving person and to reward these attributes.

The shallowness of parent-child relationships leaves such a child few
or no anchorages other than to be "in," and to have status in the eyes of
his peers. Never having had the stimulation to develop independent convictions or the motivation to strive to reach difficult goals, he can enjoy
the fun and games of high school in contrast with achievement, early
employment rather than advanced education, membership and popularity in playing the organization game rather than aiming for success-
through-contribution.

Another source of guidance is from whichever child development experts are in vogue at any particular point in time. The experts, who give
information about when motor skills appear and at what rates and sequences, when and how a child plays with other children, and when particular intellectual capacities can be anticipated to appear, give 5,5-

oriented parents a basis for building their expectations. When their child fits the model, parents feel secure.

## Facades

A 5,5-oriented facade strategist gives the appearance of reasonableness and of being a smooth operator. He is ready to go along or to compromise in the interest of progress. This does not reflect the genuine pliability of a 5,5-oriented manager. Rather, he is using tactics to hide his steadfastness of pursuing his own individual purposes from others. His intention is to win the war. Losing a battle or two along the way is of no consequence. Throughout the campaign the facadist camouflages his real strategy with simulated 5,5 tactics as described below.

### "Flexibility" of Convictions

A person hiding his true intentions behind a 5,5 facade may appear open and ready to shift his views. He avoids presenting convictions clearly enough to be proven wrong. He may quote anonymous authorities or public opinion as substitutes for revealing his own beliefs. Then he can relinquish them without seeming to back down from his real positions. By expressing himself, yet keeping other alternatives open, he can easily shift course. These tactics give him the appearance of being flexible. The flexibility can be distinguished from genuine 5,5 because the facadist has intentions that are not revealed, and it is in the interest of achieving them that his apparent changes in points of view are made.

### "Compromise"

In a sense, compromise is a tool for his personal achievement, but he relies on the *appearance* of compromise rather than truly believing it to be a "reasonable" way to manage. Even if he has reservations, the facadist feels no reluctance in committing himself to halfway solutions. Compromise undercuts resistance because it makes the facadist appear to be persuaded and shift. However, the facadist does not really believe that half a loaf is better than none. He embraces compromise as a maneuver, a tactical short-term accommodation that allows him to pursue the whole loaf. As one skillful facadist said, "I compromise in order to be able to go underground with my real purpose. Then, at a later time, I come up again, and usually I win."

### Friendly Interest

Showing friendly interest in a subordinate, evidenced perhaps by inviting him for a drink after work hours to continue a discussion or over to the house for a business chat during the weekend, may be a subtle form of a 5,5 facade. The motivation is not friendly interest but a desire to get the subordinate to talk freely. Liquor, plus flattery from a higher level manager, can unlock secrets useful to a facadist in his personal pursuit of success.

## Use of Cliques

Like a person with a straightforward 5,5 orientation, the 5,5 facadist also uses informal organization cliques, but in pursuit of different objectives. By having a thorough knowledge of cliques and their members, he can not only tap into the grapevine at strategic points for information but also use them to influence the organization to his *personal* advantage. He talks with key clique members, evaluating their opinions before making decisions that affect them. By influencing *key* members he exerts unrecognized control on *other* members of the organization who follow the lead of the key members. Frequently, this can result in shaping decisions in ways that reduce or eliminate resistance points. Also, by manipulating clique action, sanctions can be brought to bear on members who are running counter to the facadist's purpose.

## Receiving and Giving Advice

The facadist frequently avoids asking for advice from people either above or below him in rank. Asking for advice may look weak. This is to be avoided whenever a person can make a decision based on his own independent judgment.

Accepting unsolicited advice is equally undesirable because doing so obligates a person to the one who provided it. The obligation arises when the advice given has been helpful. The giver can then expect reciprocity. This kind of obligation is significantly reduced by accepting advice only when it is solicited because then the recipient "told" the giver what he wanted to know. Furthermore, the information gleaned is likely to be more accurate because the person who is giving information can be kept in the dark as to how much the recipient really knows. Then the giver of advice must be doubly sure that what he says "squares." All of this takes place within a framework of 5,5 "give-and-take."

Giving advice is a two-sided affair. A facadist decides when to offer advice and counsel according to whether it will increase or decrease his influence over others. If a facadist counsels action that fails, he invites criticism and possibly even rebuke. Furthermore, it shows others that his judgment is unreliable. If he counsels action that ends in success, he may receive commendation. Yet the reward for counseling that results in success rarely equals the punishment for counseling that throws the recipient out of step. Over the long term, then, the facadist is wary of the risks involved in giving advice.

When he does give it the facadist tries to make the person who receives advice feel that he is accepting it as support for his own judgment and free choice. If all goes well, the giver gains recognition by reminding the recipient of his contribution. If things go poorly, he dissociates himself without facing the risk associated with advice that ends in failure. The fail-safe point between these extremes lies in giving advice and counsel with moderation, calmly and modestly when it becomes necessary to do so.

## The "Gamesman" Facade

A kind of pseudo collaboration is rising in popularity, particularly in high technology, knowledge-centered companies and organizations. These are organizations in which work tends to be complex, give-and-take is expected, and no one person confidently feels in charge. The exchange of technical information is necessary for valid problem solving and decision making. The nature of the work, in other words, puts a premium on collaboration, yet it is not the kind of participation, involvement, and commitment characteristic of a 9,9 teamwork approach. What is the difference?

This 5,5 facade takes its motivation from the 9,1 orientation, i.e., to dominate, control, and master, coupled with a 5,5-oriented give-and-take approach to "participation." Group meetings are used to collect data to get a problem examined from many points of view, to hear pro and con arguments, and to see where majority and minority thinking lines up. This strategist seeks to exploit every contact by being "all things to all people," but the underlying motivation is mastery.

The facade aspect is that the boss avoids showing his hand, keeping his options open until the very last minute. He may elicit open and candid discussion far beyond the point where it is useful. The reason is to keep a decision from becoming either self-evident or polarized. One manager put it this way: "To prevent one part of the team from achieving influence that might impede my progress, I keep discussions fluid far beyond the time when a decision might have been made. This can easily be done under the guise of not making a premature or unworkable decision until all possible alternatives have been tested or additional data gathered. Then the stronger faction is weakened, the weaker faction is not hurt, and when I finally make a decision, everyone is relieved and ready to move my way, thankful to get some action." Thus, he retains maximum freedom to make the ultimate decisions, often risk-taking ones that oppose advice previously given but that was not discussed or rejected at the time. Making the solo decision or taking the dramatic action, he dominates and controls and comes out a "winner." This coupling of nondecisive participation with solitary decision making creates the 5,5 facade called the "gamesman."

## Implications of 5,5 for Organizations

Circumstances prompting the emergence of 5,5 as a popular style can be viewed best from an historical perspective. Antagonistic and hostile reactions to 9,1 management for a brief period produced an overreaction into the 1,9 direction of what was thought to be excessive concern for personal feelings and attitudes. However, after a period of "the 1,9 human relations binge," counterforces developed to move people back in the opposite direction. Rather than an alternative of either 9,1 or 1,9, the pendulum was dampened and stopped in the middle of the 9,1-1,9 diagonal, where a *balance* was sought by choosing a happy medium.

Another argument presented to explain the rapid increase observed in the number of 5,5-oriented managers and organizations is related to the fragmentation and specialization of work, whether of managers or of workers. As work becomes more specialized and fragmented, pulled apart, and unconnected, it loses meaning, becomes repetitious, and has no inherent quality to which reason and problem solving can be applied. This routinization is insufficient to inspire involvement or commitment.

Another circumstance that continues to promote 5,5 as an organizational style is the transfer of concepts of decision making from politics into the industrial setting. The rightness of the majority; the significance of people with leadership giving it in a participative way; feelings of equality and respect for the individual; and a sense of one-man-one-vote democracy are values that can be translated into 5,5 or 9,9 managerial philosophy. Emphasis on lawful, orderly behavior, rooted in tradition and past practices, when the *rule* is the critical element, rather than experimentation, leads into 5,5 as the preferred managerial style.

Whyte, in his popular book, *The Organization Man,* offered a quite accurate analysis of 5,5 as the general American approach to management, and a spate of new books continues to claim that this approach is becoming increasingly popular. In the absence of a truly sound managerial base, 5,5 is seen as superior to a 9,1 system, which, *in the extreme,* often generates intense warfare that disrupts even moderate achievement of organizational and individual goals. 5,5 is also seen to be superior to the 1,9 approach of sweetness and light that results in people becoming contented and happy but which can produce a flat, fat, flabby, and ineffectual organization.

Many large organizations, whether industrial, government, military, or academic, have been unable to gear their membership to any greater accomplishment or commitment than that represented by 5,5. This style of management is here to stay and for a long time to come. It is entrenched. It is able, over long periods, to endure as a way of life in large, massive organizations.

Many aspects of organization life encourage targets of mediocrity, particularly in larger, older organizations and in bureaucracies. Young members are told, "pace yourself, don't shoot too high or, in the event of failure, you will stand out in comparison with the person who set attainable targets for himself." Pressures toward conformity surround the person or group who would strike out for higher performance. The recommended goal for a person is not to be a "flash (in the pan), but to be durable, to be with it for a long, long career; to be able to roll with the punches," and not burn himself out.

Organizations managed by 5,5 orientations are likely to be viewed as bureaucratic because rules, regulations, and red tape frequently appear to be an end in themselves. They become sacred cows. Managers are less free to interact to solve problems according to their own understanding of the situation. They have become administrators interpreting procedures and regulations. Literally they manage paper rules and regulations; not people trying to solve problems of production.

A reliance on norms and traditions can, for many of the repetitive problems of management, provide effective mechanical guidance that adequately fits a large majority of situations, particularly where mediocre productivity has come to be accepted as okay. But, there are many management situations where reliance on tradition is insufficient for getting the job done. Thus 5,5 provides a poor basis for promoting innovation, creativity, discovery, and novelty. All of these are likely to be sacrificed by adherence to tradition and "majority" standards of decision making. Long term, then, the 5,5 or *status quo*, results in a gradual slipping behind as more progressive organizations take advantage of new opportunities through better management practices. The challenge confronting modern management is to *set higher goals* than 5,5 as the basis for future accomplishment.

### Summary

The 5,5 motivations stem from the desire to be a popular member in good standing, and to avoid being a minority of one, ostracized, or out of step. Energy and initiative are expended in playing the popularity game.

A person can exercise skill in studying others, understanding what they are saying, and measuring his success by their popularity votes. The game is not deeply meaningful in itself because it does not contribute to the satisfaction of any human wants. But when meaning is absent from the work itself, it can be replaced by this substitute activity, which can create considerable enthusiasm.

A manager has as his realistic goal the achievement of workable solutions that please the majority and hopefully appease the minority. Conforming to the expectations of others can provide a significant gain in feelings of belonging for an individual, but this kind of security is characteristic of anything but sound mental health. It is the security of safety in numbers rather than the security of sound convictions and the capacity to predict consequences from acting on one's convictions. Finally, it is not the kind of security that makes one confident enough to take risks, to achieve, or to inspire others.

When initiative is called for, he prefers to rely on traditions and past practices or the judgment of others. He rarely moves out front until others have established a new direction or indicated the safest way to go. When majority thinking is unavailable and traditional reactions are unacceptable for dealing with problems, or when different approaches to problems might promote conflict, a 5,5-oriented manager searches for accommodations and compromises that involve going halfway or splitting the difference. From compromises that gain acceptance comes social approval.

Mental and physical health consequences include a new mental health hazard, called "Who am I?" and refers to a crisis of identity. Another is the constant, nagging fear that one is actually inferior, unable to play the game as expected. Peptic ulcers appear correlated to extremes of this Grid style on the physical side.

Parents who point their children toward conformity with outer expectations, and who keep the importance of the child's belonging in the focus of attention seem to create the conditions essential for the emergence of a dominant 5,5 orientation.

In Chapter 1, the *C* paragraph is the 5,5-oriented manager's self-description.

## Chapter 7

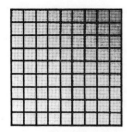

# 9,9

The 9,9 theory of managing presumes an inherent *connection* between organization needs for production and the needs of people for full and rewarding work experiences. Active participation leading to involvement and commitment to standards of excellence underlie 9,9 motivation. Production through integrating people into its achievement means involving their emotions and ideas in solving problems through teamwork. Joint effort makes synergistic consequences possible. A 9,9-oriented manager desires to make a contribution to corporate success, coupled with a commitment to involve others with and through whom he works. These values promote voluntarism, spontaneity, openness, and responsibility shared with others in accomplishing clear and challenging goals. This coupling of contribution with caring has been said to encompass head and heart.

9,9 achievement motivation comes from developing the competence required to make a positive contribution and, therefore, to search for and pursue goals and objectives that are simultaneously personal and corporate. There is a sense of gratification, enthusiasm, and excitement from making an important contribution. The closer one comes to success, the greater the sense of emotional reward.

When an effort is judged as more than a momentary failure, a 9,9-oriented manager is likely to feel self-defeat, disappointment, and discouragement. He may be disturbed, or uneasy, faced with self-doubt about his capacity to meet future problems successfully. Setbacks occur, but perspective provides the foundation for persistence. Failure in the short term is not the end of everything. The motivational motto is, "With caring, commitment, and versatility, we can solve the really tough problems. That's the meaning of managing."

## Boss Behavior

A 9,9-oriented boss thinks, "My job is to make decisions, but it is equally important to see to it that sound decisions are made." This style is seen in the following approaches:

*Planning:* "I get the people who have relevant facts and/or stakes in the outcome together to review the whole picture. We formulate a sound model from start to completion to provide an organizing framework for integrating an entire project. I get their reactions and ideas. I establish goals and flexible schedules with them."

*Organizing:* "Within the framework of the whole, we determine individual responsibilities, procedures, and ground rules."

*Directing:* "I keep informed of progress and influence subordinates by identifying problems and revising goals *with* them. I lend assistance when needed by helping to remove road blocks."

*Controlling:* "In addition to in-progress critiques to keep projects on schedule, I conduct a wrap-up with those responsible. We evaluate the way things went and see what we can learn from our experience and how we can apply our learning in the future. I give recognition on a team basis as well as for outstanding individual contributions."

*Staffing:* "Work requirements are matched with personnel capabilities or needs for development in making decisions as to who does what."

In each statement a manager is *creating* conditions that help him and his subordinates understand the problem and that give them stakes in outcomes.

Much behavioral science experimentation, extensive field studies within industrial systems, and even observations across different cultures, indicate that when people are oriented towards achieving concrete, specific goals they understand and agree with, their behavior becomes more orderly, meaningful, and purposeful. The assumption is that when individuals who must coordinate their activities are aware of organization purpose and of their real stakes in productivity, then it is possible to rely on self-control and self-direction. With effective leadership, individuals can mesh their efforts in an interdependent way.

Direction and control are achieved first by pursuing understanding and agreement concerning organization purpose and how to contribute to it. Genuine understanding of organization economic health, work goals, unity of effort, and commitment arise out of discussion, deliberation, and debate around major organization issues and by the mutual identification of sound objectives. In other words, those who are involved in the overall effort participate in creating the conditions under which full production can be accomplished. Such action can result in self-control geared to organization goals and in the autonomous regulation of action.

This may require fundamental reorientation of managerial practices. It can no longer be taken for granted, for example, that people accept profit as a legitimate organization purpose. Has anything been found that can guide complex human effort in as sound a way? It is inevitable that the concept of profit be studied, thought through, and understood in depth. Where profit motivation is not the basis for organizing work, decision making, measuring performance, and motivating people, what replaces it? The bureaucratically stiff companies and government agencies that operate on a more or less fixed budget rather than using profit or expense management tell the story of what happens when profit is eliminated as an organizing concept, as a measuring tool, and as a source of motivation.

Profit in the abstract is only one tool, however. At all levels of management greater awareness of profit and loss (P/L) circumstances also is needed within the specific organization, department, section, or unit in which one works. To accomplish this requires that detailed facts and figures be made available for discussion and understanding, which many managements are unprepared to do. This closed approach is likely to lead to uninvolvement and to stimulate resistance to change because management and the worker alike have less stake in helping the organization work more profitably.

There are other aspects, but these typify the meaning of "understanding of, agreement with, and support of organization purpose(s)."

Far greater attention is concentrated, through education, on the feelings and thoughts of people as they relate to profit motivation than has been considered possible or necessary except in a few field experiments. Ordinary classroom methods are relatively worthless for aiding understanding of concepts such as these, which are both difficult to comprehend and shrouded with emotions. Team learning methods, themselves consistent with a 9,9 approach, are available and have successfully been used to bring about such commitment.

A sense of stakes and awareness of organization purpose(s) has been achieved in situations where approaches like Grid Organization Development and the Scanlon Plan have been set into motion. Under these conditions, each organization member keenly feels the stakes he and others share in their productivity. Awareness of organization purpose(s) is possible because people interact directly or through their own representatives to influence decisions and to set organization direction. Knowledge of one's stakes and of common purpose(s) sets the conditions for releasing self-imposed control and direction.

Against this background of widespread commitment to organization goals and profit consciousness, 9,9-oriented managers make significant use of teamwork. The essentials for reaching sound decisions are present when all the data and perspectives for defining a problem are available and utilized. When those who share responsibility for specific outcomes pool information and judgment, the full complexity of the situation is more likely to be comprehended. Then the implications of alternate solu-

*MBO*

tions can be assessed through shared thinking, and decisions of high quality have the greatest possibility of being reached.

Another reason for teamwork is the need for the involvement and commitment of those who shoulder the responsibility for enacting a decision once it has been reached: this is the issue of acceptance. Having engaged in the thinking and in learning about why one solution has merit over others, they have an understanding that can make the difference when the decision is carried out. Resistance overcome in the process of discussion is no longer present to hinder successful implementation. This character of managerial effort avoids foot-dragging and the other features of inadequate managing. More about 9,9 teamwork is contained in Chapter 10.

## Management-by-Objectives

The decision to use management-by-objectives to manage in a better way comes from the widespread realization that people who are committed to achieving goals are motivated and self-directing, acting according to a sense of purpose. Then the achievement of goals is both productive and personally gratifying. Should not those employed by corporations also be motivated and self-directing? Management-by-objectives was introduced with this end in view.

Rather than presuming that people are managing by objectives simply because a program for this purpose has been introduced, it is important for managers to understand the properties that cause goals to be motivating. Properties of goals are rather well worked out and described in the behavioral sciences. Several might be mentioned to show how this goals-oriented managerial approach gains the many advantages of linking individuals together into the total organizational effort.

It goes without saying that the setting of objectives in industry is practical only when those responsible for doing so enjoy a good relationship themselves: open communication, mutual trust, sound methods of conflict resolution, a problem-solving approach to decision making, and a shared commitment to contribute to corporate success. Efforts to introduce management-by-objectives without first strengthening teamwork run a high risk of failure.

Of singular importance for effective management-by-objectives is the basic idea of psychological ownership. This means that a manager is motivated to reach a goal when it belongs to him, when he feels it as his own. Then he is involved in being successful by applying his energies toward reaching it.

An attribute of a sound goal is that it has *clarity*. Though the goal may be clear to the boss and though he may be able to give adequate directions for accomplishing it, it may be resisted by subordinates because it makes no sense to them. When a goal is unclear, subordinates are unable to join their efforts towards accomplishing it in a meaningful, sensible way. Yet when subordinates are clear as to what the goal is, because they have thought it through and have accepted its challenge, they are likely to be more fully committed to bending their efforts in its direction.

Making the activity itself a unit where all the subcomponents fit together into a whole, rather than fragmenting it so that it does not carry any inherent meaning to the person responsible for it, is an important factor in successful management-by-objectives. If the activity is a fragment, it is less likely to be motivating than if it is a whole.

Another property of a goal is related to its degree of *difficulty*. A goal that can be accomplished with little effort is not motivating. A goal which is so difficult as to be unsound also is not motivating. If it appears a goal is unattainable, it is necessary to have a complete and clear understanding of the factors that limit the achievement. Then it may become possible to deal with the limitations realistically. If problems subject to resolution are identified, there is motivation to correct them. If skill problems are the barrier, they can be rectified or compensated for. If problems genuinely beyond present control are identified, they are then understood and thus less likely to be demotivating. Furthermore, even these problems are then subject to further strategy consideration and potential future resolution.

In summary, there is no need to accommodate goals or lower them from a true standard of excellence. What is necessary is that any gap between achievement and excellence needs to be clearly understood.

Goal-setting is a way of changing, by foresight, what needs to be done to reach some objective. Without this clarification the prospect of reaching some objective, no matter how desirable, is remote indeed. Being able to foresee a goal, however, makes it possible to sequence explicit steps necessary for getting to the goal in an orderly way. The likelihood of getting there is increased when steps are set and agreed to in advance, but flexibly so they can be changed. If all of the steps can be foreordained, the goal loses an important property of a motivator because initiative cannot be exercised. However, if the steps toward the goal are unidentifiable, the goal no longer motivates because it is likely to appear unreasonable. Ideally the route to a goal should be thoroughly outlined, but specific steps on that route should be formulated by the person responsible for taking them.

The time span for reaching goals is another significant property of management-by-objectives. An individual may allow too much (or too little) time between setting a goal for himself and accomplishing it. A goal set in the too distant future is unlikely to be motivating because current activities bear little meaningful relationship to it. A goal set in the immediate future may not be motivating either because a person has 100 percent confidence that he can reach it or because time is so short there appears to be little or no hope of achieving it.

Standards are needed for deciding "how good is good?" and in managing-by-objectives the best standard is *excellence.* Excellence means, "If that goal were reached, the problem would be solved," or "That reflects the true solution," or "This is the most that can be realized under the realistic competition we face." Another way of characterizing excellence is to say what it is not: "That would be a little better than last year," or "We'd better cut down on that because you can never predict what will happen." Excellence, in other words, is the best that rigorous thinking and analysis can visualize. Often goals set on excellence standards are really no more difficult to achieve and are far more rewarding to reach. The difference is quality, which in itself is a source of motivation essential for making the extra effort.

Feedback of performance relative to the objective is another factor in successful management-by-objectives. Without frequent and valid feedback a manager has no way to evaluate whether his efforts are moving him closer to or farther from the objective. It becomes more motivating to strive when feedback is available.

Another characteristic has been identified as the completion effect. Once an individual has accepted the idea of achieving a goal, internal tensions arise towards successful completion. Barriers can arise to block an individual. Rather than sitting back with resignation and saying, "I got blocked," the individual increases his effort to remove the barrier. These tensions constitute part of the motivating force that explains why committed people don't quit simply because difficulties are encountered.

Except for momentary circumstances, hostility and anger, fear, emotional resignation, anxiety, and worry are not characteristic of a 9,9 orientation. Perspective can be maintained when there is both a realistic amount of commitment to an action and reservation about having taken it. Reservations about commitments must be decided upon because a realistic plan for the future allows for unknown factors. Thus the relative absence of unhealthy emotions may be understood to result when an affirmative approach is necessary even if its outcome cannot be forecast with certainty. These considerations help explain why the medical literature establishes no disease entities as characteristically associated with 9,9.

If a management-by-objectives approach disregards these properties of goals, it is doomed to failure because goals that are set cease to have motivating value and therefore do not influence behavior.

One way of using management-by-objectives in a 9,9 way is to give managers decision-making control over the profitability of that part of the whole for which they are responsible. It is for this reason that the trend toward local profit centers is so important. A profit center within a larger corporation is a goals system. It is the smallest unit of the organization that can be subjected to P/L accounting. Here is an example of taking organization purpose and translating it into a local profit-centered goal.

Each team member knows how his unit is doing under the profit center concept. They can study what factors, and combination of factors, go into P/L arithmetic and see how specific actions, over which he and others have some control, contribute to P/L, in either a positive or negative way. Organization purpose, in other words, has been translated into a meaningful local goal. Given a 9,9 climate, local P/L can become a·

1. Significant educational topic
2. Goal around which actions are integrated
3. Performance measure that motivates change, etc.

However, management-by-objectives has proven anything but successful, and the question is "Why?" Is the idea wrong, and if not, then what is the explanation for its all-too-common failure? Viewed from the perspective of a 9,9 Grid orientation there are several clearcut indicators as to why management-by-objectives has not worked as it might. Two are of particular importance.

**Corporate Culture.** People respond to "real" rewards and punishments and not to the "announced" rewards. If the real reward is to push for production in a 9,1 way, or to smooth differences in a 1,9 way, or to go through the motions based on 1,1, or to compromise in a 5,5 way, then management-by-objectives will be dealt with accordingly. Thus, unless the corporate culture is based on 9,9 values of participation, involvement and commitment, management-by-objectives is unlikely to succeed.

**Conflict Resolution.** Facts, data, logic and resolution of differences by confrontation are likely to release the boss-subordinate tensions that otherwise block realistic management-by-objectives. The 9,9 managerial theory links individual effort to organizational purpose(s) through goal setting. When this way of managing has become a way of life, an individual is not only working for the corporation, he is also working for himself. Individual and organization purposes have come together. Thus management-by-objectives is carried out in a 9,9 way.

Performance appraisal is an important part of the management-by-objectives program. Goal setting stimulates awareness of needs, possibilities, and opportunities. The review itself offers an opportunity for boss and subordinate to jointly discuss the subordinate's present level of goal achievement and to plot development by eliminating any barriers that may be present toward achieving previously agreed upon goals. Since people are employed not only for their qualifications relative to an entry position but also for their potential to develop additional capabilities, individual growth can be stimulated in ways that are geared to organization contribution.

### Conflict

Conflict can delay or prevent the achievement of organization objectives and personal goals, and from that standpoint it is unproductive. Yet conflict can promote innovation, creativity, and the development of new ideas which make organizational growth possible. From these standpoints, conflict is useful. The issue, then, is not in whether conflict is present. The 9,9 approach to conflict rests on the assumption that, although conflict is inevitable, it is resolvable. *The key is in how conflict is managed.* The best way to approach conflict is to anticipate it and to take steps to ensure understanding and agreement before participants take positions and freeze to them.

There are several 9,9 approaches to conflict prevention.

### Open Communication

Communication is based on the assumption that mutual understanding is the key to agreement. If an individual genuinely wants to know what is going on, he needs to tell, in a forthright and candid manner, how he understands the situation. Free two-way exchanges stimulate openness, trust, and spontaneity.

A remark by a senior manager identifies 9,9 attitudes towards communication. His comment was, "In the final analysis, words have no meanings, it is only people that have meanings." In effect, he was saying that problems of communication actually are problems of *exchanges* between people. Words are tools for achieving effective interplay, attitudes, feelings, and meanings. There is no problem of communication, per se. There are problems of people who work together in trying to communicate with one another.

The power that a boss has and the way he uses it in a boss-subordinate way is the key to communication problems. A boss who says to his subordinate, "Can we get together? I am interested in your ideas," is likely to be reflecting a 9,9 orientation. If a subordinate has reservations and doubts, these can be brought out before they fester and become chronic sources of resistance. If he has suggestions, they can be given, listened to, and dealt with rather than stifled. This approach stimulates subordinates to initiate contact when they think they have something to contribute.

It is important to know that communication has a two-way character. Like other properties of social systems, communication tends toward an equilibrium between the amount given and the amount received. For example, if an individual seeks a great deal of information but gives only a very small amount, the system is unstable. It is not likely to retain the character of one communicator asking much but giving little and of the other giving much but getting little. It is likely to drift in the direction of neither giving nor getting much. Openness, in a two-way exchange of information, stimulates openness, trust; closedness stimulates closedness; hostility provokes counter-hostility. If an individual genuinely wants to know what is going on, he needs to tell, in a forthright and candid manner, what it is that he understands about the situation. He *levels*. Mutual understanding as the basis for agreement and control places a high premium on open, two-way communication.

Based on personal history and experience, an individual is likely to listen through filters that are unique to himself. He tends to hear what he wants to hear and disregards what he considers irrelevant, trivial, or unimportant. What appears trivial to one person may seem more significant to another.

Furthermore, unless he is very unusual, a person listens defensively to negative information—explaining away or justifying what he needs most to comprehend and understand in order to increase his own effectiveness. Rationalization, projection, compensation, and other widely known mechanisms of defense come into play in the everyday dealings of bosses and subordinates. Once conditions promoting full disclosure have been achieved, there are few reasons remaining for misunderstandings, for withholding negative information, or for any of the many other communication pitfalls that are likely to arise as barriers to full effort. The goal of two-way communication is to be able to talk candidly and communicate negative information.

### Giving Rationale

A 9,9-oriented manager explains the rationale behind a requested action as well as the particulars of the action itself. Without rationale, a subordinate may carry out instructions, but for all practical purposes he is "flying blind." Background thinking provides perspective for making decisions if specific problems arise that could not have been anticipated.

When people are stimulated to think, analyze, and evaluate and can see cause-and-effect relationships, they can and do *support* assignments that they have not helped create. This increases the probability that there will be less need for constant review and correction. People give the best *of* themselves rather than keeping the best *to* themselves, as is often true when one's contributions are not sought.

## Seeking Facts, Data, and Logic

When differences do appear, a 9,9-oriented manager looks for facts, data, and logic to resolve them. As a result, answers to complex questions are likely to be approached from an attitude of fact-finding. Since finding a best solution is his objective, he has less need to deny, distort, or defend his own position and therefore is open to alternative points of view.

## Experimentation

Because of his readiness to try out novel approaches to the resolution of conflicting points of view, a 9,9-oriented manager is likely to be known as an experimenter and innovator. Experimentation for resolving differences is done when two or more courses of action appear equally attractive, when the outcome is difficult to anticipate from available facts, or when participants see a situation from different and apparently irreconcilable perspectives. Evaluating alternative ways of operating experimentally suggests moving forward into new terrain and may create a solution that previously had not been recognized. A pilot project, test run, or trial period may provide the actual basis for testing innovations that resolve the dilemma of which solution to utilize.

## Critique

Critique is critical in managing and resolving conflict because it involves two or more people in analyzing an activity and sharing their reactions to it in an open and constructive way. Critique can reveal weaknesses, doubts, and reservations that might otherwise remain hidden. These can be discussed and dealt with in a problem-solving way. Each member's insights can be compared and evaluated against other team members' alternative points of view. Then barriers, reservations, and doubts can be dealt with more intelligently. Real and potential areas of conflict can be brought to the surface and resolved. Then the 9,9-oriented boss keeps an ear tuned for good ideas, no matter who possesses them. Because he listens for implications from a problem-solving point of view, the pickup and utilization of ideas is likely to be greater than for persons acting under other managerial assumptions.

## Confrontation

Sometimes positions people take become polarized, and agreement appears impossible. Confrontation is a means of focusing on antagonisms that are created by strong win-lose kinds of disagreement, facing up to them, and bringing them out into the open where they can be resolved directly by those who are a party to them. The boss joins with subordinates to help work through their differences, challenging those in disagreement to explain to one another or to him the reasons for it. Their reactions indicate whether or not they understand the situation in the same way. If they do not, the boss keeps asking questions that allow them to confront their differences, presenting facts, counterarguments, and logic to help them test their objectivity. Once they understand their own values and assumptions, he may challenge their thinking regarding different courses of action, probing for reasons, motives, and causes to give them a clear and possibly different perspective.

Emotions that usually accompany conflict—anger, hostility, fear, anxiety, doubt, and disappointment—can also be dealt with directly. The idea of getting conflict into the open sometimes meets resistance. Frequently managers feel that conflict, openly acknowledged, will escalate out of control. Another fear is that someone will be hurt. Another attitude is that acknowledging negative feelings is weak and dealing with emotions is immature and soft. These consequences rarely happen because once tensions in a system are identified, the pressures and strains on those who felt them are relieved.

### Subordinate Reactions

The 9,9 way of integrating people into production is consistent with sound behavioral science principles as applied to management. For this reason organization members might be expected to react to this approach to management and supervision with enthusiasm. Some do. This is not always the case, however. Many people in management have never had real experience with 9,9 ways of managing and, therefore, are not in a position to evaluate it in comparison to their experiences with other ways. Thus they have learned to regard 9,9 as unrealistic from earlier experiences and from the currently existing culture of their organizations. To be in a position to evaluate 9,9 teamwork, managers need to learn the skills essential for managing in that way.

### Can-Do Spirit

One of the most common reactions is positive readiness to be involved and to make the commitments necessary for achieving the kind of excellence that 9,9 teamwork can make possible. This reaction results because many strive for a greater degree of involvement than has been possible for them under other styles of boss behavior. Involvement and commitment are indicators of health, which create a sense of camaraderie. Striving to achieve goals in which managers have a personal investment presents a challenge and results in their having a stake in seeing the organization succeed.

## It's Too Much to Ask

Another reaction acknowledges that 9,9 teamwork is a realistic possibility but claims that it expects too much of a person. The requirements of involvement, participation, and commitment are beyond what an individual is ready to consider for himself. Others might have been ready to make such commitments earlier in their employment, yet have pulled back and taken their commitments elsewhere—into the community, into sports and recreation, and so on. This is understandable because to make the effort that a 9,9 approach involves might upset an individual's current status quo, and, without experiencing the alternative, maintaining his status quo may seem preferable to him.

## It's Impractical

Another reaction is, "It's impractical. It takes too much time. It won't work. My boss manage that way? Never."

Many people have become so conditioned by their management experiences that they dismiss the 9,9 teamwork idea as hypothetical and impractical in the sense of being "too ideal" to be realized. They have seen too much of what really goes on in terms of other Grid approaches to management to believe that the values inherent in 9,9 might ever be embraced throughout an organization. Therefore, the attitude is that 9,9 ideas are unrealistic.

Embracing 9,9 values is not the same as employing the skills of 9,9 teamwork in everyday management. Thus, a learning phase is essential for bringing a 9,9 basis of teamwork into operation. The kind of learning involved is more than simply reading a book, seeing a movie, or answering questions such as those in Chapter 1. The strategies for doing so are discussed in greater detail in Chapter 13, but the following constitute a general description of the requirements for bringing change about.

### Learning 9,9 Teamwork Skills

At least five elements are essential for shifting from one of the other Grid styles to a 9,9 basis of personal management.

## Theory

Learning the theories of the Managerial Grid provides each manager a framework for recognizing alternative possibilities of managing. Since the Grid offers a basis for systematic comparison between each of the theories, it aids a manager to see ways in which 9,9 is similar to or different from the other theories. It also permits an examination of strengths and limitations of each and provides each manager a basis for convincing himself as to the best approach, rather than taking one approach or another on the basis of recommendation or faith.

## Values

When managers identify what they think good management would consist of, but without reference to the Grid, and evaluate them from most ideal to least ideal, it becomes possible to establish which practices are the most highly valued. These can then be coded to identify the Grid styles they represent. Managers almost universally agree that 9,9 actions are the soundest ways of achieving production through people. 1,9 actions are next to poorest, and 1,1 ways are the poorest, though there is widespread disagreement as to second soundest, whether it is 9,1 or 5,5.

## Reducing Self-Deception

A second condition involves helping a manager eliminate or reduce his self-deception, which often tells him he is managing in a 9,9 way when he is not. When managers have not studied the theories of the Grid, but rank the paragraphs presented in Chapter 1, approximately 75% select the 9,9 paragraph to typify themselves. When these same executives rerank themselves after an intensive learning experience in a Grid Seminar of a week's duration, self-evaluations that continue to be 9,9 have been reduced to approximately 25%.

These and other indicators suggest that self-deception is a very important barrier to learning the skills of 9,9, the reason being that if a person sees himself as managing in 9,9 ways when, in fact, he is not, he is not motivated to change. He sees himself as already doing what the values of 9,9 require.

## Gap

Recognizing that 9,9 is highly valued and acknowledging that one is unlikely to have been managing in a 9,9 way, a person can see the difference between the way he has been managing and what he would like to accomplish to become a more truly excellent manager. Gaps between the way a person currently is managing and the way he would like to manage create a tension, and relieving this tension is a strong motivation towards managing in a better way.

## Social Support

A fifth consideration is the active and positive support of one's colleagues in helping a person shift from past habits of managing toward a 9,9 style. Thus the team itself is the social support system for shifting the way the team has been led in the past into the direction of a more 9,9 style of operation.

When boss and subordinates alike learn the various Grid styles and see the differences between managing in the 9,9 way and its alternatives, basic conditions are set for bringing about change. Active participation of those who are likely to be influenced by change, and, in fact, who are directly involved in change themselves as they set goals, face and resolve conflict, and open up their communications, means that everyone is simultaneously engaged in bringing the change about. The strongest approach for bringing this about in an organized way involves Grid Team Building, as described in Chapter 13.

## Implications for Mental and Physical Health

Examination of the medical literature leads to the conclusion that neither mental nor physical health problems can be identified in association with the 9,9 Grid style. To answer the question of mental and physical health implications, therefore, we must approach the issue from different directions.

One direction involves investigations where outstandingly productive and creative people such as Einstein, Eleanor Roosevelt, or Pablo Casals, are identified as a group who, by wide acclaim, have lived rewarding and fulfilled lives. Then their actual person-to-person behavior has been described in Grid-relevant terms. Conclusions are typified in the following descriptions by Maslow.

> The first and most obvious level of acceptance is at the so-called animal level. Those self-actualizing people tend to be good animals, hearty in their appetites and enjoying themselves without regret or shame or apology. They seem to have a uniformly good appetite for food; they seem to sleep well; they seem to enjoy their sexual lives without unnecessary inhibition and so on for all the relatively physiological impulses. They are able to accept themselves not only on these low levels, but at all levels as well; e.g., love, safety, belongingness, honor, self-respect. All of these are accepted without question as worthwhile, simply because these people are inclined to accept the work of nature rather than to argue with her for not having constructed things to a different pattern. This shows itself in a relative lack of disgusts and aversions seen in average people and especially in neurotics, e.g. food, annoyances, disgust with body products, body odors and body functions.

Closely related to self-acceptance and to acceptance of others is (1) their lack of defensiveness, protective coloration, or pose, and (2) their distaste for such artificialities in others. Cant, guile, hypocrisy, front, face, playing a game, trying to impress in conventional ways: these are all absent in themselves to an unusual degree. Since they can live comfortably even with their own shortcomings, these finally come to be perceived, especially in later life, as not shortcomings at all, but simply as neutral personal characteristics.

. . . Our subjects are in general strongly focused on problems outside themselves. In current terminology they are problem centered rather than ego centered. They generally are not problems for themselves and are not generally much concerned about themselves; e.g., as contrasted with the ordinary introspectiveness that one finds in insecure people. These individuals customarily have some mission in life, some task to fulfill, some problem outside themselves which enlists much of their energies.

. . . Self-actualizing people have deeper and more profound interpersonal relations than any other adults (although not necessarily deeper than those of children). They are capable of more fusion, greater love, more perfect identification, more obliteration of the ego boundaries than other people would consider possible. There are, however, certain special characteristics of these relationships. In the first place, it is my observation that the other members of these relationships are likely to be healthier and closer to self-actualization than the average, often *much* closer. . .

. . . These people have all the obvious or superficial democratic characteristics. They can be and are friendly with anyone of suitable character regardless of class, education, political belief, race, or color. As a matter of fact it often seems as if they are not even aware of these differences, which are for the average person so obvious and so important.

They have not only this most obvious quality but their democratic feeling goes deeper as well. For instance they find it possible to learn from anybody who has something to teach them—no matter what other characteristics he may have. In such a learning relationship they do not try to maintain any outward dignity or to maintain status or age prestige or the like. It should even be said that my subjects share a quality that could be called humility of a certain type. They are all quite well aware of how little they know in comparison with what *could* be known and what *is* known by others. Because of this it is possible for them without pose to be honestly respectful and even humble before people who can teach them something that they do not know or who have a skill they do not possess. They give this honest respect to a carpenter who is a good carpenter; or for that matter to anybody who is a master of his own tools or his own craft . . .

Another meaning of autonomy is self-decision, self-government, being an active, responsible, self-disciplined, deciding agent rather than a pawn, or helplessly "determined" by others, being strong rather than weak. My subjects make up their own minds, come to their own decisions, are self-starters, are responsible for themselves and their own destinies.

Thus people who have been outstandingly productive and creative appear to have approached their relations with people from a 9,9 orientation. Even though the above research was not focused on it, findings reveal that these 9,9-oriented people were characterized by good biological functioning.

Levinson describes an approach similar to Maslow's in which fourteen senior members of the Menninger Foundation clinical staff were asked to describe people considered to be mentally healthy. Forty-one descriptions of the qualities of those people included a wide variety of sources of gratification and flexibility under stress. They also had the ability to see alternate solutions to problems, could recognize and accept personal limitations and assets, and treated other people as individuals. They were also active and productive people who sought to use their energies to do something rather than be somebody.

Another approach entails conclusions by medical biologists who have studied and researched physically healthy people and then sought to describe characteristics of their person-to-person behavior.

One of the most eminent of these studies concludes that stress of a certain kind and magnitude is essential to full living but beyond these limits it is destructive. Selye sees the man-to-man conditions resulting from a biologically healthy degree of stress as involving a coupling of two underlying values. One of these is achievement, equivalent with concern for production. The other is altruism, related to concern for people.

> ... But there is also a nonspecific resistance that can be acquired by making continuous but moderate demands upon our organs, for example, our muscles and brain. Here, the lasting gain is to keep them fit, the lasting loss is caused by over-exertion, resulting in irreparable tissue breakdown.

> In interpersonal stress, the gain is the incitement in others of friendship, gratitude, goodwill, and love toward ourselves; the loss is the creation in others of hatred, frustration, and an urge for revenge. This applies both to people around us and to ourselves, for our own positive or negative feelings toward others respectively benefit or hurt us directly, just as much as we are helped or hurt by inciting those feelings in others.

Achievement reached under conditions of altruism, rather than at the expense of altruism, or altruism carried out in the absence of achievement, is healthy. The following quotation conveys the gist of his conclusions.

> In this sense, and to my mind, the aim of life is to maintain its own identity and express its innate abilities and drives with the least possible frustration. To remain healthy, man must have some goal, some purpose in life that he can respect and be proud to work for. Each person must work out a way to relieve his pent-up energy without creating conflicts with his fellow men and, if possible, to earn their goodwill and respect.

Under 9,9 conflict solving, emotions harmful to physical and mental health are less likely to accumulate. If frustrations are resolved when they do arise, for example, the negative effect of stored anger and hostility are significantly reduced. A person who operates openly does not suffer inner conflicts or compulsions. He has the ability to handle stresses rather than having to recoil from them, or swallow them, or enlist others in sympathy. He has the capacity to establish relationships based upon trust and mutual respect in the business world and on intimacy in the family. Whether the answer to the question seeks to identify outstanding and productive people and then to determine their man-to-man characteristics, or whether it begins with concepts of biological health and then considers the person-to-person behavior of these individuals, the conclusion appears to be the same: positive mental and physical health appear to be associated with a 9,9 orientation.

## Childhood Origins of 9,9

### Systematic Model

The key to understanding child rearing that leads to a 9,9 orientation as an adult is that parents have an explicit systematic model for the kind of person toward which they intend to guide their child's development. The model contains two components. One is the capacity for autonomy, which means promoting the child's capacity for spontaneity and freedom to act according to his own choice. This means guiding a child's growth and development toward the capacity for independent self-direction based on his own sense of social responsibility. The other is the capacity for cooperation and mutual respect that can permit sound interactions with other people.

### Autonomy

Automony is rooted in parents' reactions to a child's spontaneous activities. Living in an environment in which stimulating activities take place, a child is helped to learn the natural consequences of his own actions without direct guidance or evaluation. In creating such an environment, parents maintain a structure for behavior. They are more concerned with setting the conditions of growth than channeling its direction. By emphasizing standards of performance, but resisting the temptation to tell the child what to do or what his emotions and feelings should or should not be, autonomy is strengthened as a child learns to direct his own actions with minimum control or help from others. Growth in the capacity for autonomy enables a person to make his own choices from available alternatives rather than relying on others for advice and counsel. These child-rearing circumstances also enable a child to *create* alternatives by imagining unanticipated possibilities as he or she develops the capacity to do things.

Spontaneity is respected and encouraged within the limits of safety. The need to curb a child's activity is reduced by eliminating objects and circumstances that, reacted to impulsively, might harm the child. This means providing an environment without broken or dangerous objects, which prevents children from hurting themselves and others, and about which there is no need to constantly warn him. The 9,9-oriented child also learns that limits are set to acts of self-assertion that are injurious to others. Initially, parents are the limit-setters.

No matter how carefully set, limits are likely to be exceeded. The issue, then, is how parents react to these excesses. Punishment that is rational in the sense of being predictable serves the purpose of reinforcing those limits and boundaries that parents think to be so important that they should not be violated. Punishment is, in itself, no barrier to sound development, provided that the punishment is fair and administered by parents who are generally loving toward the child.

Self-esteem is closely related to autonomy, which depends on competence to perform. A 9,9 approach to child rearing sees to it that a child is not expected to perform when he lacks the capacity to do so. Situations are created in which he is able to succeed and, therefore, to be competent and to feel confident. His own self-esteem is reinforced by parental acceptance and support which in turn promotes inner confidence and relating to others altruistically. Both are at the core of a motivation which, in adult life, is concerned with contributing to the effectiveness of others.

The question can be asked, "How old should a person be before he takes his life into his own hands or otherwise is freed to be autonomous?" The answer is sometimes, "When he leaves home," or "When he goes to college." However, there is another way of dealing with this question, which becomes clear by contrasting opposite ends of a continuum. At one end, in infancy, a child is totally dependent on others; at the other end, sometime in the late teens or early adulthood, he becomes an essentially independent adult. Along this continuum there are many points in a person's experience when he can start taking responsibility for himself: some at a very early age; others at a mature age; and others when career and marriage decisions are made. Thus the question, "When is a person capable of taking life into his own hands?" cannot be answered in a clear-cut way. Rather, a person is capable of doing so depending upon his particular stage of growth and progress in mastering the requirements of that stage at that time. Under healthy conditions it is a cumulative process rather than one which functions one day and not the next.

## Cooperation

Parents can promote cooperation by engaging in give-and-take activities in which both parents and child have the opportunity to influence outcomes. In this way, other people become a source of interest, challenge, and pleasure. Parents and child emphasize cooperation as a source of pleasure. Love and leadership in child-rearing are coupled when parents are able to enter a child's environment and engage in collaborative play with joy and laughter. This is more than responsive or supportive play; it is play that adds human stimulus to the environment of objectives and things.

Love and affection are shared in an unconditional way that promotes confidence and trust. The meaning of unconditional love is love that is not metered out in response for compliance or withheld to reflect displeasure. It is not conditioned by the behavior of the child. In other words, affection is not used to control the child by giving or withholding it. A child learns that human feelings involve caring, which means that others make a difference. The extension of a child's feelings about his own parents when they offer sympathy and help leads to the development of a concern for people as individuals worthy of dignity and respect. Adults who feel and give a child genuine love and affection in an unconditional way are setting him on a 9,9-oriented course.

As growth proceeds, definitions and delimitations of effective behavior are created verbally, but in a rational way. These include respect for one another among brothers and sisters, sharing in work and play, with parents helping children who have difficulties find solutions to their problems rather than imposing requirements.

This type of child rearing by no means eliminates conflict from the human environment of childhood, nor does it rule out the experiences of anger, fear, and anxiety. These emotions are inevitable. What it does, however, is to vastly reduce the conflicts of will that otherwise arise between parents and children and among children. It creates a basis of mutual respect for resolving the conflict of wills. This promotes a condition under which righteous indignation may develop in response to injustice but where blind anger and hate are eliminated or held to a minimum.

Underlying the development of both autonomy and cooperation are four fundamental aspects of teaching and learning. One is the parents' attitude toward *learning*, which is regarded as valuable in its own right. Second, *critique* methods are relied upon to facilitate a child's grasp of the connections between his experiences and their consequences. A third is *modeling*. This means that parents help the child to learn by demonstrating through their own behavior and conduct how to approach problems and how to do things. For example, many adults instill in their children the concept of contribution through service to others and of acting responsibly by helping those who need assistance. Thus, helping others becomes a positive motivation and serves as part of the foundation for building interpersonal attitudes based on mutual respect. The fourth is encouraging the child to act *independently or cooperatively*, depending on the circumstances. These methods help provide self-convincing evidence that he is respected.

### Systematic vs. Compensatory 9,9 Origins

The second root from which a 9,9-oriented style of managing arises in childhood is compensatory in character.

The compensatory origin arises from the fact that a young person may experience injustice and thereby become highly committed to justice. He may be protected and as a result become motivated to take risks. He may see himself as weak and desire to become strong. Thus, the closeness of opposites is proven when the experience of one extreme makes one desire to achieve something diametrically the opposite.

It can be seen why compensatory routes to an adult Grid style may more often lead to a 9,1 rather than a 9,9 adult orientation. Opposites such as feeling poor and wanting to be rich, feeling weak and wanting to be overpowering, feeling ignored and wanting to dominate, feeling defeated and wanting to win, may promote a 9,1 rather than 9,9 orientation. This depends on whether the compensation is aimed at "coming out on top rather than on the bottom" or towards contribution to and caring for those who may be less fortunate.

### Facades

A facadist may rely on several techniques to build a 9,9 image. Although some of the tactics may appear contradictory to one another, such as showering a subordinate with power and yet practicing incomplete delegation, the facadist may do these seemingly contradictory things in order to further his own personal aims and in ways that "hide" his practices. He may do one thing in one location or with a particular person and an opposite thing in another place or with a different person.

### Reputation Building

A facadist may seek to demonstrate a 9,9 orientation by building a positive reputation for commitment, caring, and contribution. When others are unable to sense what he is really like, he appears outwardly to have integrity.

Ever since Machiavelli, writers have *suggested ways to use such a reputation to hide 9,1-oriented motivations to control, master, and dominate.* The reputation is built around virtue, good deeds, and support of popular causes. Working in behalf of social causes and institutions that contribute to human dignity and reduce human suffering may be a facade. Another reputation-building strategy is expressing lofty convictions and embracing valued ideals of social justice. The reputation of the cause or movement becomes part of the facadist's reputation. Using the names and activities of respected people to bolster one's own importance is a similar technique. Toward this end, for example, a person works to bestow honor on all who actually excel. In this way he identifies with excellence.

### Concern for Others

Showing an interest in others may be a facade; being a good listener, not telling a person he is wrong even when to do so would be in the other person's own best interests, and avoiding arguments, all may be done in the interests of manipulation. Even learning and using another person's name may be manipulative. As one person says, "I make it a point to find out what someone important to me is most interested in so that I can ask questions and get him to talk. Not only does this tend to put him in a positive frame of mind, but it also makes him feel important. Because he feels friendly towards me, he is more likely to give me what I want." The intent is to gain access to another person's private point of view in order to achieve a personal advantage.

### "Trust"

The strategist may give the impression that he has complete trust and confidence in his subordinates. However, he rates subordinates as trustworthy according to their personal loyalty to him rather than their contribution to organization achievement. Trustworthy subordinates can give him candid and frank advice. This may be essential for him to achieve hidden objectives. Subordinates should know that honesty is expected and rewarded, but how can the loyalty of subordinates be tested? By showering them with power, then observing how they use it. If it is used in the interest of their boss, then they are considered trustworthy. However, if they use it for their own selfish gain, then they are not reliable.

### Incomplete Delegation

This facadist wants to be known as one who respects and trusts people and who relies on them. This can be seen in his delegation of authority.

To protect himself, however, he leaves job description boundaries fuzzy. This ensures uncertainty as to who is free to act with authority. Another tactic is to arrange overlapping responsibilities. Subordinates act as counterweights to one another, and none have sufficient authority to decide an action.

Not fully communicating technical information that would permit decisions to be made under conditions of delegating is a third tactic. Yet just enough information is given so that people feel informed, even though they may recognize that the total situation is more complicated. Another way to retain control is to operate on a one-to-one basis with subordinates or colleagues when problems require the total thinking of several or more. He avoids interaction where a free exchange of ideas and information would keep everyone informed, yet subordinates or colleagues feel "in the know" because of consultation with their boss, even though he has not explained the whole situation. Information needed by subordinates to coordinate their activities must be gained from him, and he can manipulate outcomes according to his personal gain. Subordinates are kept isolated from one another, making it difficult to track the boss's actions and discover his true motives. When these stratagems are applied skillfully, the difficulty people have in arriving at decisions appears to be caused by the system, not the administration of it. Fuzzy boundaries, overlapping responsibilities, and partial information all lead in the same direction for the final decision: upward. Then subordinates have to ask for help. Thus, the manager retains control, makes the decision himself, and is viewed as a statesman rather than an arbitrary ruler.

### Pseudo Teamwork

Appearing to involve others and share decision making, thereby gaining the advantages of seeming to practice 9,9 team management while making key decisions by oneself, is a manipulative strategy. Team action in the valid sense of involving others in problem solving, interdependent action, confrontation, and working through issues is viewed as risky and is distrusted. Thus the facadist engages in team action when it can be utilized to his own advantage. Knowledge of group dynamics is an indispensable tool for exploiting because tapping the resources of others can be facilitated through team interaction. Brainstorming, for example, is one way to elicit thoughts that makes it relatively easy for the facadist to take credit for the ideas of others without their realizing it. By cleverly hitchhiking onto others' work or thoughts, he can present them upward as his own.

He also uses team action to shift responsibilities for dangerous innovations from himself to a team. "He trusted them, but they blew it."

One way to avoid real interaction is to feel out positions and gain commitment from those concerned before the meeting takes place. In this way he can influence outcomes and achieve uniformity of opinion without open debate and deliberation. He also makes a deliberate effort to compose problem-solving teams of allies rather than of those who might have divergent points of view.

## Counseling Caution

Counseling caution through fear-provoking remarks is one of the most subtle, as well as effective, ways of immobilizing a person or team. The idea is to create anxiety about some projected course or to prevent an action from being taken. Such a statement is, "It won't work." Characteristically, such remarks are not documented with reasons or evidence, yet they give the impression of avoiding risks associated with probable failure.

Such fear-provoking remarks set off the personal anxiety of an individual relative to an action being considered. From the perspective of the person who hears it, it appears realistic. This is not objective anxiety based on healthy caution. While it may appear real under superficial examination, it is in fact a false assessment of the consequences of some proposed action.

The fear-provoking remark may be a subtle and powerful way of blocking action before testing the consequences. Such remarks as, "The boss won't buy it," "It costs too much," and "It didn't work in plant X," are examples of anxiety-provoking advice that may prevent *logical* problem solving. These remarks can be made in such a way that the person receiving the information feels it is given out of genuine 9,9 concern for his best interests rather than as a blocking tactic.

## Implications of 9,9 for Organizations

A variety of circumstances and conditions are stimulating movement in this direction. Many relate to a desire of management to avoid some of the negative consequences produced under other theories of management. Some, such as unionization, have been discussed already.

A primary condition is when a competitive advantage can be gained. Combined efforts of committed people is the only real advantage still to be realized by organizations in certain industries, where capital investment, facilities and processes, technological knowledge and skills, all tend to be relatively equal. *The only way to gain a significant competitive edge is through better management.* Also, the kind of management that can confront conflict with a problem-solving orientation holds the promise of being able to establish more effective union-management relations.

The growing appreciation and knowledge of behavioral science experimentation is promoting a shift toward 9,9. Attitudes and assumptions about how to integrate people into production are coming under critical and systematic examination through the combined efforts of managements and behavioral scientists. Management is becoming theory-based rather than relying on intuitions and common sense assumptions.

Other conditions promoting 9,9 include a gradual upward shift in the education of the general population. The basic values of the culture shift as this trend increases. Individual technical skills and knowledge are increasing, broadening, and deepening. Highly capable people now begin their working careers at low levels of entry into the organization as knowledgeable workers. People possessing such skills, together with sound and mature judgment, cannot be expected to work under unchallenging conditions, or under conditions of strict authority-obedience, or under a soft, slow-moving tempo where there is neither challenge nor opportunity.

The high technology associated with many products makes 9,9 skills important because the decisions needed for success are the ones that involve many complex factors and the pooling of information and technical knowledge of many different people. Thus the need is greater for achieving synergistic results from team action in these kinds of companies than in ones where one or a few people are the carriers of the total knowledge needed.

A way of management to stimulate the highest creativity of organization members is necessary under changing conditions. More creative and innovative thinking is required when organizations move into new or unknown areas—such as those stimulated by the nuclear age—than is required when an organization is concerned only with producing and marketing an established product under unchanging marketing environments.

Through the years the moving force has been education. As concepts and strategies of education improve, it is likely that education will play an even bigger part in the years ahead.

The long-term consequences of 9,9 remain to be seen, as this conception of management as a systematic approach is no more than twenty years old. Where the objective is that of moving in the 9,9 direction as an organization style, there is every indication that long-term, sustained growth results for the organization and its members.

Although many difficulties are encountered in the objective evaluation of organization effort, conclusions drawn to date indicate that among the gains attributable to a 9,9 change program are:

1. Contributions to organization profitability
2. The improvement of intergroup relations between headquarters and subsidiaries, headquarters and plants or sales regions, and between management and unions with which it bargains
3. Strengthening and extending the use of team action in various ways
4. Reduction of interpersonal frictions and the degree of interpersonal misunderstanding among individuals whose work requires close coordination of effort
5. Increasing individual effort and creativity and heightening personal commitment

The next decade should provide a more precise basis for evaluating the kinds of results possible from this organization style as more organizations take deliberate steps to move in a 9,9 direction.

### Summary

Contribution through commitment and caring characterizes 9,9 motivations of the positive sort, while disappointment and discouragement identify what a 9,9 manager most seeks to avoid. Involvement, participation, and commitment of those concerned with decision making and problem solving is the basis of teamwork.

The person with this predisposition places high value on sound and creative decisions. He is not interested in making a decision based only on his own convictions. He listens for and seeks out ideas, opinions, and attitudes different from his own. The 9,9 focus is on the quality of thinking and its essential validity, regardless of whether it represents his own or another person's, or emerges from discussion. He is interested in arriving at best solutions. He is a starter by initiating action, but he also follows through. Others pick up his sense of confidence enthusiastically.

A 9,9-oriented manager is likely to have clear convictions of his own, though he responds to sound ideas by changing his mind. When conflict arises, he tries to identify reasons for it and to resolve underlying causes by working them through. He rarely loses his temper, even when stirred up. His humor fits the situation. Feelings and attitudes are not regarded as barriers but as tools. They are significant elements of work and can be managed.

"A sound, solid character" is a term describing a person who can be counted on under conditions of uncertainty, stress, or crisis to do the right or valid thing. A 9,9-oriented manager is capable of acting sensibly to bring about effective results, maintaining consistency but finding innovative solutions to fit unique problems and unusual circumstances.

Grid style resilience and versatility reveal a manager's competence to maintain a problem-solving 9,9 orientation under stress. Solid managers are described in such terms as, "He is a man of principle; he has integrity."

Positive mental and physical health appear to be related to a 9,9 orientation but research evaluating this premise is only beginning to appear. However, outstandingly productive and creative people appear to conduct their person-to-person dealings in a 9,9-oriented way. Viewed from the standpoint of medical biology, the physically healthy person responds favorably to stress by seeking achievement through altruistic methods.

Childhood origins of a 9,9 orientation stem from parents, working from a systematic model, establishing conditions under which the child can develop autonomy by learning to depend on his own judgment. Parents also interact with the child in a cooperative, give-and-take way so that skills of interdependence and attitudes of mutual respect are developed.

## Chapter 8

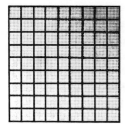

# Combinations
# of Grid Theories

Besides the five basic ones already described, additional managerial orientations can be identified. These theories are compounds or combinations of the basic or "pure" theories. They involve two or more of the basic approaches already discussed—9,9; 5,5; 9,1; 1,9; or 1,1—either simultaneously or successively.

### Paternalism

Paternalism denotes a relationship between a manager and his subordinates that involves the 9,1 direction coupled with 1,9 approval-giving, similar to that between a father and his children under certain circumstances. A paternalistic boss tends to retain tight control in work matters. He is generous and kind in a personal way when subordinates do what they are told. The spirit of paternalism is seen when a boss calls one of his men over, say, twenty minutes before the end of the shift and says, "Joe, you've put in a good day's work and finished all your assignments. Let's have a smoke."

A paternalistic manager treats his subordinates as part of his managerial family by telling them the who, what, where, when, and how for every activity. On the one hand, he encourages them to be responsible, but they are likely to avoid exercising initiative because he is unable to truly delegate, and constantly checks whenever someone seems to be involved with a problem they have not previously discussed. Subordinates soon learn that he is never happy with them unless they are handling it precisely as he would have had them deal with it had they come to him in the first place. Often he is heard to describe a subordinate in this way: "My assistant won't accept responsibility. He's bright and capable, with plenty of know-how, but he checks everything he does with me. He won't take the ball and run. It's difficult to see how he'll ever succeed." What the boss fails to realize is that his double-checking promotes a sense of uncertainty that undercuts the readiness to act autonomously.

The reward for compliance is economic and social security; thus, sub-ordinates prefer being dependent for guidance to acting on their own. Employees who buckle under are given many fine things—good pay, ex-cellent benefit programs, recreational facilities, retirement programs; even low-cost housing, to say nothing of personal acceptance. Even though these contributions to people's welfare are not directly connected to their output or productivity, they tend to increase the workers' sense of well-being. "I owe my soul to the company store," is a line from a famous song of feelings about paternalism, once a person has become so locked in that there is no escape.

The following example of paternalism emphasizes some of its harmful effects. During the Depression a decision was made in a large refinery to uncover all underground pipes and conduits, to wrap them with a protec-tive material, and to re-embed them at greater depth. While there were technical reasons for doing all this, it was by no means necessary; the major reason was to avoid laying off the wage force. It was also decided that the rate of pay for this work be reduced by one-half. Management's rationale was that the work was not necessary for safety or to maintain or to increase productivity; rather, it was intended to keep workers employed. Thus, management felt justified in reducing the rate, which in turn made it possible to employ twice the number of men in the proj-ect, thus reducing the surplus who could not be retained on the produc-tion side of the business.

What was the result? The work was accepted at the time without criticism or complaint, and with apparent appreciation. After the return of prosperity, however, employees remembered the episode for the frustration it caused them. They felt that advantage was being taken of them because of prevailing economic conditions. Wage people said, "Not only did they [the management] call upon us to do unnecessary work· they did so when we were in no position to resist. When they had us in that kind of a bind, what did they do? They cut our pay in half." Here, then, is a case where management's good intentions were not seen. The opposite result happened: their efforts to take care of people boomeranged. Their actions failed to produce respect for their thought-fulness of the needs of people to stay employed. Management thought it had done a good deed; the wage personnel felt themselves to be victims of vicious exploitation.

With consistent application, paternalism can create a highly stable organization, with minimum turnover because organization members tend to become compliantly obedient to the requirements placed on them. However, some of the worst upheavals and disruptions have oc-curred where paternalism has been extensively practiced. Against a background of what appeared to be a stable and long enduring organization, waves of resentment and retaliation have broken against the management that has for so long treated its people so well. Such a gross shift from compliant acceptance to defiant retaliation appears contradictory. It needs explanation.

One way of understanding these reactions is this: 9,1 work management that disregards the thinking and capabilities of people generates frustration and resistance and produces feelings of alienation. These feelings are difficult to express directly towards an employer who, at the same time, offers economic, social, and personal security to those who comply with his unilateral demands. Reactions to indignities, as a result, may be swallowed and bottled up, but they are there. Masking that real, seething resentment and unrest produces the appearance of docility and devotion. Under these circumstances, even a minor irritation can trigger an eruption of vitriolic and hateful reactions. *The formula for concocting hate consists of arousing frustrations under conditions of dependency.* One feels antagonized and aggressive but cannot fight back because of one's fear of losing acceptance and security. Although paternalism has failed repeatedly to solve problems of getting production through people, it is still a rather widespread attitude underlying much managerial thinking. There are many variations on paternalism that look different but actually differ only in terms of degree. Benevolent autocrat is another way of saying paternalist, and missionary is another variation on the same style.

Colonialism is the political version of industrial paternalism, and the Boston Tea Party might be regarded as a classical example of these reactions.

### Wide-Arc Pendulum

Under the wide-arc pendulum approach, either 9,1 or 1,9 may be operating but not at the same time. One follows the other.

The wide-arc pendulum swing can be seen when a manager drives for production in a 9,1-oriented way, and, in doing so, arouses resentments and antagonisms. He recognizes these negative attitudes and then overcorrects by removing all pressures and becoming exaggeratedly interested in the thoughts, feelings, and attitudes of those beneath him. Production falls, but relationships are restored to a smooth basis. Once again he becomes careless and reverts to a 9,1 manner of managing, only to back off again as tensions peak.

At least two circumstances can result in the swings of this kind of wide-arc pendulum. One is before and after a representation vote or a certification election in companies that want to remain nonunion or keep an independent union that has been challenged by an international.

Foremen say, "The signal is out. Management wants to be sure they win the election that's coming up. For the next few months let up on the tough stuff. Ease up on applying washup time and the coveralls and gloves policies. Show an interest in people. Find out what's griping them. Take whatever action is required to show employees that management is interested in them."

When the election is over and it went the way the management wanted it to, the same supervisors are told, "Get production back on line. Cut out the soft stuff."

The other circumstance is related to cyclical movements of the economy from troughs of recession to peaks of prosperity. When hard times hit, there are feverish activities to tighten up for increased output at reduced expense. Included are such efforts as cost control, waste control, rolls readjustment, and so on. Cracking down to get efficiency, then easing off to get back in the good graces of subordinates, then pushing for increased production again, etc., is the pendulum swing from hard to soft to hard. To those whom they affect, these actions seem cold and impersonal because they result in an increase in pressure. Sometimes the kind of production improvement decisions that are made do, in fact, result in an improved P/L position. But relationships become so disturbed that trouble can be seen brewing. As soon as health has been restored to the economy and company conditions improve, attention turns away from the kinds of efficiency moves previously taken. Management feels compelled to ease off and to show increased concern for the thoughts, feelings, and attitudes of people, thus shifting to a 1,9 approach to restore confidence that management cherishes human values. Control programs tend to fade out while uneconomical practices creep back in. Without the goad associated with economic threat, practices that are in fact "soft" are likely to be overlooked or accepted. After a degree of confidence and peace has been restored, another period of hard times leads to a new tightening up to regain the losses in production and efficiency suffered during the previous swing.

As people catch on to what is buffeting them, these kinds of swings sow the seeds of their own destruction. People cease to trust management's word, and the union becomes progressively more attractive as a bulwark against these kinds of ups and downs. These kinds of pendulum swings are most likely to occur when managers see people and production needs as two ends of a seesaw, where one is "up," the other is "down." An alternative formulation that they are two sides of a single coin could lead to a 9,9 solution to such problems.

### Counterbalancing

Counterbalancing is a third way of applying 9,1 and 1,9. The line organization operates on a 9,1 orientation, producing the usual negative reactions of frustration and aggression. As a safeguard against such feelings festering and breaking out with disastrous effects, a staff organization has the responsibility of keeping its finger on the pulse of the organization and providing disgruntled people the opportunity to blow off steam through ventilating their feelings. Thus the staff becomes a safety valve to prevent the entire system from rupturing under high pressure. This kind of a staff department is seen in places that have people who are called "field representatives," "personnel representatives," or "employee relations coordinators." Their responsibilities are to keep in touch with what is going on and counsel with those who are antagonistic. In some settings, staff services have taken an even more elegant form. Psychiatrists, psychologists, ministers, and other professionals skilled in listening, are employed for relieving pent-up feelings. The World War II management response to gripes—"Here's your card, take it to the chaplain and have it punched"—exemplifies the concept of counterbalancing. This "solution" has been strengthened and refined since then through the more extensive training of chaplains as counselors.

An example of the counterbalancing concept in practice comes from the Hawthorne plant of Western Electric where nondirective counseling at the work site originated in the following way. During the course of interviewing employees in an experiment on the relationship between lighting and productivity, the experimenters came to understand the benefits of the interviews for the people working in the experiment who were able to get feelings off their chests and who thereafter began to produce more. Recognizing this, management took another step by making the interview *a part* of the management approach to the maintenance of morale. The idea was to have counselors, paid by management, available to all employees but not reporting to management except to keep them apprised of trends that suggested adverse attitudes were building up toward management. Employees could feel free to talk out their problems because when they "spilled their troubles," they would not need to worry about being reported.

There are other forms of counterbalancing in addition to balancing a "hard" 9,1-oriented line with a "soft" 1,9-oriented personnel department. For example, in some organizations the line organization has become fixed into a 1,9 orientation, and is unwilling to make harsh personnel judgments. Then evaluation of managers for promotion becomes the responsibility of the "tough" 9,1-oriented personnel department, which exercises competency judgments and controls promotions. This is a reverse swing where the personnel staff serve to buck up the weak line.

The critical feature in counterbalancing is that responsibility for production and for people is not seen as a single integrated aspect of managing that rests on the shoulders of those who manage. The responsibility is divided and separated into two aspects, production responsibility on the one hand and people responsibility on the other.

Whether in industry, the military, or elsewhere, the serious disadvantage of this kind of ventilation of feelings and hostility is that it treats symptoms rather than causes. While tensions are reduced for the moment, the 9,1-oriented management responsible for generating the tensions remains unchanged.

### The Two-Hat Approach

The two-hat theory is applied by managers who separate their concern for production from concern for people while making the same persons responsible for both. Using the two-hat approach, a manager who practices 9,1-oriented management in daily work removes his production hat at six-month or yearly intervals and puts on his people hat to counsel with his subordinates in ways that deal mainly with attitudes-at-large and only incidentally as they relate to work. Job counseling is not part and parcel of work activity and individual development. Rather, it is a scheduled activity and is concentrated on when the people hat is worn. Line managers are likely to view this kind of counseling as an activity they must engage in, not because it contributes to improved work but because the personnel department has placed them under obligation to conduct these sessions as a matter of company policy.

Two-hat can be seen as an organization practice. For example, on one day, say Monday, the top team considers P/L problems and inefficient operations. Then on another day, say Wednesday, the same group meets again, this time to discuss people problems. The actions taken on Monday solve production problems. They are considered mainly in terms of technical production aspects. Even though they may be tied in with personnel problems, they are not likely to be considered in light of their effects on people. The same is true on Wednesday. The people problems considered at that time may bear significantly on production, but they are viewed mainly in the light of human needs. On Monday, problems concerning people are set aside until Wednesday. On Wednesday, production problems are delayed for discussion until the next Monday.

The two concerns are separate but equal in importance. The basic assumption again is that there are two sets of problems with the inherent connections between them frequently inadequately recognized.

### "Statistical" 5,5

It is occasionally said of a manager, "It's hard to tell anything exactly about his managerial style. He can fit every position on the Grid at one time or another." The statistical 5,5-oriented manager employs any two and sometimes all five basic styles in managing production-people dilemmas. The essential feature is that he manages according to what *he* thinks is *effective* at any particular point in time. Effectiveness is defined as behavior that is appropriate to the demands of the situation. This way of managing ignores behavioral science principles.

If a subordinate is a deadbeat, the manager does not assign him work. If a subordinate is easily upset, the manager throttles down on production pressures and praises him. If another subordinate is falling behind and isn't aware that he is courting loss of valued membership, a statistical 5,5-oriented manager points out that he is failing to carry his share of the load and that, unless he does, others will criticize him. If a subordinate has high standards and is being productive even though he may be producing conflict with others, the manager spurs him to greater effort. If his instructions are arbitrarily resisted by still another subordinate, the boss demands compliance. In other words, the statistical 5,5-oriented manager hopscotches all over the Grid. He behaves inconsistently by treating each subordinate differently depending upon the subordinate, yet he sees little or no contradiction in his actions. He assumes that each person is different and unique and that, therefore, creating widespread relationships based on mutual dignity and respect simply is not practical. Lacking a concept of change or development, the statistical 5,5-oriented manager "maneuvers," trying to adjust to whatever is expected of him within the boundaries of the status quo.

Most organizations have no one consistent organization style. Each department, division, region, or subsidiary is left to its own resources without a systematic plan for strengthening management practices. In a more or less evolutionary way, the components develop their own particular styles, and each individual manager his own within that framework. One division may be run as a tight ship to satisfy its 9,1-style manager. Another may do just enough to meet headquarters' requirements, while a third may strive for excellence. The statistical 5,5 quality in the final analysis is most probably brought about by a hands-off attitude from the top in an organization practicing the policy of extreme decentralization.

### Summary

In one respect or another, each of these compound theories recognizes the dilemma of getting production from people. Each tries in some way to handle it. However, compound theories distort the basic issue of *integrating* people into production. Their underlying limitations are that they never seek to change the status quo and, therefore, deal with symptoms rather than underlying causes. The real solution lies in learning to apply principles of human behavior to involve people and to integrate their individual goals and the goals of the organization with one another in a 9,9 way to which we now turn for further study.

## Chapter 9

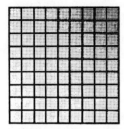

# 9,9 Versatility

Mental and physical health evidence presented in earlier chapters provides evidence that with one exception excesses in each Grid style are associated with a range of severe mental and physical illnesses. Research on career success described later in this chapter, and research on productivity and corporate profitability, to be reviewed in Chapter 13, also demonstrate that a 9,9 orientation is more positively associated with success, productivity, and profitability in comparison with any other theory.

In spite of these many lines of evidence that a 9,9 orientation is the best way to manage, a widespread belief exists that "How you lead depends on the situation, on what you are trying to accomplish, and what you're up against." Flexibility, in other words, is the key. The capacity to substitute one Grid style for another, to shift from dominant to backup or to take a statistical 5,5 approach will get the best results. Thus a manager is counseled to shift and adapt, move back and forth, dominate or yield, depending on the leadership style he thinks will move him toward his goals. This results in little more than subjective calculation or seat of pants management.

This is known as situationalism or contingency theory. It is rooted in pragmatism: if it works, do it. Adverse side effects (longer-term negative consequences for one's career and health, of an operational nature related to actual productivity, the growth and development or stunting of subordinates) are more or less disregarded. Flexibility is deemed preferable to the consistent application of a managerial style.

We need to understand this contradiction between belief and empirical evidence before examining the 9,9 orientation in greater depth.

## Principles as the Basis of Action

This rejection of "one best way" of conducting human relationships is equivalent to rejecting the proposition that effective behavior is itself based on scientific principles or laws. Yet the view that principles of behavior undergird specific events is consistent with that held in all other areas of scientific inquiry. We know that principles of physics underlie and explain a vast range of phenomena in inanimate nature. Principles of biology account for phenomena of life and make them predictable. By analogy, behavioral science principles should lie beneath human conduct, provide guidelines for soundness, and make it predictable also.

When principles are disregarded in physics, biology, or the behavioral sciences, it can be expected that side effects and longer-term operational consequences will be damaging. An aircraft designed without regard to aerodynamic principles is more likely to crash than one designed and operated consistent with those principles. The particular design varies with size, engine power, etc., but all aircraft conform to some basic principles. Gravity is a constant physical principle, but its effects on engineering design are different for space flights than for undersea exploration. Biological principles of nutrition are constant, but the actual diet of an infant of six months is different from that of a person of forty years of age. Biological principles inherent in the transfer of oxygen into the blood can be violated by an excessive smoker, but not without shortening his expected life span. Versatile applications reflect the operation of the same principle but under different conditions.

The growth and development toward effectiveness of bosses, colleagues, and subordinates can be stunted or distorted by violating 9,9-oriented behavioral science principles of participation, conflict resolution, goal setting, and so on. The larger expense is in longer-term damage to involvement, morale, and the readiness to persevere in finding valid solutions to important problems, and therefore in diminished productivity and profitability.

There appears to be, in other words, "one best way" to design an aircraft, to increase longevity, or develop strength in boss-subordinate relationships. That way is for decision making and engineering to be based on scientific principles as verified in basic experimental work and applied with versatility to specific situations.

At this point situationalists and principlists sharply contradict one another. Situationalists recommend that behavior be engineered to empirical results only. For example, if you must suppress disagreement to get grudging compliance with your wishes, you do so and save time. Principlists maintain that suppression is contrary to laws of mental and physical health and inevitably results in anger, aggression, etc., all of which take far more time to manage later on than the time saved.

There is another way to view this contradiction between belief and evidence that brings a dramatic resolution to the apparently irresolvable differences between these two approaches.

## The Concept of Versatility

The concept of versatility provides a basis for understanding how 9,9 leadership can be based consistently on sound principles of behavior and yet brought into use in creative and constructive ways that are (1) unique to particular situations, (2) unlikely to generate negative side effects, (3) optimal for problem solving and productivity, and (4) stimulating to growth and development toward maturity for those involved in the situation. Relying on behavioral science principles and implementing them through versatile applications is analogous to the relationship between scientific principles in physics and their application to engineering problems. Principles are not violated and disregarded. What changes is their application. These vary depending on the situation.

### Examples of Flexibility and Versatility

Compare the different styles of leadership, for example, in the same situation. As a boss of a new plant start-up, the person in charge may start out with a group of individuals who have never known or worked with one another. The task is to get the plant onstream. A situational leader might provide very close 9,1-oriented management in this novel situation if he assumes that even experienced subordinates don't know what to do. When they comply with his directions, he may then give them recognition. If they begin to buck, he might shift to a 1,9 sweetness and light thesis of encouragement and support, or turn to 1,1-oriented laissez-faire leadership to reduce their antagonisms.

A leader whose management is governed by 9,9-oriented principles of behavior, by comparison, knows that sound results are most likely when he and subordinates work together as a team. They can learn to analyze problems, and even though there are no tried and true answers, they seek "best" solutions by confronting differences, relieving disagreements by gathering additional data, simulating a proposal before implementing it, and so on. Beyond that, leadership may involve frequent critiques to stimulate operational as well as interpersonal learning.

Principles of behavior in the paragraph above rely on trust and respect. The engineering specifics include mutual goal-setting, openness, resolution of disagreements and conflict based on understanding and agreement, learning to change through use of critique, and so on. These are all aspects of behavior and performance that are verified in social psychology, mental health research, and clinical psychiatry as essential for a sound problem-solving relationship.

Consider a second example. Two talented subordinates submit recommendations to provide a basis for needed coordination between their departments. Their recommendations are mutually exclusive. The situationally-oriented boss might take one recommendation and veto the other, because in his view it is the easiest to implement. This 9,1 approach produces a win-lose situation between the subordinates. Recognizing this adverse effect, and in order to diminish win-lose conflict between the two subordinates, he might then shift and take a 5,5-oriented action to compromise the difference, taking something from both recommendations and putting them together, even though the final product was not as good as one of the two initially proposed. This boss might have adopted a number of other contingencies. He might have accepted both subordinates' recommendations but then procrastinated in a 1,1 way, hoping to avoid the need for decisiveness. Under any of these ways coordination breakdowns can be predicted, with antagonism and resentment felt by the defeated and arrogance by the victor, or both may feel dissatisfied and poorly motivated to make the solution work, or frustrated at the boss's inaction. Which approach the boss takes depends on his concept of what is likely to be most "effective," and, therefore, the choice is a subjective one.

What appears to a situationally-oriented manager as flexibility is likely to be experienced by his colleagues and subordinates as shifty, untrustworthy, even deceitful, whether or not dishonesty is involved or intended. The unpredictability provokes suspicion and distrust, closedness and hiding, resentment and antagonism, or calculation and tactics, depending on the Grid orientation of the colleague or subordinate who experiences it.

The 9,9-oriented boss who has a capacity for versatility might do something else to resolve the coordination problem: get subordinates together to face the contradictory character of their recommendations and help them to find a way for them to all work together and solve their problems. Shared points of view that previously had not even been recognized would begin to emerge. As areas of similarity in their coordination needs appear and areas of differences are pared down, agreements essential for coordinated effort are realized. Mutual respect is maintained throughout with confidence that the solution ultimately reached is more likely to be valid and implementable. But, if this approach did not work as anticipated, it might be necessary for a 9,9-oriented manager to shift tactics. The same strategy of managing by behavioral science leadership principles is maintained. The alternative tactics might now involve a participants' cooperating with one another to design and run through an experiment to test the operational consequences of both approaches, etc., or to put aside their introductory proposals and to formulate an "ideal" solution. Each of these different approaches is still based on 9,9 assumptions. Using a range and variety of 9,9 options identifies the versatility aspect and demonstrates in a different way why flexibility is a less preferred option to 9,9 alternatives.

## History

Where did situational flexibility come from? The ethic that undergirds situationalism is a protest against the 9,1-oriented Protestant ethic that held sway a century ago. The latter was based on arbitrary *rules* for behavior and conduct rooted in religion, philosophy, and economics. These rules failed to square with widespread feelings of a deeper sense of the possibilities of a richer life. The result was that situationalists overthrew the Protestant ethic and its arbitrary or inclusive rules to guide one's efforts toward effectiveness in given situations. Thus the situation itself, as subjectively viewed by the person responsible for it, became the sole criterion for its own management. The only constraint tolerated under the situationalist ethic is that whatever the action is, it must not *hurt* others. Thus a pessimistic view that accepts the status quo but allows great flexibility within it came into being.

Rules were confused with principles. The possibility of sound guidelines that can contribute to effectiveness was rejected and replaced with the "...it all depends..." philosophy of "subjectivism without harm to others."

Situationalism is now giving way to the principled approach that requires comprehension of laws of behavior. The manager is challenged to find solutions to production-people dilemmas that are consistent with verified laws of behavior.

### Behavioral Science Principles Basic to Effectiveness

What behavioral science laws of participation must be respected to ensure sound managing? The following examples are based on evidence from many behavioral science disciplines. The positive ends of each statement are supported in evidence from social psychology, sociology, anthropology, mental health, counseling, psychiatry, political science and history, and in field studies of business effectiveness. In addition to the above sources, the negative sides are validated in criminology, penology, in studies of slavery, indentured servitude, and so on.

Other things equal, productivity, creativity, and mental and physical health are better served when:

1. Informed free choice is the basis for personal action rather than enforced compliance.

2. Active participation in problem solving and decision making is the basis of growth and development rather than passively accepting instructions as to what to do or inactivity reinforced by social isolation.
3. Mutual trust and respect is the basis for sound human relationships rather than suspiciousness and defensiveness.
4. Open communication gives mutual understanding in contrast with one-way, hidden, closed, or Machiavellian communication that increases barriers to understanding.
5. Activities are carried out within a framework of goals and objectives for self-direction rather than direction from outside.
6. Conflict resolution is by direct problem-solving confrontation rather than by other ways (suppression, smoothing, withdrawing, compromising, or manipulation).
7. One is responsible for one's own actions rather than being responsible to someone else.
8. Critique is used to learn from experience rather than repeating one's mistakes because experience is not studied.
9. A person is engaging in complex work activities or a variety of activities in contrast with engaging in simple ones or in repetitions of the same activity.

The descriptive statements in Table 9-1 evaluate how these basic principles of behavior are dealt with by managers operating under each of the major Grid theories.

## Versatile Applications of the Informed Free Choice Principle Under 9,9

A further example might help in demonstrating that there is, in fact, "one best way" but that principles have different applications depending on specifics of a given situation.

Take the behavioral science principle concerned with *informed free choice*.

A good boss-subordinate relationship is one that honors this principle. Here is an example. A manager is needed in another location. A transfer appears to the boss to be the best solution. Is a person told to go, or else; or is subtle leverage applied? No. The subordinate is aided to see the costs and benefits for his career, family, friends, etc. of accepting the transfer vs. rejecting it. The decision is based on his informed free choice, with consequences of alternative courses of action known.

Another example of the same principle applied to a different situation involves a subordinate who is a newcomer, a person without previous ex-

**Table 9-1\***

**Behavioral Science Principles of Behavior and Conduct Evaluated by Grid Style**

| Principle | 1,1 | 1,9 | 5,5 | 9,1 | 9,9 |
|---|---|---|---|---|---|
| Informed Free Choice | Subordinates fend for themselves with insufficient information to exercise informed free choice. | Action is free, except unpopular actions that might provoke tensions in others are avoided. | Free choice is muted by conformity pressures which keep people moving together. | Requirements for compliance eliminate free choice. | Subordinates are kept informed and are encouraged to influence outcomes that affect them. |
| Active Participation | People know what to do. | Involvement in the social aspects of person-to-person relations is promoted. | Subordinates are expected to respect and embrace majority views. | Obedience rather than active involvement is expected. | Is the key to gaining the involvement, commitment, and creativity prerequisite to high productivity with morale. |
| Mutual Trust | Lack of respect between boss and subordinates prevails. | Overly-trusting managers give subordinates free rein. | Members in good standing have the boss's confidence that they won't make trouble. | Suspicion that subordinates will not follow through prevails. | Confidence is based on demonstrated competence by both boss and subordinates. |

| Principle | 1,1 | 1,9 | 5,5 | 9,1 | 9,9 |
|---|---|---|---|---|---|
| Open Communication | Messages are passed faithfully, up and down, as required. | Communication upward from subordinates is encouraged but downward flow from the boss is dampened to absorb anticipated negative reaction of subordinates to pressures. | Two-way communication is in line with what is acceptable within both the informal and formal organization. | Communication is one-way, hidden, and closed. | Open expression of thoughts and feelings is promoted. |
| Goals and Objectives | Goals are ignored as a source of direction or motivation. | The boss supports and encourages subordinates to set goals in line with what is attractive to them. | Production targets can be achieved with a reasonable effort. | Quotas are used to pressure production to the requirements decreed by the boss. | Understanding of and agreement with goals and objectives provides the basis for cooperation. |
| Conflict Resolution | Neutrality prevails in the presence of disagreement. | Agreement is sought by supporting the conclusions of others when conflict arises, differences are smoothed over or explained away. | When tradition or majority view is unavailable, compromise and accommodation through splitting the difference ensures no one loses. | Winning one's own position or suppressing disagreement demonstrates mastery over others. | When conflict appears differences are confronted and resolved. |
| Personal Responsibility | Subordinates take responsibility to the degree they want to. | Subordinates are provided whatever responsibility they want, but they are not likely to be held accountable for their actions. | Subordinates are expected to accept the status quo and to work graciously within it. | Responsibility for the subordinate is held by the manager. | Each person is responsible for his own activities as well as sharing responsibility for team effort. |

**Table 9-1 (continued)**

| Principle | 1,1 | 1,9 | 5,5 | 9,1 | 9,9 |
|---|---|---|---|---|---|
| Critique | Comments regarding subordinates' actions are rare. | Compliments for both work and nonwork-related actions over-exaggerate positive features; criticism is withheld if at all possible. | Tentative suggestions are offered which can be shifted if unacceptable. | Others are criticized for not measuring up to the boss's expectations. | Critique is used to learn from experience why actions are effective or ineffective and to learn from them. |
| Work Activities | Minimum work requirements are carried out on a catch-as-can basis. | Insofar as possible, subordinates choose the work activities they prefer. | Work is organized along conventional lines. | Work tasks are simplified and formalized in the interest of operational efficiency. | Engaging in complex work activities or a variety of activities is more conducive to mental health than is engaging in simple ones or repetition of the same activity. |

* Reproduced by permission from Blake, R.R., and J.S. Mouton. "Behavioral Science Principles to Increase Effectiveness," Austin, Texas: Scientific Methods, Inc., 1977.

perience. Informed free choice is exercised in completing the work assigned by accepting supervision in order to learn. Recognizing this, the boss demonstrates, tells the subordinate what to do and how to do it, encourages him to try and not to worry about mistakes, and coaches and supports the newcomer as he gets acquainted with the job. They critique the newcomer's performance at the beginning, during, and after work activities. The boss takes responsibility for assisting the subordinate to see angles, options, and alternatives. All along the line, he honors the individual's capacity to exercise informed free choice by creating a learning climate within which the subordinate can practice, experiment, critique, ask for help, and control the pace of his own learning.

The informed free choice principle is honored in both cases but in different ways, depending on the particular situation to which it is applied. This is versatility. It demonstrates how one leadership style can be "the best way" with variations in how it is employed to fit situations.

### Barriers to 9,9 Versatility
### and How They're Overcome

As a manager views a given situation, he may say, "A 9,9 strategy is impossible here." What may he really be saying? He could be stymied by any of the several things enumerated below.

He may insufficiently understand 9,9 concepts. This automatically eliminates the possibility of bringing a 9,9 approach into practice. The solution is in education.

He may have exhausted his ingenuity in applying a 9,9 way of leading. This does not mean it is impractical; it only means that this manager needs to acquire new skills before he can respond in a 9,9 way. The "real" solution is in training and an experimental attitude.

A third possibility is that the manager takes the status quo as given and applies little or no thought even to the prospect of *changing* it so as to be able to manage it in a 9,9 way. This limitation excludes many possibilities because of deficiencies of imagination. The "real" solution is confirmation of the issue and validation of the legitimacy and desirability of rejecting the status quo and seeking change.

A fourth reason focuses on the organization and the pressures for results on the manager, which deny the training, the time required, and the needed support to bring change about. The solution is in organization development discussed in Chapter 13.

An activity factor is the nature of the work itself, which may be so repetitive and simple as to eliminate the challenge to thinking and involvement in solving problems that is intrinsic to a 9,9 approach. The solution may be in job enrichment and strengthened management-by-objectives.

A person's private values may conflict with 9,9 values. This is conspicuous when a manager seeks to gain by employing various facades. This factor is an insidious version of flexibility that is very difficult to change, particularly if the system of relationships among those who work together has become characterized by deception and intrigue. 9,9 openness would be self-defeating. The solution is development of the social system within which work is done in such a way as to gain consensus on new social norms that reject rather than reward manipulation, and in this way change commitment of those who work together towards openness, trust, respect, and so on. This is possible by team building and organization development.

Shifting from a flexibility to a versatility concept of leadership is what managerial effectiveness training is—or should be—all about.

### Grid Style and Career Success

A 9,9 approach may be appealing, and it may square with behavioral science principles. Putting the mental and physical health evidence aside, the question is "Does it make any real life difference in personal success terms which way you manage?"

Two research investigations using the same basic measurements but in completely different circumstances, conducted independently of one another and spanning a period of fifteen years, reach the same conclusions. It makes a difference.

One of these was in 1962-64. It evaluated the rate of advancement up the promotion ladder of 713 managers in the same company as a function of their Grid styles as reported by colleagues.

High achievers, average achievers, and low achievers were identified by a specially created formula that permits any two managers to be compared for their rates of advancement, corrected for differences in their particular age and current rank in the organization progression ladder. High achievers are managers who are higher in rank than would be expected based upon their current age. Average achievers are advancing at the expected rate for their current age, and low achievers are advancing at a less rapid rate than would be expected based upon their current age. This investigation demonstrated that most rapid progress is by 9,9, followed by 9,1, with average achievers characterized by a dominant 5,5 orientation, with low achievers consisting prominently of 1,9 and 1,1-oriented people.

The second study, reported in 1976, was designed on the lines of the first one, but involved 2,000 managers from different companies. High, average, and low achieving managers were evaluated by the same basic formula. Grid style of managing was indicated for each manager by subordinates whom he supervised. High achievers were again found to be 9,9, and average achievers more in the 9,1 direction, with low achievers described as involving the 1,1 orientation.

These studies support the conclusion that a 9,9 approach to managing carries with it the greatest likelihood of career success.

### Summary

An important dilemma facing managers is concerned with whether to adopt a flexible approach, as seen in shifting from one style to another depending on the situation, or to implement a 9,9 approach in a versatile way.

A versatile 9,9-oriented approach permits a manager to deal with others in terms of principles of behavior that are applied in unique ways according to the requirements of specific situations. Research investigations demonstrate that career success is linked most closely to a 9,9 approach and we have already seen that positive mental and physical health is associated with a 9,9 Grid style and that adverse mental and physical health consequences are correlated with all other Grid styles.

Research in a later chapter provides an evaluation of the impact of an organization-wide 9,9 orientation on corporate profitability.

## Chapter 10

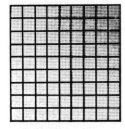

# 9,9 Teamwork

What is it that produces the need for teamwork? Organizations are made up of departments, divisions, sections, and individual assignments. Those reporting to the same boss have more or less well-defined jobs, whether the definition is written or informal, and they usually are interrelated with one another by the work they do. Yet no job description manual can possibly anticipate and arrange for solving everyday dilemmas that arise in modern complex organizations. At the team level, many such dilemmas relate directly to the issues of getting results. Under such arrangements, then, valid communication, mutual understanding, and superordinate goals, all of which rest on good teamwork, are indispensable.

9,9 teamwork, which is at the core of organizational excellence, helps members dig into, get at, and remedy underlying *causes* of operational problems. It is the key to seeing and seizing opportunities that otherwise might not be recognized. From the team member's point of view, it is one of the basic sources of satisfaction that the industrial world has to offer.

There are many adverse consequences from poor teamwork. Without mutual understanding, individual and team goals and objectives may either be nonexistent, fuzzy, too narrow, or so short-sighted as to have little or no meaning. Without effective interaction, members fail to see possibilities for synergy that can strengthen results. Individuals may be duplicating effort, with the result that much of the work is unproductive. When communication falters, work may be left undone because it falls in the crack between what each person thinks his job demands of him. Disappointments from past failures and interpersonal misunderstandings may rupture morale and cohesion. Even more stultifying problems may go unsolved because of excessive reliance on outmoded traditions, precedents, or past practices that provide insufficient guidance for what to do. The way a boss exercises his power and authority and the ways subordinates respond to it may be reducing effort and creativity, to say nothing of blocking organization members as they seek to satisfy personal values through work.

### Are You a Team Member?

The first issue that a manager might ask himself is, "Am I a member of a team?" then, "If so, which one?" "Who are the other members?" He might be tempted to say, "No, I am not a member of a team. The people who report to the same boss I do never meet together. We're a bunch of individuals. We're not a team."

Take another look. Here are some tests for whether you and they *are* or *are not* a team.

Let's say you bring up a problem with your boss. You are *not* a member of a larger team if the solution that is reached can always be implemented by you and if others who report to your boss have no need to know about it. If your job is that way, there are only two people. Your team is you and your boss. If others who report to him deal with matters that only he and each of them can solve on a one-to-one basis, then there are several two-man teams but no larger one. This situation rarely arises, except in certain staff situations where one boss oversees a number of disparate functions.

However, you are a member of a larger team if you bring a problem to your boss and he says any of the following sorts of things:

"Let me check this out with Bill first."

"Okay, but coordinate your action with Cathy."

"Don't worry. Don is taking care of that."

"Okay, but touch base with Al so he'll know what's going on."

"Go ahead. Your action supports but does not overlap what they are doing."

If a decision involves these kinds of remarks, then you are a member of a larger team. It includes you, your boss, and several colleagues. What you do touches at some point on what they do. You and they are interdependent.

You are also a member of a team if your boss says, "Do it, but don't tell anybody until it's finished. If they know in advance they'll block it." When this happens, it is not sound teamwork because members are working against the team and against one another, rather than supporting one another in their efforts to get results. Nonetheless, you are a member of a team, and there is a need for shifting the situation toward more constructive teamwork.

There is another test of whether you are a team member. Your boss doesn't say anything like the remarks above. He says, "Do whatever you want." Does this mean you're not a member of a team? No, not necessarily. You, your boss, and others may be members of the same team but your teamwork is so lacking in quality that neither he nor you feel a sense of teamness. You *should* be operating as a team but you are not. The challenge is to become one and to gain the benefits teamwork makes possible.

There is one other way you may be a member of a team without recognizing it. This is where you take an action and, having done so, other people automatically are able to take their actions; or, because you took an action, others who might have done so have no need to take an action. Things go smoothly and you do not notice how one person's effort helps another. This is excellent teamwork even though you may not recognize it as such.

### How Participation Relates to Teamwork

Teamwork does not mean everyone meeting together all the time. It may occur when a person is operating alone, or with one, several, or all members. It may occur in a face-to-face situation, when each member is separated from every other, or when one person is out of the situation and another is acting in his behalf.

### 1/All

Let's say a team has four members. Al is boss; Bill, Cathy, and Don are subordinates. Problems can only be solved by Al, Bill, Cathy, and Don working on them. Such situations are "one-to-all" (1/all). One-to-all problems bring together everyone who reports to the same boss to focus on and deal with a given problem. It involves team-wide participation. Thus, 1/all means everyone who is a member of the team. This is simultaneous teamwork. It occurs when (1) no member has knowledge, information, experience, breadth or wisdom to formulate the answer, but everyone working together can be expected to reach it; (2) coordination is required to get the job completed (every member has a piece of the action; therefore, each member's participation is significant to a successful outcome); and (3) all must understand the overall effort so that each can fit it into his other ongoing activities. Planning a budget *might* be an example.

### 1/1/1

This is more complex but no less important. What happens is that each member takes a certain action that makes it possible for another member to take a second action, and so on until everyone has contributed, in sequence, to the end result. It is one-to-one-to-one. Each team member's activity is indispensable in sequence. An example begins when a saleman writes up an order. Smooth coordination from the salesman to those who receive the order, to those who fill it, to those who prepare the invoice, and to those who help package and ship the order constitutes a complex sequence of interdependent operations. Done well, they satisfy the customer and build repeat business. Though there may be no face-to-face meetings, what they do links them together in a team effort. This is sequential teamwork.

### 1/Some

Here the work involves more than two people but not the total team. These are 1/some situations. They fall between 1/1 and 1/all and differ in number of members involved rather than in character of interdependence, whether simultaneous or sequential. Therefore, they will not be treated separately. This category is focused on to ensure that 1/some interactions are utilized when needed.

### 1/1

Team problems that involve Al and Bill together are 1/1 team actions. It's up to them to work out the solution and to take the actions that move the team toward its goals. These 1/1's between Al and Bill free Cathy and Don, who can contribute nothing, to use their time in dealing with other aspects of the team situation.

Under 1/1 situations any member may interact one at a time with any other member according to that person's specific area of responsibility and need for help, support, data, consultation, coordination, and so forth. Failure to bring in that other member can be expected to have adverse effects while bringing in anyone else would be wasteful, since additional members can contribute nothing. The mode of interdependence may be simultaneous, as just described, or it may be sequential.

### 1/0

Certain "team" problems involve *only* Al—or Bill, or Cathy, or Don— in the solution. The reasoning behind 1/0 is that Al has the responsibility, the capacity, and the information to solve the problem. Then it's in the interest of teamwork for Al (or whomever) to solve the problem alone and, thereafter, to let others know of his solution as it affects their own responsibilities. Such "team" problems, in other words, are "one-alone" (1/0). Individual effectiveness contributes to teamwork by moving the team toward its goals and avoiding duplication of effort.

When there is understanding and agreement about the conditions under which a manager does not involve others, his solo decisions are not seen as arbitrary or unilateral but as part of his responsibility. There is neither resistance nor resentment. These 1/0's may be carried out in private or in the presence of others. The point is that although they are not joint or emergent actions, they are still an essential part of good teamwork.

A special case of 1/0 occurs whenever one team member takes an action or substitutes himself in behalf of another team member. An example of this kind of supportive teamwork clarifies what is involved.

> I know you have to go to New York to arrange a loan. I'm going to see our R&D people up there next Thursday. I could also deal with the loan people and make it unnecessary for you to be away at the same time unless there is something more involved . . .

Another example is this:

> Bill is away on an extended foreign trip, but I can act in his behalf and give you an answer.

When this kind of 1/0 teamwork takes place, the initiative rests with whatever team member takes the supportive action, but the responsibility for outcomes remains with the member on whose behalf the second team member initiated action. In this sense it calls for trust to a degree beyond that required in any other kind of situation.

Thus, 9,9 teamwork may occur under 1/all, 1/some, 1/1/1, 1/1 or 1/0 conditions, depending upon three fundamental aspects. One is related to decision quality. A second is concerned with the acceptance aspect involving readiness to implement the action called for. The third deals with management development. We are now in a position to examine when 9,9 team action should be 1/all, 1/1 or 1/0.

### Testing Actions for 1/0, 1/1, or 1/All

Rules that clarify when to use 1/0, 1/1, or 1/all strategies are introduced in Table 10-1. These guidelines answer the question, "Under what conditions are 1/0, 1/1, 1/some, or 1/all approaches likely to be most effective?" The left-hand column identifies criteria that help a manager evaluate when 1/0, 1/1, or 1/all is the basis of action. The conditions for 1/some are so similar to 1/all that they are not separated for discussion, but these are actions that involve more than 1/1 but less than 1/all, where "all" means the entire membership of the team.

A boss should act without consulting others when the criteria for good decision making and problem solving, shown on the left, match the conditions in the 1/0 column. Actions that involve one other member occur when the conditions match what is said in the second column. 1/some or 1/all actions should be taken when the circumstances match those shown in the column to the right.

**Table 10-1**
**Guidelines for Approaches to 9,9 Team Action**

| Criteria | Action to be Done | | |
|---|---|---|---|
| | I.  1/0 if | II.  1/1 if | III.  1/all if (1/some also) |
| 1. Whose problem is it? | mine | his; both of us | ours |
| 2. Time to contact | unavailable | available | available |
| 3. Judgmental competence | full | low | insufficient |
| 4. Pooling of information | unnecessary | vertical or horizontal | needed both horizontally and verti- cally |
| 5. Synergy | not possible | possible | possible |
| 6. Critique | no one else involved | problem belongs to two people | problem has implications for all |
| 7. Significance to the team | low | low | high |
| 8. Involvement- commitment of others | no signifi- cance | helpful- essential | necessary- essential |
| 9. Relevance for others | none | present | present |
| 10. Understanding by others of purpose or rationale of decision | no need can be assumed | needed | needed |
| 11. Coordination of effort | unnecessary | vertical or horizontal | horizontal and vertical |
| 12. Change in team norms/ standards | not relevant | not relevant | relevant |
| 13. Representation of issue in other settings | none | pertinent | pertinent |
| 14. Delegation | possible | unlikely | unlikely |
| 15. Management development | none | present | present |

These first six criteria relate most closely in one way or another to maximizing the quality of decision by the effective and efficient use of human resources.

1. *Whose problem is it?* If in viewing a problem, an individual can say, "That problem is my sole responsibility," then the action is 1/0. If, however, the problem overlaps the responsibilities of two people, it represents a 1/1 situation. If the problem is superordinate in the sense that each individual has a piece of the problem but no one has all of it, then 1/all is the best interaction for solving it.

2. *Time to contact.* If there is no time to involve others, for whatever sound reason, the individual takes whatever action he can on a solo basis (1/0). If there are other advantages to doing so, and time is available to consult with one but not all, then it is a 1/1 situation. If time is available and there are advantages to several being involved, then it is 1/some or 1/all.

3. *Judgmental competence.* A manager may have the depth and experience to exercise sound judgment. Other things equal, he does so in a 1/0 way. If his experience is insufficient, however, and only one other person is needed to strengthen the soundness of judgment, the situation is 1/1. If the wisdom of a judgment requires participation of everyone, then it should be carried out in a 1/all team manner.

4. *Pooling of information.* When all the information needed to execute an action is available from one individual, 1/0 action is appropriate. If two people each have some of the information needed for total understanding of a situation, then pooling of information may be required on a 1/1 basis. This may be a boss-subordinate relationship or it may be between equal level colleagues. 1/all pooling may be required when all team members have unique aspects of information that need to be pooled to develop total comprehension.

5. *Synergy.* Teamwork may be desirable because of synergistic possibilities from several or all team members studying or reviewing a problem. The different perspectives team members apply to it and the clash of ideas discussion can produce may result in a solution that is better in quality than any one, two, or several members might have developed. However, 1/0 is the rule if no synergy can be anticipated and 1/1 if only one other can contribute.

6. *Critique.* Decision quality may be strengthened by discussions that study the team skills in solving problems. If a problem has no team-building application it should be studied in a 1/0 way by self-critique; 1/1 if two people can learn something about teamwork effectiveness

from it; and 1/all if the full team can benefit from studying it. *Critique* is an important 9,9 skill which is discussed more fully in Chapter 12.

The next seven criteria, numbers 7 through 13, are more closely related to the acceptance issue, i.e., the readiness of team members to implement a decision once it has been made.

7. *Significance to the team.* If the action has no team implications beyond one member alone, unless he *does not* carry it out, it should be handled 1/0. If it has far-reaching operational significance, such as shifting the reporting lines in the organization, then the entire team should understand the issues. The greater the significance of an action for changing team purpose, direction, character, or procedures, the more desirable the participation and involvement of all members.

8. *Involvement-commitment of others.* Understanding of the problem and the solution to it may be necessary to achieve acceptance from those who must implement the decision. If the action to be taken does not involve other team members, it should be made 1/0. If it affects only one other, discussion with him is necessary (1/1). When the action has team-wide implications, all should discuss the pros and cons until those whose interests are involved have full understanding. Doubts and reservations are then relieved, and everyone is in a position of agreement and support.

9. *Relevance for others.* Those whose future actions will be affected by a decision need to think through the issue and discuss its implications to see that it is understood and that they are committed to it. The larger the number of team members who have personal stakes in an action, the greater the need for them to discuss the decision.

10. *Understanding by others of purpose or rationale of decision.* There are some kinds of problems to which others cannot contribute, yet they can benefit from an awareness of the rationale employed in analyzing or solving it. When others already know the rationale or when it is not important to them, then the action should be 1/0. However, sometimes the rationale behind the action will benefit at least one other and therefore it may need to be dealt with in a 1/1 way. All the others may not be in a position to contribute to a solution but need to know the rationale, and under these circumstances the rationale should be communicated on a 1/all basis.

These guidelines are helpful to any manager in analyzing the organization of a 9,9-oriented team. They also can be useful in assisting him to see opportunities for strengthening teamwork effectiveness.

11. *Coordination of effort.* Often an action can and should be 1/0 because there is no need for coordination. When coordination is required, the matter should be dealt with jointly, on a 1/1 basis. Sometimes, several if not all team members are involved in implementing a decision; in that case the strategies for coordination need to be worked out on a 1/all basis.

12. *Change in team norms/standards.* Norms/standards that influence performance on a within-team basis may need to be established, modified, or completely changed. All team members need to be involved in order for them to know and to be committed to the new norms/standards. Because each team member adheres to team-based norms/standards, he is unlikely to take a 1/0 action if it would shift a norm/standard. The most favorable condition for reaching such decisions is where a new team norm/standard is explicitly agreed to by all team members.

13. *Representation of issue in other settings.* Sometimes one team member serves as a representative in settings outside his own team situation. Other team members may contribute little or nothing to reaching a decision, but because they are in a "need to know" position, they are brought in to increase understanding.

These next two items are concerned with using teamwork situations for management development.

14. *Delegation.* This arrangement is the opposite of 1/0, where the boss takes the problem and deals with it in a solo way. 0/1 is a situation of complete delegation. A problem should be solved by a person of lesser rank if he or she has the understanding and judgment necessary to deal with it, or if to do so would strengthen the subordinate's managerial effectiveness by increasing his or her capacity for exercising responsibility by taking on larger and larger problems. This shifts a 1/0 from one member to another. In addition, the ranking person is free to utilize his time on matters only he can solve.

A rule can be stated: other things equal, 0/1 should be relied upon rather than 1/0 when (1) subordinates can deal with a given problem as well or better than the boss, (2) a development result will accrue for the subordinate, (3) delegation, not abdication, is the motivation that propels the boss in this direction, and (4) the time made available to the boss permits him to solve another problem more important than the delegated one, under conditions where the subordinate has reasonable prospects of success.

15. *Management development.* Team members participate in analyzing managerial issues, even though they may have little to contribute to

its quality by way of information and even though their acceptance of it is immaterial. Their participation is to enable them to gain knowledge and to develop the judgment needed for dealing with such problems in the future. If a problem has no management development implications, then, other things equal, it should be dealt with 1/0; if it has management development implications for only one other it should be dealt with 1/1. If it has management development implications for all team members it should be dealt with 1/all.

Table 10-1 summarizes the major considerations that enter into determining "who should participate?" under 9,9-oriented management. One other aspect needs to be made explicit. That is, no amount of 1/all discussion will result in either high quality decisions or acceptance of the solution if skills of effective 9,9 leadership and teamwork are absent.

### Using Table 10-1 to Determine Who Should Participate

Several case studies of teamwork as it relates to 1/0, 1/1, 1/some, and 1/all follow. The first part of each case describes the problem confronting the boss, and then asks you to indicate how you would deal with it. The second part tells how the boss did deal with it, and the third part, based on Table 10-1, tells how it should have been dealt with according to the criteria suggested. One suggestion for studying these cases is that you read the case and then answer the questions *before* you read what the boss actually did in Part III. This will test your understanding before moving on to the next case.

### A. Low Production on Lines 2 and 7

**I. Problem Confronting the Boss.** Frank O'Brien, manager, had just received the weekly production reports for his department. As he studied the reports he noticed that production on the two lines that manufactured the same product, line 2 and line 7, was down 5% and 10% respectively. Even though producing different products, all other lines were at or above expected levels. Frank checked the requests for products from these two lines and saw that orders were actually up. He knew his boss would be asking why production was not able to keep up with the demand.

Check below how you would deal with the problem if you were Frank.

_____1/0          _____1/1          _____1/some          _____1/all

**II. What One Boss Did.** Frank O'Brien decided this was a 1/1 problem because he had noticed that production on only two of the lines was down. In order to be able to report this to his boss, he decided to meet with each foreman to see what the problem was and what could be done about it. He picked up his phone and called the foreman from production line 2. He asked that the foreman meet him in his office in thirty minutes. Then he called the foreman from production line 7 and asked him to meet with him an hour and a half later. He spent an hour with the foreman from production line 2, digging into how he saw the situation. The line 2 foreman didn't feel production was down sufficiently to worry about it, since it was only 5%. This was just normal variation.

Then Frank met with the foreman from production line 7, where the variation was 10%. He had realized that his production was down but he felt that it was because of late deliveries of raw materials over the past two weeks. This, again, was an unusual circumstance and his opinion was that the raw materials department was probably "off" and the situation would right itself.

After discussing the problem with both foremen, Frank decided that both of these cases were exceptions and that, therefore, no action was needed. Rather he would keep close watch on these two lines during the next several weeks and be prepared to do something if the situation did not right itself.

This was an incorrect use of two 1/1's. The reason is that both foremen had lowered production and each could feel that his own situation was unique without the possibility of synergy between the three (Criterion #5). Therefore, the possible severity of the problem was overlooked. In addition, because they were not able to compare notes directly with one another in a pooling of information way (Criterion #4), the fact that both areas were experiencing late deliveries was not brought into the open and thus this source of the problem was neglected, which might have been brought to light in a joint critique (Criterion #6).

**III. How It Might Have Been Dealt With and Why.** Frank might have used a 1/some approach and begun by phoning and requesting the foremen from the two lines concerned with these product lines to come to his office. He could begin the meeting by asking, "Is there some reason why production on lines 2 and 7 is down?" The foremen from both lines might then reply that, while there had been some problems recently, they felt that production was probably almost up to the normal level. Frank next would produce the weekly reports and suggest they study them in order to understand the numbers. A few minutes study would convince all three that production on the two lines was definitely down. After discussion it might be agreed that each foreman and his technicians would evaluate the activities under their control and another meeting be held two hours later to develop a plan of action.

The data could be evaluated in a followup meeting. It would become obvious that the problem was concerned with late deliveries of raw materials to the two lines. The next step would be for Frank and the two foremen to go over to the raw materials department to seek a solution to this problem.

This 1/some involving the two foremen but not all six foremen was a correct approach. The problem was one for which both the foremen and the manager were responsible (Criterion #1), and time was available (Criterion #2) for them to work on it together. The manager enlisted the aid of his subordinates who were involved in the problem (Criterion #8), who could jointly critique it (Criterion #6), who had the relevant information (Criterion #4), and who would be responsible for implementing whatever solution might be reached (Criteria #9 and#11).

## B. Quality Control

**I. Problem Confronting the Boss.** During a period of especially high production, a manufacturing organization found that it lacked sufficient manpower to properly carry out quality control. The quality control system consisted of a checklist of "routine" checks to be made by the operators on the products at various points in the manufacturing process, and on a less frequent basis more thorough "technical" inspections made by highly trained technicians who had graduated from the job of "routine" checks. Now they had some slack in their schedules. The great demand placed on manufacturing people to run the operations themselves caused much of the routine quality control to be left undone. Something had to be done to cover the quality control function until such time as additional workers could be trained to do the routine inspection.

Margaret Egan, the Quality Control Supervisor of the technicians, is faced with the problem.

Check below how you would deal with the problem if you were Margaret.

_____1/0      _____1/1      _____1/some      _____1/all

**II. What One Boss Did.** Margaret decided that she could make a 1/0 decision because it appeared obvious that the best solution was to require the highly skilled technicians to perform certain aspects of the routine inspection while carrying out their normal duties. She felt that this would adequately take care of the necessary inspections and that the technicians would not be unduly burdened. She announced this decision to the "touch base" morning meeting of the technicians, and passed out an assignment sheet listing the portions of the "routine" quality control inspections that were to be made by each person during their technical inspection.

The technicians, particularly Jane Hughes, did not agree with this handling of the problem. Jane was vocal about it, saying that, according to her job description, she was not required to do lesser skill work, such as the routine inspections. Margaret replied, "This is my decision. There is nothing that can be done about it. The work has to be done."

This was an incorrect use of 1/0 decision making. The boss, Margaret Egan, possessed all the information needed (Criterion #4) to make the decision, and, therefore, in the interest of time (Criterion #2), she did so. However, she did nothing to gain their involvement in the problem (Criterion #8) or to aid her technicians to understand the nature of the background situation (Criterion #10), including the high demands on manufacturing personnel.

**III. How It Might Have Been Dealt With and Why.** Had Margaret Egan handled the quality control problem in a 1/all way, she probably would have reached both a decision of high quality and positive acceptance. This could have been done in the following way.

Margaret could have convened a meeting of the technician inspectors. At the beginning she might have explained the background of the quality control problem and how the pressure on the manufacturing people was causing much of the routine quality control work to be left undone. This was an unusual circumstance caused by high production demands on the manufacturing organization and, therefore, did not warrant adding additional manpower for a short period of time.

Her next step would be to ask for the aid of the technicians in answering the following question: "What can we do to help with the routine inspection, and how is the best way to implement these actions?"

This is a correct use of 1/all decision making. Margaret presented the problem and the background information needed to make a sounder decision (Criterion #10). The technicians themselves are the ones who carry the technical inspections out and who know more about the product and the manufacturing process than the people who ordinarily do the routine checks (Criterion #3). They are in an excellent position to aid in the solution of the problem from an information and know-how point of view (Criterion #4). Also, because they would be called upon to carry additional work for a period of time, it is likely that they would be able to develop a system of routine checks which, when added to their own work, would be most convenient for them to get the job done in an excellent manner (Criteria #7 and #1).

## C. Housekeeping

**I. Problem Confronting the Boss.** Elizabeth Smith, manager of an administrative division, has five departments under her. She sits at her desk reading a one-page memorandum she has just received. The document, addressed to all division heads, is on the subject of office appearance. It is strongly worded. It lists many examples of sloppy housekeeping, such as cigarette butts, carbon paper, trash on the floor, untidy desks, boxes piled around doors waiting to be unpacked, etc. Next, it stipulates that the appearance of the division, which was housed in several buildings, is to be meticulous from now on, and it is part of a department manager's responsibility to ensure this. Failure to comply would be reflected in annual evaluations. Elizabeth knows that someone upstairs must really be riled up to issue such a strongly worded memo. Some of the offices measured up to the best standards, but others violated them to a high degree.

Check below how you would deal with the problem if you were Elizabeth.

_____1/0         _____1/1         _____1/some         _____1/all

**II. What One Boss Did.** Elizabeth decided this was a 1/all problem because housekeeping of her entire department reflected on the whole building. Reluctantly she picked up the memo and walked into her weekly staff meeting with project team leaders. She was too worried to even introduce the topic by revealing her personal concern. To get the meeting started she said awkwardly, "Look, I know this is an unpleasant subject to bring up, but we're going to have to do more about improving the appearance of the office with regard to trash disposal and ensuring that cigarette butts end up in the ashtrays. We need to start persuading our employees to take greater care of the appearance of their desks and in other ways improve our housekeeping."

Several hostile remarks were heard from the department heads, including, "We aren't paid to be janitors!" and "My section looks good; you haven't been around lately." All Elizabeth could say was, "Well, I'd appreciate whatever can be done about keeping your department as tidy as possible."

Later in the day, when passing through one section, she saw that apparently no one had done anything about starting the tidiness campaign. Trying not to be noticed, she began picking up scraps of paper and cigarette butts as she moved around.

This was an incorrect use of 1/all. Elizabeth made the assumption that housekeeping was everybody's problem, rather than recognizing that some departments were well maintained and others messy (Criterion #1). Because they were not, she was wasting the time of those who were doing a good job (Criteria #2, #9, #11).

**III. How It Might Have Been Dealt With and Why.** After Elizabeth received her memo regarding the housekeeping problem, she might have decided to take a look around her division to see precisely where the problem was present.

She might have gone to each department one after another and met with the department head, asking her for a "tour" of her section of the building. As they walked around, she might have explained that she had received a memo regarding housekeeping. If the particular department was being run in a neat and tidy manner, she would congratulate the department head. If she found untidiness, she would point this out specifically and ask for her cooperation in deciding on the best approach to take to clean up the section.

This would be a correct use of 1/1. It only involves taking corrective action in certain departments, and, because it is sounder to deal with the department heads on a 1/1 basis in order to see the uniqueness in each situation (Criteria #1 and #8), this avoids alienating those who already are doing a good job and permits her to work in specific terms where correction is needed (Criteria #6 and #11).

## D. Extra Business

**I. Problem Confronting the Boss.** Jim Jones is manager of the Container Division with six department heads reporting to him. He is on the phone with David Green, the purchasing agent of one of their largest customers.

"You say you need two hundred units by the fifteenth of this month? That's twelve working days from now. Is there any leeway in your time schedule?"

Dave replies, "The sixteenth is really squeezing all I can from my end. I'll need your hundred percent assurance within thirty minutes that we can get the units, or else I'll be in a contract bind."

"Let me study our work load for the next three weeks, and I'll be back to you with a go/no-go decision within a half-hour," responds Jim.

"Okay."

Jim hangs up the telephone. He studies the master production schedule displaying the planning and scheduling for each of his six departments. This has proven to be a reliable indicator of work flow, and it shows the combined load scheduled to 125% of rated capacity.

Check below how you would deal with the problem if you were Jim.

_____1/0        _____1/1        _____1/some        _____1/all

**II. What One Boss Did.** After glancing at the production schedule, Jim called in and asked his secretary to contact the six department heads for a meeting in the conference room in five minutes. He briefly outlined the Dave Green request and asked for their opinions as to whether it would be possible to shift current production schedules and make the deadline on the sixteenth. Each person in turn reviewed for the others what his particular schedule was, and this involved restating what was already posted on the master production schedule. By the time there was full understanding by the six of each other's commitments, the thirty minutes was up. Hastily, the men concluded that it was worth the gamble to go ahead and accept the business. Jim agreed to do so.

This was an incorrect use of 1/all. Even though the department heads would be involved in implementing a positive decision, they were not sufficiently informed of the overall picture to be able to make a quality decision in the time available (Criteria #2 and #4).

He presumed that the thirty minutes were sufficient for discussion and that pooling information (Criterion #4) would tell him more than he already knew from the scheduling board.

**III. How It Might Have Been Dealt With and Why.** Jim might have decided that this was a 1/0 decision situation because time was short and he had the available information. Because the combined workload came to 125%, this would mean that they already were into an overtime situation. He could then calculate what the additional 200 units would mean—an increased capacity utilization to 150%. With such a heavy overtime burden, taking on the additional business would reduce profit margins to nearly nothing. Also, if anything were to slip and he could not meet the deadline, this would seriously undermine his record with Dave Green.

Therefore, he should have called Dave back on a 1/0 decision basis and told him that he was sorry he could not accept his business and be 100% sure of delivery on schedule. It would have been to Dave's advantage to look elsewhere on this occasion because of his urgent need to meet a deadline on the sixteenth.

Dave would have appreciated his honesty and said he'd be back another time.

This is a correct use of 1/0, with insufficient time (Criterion #2) and with judgmental competence (Criterion #3) to make the decision. Others

could not have added anything because he had all the information necessary (Criterion #4). To involve them would be wasteful and might indeed
even lead to a wrong decision. Because his decision would have been not
to take the business, there would have been no need to bring in others
from an implementation cycle (Criteria #8, #9, #11).

Studying these problems in conjunction with Table 10-1 offers examples for the 9,9 orientation in dealing with subordinates—whether in
1/0, 1/1, 1/some or 1/all terms. Many dilemmas such as these exist in
relation to how bosses use or fail to use sound guidelines for getting decisions of high quality that result in full acceptance of those who implement them.

## Chapter 11

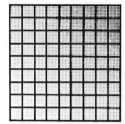

# Manager-As-Counselor

Managing under conditions of modern organizational life puts people under greater pressures and strains than ever before and has been shown to have increasingly adverse effects on mental and physical health. Adverse effects are also evident in absenteeism and mock illness to justify sick leave. It is clear in unionization—among blue- and white-collar workers and among professionals. It is obvious from vandalism, stealing, and wanton acts of destruction of materials, equipment, and products, and in political terrorism. These pressures and the stresses resulting from them are not likely to decrease in intensity simply because they are ignored or taken for granted. Rather, the opposite is likely to occur. They will probably become more intense because they occur increasingly in every advanced society that enjoys some degree of personal freedom and private enterprise.

Until recently, helping people cope with these pressures has not been a serious concern of management. Organization development, described in Chapter 13, is one way of increasing both productivity and involvement in work. Enabling managers to manage in terms of 9,9 teamwork is in itself important in avoiding pressures and stress because the values and practices involved in the 9,9 approach of openness, conflict solving, and an experimental attitude can do much to prevent pressures from building up as they are likely to do in a 9,1 produce-or-perish environment.

Where organization development has been undertaken, managers are coming to realize that they can and should give additional aid by helping others to grapple with job-created and extra-managerial problems. Every manager is expected to be a counselor and to involve himself with others in emotional problem solving.

The field of counseling is too broad to be encompassed within a book on management. However, 9,9-oriented managers may contribute to one another as counselors by taking actions to help solve more personal problems. This involves much more than simply telling another person

**Table 11-1**
**Counseling Interventions and When Applied**

| Intervention | Key Words | When Indicated |
|---|---|---|
| Acceptant | Emotional release | Pent-up feelings are blocking thought and action so that needed initiatives cannot be taken. |
| Catalytic | Strengthen perception | Poor communication has resulted in pluralistic ignorance that blocks effectiveness. |
| Confrontation | Value clarification | Values, often hidden, are having negative effects. |
| Prescriptive | Giving answers | Associate has thrown up his hands or is on the ropes, unable to exercise sufficient initiative to move. |
| Theory/ Principles | Systematic insight | Associate is ready to shift to a science-oriented basis of problem solving. |

what to do or applying common sense remedies. It involves interventions that are specific to the nature of a problem a person is having. When a manager is intervening in a counseling way with another person, the word *associate* is used to describe the person with the problem because counseling is better done between individuals whose respect and liking for each other is independent of the hierarchy implied in a boss-subordinate relationship.

### Kinds of Interventions

Five major types of interventions and the situations to which they are most appropriately applied are shown in Table 11-1.

### Acceptant

Acceptant interventions are useful when an associate has severely hurt feelings. These range from feelings of rejection at not being promoted to feelings of dejection arising from some failure such as divorce, death, and so on. Once aroused, these feelings can monopolize a person's thoughts and block the kind of clear thinking essential for him to be a productive, problem-solving person. An acceptant intervention gives an associate a sense of personal security so that he or she feels free to express personal thoughts without fear of condemnation or rejection. The associate may thus be helped to sort out his emotions and thereby to get a more objective view of the situation.

The following are some ground rules a manager-counselor might follow when helping an associate in an acceptant way:

1. Help an associate talk about the situation. "Why not just freewheel about your situation? No need to outline, just tell it as it comes out." Encourage with "tell me more" expressions.
2. Try to understand an associate's situation from his point of view, without necessarily accepting it as valid for problem solving. This may mean vicarious sharing in the sense that the associate sees that the manager-counselor "feels" the problem. As an essential minimum, the counselor may respond, "This is what I hear you saying. . . ."
3. Practice active listening. Encourage the associate to talk more, that is, look him or her in the eye, smile, nod acceptance of what is being said, say, "Uh-huh."
4. Help *clarify* his feelings and *accept* their existence. Say, for example, "You've described the situation. How do you *feel* about it?"
5. If an associate falls silent, restate his last remark in a way that lets him or her know you as counselor fully understand and accept—without judgment—what has been said.
6. Do not amend or edit the *content* of the associate's problem. Take no sides and neither agree nor disagree with what the associate says.
7. You might say, "What do you think the problem is? What ways are open to you for dealing with it?" *All* diagnosis comes from the associate.
8. Expect the associate to make progress in defining and successfully solving the *real* problem because the acceptant approach helps the associate to develop self-confidence in dealing with frustration, anger, or low self-esteem.

Nonjudgmental, supportive counseling can help a person reduce feelings and emotions that are blocking objectivity and help him gain the perspective necessary to reestablish his balance and equilibrium.

## Catalytic

Another set of problems occurs when an associate is troubled by indecision and uncertainty as to what action to take. Faced with such dilemmas he is frozen, unable to move forward or backward, right or left. Often such indecision arises as a result of insufficient data. A catalytic intervention assists an associate in collecting information to reinterpret his perceptions as to how things are. In this way, the associate may arrive at a better awareness of the problem and how to handle it.

To help in a catalytic way, the manager-counselor:

1. Starts an intervention with informal conversation to create an easy-going atmosphere, an informal give-and-take situation. "How are things?"
2. Invites the associate to describe his situation, and accepts the needs described by the associate as the frame of reference to work within.
3. Suggests procedures for gathering more information. These may be about ways to proceed ranging from giving suggestions to using action-research or survey-research methodologies. "Have you thought about using this method to get more information?"
4. Gives encouragement whenever possible by supporting the associate's efforts to define or redefine the problem.
5. Avoids specific suggestions about the problem itself or how to solve it. Even procedures for data gathering are offered in a *very* tentative way. The manager-counselor seeks to stay within the limits he thinks the associate will accept. He may know what the associate "should" do or that the associate is not "facing up," but to impose his will or to challenge the associate's self-deception could possibly promote resistance, which might shift responsibility for solving the problem from the associate to the counselor. To ensure that the associate feels and knows that he retains control over the situation the counselor does not overstep these bounds. "How about this possibility?" and "Do you think this would work?" are as far as the catalytic counselor is likely to go. He restricts himself to the role of facilitator.
6. Encourages the associate to make his own decisions. Acting as a counselor he is graceful about it, but will *not* make decisions for the associate, or even tip the balance one way or another, or even confront the associate with the fact that his definition of the situation is what is blocking progress. As a result, the associate feels that whatever action comes about is of his own choosing.

Information gathering and procedural assistance which result from catalytic intervention often can enable an associate to consider more alternatives in solving personal problems. It can also aid him in weighing and appraising one alternative over another as the better of two solutions. In either case, the associate retains a full sense of personal responsibility for the outcome.

## Confrontation

A third area of difficulty leading to poor mental health and social problems arises from value conflicts between people. Often these values are based on false premises of which the people are unaware. A confrontational intervention can help people become more aware of their own unexamined values or the premises on which they rest. This can be accomplished by challenging an associate to see how the foundations of his thinking may be coloring and distorting his view of some situations; that is, the associate may screen off one or more options which, if he were aware of them, could lead to more effective actions.

A manager-counselor utilizing confrontation as a way of helping:

1. Takes nothing for granted as the associate describes his situation. In answering questions the associate either shows that he understands the situation or that he does not. If the associate does not, the counselor keeps asking questions that "force" him to face up. "Tell me why you see the situation that way."
2. Presents facts, counterarguments, and logic to help an associate test his own objectivity.
3. Challenges the associate's thinking regarding different courses of action once the associate understands his own values and assumptions.
4. Probes for reasons, motives, and causes that give the associate a clear and possibly different perspective on his situation.
5. Gives the associate his own thoughts, particularly when these differ from or contradict the associate's values and assumptions, but in such a way that the associate does not feel personally attacked or put down.

Confrontation can bring into focus conditions that are having important yet unrecognized effects on an associate's personal problem solving. The associate retains full accountability for whatever changes come about, as the counselor's interventions are calculated to clarify values rather than to control how the associate deals with his problem.

## Prescriptive

A fourth area relates to the many traumas that seem to be inevitable in modern life. Sometimes people can anticipate and plan for adversity, and in this way avoid serious after effects. Often it comes crashing in, blocking any possibility of effective reaction and rendering an associate helpless and hopeless. A prescriptive intervention can provide a sense of direction and hopefulness by means of the manager-counselor telling the associate what to do to rectify a given personal problem or even doing it for him. This manager-counselor takes responsibility for developing the evidence for the diagnosis and formulating the solution.

The manager-as-counselor, who is dealing with an associate in a prescriptive way:

1. Interrogates to learn what he needs to know about the associate's problem and in a businesslike manner cuts through to the heart of the matter, sometimes without much concern for social delicacies. He is unlikely to explain much of his own thinking to the associate as this would be unlikely to lead anywhere.
2. Controls the situation by telling the associate how he, the counselor, perceives the problem.
3. Tells the associate in a confident, authoritative way the "best" solution to implement.
4. Expresses confidence in the plan and often offers to double check on its implementation.
5. May say, if the associate procrastinates, or tries to avoid acting on recommendations, "I don't think we can presently work together, but feel free to call back whenever you feel seriously committed to having help with your problem."

The premise of prescriptive interventions is that the manager-counselor is an expert and that the associate is prepared to accept the answers the manager-counselor provides. It should be noted that the prescriptive approach prescribes *what* to do in solving a personal difficulty. This relationship is fraught with difficulties when selected as the intervention strategy, for, even though the manager-counselor may know what is best for the associate, the associate may not be prepared to do it. This may be partly because the associate feels incapable of taking the recommended action and partly because it might result in conflict with others.

### Teaching Theories and Principles with General Application

There is a fifth area of modern industrial life where counseling can be important. It involves helping people understand personal reactions in systematic terms and thereby to avoid or rectify unnecessary human mistakes.

When a manager-counselor intervenes, he offers the associate theories pertinent to understanding his problem, then teaches the associate systematic and empirically tested ways of analyzing it. When learned, these principles permit the associate to think in more analytical, cause-and-effect fashions than had hitherto been possible. Thus the associate learns to diagnose and to plan more valid solutions to present and future personal dilemmas.

A typical series of steps in theory counseling might include the following:

*Step 1*—The associate is presented with a typical personal dilemma that he or others is likely to meet in daily living. The associate's reactions are either written down or acted out. Such reactions define his natural bent. This activity is completed *before* any theory is introduced.

*Step 2*—The associate then studies pertinent theories of behavior, either through a textbook or lecture approach, by the use of audio cassettes, or by viewing a movie or TV that introduces the theory. Questions and test examples are provided to enable the associate to check his understanding of the theory.

*Step 3*—The associate works with simulated problems where "best" solutions can be practiced by using theories learned in Step 2.

*Step 4*—Post-simulation critiques enable the associate to see how well he understood the theories and how well he was able to use them. These critiques also help him identify any inaccurate assumptions he may have made and any limitations in the theory itself.

*Step 5*—An additional series of simulations can be used to provide the associate the opportunity to compare his natural bent for dealing with situations against the theory. From such self-confrontations the associate comes to understand the theory in a personally useful way and to recognize the extent to which his second-nature assumptions take over when he is pressured to act. The associate comes to appreciate that he *does* know how to use theory effectively.

*Step 6*—If necessary, further practice is provided to enable the associate to perfect his capacity to identify and to execute the actions and practices required.

*Step 7*—The associate reevaluates the way he now solves problems in comparison with the natural inclinations revealed in Step 1. He again responds to the Step 1 circumstances, this time with theory-based actions.

*Step 8*—Generalizations regarding his natural bent are further clarified and differentiated to prevent the associate from slipping into habitual responses. This further equips the associate to handle situations from a theory-based perspective.

*Step 9*—Manager-counselor support and implementation for using a theory-based approach in dealing with personal complexities assist the changeover from what he has been doing to what he now intends to do.

The manager-counselor does become a teacher when he conveys ideas to help the associate to "see" his situation from a different perspective. With increased understanding of theories the associate is likely to be able to see a wider range of alternative solutions to his problem as well as to weigh the probable consequences of each one before selecting the best one. In addition, he is in a better position to apply the principles to other similar problems as they arise in the future.

### Management Preferences and/or "Natural Bent"

Many managers-as-counselors have personal preferences and predispositions that influence their choices or even govern their style of intervention. Often these influences are unrelated to an associate's real needs. Interventions based on counselor preferences, rather than on a valid diagnosis of the associate's real needs, are of less value than those targeted on the associate's actual problem. Table 11-2 shows how the Grid framework can be used to illustrate this.

Many considerations determine the effectiveness of an intervention. Thus use of the entire range of interventions reflect a 9,9 orientation as illustrated in Table 11-3.

Sometimes the intervention mode is more related to 9,1 assumptions on the part of the manager-counselor than to the problem-solving needs of the associate. Such a case is shown in Table 11-4.

In contrast, a 5,5 manager-as-counselor's assumptions are outlined in Table 11-5.

A manager-counselor who is oriented in the 1,9 direction is likely to exhibit the attitudes described in Table 11-6.

The "burned out," or 1,1, manager-as-counselor's assumptions are given in Table 11-7.

A special case of relying on prescriptive intervention can arise out of a manager-counselor's paternalistic orientation, as described in Table 11-8.

These various intervention modes, as evaluated by Grid styles, specify when a particular intervention satisfies the needs of the counselor, and when it is likely to be what an associate really needs to grapple successfully with his problems.

**Table 11-2**
**Types of Interventions and Grid Style(s)**

| Manager-as-Counselor's Intervention Preference | Manager's Probable Grid Style(s) |
|---|---|
| Acceptant | 1,9 (and 1,1) |
| Catalytic | 5,5 (and "statistical" 5,5) |
| Confrontation | 9,9 (and 9,1) |
| Prescriptive | 9,1 |
| Theory and Principles | 9,9 (and 9,1) |

**Table 11-3**
**The 9,9 Manager-Counselor**

| Intervention Mode | Grid style | When |
|---|---|---|
| Acceptant | 9,9 | The manager-as-counselor helps the associate to relieve immobilizing tensions and thereby to unblock barriers that have prevented constructive action. |
| Catalytic | 9,9 | By helping the associate build up his perceptions of the situation, the manager-counselor assists him in taking fundamental rather than superficial action. |
| Confrontation | 9,9 | The associate's problem can only be brought into focus and resolved through the associate coming to recognize that his own behavior and values are the cause of his problems. |
| Prescriptive | 9,9 | The associate has reached the point of impasse, hopelessness, or despair, and yet action is imperative to avoid further negative consequences. |
| Theory/Principles | 9,9 | The associate can approach and probably solve his problems based on systematic insight, and be in a better position for contending with similar future problems. |

**Table 11-4**
**The 9,1 Manager-Counselor**

| Intervention Mode | Grid Style | When |
|---|---|---|
| Confrontation | 9,1 | The manager-as-counselor derives gratification from shaking the associate up. |
| Prescriptive | 9,1 | The manager-counselor is determined that an action he sees as valid is taken and is ready to use whatever pressure he needs to muster to get the associate to take the action. |
| Theory/Principles | 9,1 | The manager-counselor is certain that theory represents the one and only way for the associate to solve his personal problem. |

**Table 11-5**
**The 5,5 Manager-Counselor**

| Intervention Mode | Grid Style | When |
|---|---|---|
| Acceptant | 5,5 | The manager-as-counselor reacts in terms of what the associate feels he needs without being convinced in his own thinking that this is the best thing to do. |
| Catalytic | 5,5 | The manager-counselor adapts his response to what the associate feels he needs, even when it is clear to him, privately, that the realistic solution entails an alternative definition of the problem. |
| Theory/Principles | 5,5 | The manager-counselor presents theory not because he thinks it useful but because he thinks the associate wants it. |

**Table 11-6**
**The 1,9 Manager-Counselor**

| Intervention Mode | Grid Style | When |
|---|---|---|
| Acceptant | 1,9 | He approaches an associate in this manner because high concern on the personal dimension is his sole way of feeling helpful. |
| Catalytic | 1,9 | He wants to please the associate. |

**Table 11-7**
**The 1,1 Manager-Counselor**

| Intervention Mode | Grid Style | When |
|---|---|---|
| Acceptant | 1,1 | The manager-counselor takes a passive, listening attitude, not of supportive orientation toward the associate but from lack of interest. |

**Table 11-8**
**A Manager-Counselor's Paternalistic Orientation**

| Intervention Mode | Grid Style | When |
|---|---|---|
| Prescriptive | Paternal-istic | He insists, and often correctly, that the associate take the recommended action "for his own good," even though the associate may not see it that way. |

## What Manager-As-Counselor Can be Helpful to Which Kinds of Associates?

A dilemma is involved in the question, "Who is the best manager-counselor to help any given associate to deal with a personal problem?"

Bosses may be in a poor position to help their own immediate subordinates, particularly regarding personal problems arising from within the company. Part of the reason is that the boss may have a vested interest in the solution and want it to come out a certain way. The other part of the problem is that, even though the boss may not have a vested interest in the solution, the subordinate may not feel free to discuss with his boss some personal problem that is disturbing him. Whether or not he should feel free to do so is another matter because such discussions may be fruitless or even harmful. In either case, boss-as-counselor to his own immediate subordinates is a special case. For example, a boss may be in an excellent position to help a subordinate when the subordinate is faced with personal problems resulting from whether to accept an external job offer. Then he can help the subordinate, often in a catalytic manner, to weigh the risk-benefit consequences of staying vs. leaving. The boss needs to be sure how much his own needs are influencing his counseling, however.

The reverse situation, that of a subordinate seeking to counsel with his own boss or others higher up the ladder than himself, is too likely to be mistaken as apple-polishing or power-seeking. Even here there are exceptions. A boss may be so "blocked" that a subordinate-as-counselor may be able to offer help that would be unacceptable coming from others. This is true when the subordinate is informed, and the boss readily accepts the idea that the subordinate's intervention has the boss's best interest at heart.

Although there are no hard and fast rules, a general principle provides useful guidance for finding out who the best manager-counselor is to help any given associate. Problems that arise within the managerial system and with regard to operations and problems of personal effectiveness related to the task itself are best dealt with by a 9,9 approach described in Chapter 7. If personal problems arising outside of work are hindering the work itself, then the answer is anyone who (1) can keep his vested interests from intruding into the counseling, (2) is respected by the associate who needs help, and (3) feels capable of bringing about the kind of intervention that can help solve the problem.

## Summary

Mental anguish, physical illness, and antisocial behavior have become more and more characteristic of modern industrial societies. This is the price that is being paid for material, technological, and social progress, but it may be possible to have progress and yet reduce these adverse consequences. To do so involves redefining the activities and responsibilities of management. Not only must bosses become more effective managers and educators, thereby decreasing the causes of serious problems, they also must learn to become counselors, helping one another to deal more effectively with the feelings, tensions, frustrations, blind spots, ignorance, and antagonisms that lead to mental and physical health problems and to antisocial behavior. Every manager is, or can become, a counselor.

Counseling used to be the special job of academics or of a few industrial personnel. No more. Every manager can learn to be helpful as a counselor because the theory and skills needed are now quite well understood, and techniques for teaching them are available. The new challenge is to enable every manager to learn to counsel. In this way there is a realistic possibility of bringing the help required today to assist those who need it.

An approach has been outlined to describe manager-as-counselor and associate-as-client. Five different kinds of problems are susceptible to solution from the use of five different counseling interventions: acceptant for emotional upset; catalytic for problems created by lack of information or faulty perception; confrontation for value difficulties; prescription for hopelessness; and theory for systematic insight.

Conclusions were drawn as to the implications of a manager-counselor's "natural" Grid style and his preference for using each mode of intervention.

The special difficulty of deciding who can counsel most effectively with whom sometimes involves combining the boss-subordinate relationship with the manager-as-counselor/associate-as-client. While this coupling may prove feasible for certain types of problems and situations, it is a barrier to efforts to be helpful unless the relationship is of a 9,9 character. When it is not tenable to be helpful within a boss-subordinate coupling, then another manager who is not directly related in a boss-subordinate way to the associate needing help may be able to make a worthwhile contribution.

## Chapter 12

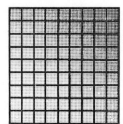 # 9,9 Team Learning from Experience Through Critique

Human values of candor, conflict confrontation, and an experimental attitude make it possible for a 9,9-oriented team to constantly learn how to improve its effectiveness. Such values open up the realistic possibility of using feedback, which is the critical factor in permitting team members to learn from critique. "Critique" is a term denoting a variety of useful ways to study and solve operational problems members face either singly or collectively as they seek to carry out their assignments.

Participants in an experience frequently know that performance is below par and they usually have little difficulty in describing what is going on, at least in mechanical terms. "We started at 10:00, and, though the project should have been completed by 12:00, we did not finish up until 12:30." Or, "Even though I needed to exchange information with Bill and Tom, they never spoke to me, or to each other. Bill always asked Nan to get the information from Tom, and Tom got his information from Bill through Ralph. By the time it got to me it was useless." Describing it is a mental reconstruction of the event, involving awareness of the way things occur as they are happening. That is important, but it is only half the picture.

As an approach to learning, critique takes place when two or more people exchange their own descriptions of an event both have directly experienced. If Bill, Tom, Nan, Ralph and others had come together and answered the question, "Why is it that when the information gets to the last man, it's useless?" then they would have been using critique to improve their situation. People also learn from critique when two or more people describe the actions of a third person and each pictures the meaning and intent of those actions as he understands them. By describing and discussing these similarities and differences with the third person, potential misunderstandings, errors of perception, or other unanticipated consequences of his actions can be corrected.

## When and How Critique Can Take Place

Critique can be used at the beginning of an activity, as it is taking place, or when it is over.

### Beginning of the Activity

Contradictory as it may seem, critique is an excellent approach to learning about problems even before the activity has taken place. Introduced before the beginning of an activity, critique helps team members think about the activity in which they are about to engage. Determining what each participant knows, what each expects to happen, and how, and what each wants to see done, can make for better utilization of human resources. In this way it is frequently possible to anticipate problems and thus to avoid them.

Consider the following. Shipbuilders routinely provide a warranty detailing the operating specifications they have built into a ship and the performance standards that the owner has a right to expect in sailing that ship. This is true for passenger ships, but it is also true for tankers, freighters, and even most pleasure craft.

The conventional practice of accepting a ship from its builder is for the captain to be designated and then for a crew to be drawn together.

Before launching, the crew takes several days to become familiar with the ship's machinery and characteristics of its operation that can only be known through firsthand examination of the ship's construction and by studying its probable capabilities.

The ship is then taken on a shakedown cruise, and as many defects are worked out as possible. The fact that a warranty specifies what the owner has a right to expect in terms of performance standards is forgotten except when there is a gross malfunction. Gross malfunctions and significant departures from the warranty are reported to the captain. Many limitations in the ship are taken for granted, with the crew working around them as best it can.

Using critique methods under these conditions, the captain would be appointed and the crew drawn together, as in the conventional case. However, before the ship is boarded, a period of time is devoted to the crew, as a team, learning in detail what specifications for ship performance and for machinery and other subcomponents are written into the warranty. Then operating manuals that specify the proper operational approach to various pieces of equipment are consulted and critiqued for standard and unique features. Only at this point does the crew go aboard to become knowledgeable about the actual properties of the ship and its equipment. During the shakedown, the ship and its equipment are to be tested to their maximum and minimum limits, rather than restricting their performance to an average range. The third step is taking the ship to sea.

## Concurrent Critique

Critique can also occur, spontaneously or according to a plan, at any time along the way when the activity is in progress. It is called concurrent because it occurs along with the activity itself. Here is an example.

| | |
|---|---|
| Frank to Joe: | "Well, getting back to Joe here for a minute. Are you suggesting in effect then that we continue discussion and, as we see people get into a situation, that we stop and test it then and there?" |
| Joe to Frank: | "Well, yes. Take the opportunity to point it out just when it happens." |
| Frank to Joe: | ". . . to observe each other as the discussion goes and see how things turn out. . . . Is that right?" (General agreement) |
| George to Joe: | "Let me try one on for size. *I just noticed you jump to an inference, real fast . . .*" |
| Joe to George: | "That's right." |
| George to Joe: | ". . . just a second ago . . . and what I meant was . . . and I can give you an example. *All of a sudden you say, 'Well I've got the answer. It isn't that at all. It's this.' You go too fast for the rest of us."* (George spots a critical example and calls Joe's attention to it right after it happens.) |
| Joe to Group: | "Well, do you deduce from that that I'm a man of action?" (Laughter and some confusion) "More seriously, I can understand why I look that way to you. I'll try to watch it, but when you see me doing it again, tell me about it." |

Such feedback increases the likelihood of Joe coming to understand how to strengthen his own effectiveness. It increases the likelihood of each member examining his own behavior and asking himself pointed questions, recognizing how his own habits might be changed to permit him to contribute more to the team's problem-solving effectiveness.

These concurrent critiques are particularly useful for identifying problems and difficulties and for introducing corrective actions before disabling problems have blocked productivity.

Informal, spontaneous, even off-the-cuff commentary on what is occurring is likely to have some value principally by virtue of its spontaneity. However, when spontaneity is replaced by impulsiveness, more often than not, the remarks made are neither well thought out nor are others prepared to accept their validity. For example, if Tom says to Bill, "You are being dogmatic. You keep repeating your opinion and don't listen to a thing I say." Tom's statement that he isn't being heard may be valid; however, it is not likely to make Bill listen better. Rather, Bill probably feels more inclined to deny or to justify his behavior. Such interventions often produce injured feelings and defensiveness. Had Tom said to Bill, "I feel that the idea I was putting forward was not heard . . . ," Bill is more likely to say, "Then repeat it and see if I understand."

This approach to learning works best when those engaged in it have some skill in giving and receiving feedback and are prepared to use critique as needed. Then false starts are avoided, wrong choices eliminated, and a whole activity can be reviewed to determine how to strengthen performance in the next cycle of experience.

## Post Critique

When critique is introduced at the end of an activity it permits participants to review and reconstruct the entire experience and to figure out what caused the results to be less than they might have been able to accomplish. It enables them to trace interpersonal influences, to identify and to evaluate critical choice points, and to verify recurring patterns. These insights are significant for deciding what is and what is not the best way to carry out a comparable activity in the future.

These end-of-the-activity critiques have been called "postmortems." Translated from its original Latin the word postmortem means "after death." In the legal sense, a postmortem is the principal way of determining causes of death. It is sometimes conducted to draw cause-and-effect conclusions so that prev ntive actions can be taken to avoid needless deaths under similar circumstances in the future. Used in everyday situations, however, a postmortem is not legalistic but a formalized critique procedure. It can range from a casual attempt to figure out what happened, usually after obtaining bad results, to a standardized set of procedures to evaluate designated events, such as a quarterly budget review, conducted on a more or less regular basis.

As participants think about a completed activity, they reach conclusions regarding performance on certain critical aspects of it.These relate particularly to procedures used and to people factors that blocked effectiveness. Sometimes a postmortem is able to piece together interactions between participants and the effect these had on performance and results. Postmortems are quite "natural," even though using a postmortem for critique is not too common.

Using a questionnaire or some other information-gathering device as a starting point for a critique can be particularly useful. The following, for example, is one of several questions answered by participants in a Grid Seminar following a problem-solving team discussion. First, individual members working separately allocate 100 points among the five alternatives to indicate their observations as the way critique did or did not occur, as shown on the left.

| Individual | | Team |
|---|---|---|
| A ____ | Little or no attention was given to analyzing team action. | A ____ |
| B ____ | Compliments were given, and any faults were not examined. | B ____ |
| C ____ | Suggestions of how to do differently or a little better to keep the meeting moving at an acceptable pace. | C ____ |
| D ____ | Fault-finding; unconstructive criticism. | D ____ |
| E ____ | Concurrent critique of teamwork was present and used for improving action and for learning from it. | E ____ |

Next, members reveal their point allocations and use them as the basis for a discussion of similarities and differences in their observations, reaching and recording team agreement as shown on the right.

If a postmortem is delayed too long after an activity is completed, recollections of what happened may be incomplete or fragmentary. The possibility of making real use of the lessons learned is remote, i.e., changes needed, even though identified, are less likely to be put into action. Maximum benefit is possible when critique follows immediately on completion of the activity.

Many companies lose much of the real benefit of postmortem critiquing. One reason is that managers rush headlong into the next activity, glad to be through with the last one. Another reason is the attitude, "Let's not look backward. That's history. You can't do anything about it. It's done and gone. Look forward and get on to the next project." This attitude rejects the notion that learning from experience is even a possibility.

### When is Critique Useful?

Critique may be used when

1. Work is bogged down and people are unclear as to the causes of their lack of progress.
2. Work practices have been relatively formal and there is a readiness to move toward informality and more spontaneous collaboration.

3. A new procedure is being introduced.
4. A group is embarking on an innovative activity.
5. A group's membership is changed, particularly by the introduction of a new boss.
6. 9,9 teamwork values are understood by team members who are motivated to learn how to increase their effectiveness.

Critique is not likely to be useful when

1. Two or more participants are overtly antagonistic to one another and would use the opportunity for destructive criticism.
2. There is a crisis and the time needed for deliberation is unavailable.
3. Activities are relatively mechanical and of such a routine nature that few benefits can be anticipated by submitting them to examination and study.
4. Participants are inexperienced in face-to-face feedback methods, or fearful of open communication.

### Strengths and Limitations of Critique as a Method for Learning from Experience

The various forms of critique ensure that those whose participation is under study become their own students and teachers. Then it is most likely that the conclusions reached will be implemented because the implications of what has been learned are well understood.

One limitation lies in the difficulty many people experience in being objective and in making sound observations when they are deeply involved in an activity itself. They are called on to observe as they are participating, that is, to participate in the problem solving but to study the progress simultaneously. Their reactions to the activity itself, as well as to the people in it, may color what they think and feel, and therefore, how they react. This is a strength as well as a limitation because when more points of view are brought to bear on analyzing an activity, there is a greater likelihood of learning from it.

Observation and feedback create a need for effectiveness and skill in communication. Participants must develop such skills if the full benefits of critique are to be realized. A systematic basis for learning to use the major approaches to critique is available elsewhere.

### Summary

When team members identify and discuss in advance the purpose, goals, or objectives of an activity and how it can best be accomplished, they are using one version of critique. This can ensure agreement as to what should happen and set the stage for effective performance. Concurrent critique is interrupting the activity as it is being carried out so that team members can analyze and give feedback regarding procedures, processes, or people's reactions. Then whatever is contributing to or hindering performance can be identified. Postmortem critique of an activity occurs when the activity has been completed. This is utilized to determine whether the accomplishment was satisfactory, and if so, why, and if not, why not. When these questions are answered, the participants have both evaluated the task just finished and improved their understanding of how to go about undertaking future activities to get better results.

The major limitation to using critique is that it is premised on 9,9 values of candor, conflict confrontation, and reliance on an experimental attitude. If these values are lacking, team members may go through the motions, but it is unlikely that the activity will be worth the effort. It may be necessary to shift values before the benefits of critique can be realized.

## Chapter 13

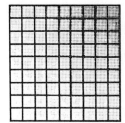 # Grid Organization Development

Purpose, people, and hierarchy are three universals of organization. They have been focused on through an analysis of the Grid style assumptions about how hierarchy is exercised to achieve production with and through people. A fourth universal of organization is *culture*. In order to increase the effectiveness of an individual manager dealing with his subordinates, as well as the organization as a whole, change must take place in the organization culture itself.

Management takes place within a culture of established expectations. Traditions, precedents, and past practices come to control people's actions rather than the requirements of the situation or their personal inclinations. These conventional ways of thinking, feeling, and acting come to govern attitudes toward profit margins, debts versus equity financing and cash flow, inventory control, production planning, plant layout, product lines, packaging, distribution, advertising and selling, employment standards, promotion procedures, and a host of other practices. They encompass attitudes that accept the status quo as okay and mental straight jackets that say, "To get along you have to go along."

To try to change procedures, processes, or products while ignoring the expectations of those who manage only provokes resistance to change and may eventually cause improvement efforts to be set aside. As a result, many organizations are being operated in ways that fit the past but are severely maladapted to the requirements of tomorrow. This makes responsiveness to future requirements even more demanding. Reliance on traditional ways of management and supervision is, in other words, failing to bring about desired and needed operational outcomes. Profitability or cost-effectiveness suffers as a consequence, as do human satisfaction, involvement, and the readiness of organization members to commit themselves to the attainment of organization goals. Managers fail to recognize how culture molds character and dictates relationships. They often are unaware of the inability of individuals and society to exploit the powerful potential for cultural change within a corporation, government agency, hospital, school or social agency.

Emphasis on the extent to which the organization culture controls individual behavior is recent in origin. Once apparent, however, an important conclusion is that the organization's culture must be a central part of any effort to change. Organization culture is usually outside direct executive control. If the corporate culture is openly hostile to change or threatened by it, or simply indifferent, then efforts to change are likely to be blunted.

### An Organization Culture Change Experiment

Can organization culture be changed in a positive, dynamic way to create a more productive organization? Figure 13-1 illustrates the success of one organization in such an effort to change. It describes the profitability of two autonomous corporations operating nationwide on opposite sides of an international border. Corporation A engaged in Grid organization development. Corporation B did not. They are owned by the same parent located in a third country. They engage in similar businesses and face the same character of competition in comparable markets.

Starting in 1961, the comparisons show that for five years prior to the introduction of Grid development, the control corporation, B, appeared to be obtaining somewhat better economic performance, but the results were well within the range of change fluctuations. Then, after introduction of Grid organization development, Corporation A experiences a continuous and rising curve of profitability during the following decade. By this time, the cumulative impact on profitability in the Grid company is 400% greater than in Corporation B, which is not engaged in Grid organization development: Corporation B has managed to hold its own over the entire fifteen-year period.

The following remarks by the president of Corporation A at a point in time when his company had been engaged in Grid OD for six years offers his evaluation of change.

> ... there is no doubt that OD has had a significant and positive effect on profits. ... A major objective of the Grid was to change behavior and values within the organization in the direction of showing a high concern for both task accomplishment and human motivation, and then to sustain these changes and institutionalize them ... there has undoubtedly been a substantial transformation in this area, with positive effects accruing through improved communication, the use of critique, profit or cost consciousness, some aspects of planning, the handling of conflict, meaningful

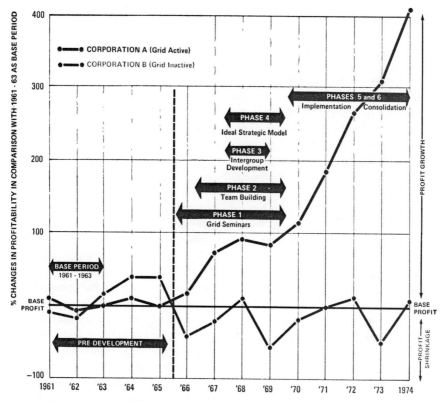

*Figure 13-1. Comparison of the profitability of two matched corporations; Corporation A is involved in Grid development, but Corporation B is not.*

participation in a group, and commitment among key managers . . . there is one other most important benefit that has accrued from the OD program and that is a substantial improvement in the working relationships between management and union officials.

Much of the work involving the union can be considered as a breakthrough in the application of OD principles and there is little doubt as to its success.

The model this organization used to change its corporate culture and thus increase profitability is based on six phases of development. However, we need first to deal with the question, "From a development perspective, what is an organization?"

### What Is an Organization?

The organization development part of Grid organization development means *organization* development. The organization is the unit of development rather than a person or a component part. The reason is that an organization is an integrated business entity. Its members and component parts must act not only independently but also interdependently to approach excellence. This statement is fundamental. Once it is understood that the whole can be more and different than the sum of its parts, possibilities for synergistic operation are recognized. With this recognition, the consequences for development efforts are great.

This line of thinking does not lead automatically to the conclusion that the corporation is the organization development unit. It may mean this but not necessarily. An "organization" in the context of "development" means a whole—an entity that is self-sufficient, possessing the essential autonomy for changing itself, as illustrated in Figure 13-2. It requires no approval from outside itself to shift key aspects of its business which might need to be changed to achieve excellence.

Some companies are led from corporate offices in such a way that the corporate office is so closely involved in the management of the business that the component is engaged in, the character of the market, the structural alignments of segments, and the policies that guide action, that the whole must then be recognized as including the corporate office as well as subordinate components. Other companies are so structured that subsidiary segments or regional divisions or plants, under a concept of decentralization, have sufficient autonomy and freedom to change the basic character of their operations in those matters that need changing. They are free to improve their return on investment or other indices of profit and productivity. By recommendation and approval they can exert weight on decisions that affect the nature of their business. They can shape the market within which they intend to concentrate business activity. They can redesign the structural relations among segments and components and interpret the major policies that govern their business decisions. Though capital expenditures undoubtedly are subject to higher level approval, the way that they are approved is the same as for any business transaction.

A subsidiary segment or a division or plant that acts under such autonomy is, from the perspective of development, a whole. The degree of autonomy is such that decisions for change are the responsibility of those who lead the operations. The corporate office's involvement in Grid organization development might be little more than consultative in this case. This issue defines perhaps the most fundamental organization

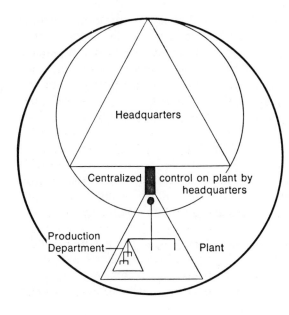

**Two Possible OD Units**
Neither plant nor produc-
tion department operates
with sufficient decentra-
lized autonomy from head-
quarters to be responsible
for itself.

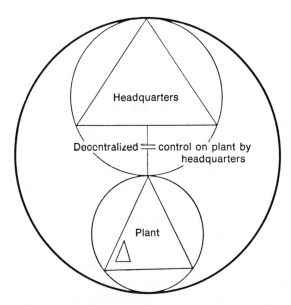

**Three Possible OD Units**
The plant has sufficient
autonomy to be responsi-
ble for internal change.

*Figure 13-2. The organization development unit is any component that is a
whole.*

development decision that can be made. It should not be glossed over or treated casually. Units that do not constitute sound development units are a work team, a section, department, or division within a plant or region. The unit is generally only a piece embedded in a larger organizational culture. It is not the whole, only a slice. It is not sufficiently independent either vertically or horizontally to change itself in significant ways without active involvement of other units.

## Grid Phase 1

In the initial phase of organization development everyone in the organization gets involved in learning the Grid and using it to evaluate their own personal style of managing through attending a five-day seminar.

Maximum impact is possible when all employees participate. Included are persons who manage others, though some companies begin by extending organization development to include technical, wage, and salaried personnel. The decision on extending Grid learning to other than managerial levels can be made at a later time.

### Grid Seminar Goals

Specifically, the goals of the seminar are for participants to:

1. Gain personal learning by
   —understanding the Grid as a framework of thought
   —gaining insight into one's own Grid styles
   —increasing personal objectivity in work behavior
   —reexamining managerial values
2. Experience problem solving in teams by
   —testing ways to increase effectiveness
   —studying the use of critique
   —developing standards for openness and candor
   —examining the need for active listening
3. Learn about managing intergroup conflict by
   —studying barriers between teams
   —examining conflict within teams
   —exploring ways of reducing or eliminating such conflicts
4. Comprehend organization implications by
   —understanding impact of work culture on behavior
   —gaining appreciation of Grid OD and possible outcomes

These seminars are conducted on both a public and an internal basis. They involve hard work. The program requires thirty or more hours of guided study before the seminar week itself which usually begins Sunday evening. Participants are involved in learning activities morning, afternoon, and evening through the following Friday.

The sessions include investigation by each person of his or her own managerial approach and alternate ways of managing which he or she is able to learn about, experiment with, and apply. Participants study methods of team action. They measure and evaluate team effectiveness in solving problems with others. A high point of seminar learning is reached when each participant receives a critique of his style of managerial performance from other members of his team. Another is when managers critique the dominant style of their organization's culture, its traditions, precedents, and past practices. A third is when participants consider steps for increasing the effectiveness of the whole organization.

Grid seminars are intended to aid managers to increase their effectiveness in many different ways. Two approaches are useful in evaluating actual impact on individuals. One is quantitative and involves field research and statistical studies. The other is qualitative and includes subjective reports.

## Quantitative Studies

The following data summarize typical kinds of changes in individual behavior that have been found in field research.

*Changes in promotion* practices following Grid ÒD favor merit over seniority.

1. Those promoted are three years younger on the average.
2. Length of service for those promoted reduced 2.8 years.
3. Promotion rate to higher positions outside plant up 31%.

*Behavior changes* are toward sounder relationships.

1. 62% better communication between bosses and subordinates.
2. 61% improvement in working with other groups.
3. 55% better relationships with colleagues.
4. 48% more leveling in one study, 21.8% in another.
5. 22% improvement in goal setting.
6. 20% more openness to influence.
7. 14% increase in delegation.

These kinds of changes all are in a more 9,9-oriented direction, and they suggest that significant changes in managerial behavior are brought about by Grid seminar participation.

## Qualitative Reports

The following comments are typical of participant reactions:

—Theories increase understanding and insight.

*Now I see a means of improving in a total way rather than a piecemeal way. A sound theoretical framework.*

—Grid seminars offer growth-giving personal experiences.

*Much greater insight into my managerial style will provide guidelines into how I can improve my effectiveness.*

—Critique is central to valid problem solving.

*Best personal learning experience ever, particularly since individuals and teams learned through experience with continuous critique and positive reinforcements.*

— Openness is basic to sound relationships.

*The frankness and openness created by the seminar experience is a significant factor in enabling useful discussions to be carried out in depth with team members.*

—Better teamwork is one of the rewarding outcomes.

*I saw synergistic action and understand now that when a group works well together, its end product is superior to the sum of its products of the same group members working individually.*

— Perspective for seeing one's own performance in more objective terms.

*It forced me to take a critical look at myself and also, through practical Grid experience in a team setting, showed me how some of my beliefs can actually be detrimental to the company.*

## Seminar Composition

Although 100% of a firm's managers may be engaged in organization development, it is rare that all can participate in Phase 1 seminars at the same time. Members of a firm are selected to participate in a particular Grid study team in terms of a *diagonal* slice of the membership.

In a diagonal slice Grid team, line and staff managers, technical and professional men, and supervisors study together. The same is true for personnel of different ages and organization functions. The only basis for grouping is that insofar as possible, each Grid team should be composed to be a miniature of the organization.

When the diagonal slice is used, several functions of the organization as well as levels of hierarchy are represented in the same study team. The composition is a replica of the company. The diagonal slice makes possible an exchange of perspective not only among persons from different functions but among those from different levels as well. A boss and a subordinate may be present in the same seminar in the diagonal arrangement, but they do not engage in learning in the same study team.

When a Grid seminar is formed, the question almost always raised is whether "lower level" members are able to participate effectively with "higher level" ones. The implication is that lower level members, because they are most likely to be men with practical experience, may not be able to learn as fast as men with college backgrounds. This is not the case, however. Lower level men often have a depth of practical experience as rich as that of technical personnel. When men who have risen from the ranks have opportunities to study and learn with college educated managers, they gain a better understanding of the technical man's thinking—how he goes about analyzing a problem, formulating alternatives, and weighing advantages and disadvantages. For a man from the ranks, this in itself can be an education. On the other hand, men from the ranks also are more likely to understand behavior in concrete terms and be able to provide insight otherwise not readily available.

Nonsupervisory personnel are often included in Grid organization development but as an extension of the initial effort, particularly in high technology, knowledge-oriented organizations. This means that those who engage together in study teams are lower level managers and wage and hourly personnel. This is particularly desirable. Participants are permitted to gain insight into the emotions surrounding the cleavage between the management organization and operating levels. Observers have often pointed to this as one of the important contributors to strengthening the effectiveness of lower level supervisors and the identification of wage and hourly personnel with corporate objectives of excellence in performance.

Another related question is, "What is the minimum education a person needs to be able to benefit from Grid seminar participation?" The level of formal education is far less important than the ability to comprehend concepts. Many persons with little formal education have effectively educated themselves. There are limits, but someone with a reading comprehension equivalent to the sixth grade public school level, whether or not he actually completed the sixth grade, usually has the skills essential for learning in a Grid seminar.

The one disadvantage of diagonal slice selection stems more from the final choice of the participants than from the method itself. It is related to level and indirectly to education. When levels are too far apart within the hierarchy—vice-president and front-line supervisor in a large company, for example—participants may find it difficult to interact in an easy and understanding way. While the diagonal slice method is the most desirable of the three, a sound selection of levels should probably be limited to three or four levels.

Sometimes the question is asked, "Should those who are nearing retirement be included in the development effort?" When a man is nearing retirement, he may not see value in increasing his further involvement with the organization within the short time remaining to him. On the other hand, many managers near retirement find gratifying personal reward in the learning itself and in the opportunity to study with others. For these reasons, managers preparing to retire certainly should be invited to participate.

There is no hard and fast answer to how many should participate in a seminar, but there are some ground rules. Achieving speed in organization learning must be balanced against ensuring that organization performance does not falter because too many people are absent from work at the same time. Company after company has found that under the diagonal slice concept of seminar composition, about 10% of the working organization can be away from the work site without undesirable effects on organization performance. Use of this proportion as a guideline also produces a minimum of disruption of working teams. The diagonal slice approach ensures that no work unit is seriously depleted.

The 10% figure should not be used automatically in organizations with more than 500 people because of its effect on seminar learning. The question is, "How many people in a seminar is too many?" The maximum number is around seventy-five for two instructors for an incompany seminar. Companies with more than 500 managers may send fewer people away at any one time, or two seminars (of forty to sixty participants) might be conducted simultaneously but independently.

### Team Building: Phase 2

Chapter 10 pointed out the value of good teamwork for increasing organization effectiveness. Phase 2 team building is specifically addressed to diagnosing specific and concrete barriers to sound teamwork and identifying opportunities of each team for improvement.

Issues of problem solving and decision making, such as when 1/0, 1/1/1 and 1/all teamwork are needed, are central. However, many more facets of teamwork are explored in sufficient depth so differences are distinguishable. These include each team member's experience of the contributions of others, the culture's assumptions about the proper form of teamwork, identification of particular problems of teamwork that are barriers to effectiveness with specific plans to remedy them, and, finally, setting team objectives to be accomplished in the near future.

Phase 2 team building begins when all members of any corporate team have completed Phase 1 Grid learning and want to apply concepts to their own managerial team culture. It starts with the key executive and those who report to him. It then moves down through the organization. Each manager sits down with subordinates as a team. They study their barriers to effectiveness and plan ways to overcome them.

## Team Building Goals

The goals of team building are to:
1. Replace outmoded traditions, precedents, and past practices with a sound team culture
2. Set standards of excellence
3. Increase personal objectivity in on-the-job behavior
4. Use critique for learning
5. Establish objectives for team and individual achievement

An analysis of the team culture and operating practices precedes the setting of goals for improvement of the team operation along with a time schedule for achieving these goals. Members learn how to become more productive through synergizing their individual contributions. Sound and enduring standards of excellence are established as benchmarks for team use in continually strengthening its problem-solving culture. Tied into the goal setting for the team is personal goal setting by team members. This might be a goal for trying to change aspects of behavior so as to increase a member's contribution to teamwork. A demonstration project is selected to enable the team to immediately apply its new problem-solving skills and standards to solve a significant actual barrier to effectiveness with which it is faced.

Grid team building is a five-day activity implemented during working hours on the job. If job considerations require it, the activities can be segmented into parts and conducted over a longer period.

## Impact on Team Effectiveness

Team building, as indicated in the following quotation, can have major impact on team effectiveness.

Phase 1 is like getting a check; Phase 2 is when you cash it . . . . The period of Phase 2's implementation in the automotive division coincided with a 300% increase in divisional profits—a significantly better profit improvement than that of the rest of the domestic organization—even though we concede that other factors, such as market conditions, expanded plant capacity, the state of the economy, and so on may have contributed to the improvement in profits. Still, top management believed that Phase 2 and the striking turn-around in the automotive division were more than a coincidence, that Phase 2 made a substantial contribution to the performance picture, even though it was impossible to measure precisely.

Taken together, Phase 1 and 2 unlock communication barriers between people, amongst other things.

In the past, when we would set budgets, I would calculate what each department would get . . . . Then they would yell and complain, "Why did you give me this?" I would say, "This is the way it is, boys, I'm the boss." Now, since we went to Grid last year, there's no such happening. Perhaps we've got to reduce our margin in meat. We know we've got to make it up somewhere else. The group comes to a decision. This year it took us an hour-and-a-half to set our budget. Before Grid, we were in there for eight solid hours table-pounding. But now we were committed. . .

One marketing manager put it this way, "I never realized our department could really work as a team. Phase 1 of the Grid was great, but it really took Phase 2 to bring it all out. Sure, I was apprehensive at first, all the guys were, but when it came right down to it, we were able to work together, solve problems, open up and really communicate with each other. It wasn't what you would call an easy experience, but it was certainly worthwhile."

The top man of each team retains full responsibility for leadership. Subordinates in the top team then lead team building in their own teams where they are leaders and this continues throughout the organization.

## Intergroup Development: Phase 3

The next step is to achieve better problem solving between groups through a closer integration of units that have working inter-relationships. The need for Phase 3 development comes about because, when each department or unit has a singular responsibility, corporate members of departments or divisions tend to think more about their components and less about the whole. They may act and react more in the interests of their departmentalized units than in the interests of the entire organization. People can see most clearly their most immediate interests. From inside the department, this is viewed as selflessly serving the corporation. Such preoccupation with their own departments may mean less of their attention is paid to other departments. Then, when one department must cooperate with another, managers in the second tend to see those in the first motivated by selfish considerations, particularly when needed cooperation does not seem to be forthcoming.

The second department may ask, "Why are they dragging their feet? Why are they unable to provide the service we need, which is the only reason for their existence in the first place? They are deliberately disregarding our requirements."

These kinds of attitudes are born of frustration and can quickly promote feelings of hostility. A man in the second department may pick up his phone in irritation, "What's the matter with you? Why can't you meet your deadlines? Don't you know how to manage?"

The answer comes back, "Who do you think you are? Can't you remember last week? One of your people miscalculated on a job that forced us into needless overtime and fouled up our schedules, but good!"

Such intergroup attitudes are easily provoked and, once formed, easily inflamed into win-lose power struggles. When this happens, needed cooperation is sacrificed, information is withheld, requests are received as unreasonable demands. When corporate members are asked what their problems are, they tend to answer, "Poor communication between departments." However, the underlying problem of relationships must be dealt with before any fundamental changes in effectiveness of communication are achieved.

**Intergroup Development Goals**

The goals of Phase 3 are to:

1. Use a systematic framework for analyzing intergroup coordination problems
2. Apply problem-solving and decision-making skills for
   —polarizing acknowledged antagonisms
   —confronting relationships based on surface harmony or neutrality that hide problem-solving intergroup difficulties
   —resisting compromise when accommodation of differences cannot solve the real problem
3. Utilize controlled confrontation and identify focal issues needing resolution to establish integration
4. Plan next application for achieving improved cooperation between units on a continuing basis

The beginning of intergroup development between any two conflicting groups is devoted to establishing a positive climate and gaining understanding of lack of cooperation, its causes, and barriers to resolution. Establishing objectives, working toward operational improvement, and designing plans for implementation and critique complete the design.

Phase 3 is only participated in by those groups where actual barriers to effective cooperation between them exist. It is not a "universal" phase that all groups automatically engage in. Intergroup development usually is undertaken after Phase 2 Grid team building has been completed.

## Impact of Intergroup Development

How Phase 3 works in resolving union-management chronic difficulties is described in the quotation that follows.

The union-management Phase 3 has been in progress for eighteen months and has been very successful. The time has been spent systematically analyzing all the important aspects of the union-management relationships. The outcome has been a mutually agreed ideal on each of these aspects plus a whole series of action steps designed to move towards this ideal. Some of the areas covered were overtime, job performance, grievances, seniority, job ownership, the Agreement, work fluctuations, job evaluation, communications, compensation, the pension plan, and objectives.

Overall, these Phase 3 activities have served to develop trust and respect between the union and management participants and have provided an excellent forum for the candid discussion of problems. Many traditions have been broken down and a new culture has emerged. There are two particularly striking features to this new atmosphere. The greatest improvement has come in the area of listening and trying to understand the other side's viewpoint. Secondly, this and the very nature of the Blake operation (management presenting how it sees itself and how it sees the union on various elements, and the union presenting how it sees itself and management) have tended to make both sides more objective. As a consequence, many of the flare-ups that occurred in the early stages are no longer happening.

That is not to say that both sides agree on everything by any means. However, where some disagreement does arise, it is approached rationally and there is a basic trust between the two groups that each is committed to finding a sound and acceptable solution.

### Designing an Ideal Strategic Organization Model:
### Phase 4

Many outmoded traditions, precedents, and past practices have been replaced by standards of excellence for judging individual performance and effective teamwork and for confronting and resolving cleavages between groups when Phases 1 through 3 have been completed. This is important to corporate excellence, but none of it is sufficient for reaching the degree of excellence potentially available to corporations based upon the systematic development of the business logic employed throughout an organization for strengthening productivity.

The key to exploiting organization potentials for excellence is in the organization having a business model of what it wishes to become in comparison with what it currently is or historically has been.

## Goals of Designing an Ideal Strategic Organization Model

The goals of ideal strategic organization modeling are to:

1. Specify minimum and optimum corporate financial objectives
2. Describe in explicit terms the nature and character of business activities to be pursued in the future
3. Define in operational terms the scope and character of markets to be penetrated
4. Create a structure for organizing and integrating business operations for synergistic results
5. Delineate basic policies that are to guide future business decision making
6. Identify development requirements for maintaining thrust and avoiding drag

The top team of a corporation is ideally situated for carrying out such a fundamental approach for examining and rejecting whatever in its current practices is outmoded and unprofitable and formulating a replacement model. The model is based on the organization's being engaged in business activity in the future that is geared to the needs of society for products and services, the needs of corporations for profitability, and the needs of employees for satisfaction with work based upon involvement, participation, and commitment, and of stockholders for a meaningful return on invested funds.

Ideal strategic organization modeling is a planning technique that enables the top team to apply rigorous business logic in designing and blueprinting what the organization is expected to become during its next stage of development.

Phase 4 engages the top team in a step-by-step process of business logic study, diagnosis, and designing of an ideal corporate model. The study step is a conceptual investigation of the most basic concepts of business logic currently available. These are drawn from, but not limited to, the writings of Sloan, who pioneered in the development of a systematic discipline of business logic.

Using agreed upon concepts of "pure" business logic, the next step is to specify the operational properties of a model to serve as a blueprint for how the corporation led by the top team is reconstructed. Phase 4 is completed when this strategic corporate model has been evaluated and agreed to by other senior executives, who have a corporate perspective but are not members of the top team, and approved as a stave for the future by the board of directors.

## Impact of Designing an Ideal Strategic Organization Model

The kinds of changes brought about through Phase 4 are described below.

> Other important outcomes of the OD effort which must be evaluated are in the area of strategy. Here there is a widespread conviction that the strategic insights that occurred during Phase 4 have been beneficial and have served to start the corporation moving in the right direction.
>
> The Phase 4 team at . . . first reached agreement on details of what actually exists in the present organization model. That is, the team developed a clear picture of . . . management, with no rationalizations, excuses or apologies; they developed simple, concise statements that picture the ideal model today. Then, using the same format, they developed statements as to how a hypothetical, ideal . . . would operate. This ideal model served to focus attention on needed changes in policy.
>
> All participants committed themselves to action based on statements of concepts and principles that were agreed upon. In support of these concepts and principles, 39 policies were drafted that are to serve as the specific basis to guide management action.

### Implementing Development: Phase 5

The Phase 5 activity moves an organization out of its traditional way of operating and into alignment with the ideal strategic model. Phase 5 is designed so that it is unnecessary to tear down the whole company and start from scratch to build a new company to meet the requirements of the model. What is done is more like remodeling a building according to a blueprint of what it is to become. Then architects and engineers study the existing structure to identify what is strong, sound, and consistent with the blueprint and can be retained, what is antiquated and inappropriate to the blueprint and must be replaced, and what is usable but needs modification or strengthening in order to bring it in line. Once these decisions have been reached, then carpenters, plumbers, and others know what must be done concretely to shift from the old to the new. Essentially the same procedure is followed for an organization.

**Goals of Implementing Development**

The goals of Phase 5 are to:

1. Study the existing organization to identify the gaps between how it operates and the way it is expected to operate according to the ideal strategic model

2. Specify which parts of the business are sound, which parts can be changed and therefore are likely to be retained, which parts are not sound and need to be divested, and identifying new or additional activities needed to meet the requirements of the ideal model

3. Design implementation steps to change from the actual to the ideal model

4. Continue to run the business while simultaneously changing toward the ideal model

Changing the organization from what it is to what it should be takes place in a series of steps. They begin with analyzing and subdividing the company into its smallest components. The mark of a smallest component is a grouping of interrelated activities that are tied together because they all are essential factors in producing a recognizable source of earnings. The company may be subdivided into many such units.

The next step is to identify all the expenses entailed in engaging in these activities. A third step is to compute the investment related to these activities that is tied up in plant, equipment, etc. Once these steps have been taken, it becomes possible to evaluate whether or not the business identified by that component meets the business specifications of the ideal strategic corporate model. Test questions such as the following are answered with regard to each of these components. Is the return currently realized on this investment consistent with the ideal strategic model? If not, are there controllable expenses or pricing factors which could be altered to bring it within specified return on investment standards? Is this area of business activity consistent with market areas identified within the ideal strategic model as areas for future growth? These test questions are typical of the many that are employed to decide whether each activity that leads to earnings should be expanded, contracted, changed, or eliminated in pursuing corporate development.

Because of the depth of change involved, the implementation of Phase 5 oftentimes contributes a quantum leap in productivity. The results shown in Figure 13-1 demonstrate the character of improvement possible.

## Impact of Implementing Development

An organization member who was intimately involved in his company's implementation project summarized his reactions.

Once we could specify how we needed to change to meet the Ideal Strategic Model we were in the management-by-objectives business in a way that wasn't limited by blind acceptance of the status quo. Some of the specific things we learned included:

1. How to approach the business in a scientific way to analyze and evaluate variables selectively
2. Taking corporate perspective as opposed to previous functional or departmental view
3. Looking at existing business more critically, growing more and more displeased with current efforts
4. Gaining a new perspective of the role of planning in effective management
5. Focusing on results expected by using return on assets as the basis for business decisions in comparison with conventional profit and loss and share of market thinking
6. Grasping the deeper implications of effective teamwork for increasing the soundness of an implementation plan
7. Developing more basic insight into the dynamics of resistance to change

## Consolidation: Phase 6

Phase 6 is a period of time which is used to stabilize and consolidate progress achieved during Phases 1-5 before recycling into another period of change.

### Goals of Consolidation

The goals of Phase 6 are to:

1. Critique the change effort to ensure that activities that have been implemented are continued as planned
2. Identify weaknesses that may have appeared that could not have been anticipated throughout the implementation and take corrective action to rectify them
3. Monitor changes in the business environment (competition, price of raw materials, wage differentials, etc.) that may indicate that fundamental shifts in the model are necessary

Three features of business life suggest the importance of a consolidating phase in organization development. Managing change is the opposite of managing the tried and true. People tend to repeat the tried and true, but people may lose interest in something that is novel as they become more familiar with it. Reduced effort in making the novel work as it was intended may cause it to fail. Phase 6 activities help to identify these drag factors.

A second reason for a period of time to consolidate progress is that by continuing study of what is new, additional improvement opportunities may be identified that can add to the organizational thrust. A third is that significant alterations in the outer environment may occur to cause changes specified in the model and implemented in Phase 5 to be more or less favorable than had been anticipated. In either case the monitoring activities of Phase 6 provide a basis for specifying the potential needs for additional change.

Phase 6 strategies and instruments enable an organization to assess its strengths and to consolidate its gains. This is done by organization members' identifying drag factors that may have cropped up and that need to be eliminated to counter their adverse effects. The same is true for thrust factors. These may need to be stressed in order to gain the full potential of OD.

The significant aspect of Phase 6 is that the consolidation phase is made explicit rather than assuming that once change has been set in motion, it will persist of its own momentum.

## How to Get Started

*How* Grid organization development is introduced is a major factor in its success. Finding a way to achieve an organization-wide awareness and conviction about the importance of Grid organization development among members without demanding participation is the dilemma. The best approach lies in a series of preliminary steps that are exploratory and are designed to orient members to Grid organization development's possibilities as shown in Figure 13-3. These steps permit the organization to test the implications of Grid organization development in a methodical way without its obligation to become deeply involved in it. If these steps are taken in a planned way, organization members have the opportunity of developing their own commitments through a series of self-convincing experiences. Orientation without obligation—the opportunity to test the temperature before plunging in—produces awareness of possibilities from which a conviction-based decision can be made.

| | |
|---|---|
| Background Reading | Gives an orientation as to how applied behavioral science is being used to strengthen organizations |
| Seeding | Provides a few organization members depth insight into Phase 1 and the Grid without the organization's being committed to doing more |
| Grid Organization Development Seminar | Gives a few managers a breadth and depth of insight into the whole of Grid organization development as the basis for evaluation and possible recommendations for next steps |
| Pilot Grid Seminar | Provides the organization a test tube trial of what would be involved were the organization to engage in Phase 1 |
| Pilot Teamwork Development | Affords the top team direct understanding of how the Grid is applied to strengthening not only its team effectiveness, but also the effectiveness of individuals as the basis for assessing probable impact of Phase 2 applied on an organization-wide basis |

There are other possible approaches to development, depending upon an organization's needs, resources, and state of readiness. These include survey research, sensitivity training, job enrichment, management-by-objectives, and others. The Grid approach is different from these in its emphasis on changing organization culture before team building, management-by-objectives, or job enrichment. Only in this way is there a reasonable prospect that new approaches to management can survive the negative pressures which otherwise cause them to be abandoned.

## Chapter 14

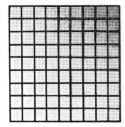

# Analyzing
# Personal
# Managerial Styles

A way to evaluate your own managerial style was provided in Chapter 1. You ranked several paragraphs from *5*, the most characteristic of your approach, to *1*, the least like you. In addition, you selected one phrase in each of the six elements of Decisions, Convictions, Conflict, Temper, Humor, and Effort.

### Identifying Managerial Styles

Before examining these rankings it may be useful to summarize the main features of each of the major Grid theories, as is done in Table 14-1. Grid styles are shown across the table. Reading down the left margin are shown basic aspects of all Grid styles: Management Functions, Boss Behavior, Consequences, Dynamics, and Childhood Origins. Reading across a row from left to right shows some feature evaluated according to each Grid style. Reading down any column permits comparison for a variety of specific considerations against Grid style. You may wish to rerank yourself after reexamining this chart in order to make it a more accurate self-assessment.

Now, transfer your initial rankings from Chapter 1 to the two left columns under *Initial* of Table 14-2. The leftmost column is for *Paragraphs*, the second column is for *Elements*. Next, put your revised ranks in their respective places under the *Revised* columns.

The first paragraph, A, in Chapter 1 is the 1,1 paragraph. It is followed, in order, by B—1,9; C—5,5; D—9,1; and E—the 9,9 paragraph. The same order applies for each element. The first phrase under *Decisions* (A1) describes the 1,1 attitude. It is followed by (B1)—1,9; (C1)—5,5; (D1)—9,1; and (E1)—9,9. The same order applies for each of the other elements.

Now it is possible to interpret your selection of Grid styles to depict your own managerial behavior. This provides one basis for you to

(Text continued on page 203)

**Table 14-1**
**Summary of Grid Style Dynamics**

| Management Functions | 1,1 | 1,9 | 5,5 | 9,1 | 9,9 |
|---|---|---|---|---|---|
| Planning | I give broad assignments though I avoid specifying goals or schedules when possible. Each subordinate fends for himself. | I suggest assignments and convey my confidence by saying, "I'm sure you know how to do this and that all will go well." | I make my plans according to what I know my subordinates will accept and what they will resist. Then I plan for each subordinate according to what he will think is okay. | I do the planning by setting production quotas and detailing plans to achieve them. | I get the people who have relevant facts and/or stakes in the outcome together to review the whole picture. We formulate a sound model from start to completion to provide an organizing framework for integrating an entire project. I get their reactions and ideas. I establish goals and flexible schedules with them. |
| Organizing | If left alone, they carry out assignments, as they know their own jobs and their capabilities better than anyone else. | Subordinates know what to do and how to coordinate with each other. If they need my suggestions, I'm ready to listen and offer to them and offer whatever help I can. | After explaining aims and schedules, I make individual assignments. I double check to make sure my subordinates think what I request is okay. I encourage them to feel free to come back if they don't understand what to do. | I make assignments and tell subordinates what to do, how, when, and with whom. | Within the framework of the whole, we determine individual responsibilities, procedures, and ground rules. |

| | | | | | |
|---|---|---|---|---|---|
| **Directing** | I carry the message from those above to those below. I pass the story as straight as I can and with as little embroidery or interpretation as possible. | I see my subordinates frequently and encourage them to visit. My door is always open. My desire is always to get them the things they want without their having to ask. That's the way to encourage people. | I keep up with each person's performance and review his progress from time to time. If a subordinate is having difficulty, I try to reduce pressure on him by rearranging conditions of work whenever possible. | I keep in close touch with what's going on to ensure that what I have authorized is being followed. | I keep informed of progress and influence subordinates by identifying problems and revising goals *with* them. I lend assistance when needed by helping to remove road blocks. |
| **Controlling** | I make the rounds, but I take little on-the-spot action if I can avoid it. They like it that way. I do, too. | I rarely need to check on how things are going since my subordinates will try their best. I place emphasis on congratulating each individual for his good efforts. Our discussions usually end by talking about why we did as well as we did and how we can help things to go as smoothly or more so in the future. | I meet informally to discuss how things are going. I tend to emphasize good points and avoid appearing critical, though I do encourage subordinates to identify their own weak points. My subordinates know I take their thoughts and feelings into account in planning next assignments. | I ensure that schedules are being met and move people along faster if progress permits. I criticize, assign blame for deviations, and impose corrective actions. | In addition to in-progress critiques to keep projects on schedule, I conduct a wrap-up with those responsible. We evaluate the way things went and see what we can learn from our experience and how we can apply our learning in the future. I give recognition on a team basis as well as for outstanding individual contributions. |

**Table 14-1 (continued)**

| Management Functions | 1,1 | 1,9 | 5,5 | 9,1 | 9,9 |
|---|---|---|---|---|---|
| Staffing | You take whoever they give you. | Even though it's not possible to please everyone, I try to ensure that subordinates are in the jobs they like best and working with those they enjoy. | I seek people who will fit in. | I get strong people and weed out weak ones. Management development that concentrates on personnel issues may be useful, but on-the-job learning is what counts. | Work requirements are matched with personnel capabilities or needs for development in making decisions as to who does what. |
| Management-by-Objectives | Empty "shells" | "Good" intentions, under least common denominator agreements | Targets | Quotas, deadlines | Goals and objectives |
| Performance Appraisal | "Go through the motions" | Compliments | Sandwich technique | Criticism | Progress studied against goals |
| **Boss Behavior** | **1,1** | **1,9** | **5,5** | **9,1** | **9,9** |
| Communication | Message-passing | One-way, up | Tentative, informal | One-way, down | Two-way, open, candid, full |
| Conflict | Neutrality, double-talk | "Yes man," keeping in touch, yielding, smoothing | Splitting the difference, compromise, straddle the fence, tentativeness, testing the wind | Fixed position-taking, downgrading, taunts, suppression | Experimentation; facts, data, logic, confrontation; "law of the situation" |
| Counseling Biases, if any | Inaction or acceptant | Acceptant | Catalytic, facilitative | Prescriptive, confrontation | Confrontation, theory |

| Facades | Don't care | Praise, flattery, "yes man" | Flexibility, friendliness, using cliques, "gamesman" | Tough guy, intimidation | Reputation-building, showing concern for others, incomplete delegation, psuedo-team-work |
|---|---|---|---|---|---|
| **Consequences** | **1,1** | **1,9** | **5,5** | **9,1** | **9,9** |
| Basis for Boss-Subordinate Coordination | Acquiescence | Dependence | Consent | Compliance | Consensus |
| Subordinate Reactions | Going all out, leaving, apathy | Security; resentment and frustration, stifle creativity, leaving | Like begets like, "statistical" 5,5 drifting into 1,1 | Fighting back, resentful, anti-organization creativity; passive-compliance, hiding and forgetting, escape | "Can do" spirit, "it's too much to ask…it's impractical." |
| Organization Characteristics | Bankrupt, caretaker situation | Welfare state orientation, country club | Bureaucracy, establishment "politics" | Command structure, reinforced by inspection | Functional, dynamic, purposeful |
| Longer-Term Organization Implications | Drift towards actual bankruptcy | High expense, low production | Average production | Good production, short run | High production and return on investment |
| Career Success | 5th, poorest | 4th, next to poorest | 3rd or 2nd best | 2nd and 3rd best | 1st, best |
| Mental | Emotional resignation | Masochism | Excessive worry | Sadism | Good spirits, respect and admiration |
| Physical | TB, cancer, "premature" death. | Asthma, diabetes, hypertension (with 9,1 backup) | Peptic ulcer | Heart attack, migraine | Good health |

**Table 14-1 (continued)**

| Dynamics | 1,1 | 1,9 | 5,5 | 9,1 | 9,9 |
|---|---|---|---|---|---|
| +Motivations | Survival | Gaining acceptance, approval | Belonging, being popular, "in" | Control, master, dominate | Contribution, caring |
| –Motivations | Avoidance of dismissal or expulsion | Fear of rejection | Worry about ostracism, being "out" | Dread of failure | Disappointment |
| Core Emotions | "Empty," numb | Fear | Anxiety | Anger, temper, rage | Love, affection, and appreciation |
| Thinking modes | Repetitious, sluggish | "Soft," spongy | Stereotypical, mechanical | Rigid, dogmatic, categorical, black-white | Systematic, creative, innovative |
| **Childhood Origins** | 1,1 | 1,9 | 5,5 | 9,1 | 9,9 |
| | Extreme coerciveness, deprivation and neglect, inconsistent expectations; complete indulgence. | Close direction provided with obedience rewarded; rejection with little or no approval given. | Emphasis on being "popular," and living up to expectations of one's peers. | Achievement demanded but is never "enough"; relative deprivation, partial pampering with disobedience punished. | Parents have a systematic model of development; unconditional love with cooperative parent/child activities, autonomy for actions with limits. |

**Table 14-2**
**Assessment of My Grid Styles**

| Initial | | | Revised | | |
|---|---|---|---|---|---|
| Paragraphs | Elements | | Paragraphs | Elements | |
| A(1,1) ____ | 1. Decisions | ____ | A(1,1) ____ | 1. Decisions | ____ |
| B(1,9) ____ | 2. Convictions | ____ | B(1,9) ____ | 2. Convictions | ____ |
| C(5,5) ____ | 3. Conflict | ____ | C(5,5) ____ | 3. Conflict | ____ |
| D(9,1) ____ | 4. Temper | ____ | D(9,1) ____ | 4. Temper | ____ |
| E(9,9) ____ | 5. Humor | ____ | E(9,9) ____ | 5. Humor | ____ |
| | 6. Effort | ____ | | 6. Effort | ____ |

evaluate how you were thinking about your approach to management before studying this book, and the choices as you have just reranked them to evaluate your managerial approach. In addition, it provides opportunity to consider whether you wish to change your managerial behavior, and if so, in what direction.

Did you come out as predominantly 9,9? Or was it 9,1; 1,9; 1,1; or 5,5? If what you saw was 9,9, is that the real you? Is your approach really from a 9,9 direction, or is it possible that you have misread yourself? We know that self-deception is common, as indicated in the following study.

### Deception in Self-Assessment

Managers from all organization levels evaluated themselves by choosing Grid paragraphs just as you did in Chapter 1. Then they attended a Grid seminar to study their own Grid style assumptions, similar to the Seminar described in Chapter 13. Each participant received written feedback from his colleagues concerning the dominant and backup Grid styles they had observed in his problem-solving and decision-making behavior during the week's discussions. The feedback was in the form of paragraphs written around the elements: Decisions, Convictions, Conflict, etc. Yet it was a tailor-made description of his specific and concrete behavior. Then, he reexamined himself by reranking the Grid paragraphs again to describe what he saw to be his own dominant and backup Grid styles.

As can be seen in Table 14-3, a large shift in self-assessment, particularly with respect to the 9,9 Grid style, occurred between the first self-assessment and the second. Prior to the seminar 69.2% saw themselves as having a 9,9 orientation. After the Grid seminar 24.6% saw themselves as being 9,9.

**Table 14-3**
**Self-Ranking of Dominant Grid Styles**
**Pre and Post Seminar Attendance**

| Grid Styles | % Self-Rankings of Dominant Grid Style | |
|---|---|---|
| | Pre | Post |
| 9,9 | 69.2 | 24.6 |
| 9,1 | 14.0 | 34.9 |
| 5,5 | 14.7 | 34.5 |
| 1,9 | 1.8 | 4.8 |
| 1,1 | 0.3 | 1.2 |

How can we account for this reduction of 44.6%? There are several explanations:

1. *Better understanding.* A more thorough comprehension of the concepts makes it possible to be more objective. You can't see as well in a foggy mirror.
2. *Self-deception.* When a person looks inside himself, he is likely to misjudge what he finds. He looks at his intentions. Most people have good intentions that correspond generally with a 9,9 orientation, but the individual is unlikely to see his own behavior which may be, and often is, contradictory to his good intentions.
3. *New data.* When people receive feedback as to how others see their behavior, they may learn things about themselves which they previously had not recognized. With this new information, they can see themselves more objectively.

It is important that this tendency toward self-deception be considered in examining your rankings in Chapter 1. You may very well be accurate if you designated the 9,9 paragraph as your first choice. But the data indicate that there is a 50-50 chance that such a choice is inaccurate.

If your first choice is still 9,9, with these cautions in mind, you may wish to rethink your rankings of the paragraphs to see if they reveal your most objective reflection of your management.

Evidence suggests that the best managers—those who get to the top in terms of career progress at a faster than average rate—tend toward a pattern of 9,9; 9,1; 5,5; 1,9; and finally 1,1. If you want to figure out your Managerial Achievement Quotient (MAQ), the formula is

$$MAQ = \frac{5(9-L)}{60-A} \times 100$$

where $L$ represents your level in the organization hierarchy, with the top man being at level 1 and the first-line supervisor at level 8. If you are neither at the top nor at the front line, see how many levels you are down from the top and use that number. However, if yours is a very steep organizational structure and there are more than eight levels, then estimate where your level would be relative to an eight-level organization. $A$ represents age up to 59 years. If you are under 20 years of age, use 20 for $A$. This means that if you are 59 and at the top you have an MAQ of 100. If you are 59 years old and not at the top, your MAQ is less than 100. If you are less than 59 and at the top, your MAQ is greater than 100. If you are, say, a vice-president at the age of 39, your MAQ would be 166, indicating that your rate of advancement is far greater than the average. Middle achievers have scores in the neighborhood of 100, say from 90 to 110, while high achievers are in the range above. Low achievers are below that range.

5,5 seems to be the backup theory for those who achieve average success. Compare the two paragraph descriptions which follow to get a feel for the difference between Manager A, who has a dominant 9,9 orientation with a 9,1 backup and Manager B, who has a dominant 9,9 orientation with a 5,5 backup.

*Manager A* places high value on reaching agreement towards sound, creative decisions. He looks for and seeks out opinions from others to thoroughly explore a point. He responds to sound ideas by changing his mind. His manner creates an open and stabilizing effect on the group and he displays an evenness of temper. His humor is used to give perspective. He is aggressive and if continually opposed, will hold out for his ideas at the expense of good feelings.

*Manager B* is very active in promoting and seeking out ideas from others that result in agreement, understanding, and sound decisions. He does not avoid conflict even when it does occur. He tends at times to fall back on precedent and established procedures. His temper is well controlled but he evidences impatience at times. He retains a sense of humor even under stress.

The differences between the descriptions of Managers A and B make it clear that Manager A makes a stronger contribution to quality decisions. Manager A creates an openness through which differences can be explored, while Manager B falls back on precedents and procedures to resolve disagreements.

The pattern of 9,1 followed by a 9,9 backup reverses the pattern of 9,9 followed by a 9,1 backup. Though the strategies of management are the same, they are in different sequences and proportions. 9,1 followed by 9,9 is the less successful. An examination of a paragraph for Manager C offers suggestions as to why this is so.

*Manager C* places high value on getting sound decisions that are understood and agreed upon. He knows he can make good decisions, and occasionally is too aggressive and too quick to allow the group to develop to its full potential. He tends to go too fast, anticipating others' viewpoints and tending to suppress them in this manner. When faced with conflict, he tries to identify reasons for it and to resolve it. He uses conflict to gain understanding; can be stimulated by conflict, causing occasional trends toward suppressive tendencies. He rarely loses his temper, even when stirred up, but tends to be impatient when things are not moving. His humor tends to be hard hitting—could be used more often to good advantage.

Manager C is dedicated to outcomes, but the abrasiveness with which he involves others in deliberations and his tendency to shut out ideas may explain to some extent why the 9,1 followed by 9,9 sequence is less frequently characterized by those whose rate is most rapid.

Managers with the highest rate of advancement are rarely characterized by a 1,9 or 1,1 dominant Grid style-orientation regardless of backup. An indication of why this is so can be seen by evaluating the following paragraphs for Managers D, a manager with a dominant 1,9 approach, and E, a manager with a dominant 1,1 approach.

*Manager D* works very hard to keep everything harmonious. Even though he expresses his opinions, he does it without being "pushy." He is the first to soothe feelings when conflict arises by injecting humor which shifts the controversy. He never allows himself to lose his temper, but espouses a philosophy of forebearance.

*Manager E* is a very methodical person who keeps to himself as much as possible. He makes decisions alone only when he must. He never expresses his opinions but remains silent in the midst of conflict. When he becomes disturbed, he withdraws from the situation in order to avoid losing his temper. He is completely humorless.

Neither Manager D nor E is characterized by the kind of strength that is likely to result in bosses choosing them for rapid advancement. How do your rankings compare? How did you order the paragraphs to depict yourself?

## Choosing Grid Elements

Next, you should examine the Grid elements you selected in Chapter 1 to picture your most characteristic approach to Decisions, Convictions, Conflict, Temper, Humor, and Effort.

Do your elements fit together, that is, do they all come from the same Grid style or are they picked from different positions? Again you will have to judge the meaning of consistency or discrepancy. Analyzing your elements will aid you in identifying your strengths and weaknesses.

*Manager F* has a 9,1 dominant theory. He enjoys the competition inherent in decision-making, taking a determined stand toward making decisions which stick. He strongly defends convictions and manipulates the group to prove a point. He enjoys conflict that he can stimulate; his baiting approach is generally used to control unproductive conflict, but frequently acts to the detriment of discussion progress. Occasionally he is impatient to the point of detracting from listening ability. He uses a generally hard-hitting humor to sell himself.

*Manager G:* This description is of a manager with a 9,1 dominant theory and a 9,9 backup. He drives aggressively towards making decisions, using the contributions of others if possible, but not if delay is involved in obtaining them. His standards are high, and although he recognizes the high value of decisions based on understandings and agreement under pressure, he will rely on confidence in his own judgment. He is deliberate, precise, determined, and self-confident. In the face of conflict, he will try to win his own position immediately unless the opposing point of view has strong merit. His temper and impatience are well controlled. His humor fits the situation, and he retains it under pressure.

The paragraph describing Manager F is internally consistent in that each element contains 9,1 assumptions. In comparison, Manager G has a 9,9 backup reflected in the Decisions and Conflict element and in Temper and Humor elements where 9,9 is dominant.

To give you a basis of comparison for the ways in which the various elements fit together, here are several additional paragraph descriptions.

*Manager H* has a 1,9 dominant theory and a 5,5 backup. He prides himself on being known as the "peacemaker" and strives to create a jovial atmosphere at work at all times. Before making a decision, he gets the opinions of all his group and leans in the majority direction. If conflict arises, he is immediately on top of things, soothing feelings. He has a joke for every occasion. He never loses his temper but has a way of shifting the topic of conversation when he is confronted with a controversial issue.

*Manager I* has a dominant 1,1 and a backup 5,5 theory. He participates in discussions in a procedural way by asking others for their opinions and summarizing their viewpoints. When pinned to the wall for an opinion, he always balances a positive statement with a negative one. Where tension arises he suggests ways in which action can be tabled until things "cool off." He does not appear to respond to pressure but always remains calm and optimistic.

*Manager J* has a dominant 1,1 and a 1,9 backup theory. He usually accepts the opinions and attitudes of others, especially if he feels that to express his own opinion might cause personal rejection. If conflict does arise, however he tries to remain neutral. Even though a situation tends to disturb him, he pouts or withdraws instead of openly losing his temper. He is either humorless or aims at maintaining friendly relations.

You may want to stop reading and, using the elements of Decisions, Convictions, Conflict, Temper, Humor, and Effort, write a single paragraph that really fits you.

You can compare this with those just given and draw your own conclusions as to whether or not any changes would enable you to become a more effective manager.

## Chapter 15

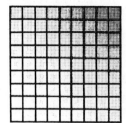

# Trends and Practices Likely in the Future

Archaeological findings have established that man in essentially his current physical form and brain capacity has existed for millions of years. The history of organizing production to benefit society cannot be more than 15,000 years old. So what we think of as "modern" culture is actually a quite recent development. By the time of Christ the transition was well advanced, marked by many shifts from precultural to cultural ways of doing things as we now know them. Two of these changes are of utmost importance in understanding where we stand today and the direction in which things are likely to develop.

### Precorporate Evolution

The first shift was from man the hunter to man the herder. As a hunter he had lived from day to day and hand-to-mouth to supply himself with food and clothing. As a herder he captured the notion of building and maintaining a reserve of food that ensured a supply over extended periods of time. The second great change parallels the first shift. This was transformation from gathering food from nature fortuitously, that is, picking berries, fruits, slugs, and so on, to planting, harvesting, or, in other words, agriculture. Agriculture had the same effects as the shift from hunting to herding. It further helped to stabilize populations, and it created a need to plan, organize, direct, and staff to control records, inventory, money, and other resources.

Beyond these influences that produced the foundations of modern society was the development and commercialization of whole crops of vegetables that had only previously existed in a wild state. Thus, vegetables we find on our tables today were unknown before this time, including beans, lettuce, cauliflower, and potatoes. Wheat and rice may have grown previously under natural conditions, but their use could now be expanded. Eventually these two sources of nutrition became more important to the expanding population than most of the rest.

Another impact was that populations stabilized. People ceased to be wanderers in food-gathering families and tribes. In turn, the regularities of the lunar year were recognized, possibly because they were important benchmarks for planting and had to be explained. This introduced possibly the first science, astronomy. Another development, education, became necessary so that some could maintain records by writing, assess quantities by counting, and engage in transactions, using symbols and mental processes rather than relying upon direct perception.

A system of commercial exchange led to a mercantile society, which used the counting systems, writing systems, records. and so on. It followed that the accountant and the need for a currency to keep accounts in balance was introduced to the world scene.

How all this happened and why it occurred at the particular time and place that it did—probably the Mesopotamian Basin—is unclear to historians, archaeologists, and anthropologists. What is clear is that a chain of events was set in motion, possibly triggered by the discovery of abstract writing, which continues to develop and change quite rapidly.

As can be imagined, these activities taking place in food-producing villages, but without an organized social system designed to regulate their interactions, raised the question of how men should treat one another to gain the material benefits possible and yet retain independence from the influence of others to direct and control them. In turn, both of these shifts created many of the other ingredients of an industrial society. For example, the problem of ownership arose. The land that made herding and farming possible became more valuable than land that was unsuited for such purposes. In the absence of rules of order and justice such that lands might have been held in a common trust or shared in some cooperative way, private ownership came to those who could protect what they held.

These aspects of the development of business and the commercialization of life during the last couple of centuries probably led to the crystallization of free enterprise as a way of acknowledging initiative. Most important, these changes created the need for organizations to protect property and mediate disputes, as well as to regulate orderly relationships and arrangements among those engaged in commercial and other transactions. Initially, a government controlled only a city. Then cities became city-states, then they expanded further, taking on the shapes and boundaries and characteristics that governments of nations have today.

Taking the multimillion-year span of man's life and placing it beside the 12,000 to 15,000-year period during which industrial cultures have been taking shape provides a dramatic picture of how young the societies we call "modern" actually are.

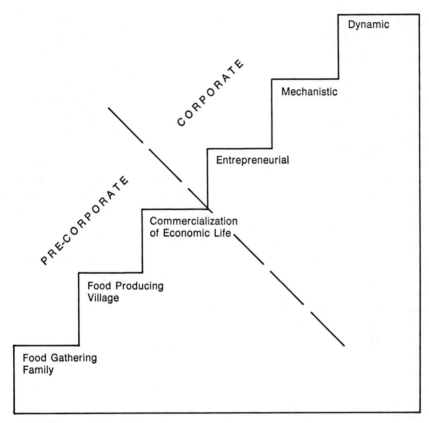

*Figure 15-1. Stages of corporate evolution.*

The changes occurring through this period are reflected in the six-stage chart shown in Figure 15-1.

## Corporate Evolution

After the first three stages another aspect of modern society emerged that is critical to the manner in which society operates. The corporation was a social discovery of first importance and one that permitted the further commercialization of economic life. The first charter that might be called a legal basis for organizing an economic corporation was issued at some unrecorded time, but experts place its real beginning within the past 500 years. This charter possibly authorized commercial trade under the Hanseatic League. It probably had earlier precedents in the organization of the Catholic Church and may have been modeled on the notions of organization used by the Church. However that may be, corporate commercial life was made possible by governments that authorized individual persons or groups of members of the country to engage in commercial activities, not as individuals and not as direct representatives of the government, but as indirect "organisms" of society created by government and operating under its protection but subject to minimum regulations. The procedure of issuing charters became popular and served as the basis for expeditions, such as that by Columbus, educational institutions such as Oxford, Cambridge, Heidelberg, or Harvard, and other arrangements of society no longer left to private enterprise. For example, there were tax farmers who would buy from the king the right to collect the country's taxes, hoping that the king had underestimated the amount of revenue available. In the 1700's there were even proprietary army regiments, regular army regiments raised by a private gentleman under contract from the government.

As shown in Figure 15-1, it would appear from an evolutionary point of view that the original organizations were highly entrepreneurial, characterized by a 9,1 orientation. Strong-willed men exercised initiative for their own selfish gain. This may explain the emergence of the industrial revolution, which, as we now look back on it, was a highly entrepreneurial and highly exploitative period in the history of Western societies. For example, many of the great entrepreneurs lived and died within the current century: Henry Ford, inventor of the Model T; Sewell Avery, the dominating personality of Montgomery Ward; Jay Gould, the railroad baron; Will Durant, who created the General Motors Company, as well as the Rockefellers, Mellons, DuPonts, and so on.

With the growth of organizations came the introduction of government restraints to curb excesses of exploitation, the expansion of education, the introduction of new technology, and other influences. Entrepreneurial initiative became insufficient. Not only did size alone make it impractical for one person to direct a particular organization, but the later generations of leadership rarely had the initiative displayed by the first. As a result, organizations began to develop rationale for their operations by designing tables of organization, by preparing policies, procedures, regulations and rules, and by creating job descriptions. As leadership became less centered in one "great man," increased reliance was placed on organization structure, policies, procedures, etc. This moved commercial life into the 5,5-oriented mechanistic or bureaucratic era, which is very characteristic of present-day large organizations. In broad terms the shift was from a dominant 9,1 style of managing to a more 5,5-oriented role-established, norm-regulated basis for conducting modern business and government agencies.

Many observers see the current strong emphasis upon a 5,5 orientation as a relatively new and yet important organization style. It is a conservative approach to progress and change that relies on many infinitely small changes from the status quo, with change by reasonable men adjusting their differences through compromise.

The great risk, however, is that change approached in this manner may be too slow. As this trend strengthens, it may create such a heavy burden of unsolved problems as to promote new crises. Evidence of the likelihood of this is everywhere and points with clarity to the conclusion that 5,5 mechanistic, bureaucratic organizations are less productive, and employment in them less gratifying to their members than it could be through involvement, participation, and commitment to problem solving.

Some few organizations in the third stage are approaching the character and dynamics of a 9,9 organization as described in Chapter 7.

## Evolutionary Trends

Changes in managerial relations among those who perform within organizations parallel these broader changes.

### Away from 9,1

From an historical point of view, change seems to be away from the raw 9,1 control of master-slave, knight-serf, foreign master-native, entrepreneur-worker arrangements. It also seems to be away from the Protestant ethic of hard work, self-control, and the denial of enjoyment in the pursuit of perfection. Furthermore, the 9,1 spirit seems less able to exert itself against the rules and regulations of legislation in the temper of the times. However, 9,1 remains the most common approach. Much of it is to be found in the more polished 9,1 orientation, as described in Chapter 3. Competitive economic pressures being what they are, particularly from recessions, etc., substantial managerial actions continue to be the sort that gets production or else, even as the "raw" 9,1 did. However, in spite of the increased number of managers operating today, 9,1 practice is probably less evident than before.

If this conclusion is correct, then a critical question is, "Toward what kind of managerial relationships is the management of work likely to move and why?" A related question is, "Can thoughtful men exercise deliberate influence over the direction of development, rather than allowing themselves to be carried into its next phases, unable to shape the currents of corporate culture that guide and control their action?"

In addition to those factors already mentioned that tend to preserve or reinforce a 9,1 orientation, there are other forces that press for a shift of managerial practices into all of the other styles.

## Toward 1,1

Some factors are driving evolution in the 1,1 direction, such as machines, the simplification of work, and assembly techniques that completely control decision making and eliminate the thinking part of work. This leaves men idle—watching and monitoring but neither thinking nor acting with emotion or involvement. However, actual automation, as opposed to mere mechanization, almost always frees people from repetitive, mind-deadening tasks. A result is that men at all levels of organizations are being released from doing work that is better done by machines. Beyond that, complex developments such as the revolution in technology, tools, and materials introduce new problems and possibilities that require more thought, effort, and challenge than ever. Barring an international holocaust, a severe depression, or an energy catastrophe, the possibility of evolution trending mainly in the 1,1 direction seems quite remote.

## Toward 1,9

A welfare society, in the extreme of its development, makes few or no demands and provides unqualified approval, comfort, and social togetherness while asking little or no effort in return. This seems to constitute a major trend particularly in modern political democracies that exchange votes for welfare security. As private ownership and antitrust laws erode and free enterprise profit motivations lose genuine meaning, the 1,9 style is likely to spread. Certain utilities and near monopolies are drifting in this direction. When competition is no threat, effort carries little real reward. Convenience and congeniality become their most characteristic feature. Over the longer term even these possibilities of evolution are likely only to be arrested if the self-correcting counterforces of competition are strengthened.

## Toward 5,5

As described earlier in connection with the mechanistic stage, many pressures are promoting trends of evolution in the direction of 5,5. One factor is the increasing unpopularity of 9,1. As managers abandon this style, while lacking the skills to shift to 9,9, they choose 5,5 over 1,1 and 1,9, thus creating a strong trend in the 5,5 direction. Indeed, 5,5 appears to be the second most widely practiced organization theory today, and this is a substantial increase since the 1950s, at least in large corporations.

Forces that culminate in a 5,5 adjustment are powerful and increasing. As companies grow, they rely more on bureaucratic arrangements for management and supervision. Systems, guidelines, and handbooks define the status quo, and majority-oriented decision making ensures that conformity and uniformity prevails. The institutionalization of rewards distributed mechanically by seniority, rather than according to merit and contribution, tends to reinforce conformity and adherence to the status quo and the safety it seems to confer.

Another push toward 5,5 comes from adopting as natural the concepts and procedures of politics and using them in managerial situations. Compromise and emphasis on the majority rule, as contrasted with genuine understanding and agreement, have far different and less desirable consequences for managerial problem solving and decision making.

In a similar manner, the 5,5 tactics of bargaining, prevalent in union-management relations between autonomous groups of relatively equal power, seem to fall short when they become the model for relations between individuals and groups within a management system. Union-management agreements tend to reinforce 5,5 problem solving because many give security and consideration in exchange for some managerial flexibility without actually solving many of the real problems associated with production or security. As a result, solutions to problems of people and production are approached with a 5,5 attitude, thus producing un-witting transference into other walks of managerial life. The transfer of such strategies from politics and union-management relations to manager-manager relations seems to be taking place without too much thought for the consequences.

Finally, the 5,5 style, even though lacking in excellence, is more or less "acceptable." From the performance side, it does get some of the job done, albeit imperfectly. From the managerial side, it gives people, if not genuine personal gratification and reward, many of the symbols of status and a reasonably acceptable level of security. 5,5, embracing ex-pedience and empiricism, is bound to produce mediocrity. 5,5 does repre-sent conformity and adjustment because it responds to the need for change while searching for a precedent. Through the emergence of the large public corporations and the disappearance of the entrepreneur, the period ahead may well be one where this nature and amount of adjust-ment is accepted as enough. 5,5 may become the new status quo, the new point of equilibrium among men in organizations, the established way.

## Toward 9,9

There are other pressures, however, against 9,1 domination and mastery, 1,1 resignation and abandonment, 1,9 support and approval, or 5,5 accommodation and adjustment. They point toward the 9,9 direction.

Education, constantly on the march, provides new insight and skills, introduces new possibilities, and excites new appetites for something better than that which now exists. Cultural concepts of excellence leave people uneasy with conditions that fail to match what they know is attainable. Standards from advanced education place high value on doing things in the "best" way. Another trend is the steady improvement in merit-based compensation systems that result in their rewarding 9,9 contribution and commitment, which lead to relations that are open, communicative, and problem solving, rather than closed, suspicious, and problem generating.

The search goes on unceasingly for better ways to manage than anything known in the past. As important as any factor in establishing 9,9 as an evolutionary trend is the emergence of applied behavioral science education-within-industry through organization development of the kind described in Chapter 13. These methods, coupled with a growing body of behavioral science concepts, are exerting a definite pull in the direction of 9,9.

Evaluating the strength of each of these trends in comparison with the others leads us to believe that the 5,5 orientation will continue to rise. It will peak some years ahead when managers come to recognize the erosion of will that it produces and the adverse consequences of it for a business society that continues to lose its capacity to compete. The direction evolution eventually will take seems clear although attitudes about 9,9 vary. The 9,1 attitude toward it is pessimistic. 5,5 sees it as impractical, 1,9 as too demanding, and 1,1 as impossible.

Those who have studied and experimented with 9,9 as an organizational style recognize that it is attainable. Those who come by it naturally know what they want. They want the self-respect that comes from respect for others at work. They want meaningful relationships with the productivity and creativity that only mutual respect built around common purpose can sustain. The trend toward 9,9 is sound, and the great challenge is to create conditions so that it can be brought into use on a wider scale.

## Summary

Managerial styles based on 9,1 direction with compliance, 5,5 conformity with compromise, 1,9 security and comfort, or 1,1 acquiescence, resignation, and abandonment are no more than second best. They are unacceptable in the long-term. Compared with performance under a 9,9 orientation, with its condition of candid communication based on conviction, commitment, and creativity, and boss-subordinate relationships based on mutual respect, other approaches fall far short. The deeper trends of social evolution seem to move in directions that add meaning to mental effort and social experience.

A 9,9 orientation defines a trend leading to mature relationships and many production organizations seem to be moving toward this direction. Achievement of such a 9,9 orientation may be the key to strengthening the free enterprise system and the political democracy on which it rests. Then, a thinking society—which is also thoughtful—will have been achieved.

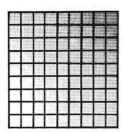

# Appendix

## Use of the Grid to Analyze Behavioral Science Approaches to Human Relationships

The original use of the Grid to analyze interactions between significant variables of management—production and people—occurred in our efforts as consultants to understand a basic conflict in a top management group. One faction maintained that, "If we don't put the pressure on for higher production, we're going to sink." The other faction said, "We must ease up on the pressure and start treating people in a nicer way." Thus, a 9,1 orientation met a 1,9 orientation. This either production *or* people way of conceiving the problem eliminated perception of other possibilities such as getting people involved in the importance of being more productive.

By treating these variables of production and people as independent yet interacting, we came to see many alternative ways of managing: not only 9,1 and 1,9 but also 1,1, 5,5, 9,9, paternalism, counterbalancing, two-hat, statistical 5,5, and facades as presented earlier.

A way of thinking about human relationships that permitted such clear comprehension and comparison of alternatives led us to believe this formulation to be of general significance for understanding other human relationships. Thus we evaluated in greater detail how others had tried to deal with the same kind of question.

We found no systematic use of a two-dimensional geometric space as the foundation for conceptual analysis of assumptions about how to manage, but we were struck by the extent to which such a basis of analysis was being used, either implicitly or statistically. Theorists who used two variables *implicitly*, and without identification of the variables involved, included Horney and Fromm. Other theorists who approached the situation *statistically*, without explicit analysis of how assumptions and therefore behavior may change as a function of the character of the interaction of these variables, included Likert and Fleishman.

Table A-1 shows the various implicit or statistical approaches for comprehending human relationships that can be fitted into a Grid

*(Text continued on page 231)*

**Table A-1***

**Catalog of Approaches**

**to Human Relationships Through**

**a Grid Framework**

| Investigator | Source | Field | 9,1 | 1,9 | 1,1 | 5,5 | 9,9 | Statistical 5,5 | Facades | Paternalism | Other |
|---|---|---|---|---|---|---|---|---|---|---|---|
| Argyris, C. | *Management and Organizational Development: The Path From XA to YB.* New York: McGraw-Hill, 1971. | Organization Behavior | xi,xii,6-15,66-70, 73-74,77-78,85-88, 105,107, 134,135, 138-140 | | | 13-14, 30-34, 56-57 | xi,15-20,21-22,24, 42,57-61,67-70,85-89 | | 19 | 3,62 | |
| Argyris, C. & Schön, D. A. | *Theory in Practice: Increasing Professional Effectiveness.* San Francisco: Jossey-Bass, 1974. | Business Administration | 66-84, 101-102, 104, 105-106, 107-108, 149-155 | | | | 85-95, 101,102-104,105, 106-107, 108-109 | | | | |
| Bach, G. R. & Wyden, P. | *The Intimate Enemy.* New York: William Morrow and Company, Inc., 1969. | Psychology | 8-9,45-46,48-49, 71-73,75, 83,109-117,129, 141-150, 256-257, 311,312, 314 | 5,48,71-73,84-85, 97,102-108,311, 314,321-322 | 31-32, 312 | 5, 53-54, 135-136 | 36,43, 53,91, 119,123, 137,161-165,257-258,343-348 | | 7,10,13, 19,36, 103,120, 159,196-197,222-223,253-254 | 113 | Sick 9,1: 112-113, 151,158, 160,260 Distorted 1,9: 75, 112,154, 158,160, 260,331 Change: 173-174 |
| Bales, R. F. | *Personality and Interpersonal Behavior.* New York: Holt, R..ne-hart & Winston, 1970. | Sociology | 193-199, 213-219, 220-229, 230-237 | 200-207, 252-257, 313-319, 320-326, 369-376 | 289-296, 332-339, 340-346, 347-353, 354-360, 361-368, 377-386 | 191, 258-264, 265-272, 327-331 | 208-212 | 190, 273-281 | | | Balanced 5,5: 191 Machiavellianism: 238-244 |

*Reproduced by permission from Blake, R. R., and J. S. Mouton. *"The Grid as a Comprehensive Framework for Analyzing Human Relationships."* Austin, Texas: Scientific Methods, Inc., 1977.

**Table A-1 (continued)**

| Investigator | Source | Field | 9,1 | 1,9 | 1,1 | 5,5 | 9,9 | Statistical 5,5 | Facades | Paternalism | Other |
|---|---|---|---|---|---|---|---|---|---|---|---|
| Barber, J. D. | *The Presidential Character.* Englewood Cliffs, N.J.: Prentice-Hall, 1972. | Applied Politics Political Science | 12-13,17-57,58-98, 99-142, 347-395, 413-442, 446-448 | 13,91, 173-206, 448-450 | 13,145-163,165, 166-167 | 170-173 | 12, 209-343, 452-454 | 79,86, 92-93 | 83 | 60,91 | Two Hat: 86,87 Critique: 277-278, 331 |
| Bell, G. D. | *The Achievers.* Chapel Hill, N.C.: Preston-Hill, Inc, 1973. | Business | 23-38, 39-59, 132-152 | 73-83, 164-171 | 60-72, 153-163 | | 104-124, 181-187 | | 84-103, 172-180, 188-195 | | |
| Benne, K. D. & Sheats, P. | "Functional Roles of Group Members." *Journal of Social Issues* 4, no. 2 (1948): 41-49. | Clinical Psychology | 45,46 | 44,45, 46 | 45 | 44 | 44 | | 46 | | |
| Bennett, D. | *TA and the Manager.* New York: AMACON, 1976. | Business Consultant | 14,19,26-27,30-32, 122,145, 146-150, 161-162, 164-165, 230 | 14,26-27,32, 122,160-161,168-170,230-231 | 79,80, 145, 153-154, 160-161 | 18-19, 79-82, 129-137, 145,150-153 | 26-27, 81,82-83,139-140,145, 154-157, 178,194-196,230 | | 81,82, 91-116 | 231 | Dom/Backup: 151-152,181 Wide Arc: 230 |
| Berne, E. | *Games People Play.* New York: Grove Press, 1964. | Psychiatry | 27,112, 113 | 25-26 | | | 27, 178-179, 180-181, 182-183, 184 | | 48-168 | | |
| Bion, W. R. | *Experiences in Groups.* New York: Basic Books, 1959. | Psychoanalysis | 152-153 | 147-150 | 152-153 | 150-152 | 156-158, 169 | | | | Dom/Backup: 160-165 |
| Blake, R. R. & Mouton, J. S. | *The Grid for Sales Excellence: Benchmarks for Effective Salesmanship.* New York: McGraw-Hill, 1970. | Social Psychology | 45-58 | 59-69 | 70-79 | 80-94 | 95-118 | 187 | 125-136 | 188 | Dom/Backup: 13-15 |

| | Reference | Discipline | 11-28 | 29-43 | 44-58 | 59-78 | 79-107 | | | | Dom/Backup |
|---|---|---|---|---|---|---|---|---|---|---|---|
| Blake, R. R. & Mouton, J. S. | *The Grid for Supervisory Effectiveness.* Austin: Scientific Methods, Inc., 1975. | Social Psychology | | | | | 79-107 | | | | Dom/Backup: 8-9 |
| Branden, N. | *The Psychology of Self-Esteem.* New York: Bantam Books, 1969. | Psychiatry | 188-190 | 150,151 | 194-195 | 185-188 | 109-139, 146 | | | | |
| Burns, T. & Stalker, G. M. | *The Management of Innovation.* New York: Barnes & Noble, Social Science Paperbacks, 1961. | Organization Behavior | 96-125 | | | | 96-125 | | | | |
| Buzzotta, V. R., Lefton, R. E., Sherberg, M. | *Effective Selling Through Psychology: Dimensional Sales and Sales Management Strategies.* New York: Wiley Interscience, 1972. | Clinical Psychology | 36-53, 99-100a, 120-121, 127,264-270,285-286,301-318,319, 320-324,338-339,344-347,357-358,358-359 | 68-82, 99-100a, 122-124, 127,274-277,287-288,301-318,319,327-331,340-341,344-347,358,359 | 54-67, 99-100a, 121-122, 127,270-274,286-287,301-318,319,324-327,339-340,344-347,358,359 | | 83-98, 99-100a, 124,125, 127,199-224,277-283,288-289,301-318,319,331-334,341-343,344-347,358,359-360 | | 113-117, 291-292 | | Dom/Backup: 101-112, 289-291 |
| Durkheim, E. | "On Anomie." In C. W. Mills, ed., *Images of Man: The Classic Tradition in Sociological Thinking.* New York: George Braziller, Inc., 1960, pp. 449-485. | Sociology | 455-461 | 460 | 460-461 | 449-461 | | | | | |

**Table A-1 (continued)**

| Investigator | Source | Field | 9,1 | 1,9 | 1,1 | 5,5 | 9,9 | Statistical 5.5 | Facades | Paternalism | Other |
|---|---|---|---|---|---|---|---|---|---|---|---|
| Etzioni, A. | *A Comparative Analysis of Complex Organizations*, (Rev. ed.). New York: Free Press, 1975. | Sociology | xxiv,5-6, 8,12,15, 27-31,56-59,60-61, 66-67,75-82,84,106, 115,116-118,133, 287,455-460,471, 479,486-490,500-504 | | 28,289 | xxiv,5-6 6-8,12, 15,40-54, 56-59,61-72,78,81-82,89,92, 106,114 11?,169, 305-311, 426-427, 455-460, 471,479 486-490 500-504 | 471 | 433-436, 437-438 | | xxiv,5, 6-8,12, 15,31-39, 62-67,72-75,78-82, 84-87,89, 106,112-113,116, 271,389-391,426-427,455-460,471, 479,486-490,500-504 | Machiavellianism: 387 |
| Fleishman, E. A. | "Twenty Years of Consideration and Structure." In E. A. Fleishman and J. G. Hunt, eds., *Current Developments in the Study of Leadership.* Carbondale: Southern Illinois University Press, 1973, pp. 1-40. | Industrial Psychology | 25-26, 26-27, 29,32 | 23,25, 26-27, 29 | 26-27, 29,32, 36,37 | 29 | 23-24, 24-25, 26-27, 27-29, 32,35, 37 | 37 | | | |
| Fromm, E. | *The Art of Loving.* London: Unwin Books, 1957. | Psychiatry | 23,25, 31,43, 54-55 | 9,23,25, 42-43, 55-56 | 15-16, 23,83-84 | 10-11, 18-22, 25,74-76,80 | 24,26-28,29, 42,53-54,87, 104-109 | | | 82-83 | |

| Author | Title | Discipline | | | | | | | | |
|---|---|---|---|---|---|---|---|---|---|---|
| Gordon, T. | *Parent Effectiveness Training.* New York: Peter H. Wyden, 1970. | Counseling Psychology | 10-11,41-44,83-86,110-112,113,151,152,153-159,174-183,195,207,248,260-261,263,280,321-322,323-324,325,326-327 | 11,13-14,43-44,151,152,154-155,159-161,184,190-193,248,251-253,324-325,326 | 44,152,183,185,327 | 42-43,110,113,184,289,322-323,324,325-326,327 | 12,30-31,33,47-61,194-264,280-282,305-306 | 261-263 | 22-25 | 11,166,168-169,177-178,190-191 | Wide Arc: 11,161-163 |
| Gordon, T. | *T.E.T.: Teacher Effectiveness Training.* New York: Peter H. Wyden, 1974. | Counseling Psychology | 27-29,48-49,80-84,84-85,86-87,184-185,186,189,191,192-194,198-206,211-216 | 49,85-86,184,186-188,189-190,191,206-207 | 49,87,206-207,208-209 | 208 | 220-282 | | | 194-195,213 | Dom/Backup: 23-24 Wide Arc: 190-191 |
| Harrington, A. | *The Immortalist.* Millbrae, Calif.: Celestial Arts, 1977. | Philosophy | 114,117,118,119,123-127,137,139 | | 117,118,129-130 | 100-101,114-115,117,118,127-129 | 136-139 | | | 120-121 | |
| Harris, T.A. | *I'm OK—You're OK.* New York: Avon, 1969. | Psychiatry | 72-73,263 | 67-69 | 69-71,142-143,152 | 143-146,153 | 74-77,151-152,153,302-304 | | 75-76,146-151,152,262-263 | | |
| Heath, R. | *The Reasonable Adventurer.* Pittsburgh: The University of Pittsburgh Press, 1964. | Clinical Psychology | ix-x,xii,5-6,20-24,38,39,63-67 | 28-29 | | ix,xi,4-5,10-11,14-20,37-38,39,57-63 | ix,x,7,8-10,30-36,39 | x,xii-xiii,6-7,24-28,38,39,67-69 | | | |

**Table A-1 (continued)**

| Investigator | Source | Field | 9.1 | 1.9 | 1.1 | 5.5 | 9.9 | Statistical 5.5 | Facades | Paternalism | Other |
|---|---|---|---|---|---|---|---|---|---|---|---|
| Hersey, P. & Blanchard, K. H. | *Management of Organizational Behavior: Utilizing Human Resources.* (2nd. ed.). Englewood Cliffs, N.J.: Prentice-Hall, 1972. | Education | 35-37,46-48,61,63,70-76,92-93 | 61,63,74-76 | 70-76 | 74-76 | 46-48,61,63,70-76 | 83-86,121-123,127-131 | | 61,63,133-143 | Machiavellianism: 92-93 Wide Arc: 125 Change: 149-171 |
| Horney, K. | *Neurosis and Human Growth.* New York: W. W. Norton & Co., 1950. | Psychoanalysis | 17-39,76,97,191-213,214-215,304-306,311-316 | 76-77,97-98,215-238,239-243,316-324 | 43-44,77-78,259-290,304,324-328 | | | 312-315 | | | Dom/Backup: 232-234 Sick 9.1: 247-256 Distorted 1,9:243-256 |
| Horney, K. | *The Neurotic Personality of Our Time.* New York: W. W. Norton & Co., 1937. | Psychoanalysis | 39,81-82,98,162-187 | 36,85-87,96-98,102-161 | 99,191-192,212-213,237 | 28,96-97 | 104,107,108,109,113,163,273-274 | 100-101 | | | Distorted 1,9:259-280 |
| Horney, K. | *Self-Analysis.* New York: W. W. Norton & Co., 1942. | Psychoanalysis | 44,47-48,56-57,57-58,58-59 | 54-55 | 48-52,55-56,57,58,59-60,62,108 | 58,108 | | | | | Wide Arc: 44 |
| James, M. | *The OK Boss.* Reading, Mass.: Addison-Wesley, 1975. | Adult Education | 10-11,16-17,20-21,35,36,39,40,54,55,56,57,59,61,62,75,76,77,131,139 | 13,18-19,37,39-40,75 | 14-15,35,55,56,57-58,59-61,62,75-76,135,139-140 | 19,37,77,132,144 | 17,21,54,55,56,57,59,61,62,69,76-77,132-133,139,144-145,161-163 | 27,38,64 | 106-121,124-127 | 12-13,35,36,39,73-75 | Dom/Backup: 8-9 |

| | | | | | | | | | | |
|---|---|---|---|---|---|---|---|---|---|---|
| James, M. & Jongeward, D. | *Born To Win: Transactional Analysis with Gestalt Experiments.* Reading, Mass.: Addison-Wesley, 1971. | Education | 18,36,68-100,101-126,230 | 18,37, 127-159, 230-231 | 37,50, 56-57 | 18,57-58, 58-59, 224-226 | 18,36, 56-62, 235-238, 263-274 | 2-3, 227-228 | 29-35, 58 | 86, 229-230 | |
| Jennings, E.E. | *The Executive: Autocrat, Bureaucrat, Democrat.* New York: Harper & Row, 1962. | Business Education | 2,4,20-21,25,66-70,75-77, 83-86,86-90,114-163 | | | 2,4,90-91,91-97, 105-106, 164-195, 228-232 | 2-3,4, 59-61, 97-106, 196-234 | 77-80, 256-266 | 85,250 | 25-26, 149, 157-160 | Dom/Backup: 117 |
| Jung, C. G. | *Psychological Types.* Princeton: Princeton University Press, 1971. | Psychiatry | 346-354, 383-387 | | 385-386, 388-391, 395-398, 401-403, 403-405 | 334-335, 354-355, 356-359, 363-366 | | 368-370 | 384 | | Dom/Backup: 355-356, 362-363, 405-407 |
| Kangas, J.A. & Solomon, G. F | *The Psychology of Strength.* Englewood Cliffs, N.J.: Prentice-Hall, 1975. | Psychology | 7-9,10-11, 14,15-17, 55-56, 56-57, 135-136 | 18-19,22, 24,78 | 20-21, 21-22, 23 | 11-12, 19, 57-58 | 3,9,12, 21,23-24,24-25,68-69,117, 130-135, 136-141, 142-145, 146-150, 151-168 | 26-27 | 13-14,17-18,19-20, 24-25,29-30,56,77 | | Wide Arc: 136 |
| Kovar, L. C. | *Faces of the Adolescent Girl.* Englewood Cliffs, N.J.: Prentice-Hall, 1968. | Adolescent Psychology | 11-12, 73-83, 103-106 | 9-10, 53-68 | 79 | 10-11, 35-51, 83, 148-149 | 4-9, 107-125, 148-149 | | | | |
| Kunkel. F. M. & Dickerson, R.E. | *How Character Develops: A Psychological Interpretation.* New York: Charles Scribner & Sons, 1946. | Psychology | 68-81 | 60-67 | 80-82 | | 125-140, 157-159, 176-178 | | | | |

**Table A-1 (continued)**

| Investigator | Source | Field | 9,1 | 1,9 | 1,1 | 5,5 | 9,9 | Statistical 5,5 | Facades | Paternalism | Other |
|---|---|---|---|---|---|---|---|---|---|---|---|
| Leary, T. | *Interpersonal Diagnosis of Personality.* New York: Ronald Press, 1957. | Clinical Psychology | 19,64-65, 104,105, 135,137, 233,269-281,324-331,332-340 | 64-65, 104,105, 135,233, 292-302, 303-314 | 19,23-24, 64-65,95-96,104, 105,135, 233,282-291 | 19,64-65, 135,202-203,233, 315-322 | 21,64-65, 135,233, 323-324 | | 181-186, 188-191, 282-283, 284-285, 316,317, 318,324, 325,326 | 64-65, 93 | Dom/Backup: 225-227 Distorted 1,9:284-286,288-289,367 Sick 9,1: 341-350, 364,372 |
| Likert, R. | *The Human Organization: Its Management and Value* New York: McGraw-Hill, 1967. | Organization Behavior | 3-12, 13-46 | | | 3-12, 13-46 | 3-12, 13-46, 47-100 | | | 3-12, 13-46 | |
| Likert, R. & Likert, J. G. | *New Ways of Managing Conflict.* New York: McGraw-Hill, 1976. | Organization Behavior | 19-40, 59-69 | | | 19-40 | 16-17, 19-40, 49-51, 51-56, 71-324 | | | 19-40 | |
| McClelland, D. C. | *Power: The Inner Experience.* New York: Irvington Publishers, 1975. | Individual Psychology | 7-8,8-12, 13-21,27, 49-51,52-76,77-78, 249,252-254,255-256,257, 258,260-261,264, 266,274-275,295-297,324, 326,328 | 27,104-122,255, 264,274, 289,322-323,325, 328 | | 27,155, 157-158, 249 | 27,257, 258,260-261,261-263,263-266,269, 288,301-302,324-325,329 | | 301-302 | 35-36, 142-144, 260,289-290 | Distorted 1,9: 102, 104 Sick 9,1: 255 OD: 254, 255 |
| McGregor, D. | *The Human Side of Enterprise.* New York: McGraw-Hill, 1960. | Psychology | 33-43 | | | | 45-57, 61-246 | | | | |

| | | | | | | | | | | | |
|---|---|---|---|---|---|---|---|---|---|---|---|
| McGregor, D. | *The Professional Manager.* New York: McGraw-Hill, 1967. | Psychology | 59-63, 79-80, 117-118, 118-125, 136-137, 138-140, 148-149 | 59-63 | 59-63 | 59-63, 144-145 | 29-30, 59-63, 79-80, 118,127-130,130-133,140, 162-182, 191-195 | | | 7-10, 142-144 | Dom/Backup: 60 |
| Maccoby, M. | *The Gamesman.* New York: Simon & Schuster, 1976. | Psychiatry | 34,47-48, 76-85, 181-182, 183-184, 187-189, 212-213 | 183-187 | 94 | 34,35, 46-47, 48,50-75,86-97,189-209 | 179,212, 213-217 | 100,149 | 48-49, 91,92-93,98-120,121-171 | 240-241 | |
| May, R. | *Love and Will.* New York: W. W. Norton & Co., 1969. | Clinical Psychology | 45-48, 57-59, 276-278 | 278-279 | 27-33 | 40-45, 279 | 55-56, 91-92, 146,283-286,303-304,306, 310-311 | | | | |
| Meininger, J. | *Success Through Transactional Analysis.* New York: New American Library, 1973. | Business Consultant | 26-27, 28-29, 33,39-40,43-44,64-67,73-75,87-90,128-129 | 29-30, 34-36, 38,43-44,45-46,67-71,75-76,90-92,105-106,166-170,186-190 | 36,39-40,40-42,43-44,56-57,100-101,105-106,110-113,153,157 | 30-31, 57-60, 76-77 | 26-27, 36-37, 63-64, 101,113-114,129-130,158-160,165-166,175-177,178-185,186-206 | 66 | 7-10,60-63,78-99,106-109,173-175 | 153, 160-161 | Wide Arc: 66 Change: 132-139, 194-204 |
| Metcalf, H. C. & Urwick, L. | *Dynamic Administration: The Collected Papers of Mary Parker Follett.* New York: Harper & Bros., 1940. | Government and Administration | 31,50-58, 96-101, 272-277 | | | 31-32,35, 210-213, 239 | 31, 33-49, 58-70, 111-116, 198-202 | | 213-225, 240-246, 260-269, 279-281 | | |

**Table A-1 (continued)**

| Investigator | Source | Field | 9,1 | 1,9 | 1,1 | 5,5 | 9,9 | Statistical 5,5 | Facades | Paternalism | Other |
|---|---|---|---|---|---|---|---|---|---|---|---|
| Missildine, W. H. | *Your Inner Child of the Past.* New York: Simon & Schuster, 1963. | Psychiatry | 77,85-100,103, 106,108-109,125-126,130-133,138-139 | 77,133-136,157, 166,171-191,259-260,266-267,271-272 | 78-79, 101-103, 104-105, 107-108, 109-111, 121-124, 145-155, 156-159, 165-166, 166-167, 243-252, 254-259, 261 | | | | | | |
| Missildine, W. H. & Galton, L. | *Your Inner Conflicts— How To Solve Them.* New York: Simon & Schuster, 1974. | Psychiatry | 35-36,37, 38-39,39-40,62,72-74,76,77, 81-82, 83-86, 131-133, 145-146, 154-155, 171-172, 172-180, 187-191, 196-201, 205-207 | 36,37-38,61, 76-77, 130 | 37,39, 53-59, 60-61,62, 62-63, 77, 120-127, 157-160, 162-163, 184-187 | | 33-34, 262-263, 308-313 | | | | |
| Moment, D. & Zaleznik, A. | *Role Development and Interpersonal Competence.* Boston: Harvard University Press, 1963. | Business Administration | 20,38,56, 62-63,67, 72,77,80, 85-86,87-88,89, 104-105, 122-123, 158-159, 160 | 20,39, 56,62-63,67, 72,77, 78-79, 80,83, 86-87, 89, 105-106, 123-124, 159,160 | 20,36-37,39, 56,62-63,67, 72,80, 83,87, 89-90, 106-107, 124-125 | | 19-20, 36-37, 38,41, 53,56, 62-63, 68,72, 77,80, 85,89, 104, 120-122 | | | | |

| | | | 41-67 | 97-113 | 123-137 | 151-169 | 181-201 | 80-85 | 76-80 | 69-74 | Dom/Backup |
|---|---|---|---|---|---|---|---|---|---|---|---|
| Mouton, J.S. & Blake, R.R. | *The Marriage Grid.* New York: McGraw-Hill, 1971. | Social Psychology | | | | | | | | | Dom/Backup: 15-17 |
| Reddin, W.J. | *Managerial Effectiveness 3-D.* New York: McGraw-Hill, 1970. | Business Administration | 27,28-29, 31-32,42, 47,73-74, 94,95, 161,177, 192,194, 194-195, 221-227, 262-263, 268-259 | 27,28-29, 31,42,68, 73,94, 194,215-219 | 43,48, 54,194, 209-212, 258-259, 263,264 | 27,28-29, 30-31,41, 42-43,48, 72-73, 93-94, 194,205-209,213, 231-233 | 27,28-29,32, 41,48, 74-75, 94,95, 192,194, 230-231, 233-234 | 52,53-54, 139-140, 149-150, 159-160, 169-178, 181-185, 256-257 | | 42,47 | Dom/Backup: 46-47,48, 49,152 Change: 163,307 |
| Riesman, D., Glazer, N., & Denney, R. | *The Lonely Crowd.* Garden City, N.Y.: Doubleday & Co., 1953. | Sociology Political Science Economic History | 23,28-32, 41,57-63 | | 278,281 | 23,24-28, 33,34-40, 41-42, 63-74, 278 | 33,278, 282,286-298,328 | | 302-305, 305-307 | 303 | |
| Schutz, W.C. | *The Interpersonal Underworld* (originally titled *FIRO: A Three Dimensional Theory of Interpersonal Behavior*). Palo Alto, Calif.: Science & Behavior Books, 1966. | Psychology | 29,41,45, 47-48,89 | 31,36,41, 47,48,89 | 25-26, 28-29, 30-31, 41,42, 45-46, 47,48, 89 | 26-27 | 27,29-30,31, 37,41, 43,48, 87-89 | | | 43 | Sick 9,1: 43 Distorted 1,9-42-43 |
| Steiner, C. M. | *Scripts People Live: Transactional Analysis of Life Scripts.* New York: Bantam Books, 1974. | Therapy | 53,54-56, 78-81, 115-119, 188-193, 197-198, 231-234, 236-237, 253-261 | 54,56, 76-78, 198-201, 211-213, 222-224 | 92-95, 115-119, 178-181, 218-220, 243-245 | | 3,85-86, 352-361, 362-370, 382-383, 384 | | 44-50, 121, 175-178, 304-305 | | Wide Arc: 39 Dom/Backup: 37-38 |

**Table A-1 (continued)**

| Investigator | Source | Field | 9,1 | 1,9 | 1,1 | 5,5 | 9,9 | Statistical 5,5 | Facades | Pater-nalism | Other |
|---|---|---|---|---|---|---|---|---|---|---|---|
| Thomas, W. I. & Znaniecki, F. | "Three Types of Personality." In C. W. Mills, ed., *Images of Man: The Classic Tradition in Sociological Thinking.* New York: George Braziller, Inc., 1960, pp. 405-436. | Sociology | 427 | | | 407-408, 409,411, 418-419, 421,423, 425,427, 428,434, 435-436 | 408,409, 411,418, 423,435, 436 | 408-409, 418,423, 433,435, 436 | | 420 | |
| Wheelis, A. | *The Quest for Identity.* New York: W. W. Norton & Co., 1958. | Psychiatry | 18,85 | | | 18-19, 48-49, 85-89, 91-93, 126 | 19,20 | 85 | | | |
| White, R. & Lippitt, R. | "Leader Behavior and Member Reaction in Three 'Social Climates.'" In D. Cartwright and A. Zander, eds., *Group Dynamics: Research and Theory.* (2nd ed.) Evanston, Ill.: Row, Peterson, & Co., 1960, pp. 527-553. | Social Psychology | 528-529, 529-532, 537,540-541,541-546,549-553 | | 528-529, 530,531, 533-534, 539-540, 549-552 | 528-529, 530,531, 532-538, 539-541, 546-549, 549-553 | | | | | |

framework. Several explicit efforts to modify the Grid also are included and are commented on later.

As shown in Table A-1, regardless of their field of specialization, and with but a few exceptions, all investigators describe behavior as if relying on a two-dimensional framework. Factor analytic approaches reinforce conceptual analysis and lead to the conclusion that most meaningful variance in behavior can be accounted for by two factors.

There are exceptions, however. One is Bales who described behavior in a three-variable geometric space, the third variable being related to a person's being group centered in beliefs and values or individualistic in orientation. The added complexity did little by way of extending understanding of behavior. Another, by Schutz, added *inclusion* as a third dimension, but little use has been made of it in experimental, clinical, or applied work. Reddin and Hersey and Blanchard have added effectiveness as a third Grid dimension, but this is not a true third dimension because effectiveness is already determined by the first two and therefore is not independent of them.

There is an implicit third dimension within the Grid framework, however, as commented on in the introductory section of each Grid chapter. It involves identification of motivation as a bipolar scale, ranging, in the 9,1 case for example, between control, mastery, and domination on the plus end to dread of failure on the minus end of the scale. While adding a third dimension of motivation introduces further clarification as to what a 9,1 orientation is like, little in predictive utility is gained over that already available in a two-dimensional system.

A further comment of importance in understanding the Grid is the concept of *interaction*. Interaction between these variables can occur in either of two ways. The combination of any two quantities can occur in an arithmetic way. This needs to be distinguished from the fusion of two quantities in a "chemical" way. Hersey and Blanchard, for example, might see 9,9 as a combination of 9 units of task orientation, telling a subordinate in great detail "who, what, where, and how . . ." added to 9 units of relationships, involving extensive compliments and appreciation expressed in response to subordinate compliance. The "chemical" view, by comparison, produces a 9,9 character of interdependence in which shared participation, involvement, and commitment produce consensus-based teamwork. In the former case combination of variables is quantitative and arithmetic; in the latter, it is qualitative and organic, *i.e.*, the *character* of the behavior itself changes, not just relative to the amounts of the same behavior.

Because most investigations have found a two-dimensional basis sufficient and three-dimensional formulations have added little to understanding beyond that already available from the use of two, we conclude that a framework for analyzing behavior that results from two variables is a sound and sufficient basis for comprehending managerial assumptions and practices.

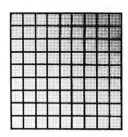

# References

### Chapter 1

| Page | Line |
|------|------|
| 1 | 7 | Blake, R.R., and J.S. Mouton. *Grid Seminar Prework. The Managerial Grid: An Exploration of Key Managerial Orientations.* Austin, Texas: Scientific Methods, Inc., 1962 (revised 1978). Reproduced by permission. |
| 1 | 20 | For quantitative norms, see Grid Seminar Materials. Austin, Texas: Scientific Methods, Inc. 1978 revised edition. |
| 4 | 17 | The role of assumptions in guiding behavior is widely recognized in the behavioral sciences. Typical are Bion, W.R. *Experience in Groups.* New York: Basic Books, McGraw-Hill, 1959; McGregor, D. *The Human Side of Enterprise.* New York: McGraw-Hill, 1960, pp. 6-8; Steiner, C.M. *Scripts People Live: Transactional Analysis of Life Scripts.* New York: Bantam, 1974, pp. 59-111; Dreikurs, R., and L. Grey. *Logical Consequences: A New Approach to Discipline.* New York: Meredith Press, 1968, pp. 23-27; Barber, J.D. *The Presidential Character: Predicting Performance in the White House.* Englewood Cliffs, N.J.: Prentice-Hall, 1972, pp. 7-9. |
| 5 | 28 | In addition to the two dimensions already introduced, every Grid style has a third dimension related to personal motivation. Each of these unique motivations can be pictured as a bipolar scale with a positive end that identifies what a manager seeks to attain and a negative end that is characterized by what a manager seeks to avoid. These motivational aspects are introduced in more detail at the beginning of each chapter. |

How this third dimension intersects the other two is shown in Figure R-1. The intermediate position,

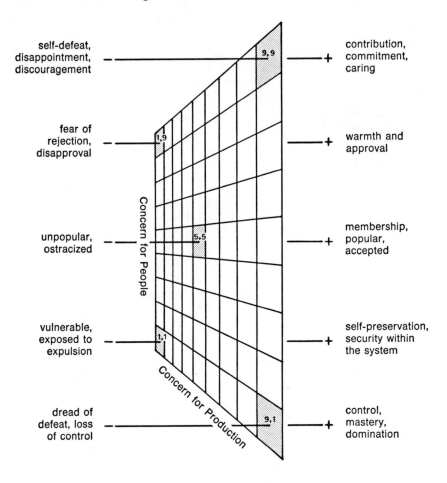

self-defeat, disappointment, discouragement — ⊟ 9,9 ⊟ + contribution, commitment, caring

fear of rejection, disapproval — ⊟ 1,9 + warmth and approval

Concern for People

unpopular, ostracized — ⊟ 5,5 + membership, popular, accepted

vulnerable, exposed to expulsion — ⊟ 1,1 + self-preservation, security within the system

Concern for Production

dread of defeat, loss of control — ⊟ 9,1 + control, mastery, domination

*Figure R-1. Every Grid style has a third dimension of personal motivation, which can be negative, neutral or positive.*

where the motivational scale intersects the other two, defines a point of indifference. At that point the activity a person is engaged in does not signal a motivational pull or a repulsion. The positive pole extends into the far side of the Grid surface and the negative pole is shown on the near side of the surface (towards the viewer).

See also Deci, E.L. *Intrinsic Motivation.* New York: Plenum Press, 1975.

## Chapter 2

| Page | Line | |
|------|------|---|
| 7 | 5 | A number of terms are used more or less interchangeably in referring to who has leadership responsibilities: administrator, executive, manager, supervisor. They all refer to the activity of achieving results with and through other people. |
| 7 | 12 | In addition to the three universals introduced here, the following identifies several others: structure, financial resources, "know-how," organization culture, results, and *environment*. See Mooney, J.D. *The Principles of Organization.* New York: Harper, 1947; Blake, R.R., and J.S. Mouton. "Grid Organization Development." *Personnel Administration,* 30, No. 1 (1967) pp. 7-14. |
| 8 | 26 | The impact of various patterns of organization and communication networks on behavior, reactions, productivity, and satisfaction of members in a hierarchy is shown in result. See Bavelas, A. "Communication Patterns in Task-Oriented Groups." *Journal of the Acoustical Society of America,* 22, (1950) pp. 725-730; Cartwright, D., and A. Zander, eds. *Group Dynamics: Research and Theory.* Evanston, Ill.: Row, Peterson, 1956, pp. 496-506; Pfiffner, J.M., and F.P. Sherwood. *Administrative Organization.* Englewood Cliffs, N.J.: Prentice-Hall, 1960, pp. 52-73; Kelley, H.H. "Communication in Experimentally Created Hierarchies." *Human Relations,* 4, (1951) pp. 39-56; Korda, M. *Power! How to Get It, How to Use It.* New York: Random House, 1975; Leavitt, H.J. "Some Effects of Certain Communication Patterns on Group Performance." *Journal of Abnormal & Social Psychology,* 46, (1951) pp. 38-50; Kelley, H.H. "Communication in Experimentally Created Hierarchies." *Human Relations,* 4, (1951) pp. 39-56; Heise, G.A., and G.A. Miller. "Problem Solving by Small Groups Using Various Communication Nets." *Journal of Abnormal & Social Psychology,* 46, (1951) pp. 327-336; and Cartwright, D., and A. Zander, eds. *Group Dynamics: Research and Theory.* Evanston, Ill.: Row, Peterson, 1956, pp. 493-506. |
| 8 | 32 | Some behavioral scientists have sought to solve the dilemma inherent in change and development by drawing sharp and fast distinctions between managing and leading. Bennis, for example, thinks that *managing* is related to acceptance of the status quo and that *leading* includes changing the status quo. In our view this is a false distinction. Leading is an essential component of managing, particularly in a |

**Page**      **Line**

9,9 orientation. See Bennis, W.E. *The Unconscious Conspiracy.* New York: AMACOM, 1976.

The same separation of management from leadership is to be found in Jay, A. *Management and Machiavelli: An Inquiry into the Politics of Corporate Life.* New York: Holt, Rinehart, & Winston, 1967, p. 26. "Management techniques are obviously essential, but what matters is leadership." The implication is that when a boss is implementing a management technique he is not leading, and when he is leading there is no scientific aspect.

8          39

Attention is not to be focused on organization and managerial principles and functions *per se,* such as unity of direction, span of control, delegation of authority, etc. Rather, consideration is concentrated on examining the assumptions a manager operates under when, for example, he delegates authority or plans a given work activity. Organization principles and management functions are treated as neutral or as givens. The *ways* in which they are applied under different managerial styles *are* subject to examination and study because the style of application determines effectiveness.

9          10

Current scholarly evaluations of the Grid as a strategy for comprehending and changing boss-subordinate relationships are available in a number of sources. See Huse, E.F., and J.L. Bowditch. *Behavior in Organizations: A Systems Approach to Managing,* 2nd ed. Reading, Mass.: Addison-Wesley, 1977; Todes, J.L., J. McKinney, and W. Ferguson, Jr. *Management and Motivation: An Introduction to Supervision.* New York: Harper & Row, 1977; Sanford, A.C., G.T. Hunt, and H.J. Bracey. *Communication Behavior in Organizations.* Columbus, Ohio: Charles E. Merrill Publishing Company, 1976; Cribbin, J.J. *Effective Managerial Leadership.* New York: American Management Association, Inc., 1972; Harris, O.J., Jr. *Managing People at Work.* New York: John Wiley & Sons, Inc., 1976; Tubbs, S.L., and S. Moss. *Human Communication,* 2nd ed. New York: Random House, 1974; Filley, A.C., R.J. House, and S. Kerr. *Managerial Process and Organizational Behavior,* 2nd ed. Glenview, Ill.: Scott, Foresman and Company, 1976.

9          15

The Grid strategy of analyzing and solving production/people dilemmas came about as a result of trying to understand conflict among senior managers in the original organization development project. See Blake, R.R., and J.S. Mouton. *Diary of an OD Man.* Houston: Gulf, 1976. Nothing is truly independent, however, and the line of thinking on which the Grid is based is consistent with much independent scholar-

| Page | Line |
|------|------|

ship of the last quarter century. Table A-1 summarizes major works that in some significant ways parallel one or more aspects of the Grid. The first publications on the Grid as an organizing framework were: Blake, R.R., J.S. Mouton, and A.C. Bidwell. "The Managerial Grid." *Advanced Management—Office Executive*, 1, (1962) pp. 12-15, 36; Blake, R.R., and J.S. Mouton. "The Developing Revolution in Management Practices." *ASTD Journal*, 16, (1962) pp. 29-50; Blake, R.R., and J.S. Mouton. *The Managerial Grid.* Houston: Gulf, 1964.

**10    27**    For impacts of the external environment as a universal property of an organization on its internal operations, see Johnson, R.A., R.J. Monsen, H.P. Knowles, and B.O. Saxberg. *Management, Systems, and Society: An Introduction.* Pacific Palisades, Ca.: Goodyear Publishing Company, Inc., 1976.

**10    29**    The relationship analyzed in this book is between boss and subordinate. Elsewhere many other relationships have been examined from a Grid point of view. See Blake, R.R., J.S. Mouton, and E.D. Bryson. "The Military Leadership Grid." *Military Review*, 48, No. 6 (1968) pp. 3-18; Blake, R.R., and J.S. Mouton. *The Grid for Sales Excellence: Benchmarks for Effective Salesmanship.* New York: McGraw-Hill, 1970; Blake, R.R., and J.S. Mouton. *The Grid for Supervisory Effectiveness.* Austin, Tex.: Scientific Methods, Inc., 1975; Mouton, J.S., and R.R. Blake. *The Marriage Grid.* New York: McGraw-Hill, 1971.

**11**    The word Grid is a trademark property of Scientific Methods, Inc., Austin, Texas. Used by permission.

**12    7**    An alternative leadership formulation shows behavior available to a boss as running along a continuum from 9,1 (boss-centered) through varying degrees of 5,5 to 1,9 (subordinate-centered). 1,1 and 9,9 are not considered as alternative modes of leadership behavior. See Tannenbaum, R., and W.H. Schmidt. "How to Choose a Leadership Pattern." *Harvard Business Review*, 36, No. 2 (1958) pp. 95-98. Another continuum involves Systems 1-4 as pictured in Likert, R. *The Human Organization.* New York: McGraw-Hill, 1967.

**13    17**    Jay alludes to a point regarding policy and sound practice when he points out that overall efficiency is made up of many bits of behavioral and operational skills that are in short supply. However, as he sees it, limited natural managerial ability can be supplemented because most sound practices can be taught, explained, and written down. What Jay does not see is that top level leadership also is subject to a person learning how to do it. ". . . leading the whole organization needs wisdom and flare and vision and they are another matter; they cannot be reduced to a system and incorporated into a training manual." Thus, Jay has a vocational concept of training as contrasted with education that facilitates a person's skills for exercising initiative, resolving conflict, promoting thoroughness of preparation, viewing problems in a systematic perspective, etc. See Jay, A., op. cit., p. 28.

13          28

In a factor analysis of 52 leadership studies, Stogdill concludes that there are 26 factors that appear in three or more studies indicating variables associated with leadership behavior. Stogdill, R.M. *Handbook of Leadership.* New York: Free Press, 1974, p. 96.

14          11

A force-field analysis is possible for identifying the conditions under which a shift from dominant to backup are likely to occur. See Lewin, K. *A Dynamic Theory of Personality.* New York: McGraw-Hill, 1935; Lewin, K. *Field Theory in Social Science.* New York: Harper & Bros., 1951.

15          4

The idea that to influence behavior a motive must be conscious was abandoned in the last century. One of the earliest of the "moderns" to acknowledge that influences may not be consciously appreciated is Le Bon, Gustave. *The Crowd: A Study of the Popular Mind.* London: Ernest Benn, 1896. This idea was developed in psychoanalysis and has become a standard proposition in clinical psychology. See Strachey, J. *Standard Edition of the Complete Psychological Works of Sigmund Freud.* London: Hogarth Press, 1961. See also Christie, R., and F.L. Geis. *Studies in Machiavellianism.* New York: Academic Press, Inc., 1970.

## Chapter 3

16          4

The behavior and concerns of "inner-directed" men at work as described by Riesman are characteristic of 9,1 assumptions and actions. See Riesman, D. *The Lonely Crowd.* New Haven: Yale University, 1961, pp. 111-126.

16          6

McClelland and associates have investigated personal behavior and characteristics, latent motives, childhood origins, and socialization processes characteristic of individuals with high needs for achievement (*n ach*). High achievement needs, high fear of failure, and relatively low regard for social interaction is most like the 9,1 behavior pattern described here. See McClelland, D.C., J.W. Atkinson, R.A. Clark, and E.L. Lowell. *The Achievement Motive.* New York: Appleton-Century-Crofts, 1953; Atkinson,

| Page | Line | |
|---|---|---|

J.W., ed. *Motives in Fantasy, Action, and Society.* Princeton: D. Van Nostrand, 1958; McClelland, D.C. *The Achieving Society.* Princeton: D. Van Nostrand, 1961.

The orientations and actions of the 9,1 managerial style also are called the "Technical Specialist." See Moment, D., and A. Zaleznik. *Role Development and Interpersonal Competence.* Boston: Harvard University Press, 1963, pp. 122-123.

| 16 | 8 | For a comprehensive analysis of research into a personality syndrome characteristic of many 9,1 aspects of behavior, see Adorno, T.W., E. Frenkel-Brunswick, D.J. Levinson, and R.N. Sanford. *The Authoritarian Personality.* New York: Harper, 1950. |

| 17 | 4 | In their work with small groups, Bales and others identified two distinct roles assumed by various members in problem-solving groups—"task" role and "social" role. Both sets of role behavior were rarely observed in the actions of any one individual, *i.e.*, a person was either concerned for the task (production) or his concern is for the social (people) aspects of a group's activities—seldom both *at the same time.* 9,1 is the task orientation and 1,9 (next chapter) is the social orientation. The integration of these two roles within the behavior of one person, the 9,9 orientation, as described in Chapter 7, is not considered as a possibility. See Bales, R.F. "The Equilibrium Problem in Small Groups." In T. Parsons, R.F. Bales, and E.A. Shils, *Working Papers in the Theory of Action.* Glencoe, Ill.: Free Press, 1953, pp. 111-161. (Also abridged in Hare, A.P., E.F. Borgatta, and R.F.Bales, eds. *Small Groups.* New York: Knopf, 1955, pp. 424-456). The most recent spokesman for this point of view is D.C. McClelland, who maintains that high power needs are irreconcilable with high affiliation needs except through religious conversion. McClelland, D.C. *Power: The Inner Experience.* New York: Irvington Publishers, 1975. |

The needs of the "formal" organization for production and the needs of individuals for mature growth and "self-actualization" are treated by Argyris. Production and people needs are viewed as incongruent. See Argyris, C. *Personality and Organization.* New York: Harper, 1957; Argyris, C. *Understanding Organizational Behavior.* Homewood, Ill.: Dorsey, 1960; and Argyris, C. *Interpersonal Competence and Organizational Effectiveness.* Homewood, Ill.: Dorsey, 1962.

McGregor's "Theory X" also provides a fundamental analysis of 9,1 assumptions and organizational behavior. McGregor, D. *The Human Side of Enterprise.* New York: McGraw-Hill, 1960, pp. 33-43. McGregor

| Page | Line | |
|------|------|---|

acknowledges the importance of integrating the needs of organizations and the needs of people (see pp. 45-57).

| 17 | 9 | The work of Likert, Katz, Kahn, Maccoby, Morse, and others at the University of Michigan Institute for Social Research has brought to light many basic assumptions underlying the concerns and actions of "job-centered" supervisors (9,1). A comprehensive review and summation is in Likert's *New Patterns of Management.* New York: McGraw-Hill, 1961. See also Likert, R. *The Human Organization.* New York: McGraw-Hill, 1967; and Likert, R., and J.C. Likert. *New Ways of Managing Conflict.* New York: McGraw-Hill, 1976, pp. 20-39, 59-69. |

| 17 | 12 | This concept of authority and obedience in the work situation has been examined by Taylor, F.W. *The Principles of Scientific Management.* New York: Harper, 1947; Argyris, C., op. cit., 1957; McGregor, D., op. cit., pp. 15-32; and Roddick, P.M. "Authority, Responsibility, Leadership." *Advanced Management,* January, 1960, pp. 12-15. |

| 17 | 15 | Sometimes it is useful to analyze the particular power base being used by a manager. Power of one person to influence another may be derived from a number of sources: referent power, expert power, reward power, coercive power, and legitimate power. Generally speaking, however, 9,1 power is based upon hierarchy and coercive power. A 5,5 orientation is likely to rely on playing rewards and punishments against one another. A 1,9-oriented manager is likely to base his exercise of influence on liking. A 9,9-oriented manager is more likely to gain the capacity for exercising influence from expertness and legitimate sources. See French, J.R.P. "A Formal Theory of Social Power." *Psychological Review,* 70, (1963) pp. 181-194; and French, J.R.P., and B. Raven. "The Bases of Social Power." In D. Cartwright, ed., *Studies of Social Power.* Ann Arbor, Mich.: Institute for Social Research, 1959, pp. 150-167. |

| 17 | 16 | The fundamental functions of a manager are most often categorized as planning, directing, organizing, controlling, and staffing. These are treated in an undifferentiated way with respect to the leadership style by which they are exercised. For a classic description of management functions, see Koontz, H.C., and C. O'Donnell. *Principles of Management.* 2nd ed. New York: McGraw-Hill, 1959. |

| 17 | 32 | Guest provides a detailed account of the 9,1 use of hierarchy in his description of a plant during the plant's "Period of Disintegration." Guest, R.H. *Orga-* |

**Page**        **Line**

*nizational Change: The Effect of Successful Leadership.* Homewood, Ill.: Dorsey, 1962, pp. 17-37 (see especially p. 23).

17          33          *The Managerial Grid: A Self-Examination of Managerial Styles.* Austin, Tex.: Scientific Methods, Inc., 1962 (revised, 1978). Reproduced by permission.

18          37          Poor vertical communication—9,1—results in reduced satisfaction especially at the lower levels of organization. See Ulrich, D.N., D.R. Booz, and P.R. Lawrence. *Management Behavior in Foreman Attitude.* Boston: Harvard University Graduate School of Business Administration, 1950.

19          38          Levinson recognizes and describes how management-by-objectives can be predicated upon a reward-punishment, 9,1-oriented psychology where compliance is based upon power rather than reciprocity. The underlying MbO and performance appraisal system can be both organizationally and personally damaging. See Levinson, H. "Management by Whose Objectives?" *Harvard Business Review,* 48, No. 4 (1970) pp. 125-134.
One study claims some advantages of managing-by-objectives short-term, *i.e.,* over eighteen months and even after two and one-half years. Thereafter, however, undesired consequences became more obvious, including many evidences that the 9,1-oriented culture maneuvers MbO into use consistent with its 9,1 values. These included inadequate use at lower levels, over-emphasis on production goals and targets, the occasional use of the program as a whip, and the heavy burden on administrative personnel with consequent large amounts of paper work. See Raia, A.P. *Managing by Objectives.* Glenview, Ill.: Scott, Foresman, 1974.

19          40          Early experimental work of Lewin, Lippitt, and White with groups of children evaluated goal setting under the "authoritarian" leadership style, which corresponds to the 9,1 approach, and laissez-faire and democratic approaches, which correspond with the 1,1 and 5,5 orientations respectively. 5,5 leadership produced the most favorable outcome of the three. This study led to increased experimental work and better understanding of the concepts of group locomotion, productivity, cohesiveness, creativity, and the effects of varying degrees of participation. See Lewin, K., R. Lippitt, and R.K. White. "Patterns of Aggressive Behavior in Experimentally Created 'Social Climates.'" *Journal of Social Psychology,* X, (1939) pp. 271-299; Lippitt, R. "An Experimental Study of Authoritarian and Democratic Group Atmospheres." *Studies in Topological and Vector Psychology, I. University of Iowa Studies in Child Welfare,*

| Page | Line |
|------|------|

16, (1940); Lippitt, R. "Field Theory and Experiment in Social Psychology: Authoritarian and Democratic Group Atmospheres." *American Journal of Sociology*, XLV, (1939) pp. 26-49; and Lippitt, R., and R.K. White. "An Experimental Study of Leadership and Group Life." In E.E. Maccoby, T.M. Newcomb, and E.L. Hartley, eds., *Readings in Social Psychology*. 3rd ed. New York: Holt, 1958, pp. 496-511; Lewin, K. "Group Decision and Social Change." In E.E. Maccoby, et al, eds., op. cit., pp. 197-219.

20    4    When performance appraisal has a 9,1 character and utilizes criticism as one of the tools to induce change, the result may lead to cynicism, alienation, and discouragement on the part of the employee being appraised. Thus, it is again demonstrated that a 9,1-oriented character of managing subordinates is likely to induce a 1,1 reaction. Huse, E.F., and J.L. Bowditch. *Behavior in Organizations: A Systems Approach to Managing.* 2nd ed. Reading, Mass.: Addison-Wesley Publishing Company, 1977, p. 198.

20    10    Work-induced conflict is discussed in Pages, M. "The Sociotherapy of the Enterprise." In W. Bennis, K. Benne, and R. Chin, eds., *The Planning of Change.* New York: Holt, Rinehart & Winston, 1961, pp. 176-177.

20    12    A clinical study of consequences from boss-based 9,1-oriented resolution of conflict between a 5,5-oriented subordinate and a 9,9-oriented subordinate, decided in favor of the 5,5-oriented manager's recommendation, is reported by Rotondi, T. "The Innovator and the Ritualist: A Study in Conflict." *Personnel Journal*, 53, No. 6 (1974) pp. 439-444.

20    15    Experiments on the effect of 9,1 win-lose disagreements on protagonists are reported. See Blake, R.R., H.A. Shepard, and J.S. Mouton. *Managing Intergroup Conflict in Industry.* Houston: Gulf Publishing Company, 1964; Blake, R.R. "Psychology and the Crisis of Statesmanship." *The American Psychologist*, 14, (1959) pp. 87-94; Bennis, W.G., K.D. Benne, and R. Chin, eds. *The Planning of Change.* New York: Holt, Rinehart & Winston, 1951, pp. 466-477; and Blake, R.R., and J.S. Mouton. "The Intergroup Dynamics of Win-Lose Conflict and Problem-Solving Collaboration in Union-Management Relations." In M. Sherif, ed., *Intergroup Relations and Leadership.* New York: Wiley, 1962, pp. 94-140.

21    5    Empathic, or 9,9-oriented listening, is contrasted with 9,1 critic-oriented listening. If a speaker is addressing an empathic listener, then maximum understanding of the speaker's comments from the speaker's point of view is likely, and this assists the

| Page | Line | |
|---|---|---|
| | | listener in recalling critical issues, in identifying areas of disagreement, and conclusions. If the speaker is speaking to a 9,1-oriented, critic-type listener who has a predisposition to criticize and disagree, then it is more likely that the listener will gain minimum understanding of the speaker's comments from the speaker's point of view. Kelly, C.M. "Empathic Listening." In R.S. Cathcart, and L. Samovar, eds., *Small Group Communication: A Reader*. Dubuque, Iowa: Wm. C. Brown, 1974, pp. 340-348. |
| 21 | 8 | An experimental study demonstrating the outcomes from differences in Grid style between two people who are in conflict but seeking to reconcile their differences shows that when a 9,1-oriented and a 1,9-oriented person are pitted against one another, the direction is controlled by the 9,1-oriented member. Two 1,9-oriented persons have the greatest likelihood of reconciling their disagreements and liking one another thereafter. The least likelihood of such outcomes is between 9,1-oriented persons. See Oltman, P.K., D.R. Goodenough, H.A. Witkin, N. Freedman, and F. Friedman. "Psychological Differentiation as a Factor in Conflict Resolution." *Journal of Personality and Social Psychology*, 32, No. 4 (1975) pp. 730-736. |
| 24 | 15 | Evidence is offered showing that 9,1-oriented subordinates are more acceptable to 9,1 bosses than is the case for subordinates who are not 9,1 in their own orientations. Medalia, N.Z. "Unit Size and Leadership Perception." *Sociometry*, 17, (1954) pp. 64-67. |
| 26 | 13 | When subordinates are required to work with a domineering (9,1) supervisor, they tend to identify with the supervisor. However, when the same subordinates interact with same-level colleagues, they become more independent of the power figure and show more hostility toward him. Stotland, E. "Peer Groups and Reactions to Power Figures." In D. Cartwright, ed., *Studies in Social Power*. Ann Arbor: Institute for Social Research, 1959, pp. 53-68. |
| 26 | 19 | How this slowdown comes about is described in Roy, D. "Quota Restrictions and Goldbricking in a Machine Shop." *American Journal of Sociology* (1952) pp. 427-442. |
| 27 | 11 | Other things equal, persons who feel competitive with one another take opposite sides at a discussion table and in fact do show more disagreement and conflict across the table. See Cummings, L., G. Huber, and E. Arendt. "Effects of Size and Spatial Arrangements on Group Decision Making." *Academy of Management Journal*, 17, No. 3 (1974) pp. 460-475. |

| Page | Line | |
|------|------|---|
| 27 | 22 | A 9,1/1,1 cycle may occur in the following way. As subordinates' behavior keeps shifting in a 1,1 direction, the accompanying low production, waste, and inefficiency tend to produce increased pressure in a 9,1 direction. That is, one level of management reacts to the 1,1 response of other levels by increasing the "9,1-ness" of its centralized work direction and tight control. This increase in 9,1 tactics causes those to whom it is applied to become even more 1,1, which, in turn, causes those above to become even more 9,1 in orientation. And so, the 9,1/1,1 cycle runs its course. Like the dog that chases its tail, yet never catches it, management may spend tremendous effort, time, and money in a futile effort to enforce obedience to its wishes through the exercise of authority. |

Examples of the 9,1/1,1 cycle are found in Argyris, C. op. cit., 1957; Argyris, C. "Understanding Human Behavior in Organizations: One Viewpoint." In M. Haire, ed., *Modern Organization Theory.* New York: Wiley, 1959, p. 143; Argyris, C., op. cit., 1960, pp. 17-18.

| | | |
|------|------|---|
| 28 | 8 | Leaders exercising coercive power (9,1) are found less attractive than those using other methods of influence. See Zander, A., and T. Curtis. "Effects of Social Power on Aspiration Setting and Striving." *Journal of Abnormal Social Psychology,* 64, No. 1 (1962) pp. 63-74. |
| 28 | 34 | A review of correlations between organizational stress and individual strain considered from a psychological point of view is by French, John R.P., Jr., and R.D. Caplan. "Organizational Stress and Individual Strain." In A.J. Marrow, ed., *The Failure of Success.* New York: AMACOM, 1972, pp. 30-66. |
| 28 | 36 | Evidence connecting a given Grid-like style to a specific mental or physical health condition in most cases is extensive, complex, and difficult to interpret. There are several reasons for this. |

The most important limitation is the inaccuracy of self-description. As already reported, self-descriptions are notoriously inaccurate, regardless of whether the data are collected through interviews, self-descriptive paragraphs, or by answering test questions. The inaccuracy factor connected with these sources of data may be larger than the 44% as reported in Chapter 14. Another source of inaccuracy is the fact that medical experts, though skilled in health diagnosis, are usually untrained in behavioral observation, and thus they may "see" what they wish to observe rather than describing what is "there" in objective terms. Given these limitations, we have

| Page | Line |
|------|------|

utilized statistical, observational, clinical, and quantitative test data and cross-checked one approach against others whenever possible. The relationships described appear to be consistent over a range of techniques of observation and diagnosis. Where important contradictions have been seen, they are pointed out. However, these limitations make it important to emphasize the tentative character of the findings, and to emphasize that the kinds of interrelationships, even though they seem to be sound, cannot be used for individual diagnosis.

It goes without saying that factors in addition to Grid style are significant in predisposing an individual to a given illness. As is true in most circumstances, it may be essential for several factors, such as heredity, exposure, present susceptibility, and often a predisposing crisis event, to come together in some particular combination before a mental or physical result is precipitated.

| 29 | 34 | A high degree of stress and the problem which a person sees to be the cause of it may so occupy a person's thinking that sleep is impossible. He can't "turn it off." Horney, K. *Neurosis and Human Growth.* New York: W.W. Norton & Co., 1950, p. 234. |

| 30 | 27 | The term "sadistic" emphasizes satisfaction experienced from subjecting others to pain or indignity, thus reaffirming to an individual his capacity for control, mastery, and domination. Horney, K. ibid., p. 199. |

| 31 | 13 | This tendency of "extreme" 9,1-oriented people to see others as blockers to their own control, domination, and mastery results in "reading" derogatory motives and insidious plans into their actions. Kisker, G. *The Disorganized Personality.* New York: McGraw-Hill, 1972, pp. 341-342. |

| 31 | 18 | An explanation of suicide is by Durkheim, who argues that suicide is found only under conditions of society where it is possible for people to compete, and yet there is no success possible from high achievement when there is no social structure which defines how much is enough. A 9,1-oriented manager is likely to be more susceptible to suicide as an expression of intolerable failure. Durkheim, E. "On Anomie." In C.W. Mills, ed., *Images of Man: The Classic Tradition in Sociological Thinking.* New York: George Braziller, Inc., 1960, pp. 449-485, specifically pp. 455-456. |

While suicide is encountered among the aged and terminally sick and therefore occurs for a number of different reasons, the conclusion here relates to investigators where the dynamics appear to be more

| Page | Line | |
|------|------|---|
| | | directly Grid related. See Shaffer, J.W., S. Perlin, C.W. Schmidt, Jr., and M. Himmelfarb. "Assessment in Absentia: New Directions in the Psychological Autopsy." *Johns Hopkins Medical Journal,* 130, (1972) pp. 308-316. Similar dynamics have been pointed to in the incidence of suicide among senior business executives during the Great Depression, when death was preferable to defeat. |
| 31 | 28 | Migraine sufferers are characterized by this 9,1 orientation of drive and mastery, and as individuals who bottle up frustrations during work only to suffer migraine attack during leisure periods. Wolff, H.G. *Headache and Other Head-Pain.* New York: Oxford University Press, 1963. |
| 31 | 29 | Seeing the migraine sufferer as "boxed in" between efforts at domination and mastery on the one side, but fear of failure on the other, Pelletier concludes that borderline panic is stimulated and that this is a common precursor of the attack itself. See Pelletier, K.R. *Mind as Healer, Mind as Slayer.* New York: Delta Publishing Company, 1977, pp. 171-172. |
| 31 | 31 | One investigation sought to replicate the findings reported by Wolff, but concluded that Wolff's generalizations had relevance to only a proportion of the migraine patients studied. Sacks, O.W. *Migraine: The Evolution of a Common Disorder.* Berkeley: University of California Press, 1970, p. 181. See also Lance, J.W. *Headache: Understanding, Alleviation.* New York: Charles Scribner's Sons, 1975, p.110. |
| 32 | 13 | This work is regarded as definitive by experts in the field: Friedman, M., and R.H. Rosenman. *Type A: Behavior and Your Heart.* Greenwich, Conn.: Fawcett Crest, 1974. The renowned heart surgeon, Michael DeBakey, interprets the Friedman-Rosenman findings in much the same way as do the original investigators. See DeBakey, M., and A. Gotto. *The Living Heart.* New York: David McKay Company, 1977. |
| 33 | 24 | A variety of studies correlate demand for performance and acceptable behavior with the strict manner in which this demand is invoked. They reveal different facets of how a 9,1 orientation evokes a 9,1 response on the part of the child. See Barker, R.G., T. Dembo, and K. Lewin. "Frustration and Regression: An Experiment with Young Children." *University of Iowa Study in Child Welfare,* 18, No. 1 (1941); Meyers, C.E. "The Effect of Conflicting Authority on the Child." *University of Iowa Study in Child Welfare,* 20, (1944); Bishop, B.M. "Mother-Child Interaction and the Social Behavior of Children." *Psychological Monograph,* 65, No. 11 (1951). Some person- |

| Page | Line | |
|------|------|---|

ality differences in children are related to strict or permissive parental discipline. See Baldwin, A.L. "Socialization and the Parent-Child Relationship." *Child Development*, 19, (1948) pp. 127-136. For a comprehensive review of experimental work on child-rearing practices as they relate to overt 9,1 behavior, as well as other orientations to be discussed, see Sears, R.R., E.E. Maccoby, and H. Levin. *Patterns of Child Rearing*. Evanston, Ill.: Row, Peterson, 1957.

33    29    A view of how the power orientations of society are related to child rearing and how these, in turn, influence adult patterns of adjustment is provided in Riesman, D., N. Glazer, and R. Denney. *The Lonely Crowd*. Garden City, New York: Doubleday, 1953, pp. 59-63; and Bell, G.D. *The Achievers*. Chapel Hill, N.C.: Preston-Hill, Inc., 1973, pp. 24-27.

33    31    The more 9,1 are the assumptions of parents regarding child rearing, the greater the likelihood that, because of their own needs, they compel their children to work, to save, to clean house, to study, and so on, all to prove themselves "acceptable." See Winterbottom, M.R. "The Relation of Childhood Training in Independence to Achievement Motivation." In J.W. Atkinson, ed., *Motives in Fantasy, Action, and Society*. Princeton: D. Van Nostrand, 1958, pp. 453-478; Hoffman, L.W., S. Rosen, and R. Lippitt. "Parental Coerciveness, Child Autonomy, and Child's Role at School." *Sociometry*, 26, (1960) pp. 15-22.

33    43    One of the richest analyses of parent influences on children and how these in turn emerge as adult styles is by Horney, K. *The Neurotic Personality of Our Time*. New York: W.W. Norton & Co., 1937, p. 170.

34    5    How parents stimulate a child's motivations to dread failure is discussed by Missildine, W.H., and L. Galton. *Your Inner Conflicts—How to Solve Them*. New York: Simon & Schuster, 1974, pp. 196-201.

34    6    Parent behavior may become a model to the child for how he should treat others. This is discussed by Horney, K., op. cit., p. 87.

34    18    That child misbehavior can produce additional punishment and additional punishment promotes more misbehavior as a reaction of rebelliousness is analyzed by Missildine, W.H., and L. Galton, op. cit., pp. 171-174.

34    20    There is general agreement that punitive 9,1-oriented parents produce hostile and aggressive children who can also be punitive on a "like begets like" basis. See Missildine, W.H. *Your Inner Child of the Past*. New York: Simon & Schuster, 1963, pp. 204-209; Missildine, W.H., and L. Galton, op. cit., pp. 38-39; and Bell, G.D., op. cit., pp. 41-43.

| Page | Line |
|------|------|
| 35 | 35 |

How learning to overcome deprivation feeds naturally into motivations that become control, mastery, and domination-oriented is commented upon extensively by Missildine, W.H., op. cit., pp. 240-241; and Missildine, W.H., and L. Galton, op. cit., pp. 186-187.

| 35 | 5 |

When parents communicate that a child is "perfect" via the route of indulging his every desire, this pampering, when complete, is likely to produce an adult style which might be called "perfectionistic 1,1." This child avoids involving himself for fear of testing his "perfection." When it is incomplete pampering, however, the child learns to be demanding in order to gain from parents what he wishes. In this manner he learns 9,1-oriented skills. See Adler, A. *Social Interest: Challenge to Mankind.* New York: Capricorn Books, 1964, p. 149; Horney, K., op. cit., 1937, p. 87; and Missildine, W.H., op. cit., p. 132.

| 35 | 26 |

The point is made that delinquency is something that parents teach their children in the sense that through labeling them as "bad," the child comes to accept this self-image and in turn to act consistent with it. See Kovar, L., *Faces of the Adolescent Girl.* Englewood Cliffs, N.J.: Prentice Hall, 1968, pp. 70-71.

| 36 | 22 |

Demonstrating the free-floating character of hostile feelings under experimental conditions was made possible in the following way. One group of children played a game of Murder while a comparison group did not. Those who played the game, and who had for the most part become quite aroused and involved in it, subsequently saw significantly greater tendencies toward violence and malice in some photographs of people than did those who had not played the game. Since the photographs viewed by both groups were the same, the differences must be explained as carry-over effects of hostility feelings aroused in one situation expressing themselves in another. See Murray, H.A., Jr. "The Effect of Fear Upon Estimates of the Maliciousness of Other Personalities." *Journal of Social Psychology,* 4, (1933) pp. 310-329.

| 36 | 37 |

How attack behavior of the 9,1 kind is learned is demonstrated by investigators who showed groups of young children a film in which a model struck a large rubber doll with a mallet, or sat on it and screamed at it. When children who had seen the film were given the same kind of doll and mallet, they acted aggressively toward the doll, repeating the kinds of actions that had been observed in the movie. There are many demonstrations that when children have observed or experienced hostility from their parents, they repeat the same action with others on whom they can exercise aggression. See Bandura, A., D.

| Page | Line | |
|------|------|---|

**37**      **4**

Ross, and S.A. Ross. "Imitation of Film-Mediated Aggressive Models." *Journal of Abnormal and Social Psychology*, 66, No. 1, (1963) pp. 3-11.

"Games" are facade behaviors where ulterior motives are unexpressed. Berne, E. *Games People Play: The Psychology of Human Relationships*. New York: Grove Press, 1964. For example, Uproar is a 9,1-oriented game played by the boss who, in effect, is saying, "You stupid clod, you never do anything right." Other games involve Let's You and Him (Her) Fight. The game of Harried, which is the overly busy executive who collapses with depression, heart attack, and so forth, and leaves others in a mess to straighten out the problems he created, and yet feels self-righteous, is described by James, M. *The OK Boss*. Reading, Mass.: Addison-Wesley, 1975, p. 113.

**38**      **19**

The historical antecedents of 9,1 are commented on in Taylor, F.W., op. cit.; Fayol, H. *General and Industrial Management*. New York: Pitman, 1949; Mooney, J.D., and A.C. Reiley. *Onward Industry*. New York: Harper, 1931, p. 31; Anderson, E.A. "The Meaning of Scientific Management." *Harvard Business Review*, 27, (1949) pp. 678-692; Gellerman, S.W. *People, Problems and Profits*. New York: McGraw-Hill, 1960, p. 164; Urwick, L. *Dynamic Administration: The Collected Papers of Mary Parker Follett*. New York: Harper, 1940, pp. 31-32; Simon, H.A. *Administrative Behavior*. New York: Macmillan, 1947, p. 127; McGregor, D. "An Uneasy Look at Performance Appraisal." *Harvard Business Review*, 35, (1957) pp. 89-94; and Broom, L., and P. Selznick. *Sociology*, 3rd ed. New York: Harper, 1963, pp. 627-635.

**39**      **9**

The role of economic conditions in labor market is reviewed by Goode, W.J., and I. Fowler. "Incentive Factors in a Low Morale Plant." *American Sociological Review*, 14, (1949) pp. 618-624.

**39**      **19**

Support for this point is found in McGregor, D. "Conditions of Effective Leadership in the Industrial Organization." *Journal of Consulting Psychology*, 8, (1944) pp. 55-63; McGregor, D., op. cit., 1960; Argyris, C., op. cit., 1957, pp. 103-107.

**39**      **24**

Some problems of consensus development are demonstrated by Riecken, H.W. *Rural Sociology*, 17, (1952) pp. 245-252; Argyris, C., op. cit., 1957, pp. 77-100.

**40**      **17**

Short-term effects of 9,1 on productivity are reported in Katz, D., N. Maccoby, and N.C. Morse. *Productivity, Supervision, and Morale in an Office Situation*. Part I. Ann Arbor: Institute for Social Research, University of Michigan, 1950; Gibb, C.A. "An Experimental Approach to the Study of Leadership." *Occupational Psychology*, 25, (1951) pp. 233-248;

| Page | Line | |
|------|------|---|
| | | Likert, R. "Measuring Organizational Performance." In K. Davis, and W. Scott, eds., *Reading in Human Relations.* New York: McGraw-Hill, 1959, pp. 276-277; and Likert, R., op. cit., 1961, p. 59. |
| 40 | 19 | Seventy-two decision-making conferences were studied by observers who rated self-oriented need behavior (frequently 9,1-oriented). This behavior was in turn shown to be related to high group conflict and negatively related to participant satisfaction, group solidarity, and task productivity. See Fouriezos, N.T., M.L. Hutt, and H. Guetzkow. "Measurements of Self-Oriented Needs in Discussion Groups." *Journal of Abnormal and Social Psychology,* 45, (1950) pp. 682-690. |

## Chapter 4

| Page | Line | |
|------|------|---|
| 41 | 3 | The contradictory character of 9,1 and 1,9 being characteristic of the same person is recognized and commented upon by McClelland, who feels that the only way they can come together in something approaching a 9,9 orientation is through religious conversion. See McClelland, D.C. *Power: The Inner Experience.* New York: Irvington Publishers, 1975, p. 322. |
| 41 | 8 | The 1,9 orientation toward others is consistent with the "Social Specialist" role identified by Moment, D., and A. Zaleznik in *Role Development and Interpersonal Competence.* Boston: Harvard University, 1963, pp. 123-124. A clinical examination of the 1,9 orientation is in Horney, K. *Neurosis and Human Growth.* New York: W.W. Norton & Co., 1950, pp. 214-238; Horney, K. *The Neurotic Personality of Our Time.* New York: W.W. Norton & Co., 1937, pp. 96-97, 102-161; and Horney, K. *Self-Analysis.* New York: W.W. Norton & Co., 1942, pp. 54-55. |
| 42 | 4 | A 1,9 orientation is not limited to management. A 1,9-oriented teacher may give little or no homework to avoid creating frustrations, promote friendly discussion in the classroom to avoid pressures, and give easy exams to avoid creating tensions. These conditions are frequently spoken of as "permissive" education where the teacher seeks the affection and approval of students by being friendly and by avoiding putting any performance pressures on students. The teacher thereby makes them feel secure, and accepting and approving relationships are expected to result. Albert Shanker, head of the American Federation of Teachers, pictures the attitude of the "soft curriculum" that came about partly as a result of a protest of the Sixties. Rather than teaching |

| Page | Line | |
|------|------|---|
| | | mathematics, he says, children were invited to engage in activities of the fun-and-games type. The consequences for their capacity of strengthening undeveloped basic skills in more advanced work is disregarded in the interest of the general 1,9-oriented attitude, "We don't care what they learn as long as they're happy." From *Issues and Answers*, TV Channel 3, September 12, 1976, Austin, Texas. |
| 42 | 16 | A manager's emphasis on providing good working conditions is discussed in Gellerman, S.W. *People, Problems and Profits.* New York: McGraw-Hill, 1960, p. 165; Cleeton, G.U. "The Human Factor in Industry." *The Annals of the American Academy of Political and Social Sciences,* 274, (1951) pp. 17-24; and Heckmann, I.L., Jr., and S.G. Huneryager, eds. *Human Relations in Management.* Cincinnati: South-Western, 1960, pp. 17-26. |
| 42 | 18 | Identification of non-work-related motivations and rewards is demonstrated in research by Herzberg, F., B. Mausner, and B.B. Snyderman. *The Motivation to Work,* 2nd ed. New York: John Wiley, 1967. Specific discussion of hygiene motivations and rewards that cause them to appear as characteristic of a 1,9 orientation is to be found on pages 113-119. |
| 42 | 24 | *The Managerial Grid: A Self-Examination of Managerial Styles.* Austin, Tex.: Scientific Methods, Inc., 1962, (revised 1978). Reproduced by permission. |
| 44 | 3 | Criticizing the human relations orientation, some authors point out that such factors as organization power structures, technological constraints within which jobs must be designed, and market competition are ignored in a 1,9 orientation. These authors maintain that all problems cannot be reduced to matters of personal feelings with minimal attention to rational problem-solving processes. See Hellriegel, D., and J.W. Slocum, Jr. *Management: A Contingency Approach.* Reading, Mass.: Addison-Wesley, 1974; and McNair, M.P. "Thinking Ahead: What Price Human Relations?" *Harvard Business Review,* 35, (1957) pp. 15-39. |
| | | Also criticizing the human relations school, Krupp claims the group is naive and utopian in emphasizing the integrating aspects of diverse and conflicting perspectives, and in its inattention to mechanisms for conflict resolution. See Krupp, S. *Pattern in Organization Analysis: A Critical Examination.* New York: Holt, Rinehart, and Winston, 1961. |
| 44 | 32 | How opinions expressed by others can influence a naive person's objectivity is reported in Asch, S.E. "Effects of Group Pressure Upon the Modification and Distortion of Judgments." In H. Guetzkow, ed., |

| Page | Line | |
|------|------|---|

*Groups, Leadership, and Men.* Pittsburgh: Carnegie, 1951; Hurwitz, J.I., A.F. Zander, and B. Hymovitch. "Some Effects on the Relations Among Group Members." In D. Cartwright, and A. Zander, eds., *Group Dynamics: Research and Theory.* Evanston, Ill.: Row, Peterson, 1953; Lippitt, R., N. Polansky, and S. Rosen. "The Dynamics of Power: A Field Study of Social Influence in Groups of Children." *Human Relations,* 5, (1952) pp. 37-64; and Cole, D. " 'Rational Argument' and 'Prestige-Suggestion' as Factors Influencing Judgment." *Sociometry,* 17, (1954) pp. 350-354.

**44   35**   Desensitization training is intended to aid an individual to experience what he fears and thereby to feel more comfortable with what he ordinarily avoids. By experiencing it, he then tests whether the consequences that he dreaded are different than what he had come to expect.

1,9-oriented managers often fear the rejection and disapproval that will come to them if they take a stand and thus they avoid taking a position. Successful desensitization training permits them to take a stand under protected conditions in order to test whether the anticipated disapproval and rejection is, in fact, what taking a stand might produce. See Wolpe, J. *The Case of Mrs. Schmidt: An Illustration of Behavior Therapy.* Nashville: Counselor Recordings & Tests, 1965; Wolpe, J. *The Practice of Behavior Therapy,* 2nd ed. New York: Pergamon Press, 1973; Wolpin, M. "Guided Imagining in Reducing Fear and Avoidance Behavior." In California Mental Health Research Symposium No. 2, *Behavior Theory and Therapy.* State of California, Department of Mental Hygiene, Bureau of Research, 1968, pp. 40-41.

**45   28**   These authors describe assertiveness training to aid individuals who cannot express themselves openly or in situations of conflict to be more candid and more self-expressive. Thus, 1,9-oriented persons are most likely to benefit from assertiveness training. See Fensterheim, H., and J. Baer. *Don't Say Yes When You Want To Say No.* New York: Dell, 1975; and Lazarus, A., and A. Fay. *I Can If I Want To.* New York: William Morrow & Co., 1975.

**46   26**   Smoothing as a way of dealing with conflict is found in Roethlisberger, F.J. "The Foreman: Master and Victim of Double Talk." *Harvard Business Review,* 23, (1945) pp. 283-294; and Zentner, H. "Morale: Certain Theoretical Implications of Data on the American Soldier." *American Sociological Review,* 16, (1951) pp. 297-307.

| Page | Line |
|------|------|
| 47 | 4 |

Representative experimental work on tension, anxiety, threat, negative feedback, and similar interpersonal conditions may aid the reader to place in perspective the underlying assumptions of 1,9 "supportive" and conflict-free behavior, *e.g.*, see Shaw, M.E. "Some Effects of Problem Complexity Upon Problem Solution Efficiency in Different Communication Nets." *Journal of Experimental Psychology*, 48, (1954) pp. 211-217; Lanzetta, J.T., D. Haefner, P. Langham, and H. Axelrod. "Some Effects of Situational Threat on Group Behavior." *Journal of Abnormal & Social Psychology*, 49, (1954) pp. 445-543; Festinger, L., and H.A. Hutte. "An Experimental Investigation of the Effect of Unstable Interpersonal Relations in a Group." *Journal of Abnormal & Social Psychology*, 49, (1954) pp. 513-522; Cervin, V. "Individual Behavior in Social Situations: Its Relation to Anxiety, Neuroticism, and Group Solidarity." *Journal of Experimental Psychology*, 51, (1956) pp. 161-168; French, E.G., and I. Chadwick. "Some Characteristics of Affiliation Motivation." *Journal of Abnormal & Social Psychology*, 52, (1956) pp. 296-300; de Charms, R. "Affiliation, Motivation, and Productivity in Small Groups." *Journal of Abnormal & Social Psychology*, 55, (1957) pp. 222-226; Harvey, O.J., H.H. Kelley, and M.M. Shapiro. "Reactions to Unfavorable Evaluations of the Self Made by Other Persons." *Journal of Personality*, 25, (1957) pp. 393-411; Pepinsky, P.N., J.K. Hemphill, and R.N. Shevitz. "Attempts to Lead, Group Productivity, and Morale Under Conditions of Acceptance and Rejection." *Journal of Abnormal & Social Psychology*, 57, (1958) pp. 47-54; Schachter, S. *The Psychology of Affiliation.* Stanford, Ca.: Stanford University, 1959; Likert, R. *New Patterns of Management.* New York: McGraw-Hill, 1961, pp. 7-8; and Herzberg, F., et al., pp. 87, 113-114, 125.

| Page | Line |
|------|------|
| 48 | 2 |

Passing distorted information upward is greater for a 1,9-oriented subordinate than by a 9,9- or 9,1-oriented subordinate whose job security is high. See Athanassiades, J.C. "The Distortion of Upward Communication in Hierarchical Organizations." *Academy of Management Journal*, 16, (1973) pp. 207-226.

| Page | Line |
|------|------|
| 49 | 18 |

A technical study of masochism is provided in Horney, K., op. cit., 1937, pp. 259-280.

| Page | Line |
|------|------|
| 50 | 5 |

Levinson, H. *Emotional Health: In the World of Work.* New York: Harper & Row, Publishers, 1964, pp. 123-125.

| Page | Line |
|------|------|
| 50 | 25 |

Missildine, W.H. *Your Inner Child of the Past.* New York: Simon & Schuster, 1963, p. 191.

| **Page** | **Line** | |
|---|---|---|
| 51 | 6 | Several clinical investigations and controlled experiments confirm the close association reported. See Alexander, F. *Psychosomatic Medicine: Its Principles and Applications*. New York: W.W. Norton & Co., 1950; Fine, R. "The Personality of the Asthmatic Child." In H.I. Schneer, ed., *The Asthmatic Child*. New York: Hoeber, 1963; Harris, I.D., L. Rapaport, M.A. Rymerson, and M. Samter. "Observations on Asthmatic Children." *American Journal of Orthopsychiatry*, 20, (1950) p. 490; Jessner, L., J. Lamont, R. Long, N. Rollins, B. Whipple, and N. Prentice. "Emotional Impact of Nearness and Separation for the Asthmatic Child and His Mother." *Psychoanalytic Study of the Child*, 10, (1955) p. 353; and Rees, L. "The Importance of Psychological, Allergic, and Infective Factors in Childhood Asthma. *Journal of Psychosomatic Research*, 7, (1964) p. 253. |
| 51 | 13 | McMahon, A.W., P. Schmitt, J.F. Patterson, and E. Rothman. "Personality Differences Between Inflammatory Bowel Disease Patients and Their Healthy Siblings." *Psychomatic Medicine*, 35, No. 2, (1973) pp. 91-103. Other studies confirm these findings. See Engle, G.L. "Ulcerated Colitis." In A.E. Lindner, ed., *Emotional Factors in Gastrointestinal Illness*. Amsterdam: Excerpta Medica, 1973; Sperling, M. "Psychoanalytic Study of Ulcerative Colitis in Children." *Psychoanalytic Quarterly*, 15, (1946) p. 302; and Sperling, M. "Ulcerative Colitis in Children." *Journal of the American Academy of Child Psychiatry*, 8, (1969) p. 336. |
| 52 | 7 | The correlations between Grid-related dynamics and hypertension have been repeatedly reported by medical experts and investigators who have drawn conclusions under control conditions. See Alexander, F., op. cit.; Pilowsky, I., D. Spalding, J. Shaw, and P.I. Korner. "Hypertension and Personality. *Psychosomatic Medicine*, 35, No. 1, (1973) p. 56; Wolf, S., and H.G. Wolff. "A Summary of Experimental Evidence Relating Life Stress to the Pathogenesis of Essential Hypertension in Man." In E.T. Bell. *Essential Hypertension*. Minneapolis: The University of Minnesota Press, 1951; Matarazzo, J.D. "An Experimental Study of Aggression in the Hypertensive Patient." *Journal of Personality*, 22, (1954) pp.423-447; Dunbar, F., op. cit., pp. 147-149; Innes, G., W.M. Millar, and M. Valentine. "Emotion and Blood Pressure." *Journal of Mental Science*, 105, (1959) pp. 840-851. |
| 52 | 12 | Dunbar, F., op. cit., pp. 199-200. |
| 52 | 30 | A similar conclusion is by Kisker, who says that diabetes is found among passive and immature persons who are frequently frustrated in their seek- |

| Page | Line | |
|------|------|---|
| | | ing of affection and approval. See Kisker, G. *The Disorganized Personality*, 2nd ed. New York: McGraw-Hill, 1972, p. 303. |
| 53 | 1 | How paternalistic control is exercised over a child is documented in Kovar, L.C. *Faces of the Adolescent Girl.* Englewood Cliffs, N.J.: Prentice-Hall, 1968, pp. 53-56. |
| 53 | 5 | Parents who over-control a child are likely to develop dependency in him. Thus, autonomy and the capacity for self-direction have little or no opportunity to develop. Evidence is presented in Fensterheim, H., and J. Baer, op. cit., p. 27; Wylie, P. *Generation of Vipers*. New York: Pocket Books, Inc., 1955, pp. 197-198; Bell, G.D. *The Achievers*. Chapel Hill, N.C.: Preston-Hill, 1973, pp. 74-75. |
| 53 | 11 | How attitudes of dependence are reinforced by parental expressions that threaten loss of love for non-compliance is found in Kovar, L.C. op. cit., pp. 62-63. |
| 53 | 18 | Horney, K. also comments on how a child's confidence can be undermined. Op. cit., 1937, pp. 85-86. |
| 54 | 9 | This origin of a 1,9 orientation is emphasized in particular by Missildine, W.H., op. cit., pp. 266-271. |
| 54 | 26 | Facades are analyzed in detail by Berne. For example, a 1,9-oriented game is called, "Look How Hard I'm Trying." Another is "Poor Me." In both of these, the subordinate's role in game playing is to avoid disapproval and to curry favor by arousing sympathy. In doing so, he wins without putting forth the realistic effort required to merit success. Other games include, "If It Weren't For Him (Her)" and "I'm Only Trying to Help You." See Berne, E. *Games People Play: The Psychology of Human Relationships*. New York: Grove Press, 1964. |
| 54 | 34 | Carnegie, D. *How to Win Friends and Influence People*. New York: Simon & Schuster, 1964, p. 27. |

**Chapter 5**

| Page | Line | |
|------|------|---|
| 59 | 31 | This concept of anomie is described in Broom, L., and P. Selznick. *Sociology*. New York: Harper & Row, 1963, p. 717; Durkheim, E. *The Division of Labor in Society*. Glencoe, Ill.: Free Press, 1947; McGee, R. *Social Disorganization in America*. San Francisco: Chandler, 1962, pp. 66-78. |
| 59 | 41 | Several studies point in the same direction. Blau, P.M. "Patterns of Interaction Among a Group of Officials in a Government Agency." *Human Relations*, 7, (1954) pp. 337-348; Fouriezos, N.T., M.L. Hutt, and H. Guetzkow. "Measurement of Self-Oriented Needs in Discussion Groups." *Journal of Abnormal & Social* |

| Page | Line | |
|------|------|---|

*Psychology*, 45, (1950) pp. 682-690; Moment, D., and A. Zaleznik. *Role Development and Interpersonal Competence.* Boston: Harvard University, 1963, pp. 124-125; Hickson, D.J. "Motives for Workpeople Who Restrict Their Output." *Occupational Psychology*, 35, (1961) pp. 111-121.

**62    23**    *The Managerial Grid: A Self-Examination of Managerial Styles.* Austin, Tex.: Scientific Methods, Inc., 1962, (Revised 1978). Reproduced by permission.

**62    36**    Consequences of failure to exercise responsibility on the part of the boss is described in Guest, R.H. *Organizational Change: The Effect of Successful Leadership.* Homewood, Ill.: Dorsey, 1962, pp. 17-38; Lippitt, R., and R.K. White. "The 'Social Climate' of Children's Groups." In R.G. Barker, J.S. Kounin, and H.F. Wright, eds., *Child Behavior and Development.* New York: McGraw-Hill, 1943, pp. 485-508; Lippitt, R., and R.K. White. "An Experimental Study of Leadership and Group Life." In G.E. Swanson, T.M. Newcomb, and E.L. Hartley, eds., *Readings in Social Psychology*, 2nd ed. New York: Holt, 1952, pp. 340-355.

**63    1**    Strategies of isolation are discussed in Argyris, C. "Human Relations in a Bank." *Harvard Business Review*, Sept.-Oct. (1954) pp. 63-72; and Lawrence, P.R., J.C. Bailey, R.L. Katz, J.A. Seiler, C.D. Orth, J.V. Clark, L.B. Barnes, and A.N. Turner. *Organizational Behavior and Administration: Cases, Concepts, and Research Findings.* Homewood, Ill.: Dorsey, 1961, pp. 237-238.
For factors in minimum communication see Hurwitz, J.I., A.F. Zander, and B. Hymovitch. "Some Effects of Power on the Relations Among Group Members." In D. Cartwright, and A. Zander, *Group Dynamics: Research and Theory.* Evanston, Ill.: Row, Peterson, 1953, pp. 483-492; Kelley, H.H. "Communication in Experimentally Created Hierarchies." *Human Relations*, 4, (1951) pp. 39-56.

**63    3**    "Lost" identity is examined in Buber, M. "Productivity and Existence." In M.P. Stein, A.J. Vidich, and D. Manning, eds., *Identity and Anxiety.* Glencoe, Ill.: Free Press, 1960, p. 630.

**64    5**    Conflict avoidance mechanisms of the 1,1 kind such as explanations based on "fate," coin-flipping, and so on, are identified in Blake, R.R., H.A. Shepard, and J.S. Mouton. *Managing Intergroup Conflict in Industry.* Houston: Gulf Publishing Company, 1964.

**64    9**    Factors of morale in 1,1 are commented upon in Guion, R.M. "Some Definitions of Morale." In E.A. Fleishman, ed., *Studies in Personnel and Industrial Psychology.* Homewood, Ill.: Dorsey, 1961, pp. 301-304.

| Page | Line |
|------|------|
| 64 | 38 |

64    38    Performance may falter not only when initiative is called for but also when change is needed. If a change recommendation comes from the top, it is resisted with responses like, "The present method has served us well for a long time. Why do you want to change it?" This is not the traditions/past practices/slow-change-by-evolution resistance of 5,5 but the total discounting of the need for excellence, or improvement even, that is characteristic of 1,1 when its own personal comfort and convenience are threatened.

65    6    1,1-oriented message passing is discussed in Kipnis, D., and W.P. Lane. "Self-Confidence and Leadership." *Journal of Applied Psychology*, 46, (1962) pp. 291-295; and Roethlisberger, F.J. *Management and Morale.* Cambridge: Harvard University, 1952, pp. 89-105.

66    6    Further discussion of 1,1 dynamics is found in Riesman, D., N. Glazer, and R. Denney. *The Lonely Crowd.* Garden City, N.Y.: Doubleday, 1950, p. 144. Uninvolvement may also be camouflaged by active—a noisy, energetic 1,1 response—as well as passive behavior where energy and argumentation are mistaken for 9,1. This occurs when it is directed toward the attainment of the 1,1-oriented person's personal goals, which are disadvantageous to the real goals of the group. Thus his true uninvolvement is unnoticed. Managers who resist change out of apathy and self-interest, whether they are withdrawn and quiet, noisy and argumentative, or more polished, are like this. So are politicians whose goal is to retain votes and party political power rather than to manage the affairs of a nation to its own economic and social well-being. These aspects of 1,1 certainly have been experienced in Grid OD projects in the last decade.

67    33    WPA "make work" during the Great Depression is described by Tannenbaum, F.A. *A Philosophy of Labor.* New York: Knopf, 1951. The "leaving" dynamic is amplified in Marrow, A.J., and G. David. "Why Do They Really Quit?" *Management Review,* 41, (1952) pp. 157-158; Argyris, C. *Personality and Organization.* New York: Harper, 1957, pp. 76-122.

68    3    "Like begets like" on a 1,1 basis. See Kelley, H.H. "Communication in Experimentally Created Hierarchies." *Human Relations,* 4, (1951) pp. 39-56; Guest, R.H., op. cit.; and Smith, E.E. "The Effects of Clear and Unclear Role Expectations on Group Productivity and Defensiveness." *Journal of Abnormal & Social Psychology,* 55, (1957) pp. 213-217.

68    9    The "goldbrick" is a classic example of 1,1. See Roy, D. "Quota Restriction and Goldbricking in a Machine Shop." *American Journal of Sociology,* 57, (1952) pp. 427-442; Whyte, W.F. *Money and Motivation.* New

| Page | Line | |
|------|------|---|
| | | York: Harper, 1955; Hickson, D.J. "Motives for Workpeople Who Restrict Their Output." *Occupational Psychology*, 35, (1961) pp. 111-121. |
| 69 | 5 | The relationship between hopelessness and premature death is found in Frankl, V.E. *Man's Search for Meaning*. New York: Washington Square Press, Inc., 1963. |
| 69 | 29 | This point of view is formulated in Kisker, G.W. *The Disorganized Personality*, 2nd ed. New York: McGraw-Hill, 1972, p. 295; Dunbar, F. *Mind and Body: Psychosomatic Medicine*. New York: Random House, 1950, pp. 233-239; Derner, G.F. *Aspects of the Psychology of Tuberculosis*. New York: Hoeber, 1953. |
| 69 | 37 | LeShan, L. *You Can Fight for Your Life*. New York: M. Evans & Co., 1977, pp. 64-66. |
| 70 | 28 | Other descriptions of personal characteristics and cancer are in Dunbar, F., op. cit., pp. 233-239; Friedman, S.B., and L.A. Glasgow, "Psychological Factors and Resistance to Infectious Disease." *Ped. CL. N. Amer.*, 13, (1966) pp. 315-335; Goldfarb, B.O., J. Driesen, and D. Cole. "Psychophysiologic Aspects of Malignancy." *American Journal of Psychiatry*, 123, June (1967) pp. 1545-1551; Kissen, D.N. "Psychosocial Factors, Personality, and Lung Cancer in Men Aged 55-64." *British Journal of Medical Psychology*, 40, (1967) pp. 29-42; and Pelletier, K.R. *Mind as Healer, Mind as Slayer*. New York: Delacorte Press, 1977, pp. 134-139. |
| 70 | 29 | LeShan, L. op. cit., p. 34. |
| 70 | 41 | Organization conditions promoting 1,1 are pictured in Argyris, C., op. cit., 1957; Mills, C.W. *The Sociological Imagination*. New York: Oxford University, 1959, pp. 165-176; Bensman, J., and B. Rosenberg. "The Meaning of Work in Bureaucratic Society." In M.P. Stein, A.J. Vidich, and D. Manning, eds., *Identity and Anxiety*. Glencoe, Ill.: Free Press, 1960, pp. 181-197. |
| 71 | 2 | Task simplification carried to the extreme can promote a 1,1 reaction. See Horwitz, M., R.V. Exline, and F.J. Lee. *Motivational Effects of Alternative Decision-Making Processes in Groups*. Urbana, Ill.: University of Illinois, 1953; Fromm, E. *Escape From Freedom*. New York: Holt, Rinehart and Winston, p. 295; and Smith, E.E. "The Effects of Clear and Unclear Role Expectations on Group Productivity and Defensiveness." *Journal of Abnormal & Social Psychology*, 55, (1957) pp. 213-217. |
| 71 | 6 | An interview study of over 500 people who were asked to describe their work leads to the conclusion that the dominant reaction of individuals in rank and file jobs of today is that they are both lonely and bored. |

**Page**        **Line**

Evidences drawn from these interviews include excessive fatigue, fantasy, playing games, anti-organization creativity, absenteeism, tardiness, social gossip, forgetting, daydreaming, engaging in outside hobbies, turnover, teasing, and drugs. Terkel, S. *Working.* New York: Pantheon Books, 1974. See also Blau, P.M. *The Dynamics of Bureaucracy.* Chicago: University of Chicago, 1955, pp. 172-179, 184-188; Collins, O., M. Dalton, and D. Roy. "Restriction of Output and Social Cleavage in Industry." *Applied Anthropology,* 5, No. 3 (1946) pp. 1-14; Whyte, W.F. *Money and Motivation.* New York: Harper, 1955; Argyris, C. *Personality and Organization.* New York: Harper, 1957. 1,1 implications in the larger society are discussed in McGee, R. *Social Disorganization in America.* San Francisco: Chandler, 1962, pp. 66-78.

71        9

Technological innovation can result in people filling meaningless jobs. See Lincoln, J.F. *Lincoln's Incentive System.* New York: McGraw-Hill, 1946, p. 20; Riesman, D., op. cit., p. 268.

71        29

Experimental studies and observations of children and adults have demonstrated reactions of individuals to situations of prolonged frustration. Behavior described is most like the 1,1 orientation as discussed in this chapter. See Eisenberg, P., and P.F. Lazarsfeld. "The Psychological Effects of Unemployment." *Psychological Bulletin,* 35, (1938) pp. 358-390; Lewin, K., R. Lippitt, and R.K. White. "Patterns of Aggressive Behavior in Experimentally Created 'social climates.'" *Journal of Social Psychology,* 10, (1939) pp. 271-299; Dollard, J., L.W. Doob, N.E. Miller, O.H. Mowrer, and R.R. Sears. *Frustration and Aggression.* New Haven: Yale University, 1939; Barker, R.G., T. Dembo, and K. Lewin. "Frustration and Regression: An Experiment with Young Children." *University of Iowa Studies in Child Welfare,* 18, I (1941); Merrill, M.A. *Problems of Child Delinquency.* Boston: Houghton, 1947; Marquart, D.I. "The Pattern of Punishment and Its Relation to Abnormal Fixation in Adult Human Subjects." *Journal of Genetic Psychology,* 39, (1948) pp. 107-144; Write, M.E. "The Influence of Frustration Upon the Social Relations of Young Children." *Character & Personality,* 12, (1943) pp. 111-112; Maier, N.R.F. *Frustration: The Study of Behavior Without a Goal.* Ann Arbor: University of Michigan, 1949; Heber, R.F., and M.E. Heber. "The Effect of Group Failure and Success on Social Status." *Journal of Educational Psychology,* 48, (1957) pp. 129-134; Pepitone, A., and R. Kleiner. "The Effects of Threat and Frustration on Group Cohesiveness." *Journal of Abnormal & Social Psychology,* 54, (1957) pp. 192-199; Moment, D., and

A. Zaleznik. *Role Development and Interpersonal Competence.* Boston: Harvard University, 1963, pp. 124-125. Lewin, et al., speaks of "laissez-faire" leadership and Moment and Zaleznik speak of an "Underchosen" role, but they are approximately the same. Branden, N. *The Disowned Self.* New York: Bantam, 1973; Slater, P. *The Pursuit of Loneliness.* Boston: Beacon Press, 1970.

71    35    An analysis and interpretation of worker motivation in the industrial situation, with recommendations consistent with a 9,9 orientation for sound motivation to replace 1,1 lack of interest and 1,9 "hygienic" concepts that are ". . . not related to the actual conduct of work [which] are the major sources of satisfaction . . ." is found in Herzberg, F., B. Mausner, and B.B. Snyderman. *The Motivation to Work.* New York: Wiley, 1959, p. 131.

71    39    Excessive punishment as a parental basis of child rearing is described in Missildine, W.H. *Your Inner Child of the Past.* New York: Simon & Schuster, 1963, pp. 121-122; Missildine, W.H., and L. Galton. *Your Inner Conflicts—How to Solve Them.* New York: Simon & Schuster, 1974, pp. 120-121.

72    3    A child's withdrawal as a means of reacting to coercive parental practices is described by Horney, K. *Neurosis and Human Growth.* New York: W.W. Norton & Co., 1950, p. 275.

72    11    Threat of desertion is a mechanism for controlling the child. See Branden, N. *The Disowned Self.* New York: Bantam, 1971, pp. 8-9.

72    15    A 1,1 orientation can be created during the first year of life when a child experiences nothing but an "emotional vacuum." Even though physically and nutritionally provided for, if the child remains untouched, uncarried, uncraddled, unsmiled at, unlaughed with, unplayed with, then it can be predicted that a nonresponse reaction comparable with apathy will emerge. The child becomes less able to make spontaneous, free, open contact with other children or with adults. This kind of child rearing, sometimes found in "sanitary" orphanages, has been verified in child research. It is the basis for some aspects of a 1,1 orientation in adults, who themselves may feel emotionally withdrawn, disinterested, and unable to gain interest or involvement in their child. See Spitz, R.A., and K.M. Wolf. "Anaclitic Depression: An Inquiry into the Genesis of Psychiatric Conditions of Early Childhood." *The Psychoanalytic Study of the Child,* 2, (1946) pp. 313-342.

72    18    Parental neglect resulting from environmental pressures on the parent for adult activities has been described by Missildine, W.H., op. cit., pp. 231-233.

| Page | Line | |
|------|------|--|
| 72 | 21 | Withdrawal, indifference, and uninvolvement is a childhood reaction to parental neglect. See Branden, N., op. cit., pp. 7-9. |
| 72 | 27 | Institutional neglect and its impact upon the affective and intellectual development of the child is described in Bakwin, H.L. *American Journal of Diseases of Children*, 63, (1942) p. 30; Spitz, R.A. "Hospitalism." In O. Fenichel, ed., *The Psychoanalytic Study of the Child*. New York: International University Press, 1945; Goldfarb, W. "Effects of Early Institutional Care on Personality, Behavior." *Child Development*, 14, (1943) p. 213; Missildine, W.H., op. cit., pp. 234-235, 243; Missildine, W.H., and L. Galton, op. cit., pp. 184-187; Bowlby, J. "Some Pathological Processes Set in Train by Early Mother-Child Separation." *Journal of Mental Science*, 99, (1953) pp. 265-272. |
| 72 | 42 | Unpredictable parental behavior may result in 1,1 withdrawal by the child. See Horney, K., op. cit., p. 275; and Bell, G.D. *The Achievers*. Chapel Hill, N.C.: Preston-Hill, 1973, pp. 61-62. |
| 73 | 13 | Overindulgence and complete pampering, which leads to a child's feeling perfect from being the center of adult attention, has been described in Adler, A. *Social Interest*. New York: Capricorn Books, 1964, pp. 21, 45-48; Missildine, W.H., and L. Galton, op. cit., pp. 157-159; Missildine, W.H., op. cit., pp. 145-159. |
| 73 | 34 | Games which are 1,1 in character include "Kick Me," in Berne, E. *Games People Play: The Psychology of Human Relationships*. New York: Grove Press, 1964, p. 84. |

### Chapter 6

| Page | Line | |
|------|------|--|
| 75 | 2 | Several basic inquiries into the 5,5 orientation have appeared since World War II. These include Whyte, W.H. *The Organization Man*. New York: Simon and Schuster, 1956; Wheelis, A. *The Quest for Identity*. New York: W.W. Norton & Company, Inc., 1958; Riesman, D., N. Glazer, and R. Denney. *The Lonely Crowd*. Garden City, N.Y.: Doubleday & Co., Inc., 1953; Putney, S., and G.J. Putney. *The Adjusted American*. New York: Harper & Row, 1964; Harrington, A. *Life in the Crystal Palace*. New York: Alfred A. Knopf, 1959; and Kilpatrick, W. *Identity and Intimacy*. New York, N.Y.: Dell Publishing Co., Inc., 1975. |
| 75 | 3 | This means of obtaining personal feelings of security is studied in Hochbaum, G.M. "The Relation Between Group Members' Self-Confidence and Their Reactions to Group Uniformity." *American Sociological Review*, 19, (1954) pp. 678-687. |

| Page | Line | |
|------|------|---|
| 75 | 5 | Fromm speaks of the 5,5 approach as having a "market orientation," where the manager's aim is to sell himself successfully in the corporate managerial market. ". . . His sense of self does not stem from his activity as a loving and thinking individual, but rather from his socio-economic role. . . . His sense of value depends on his success: on whether he can sell himself favorably . . . . Human qualities like friendliness, courtesy, kindness, are transformed into commodities, into assets of the 'personality package,' conducive to a higher price on the personality market. . . . Clearly, his sense of his own value always depends on factors extraneous to himself, on the fickle judgment of the market, which decides about his value as it decides about the value of commodities. He, like all commodities that cannot be sold profitably on the market, is worthless as far as his exchange value is concerned, even though his use value may be considerable." Fromm, E. *The Sane Society.* Greenwich, Conn.: Fawcett Publications, Inc., 1955, pp. 129-130. |
| 75 | 16 | Fromm sees the 5,5 orientation as a bipolar system. His paramount aim is to be popular with others; his central fear that he may not be. To find himself in the minority is a danger which threatens his sense of security. Hence, a craving for limitless conformity. Fromm, E., op. cit., p. 175. |
| 75 | 25 | The language by Riesman for understanding motivations underlying Grid styles needs revision in the following way. Tradition-directed and other-directed are two aspects of 5,5. Tradition-directed characterizes 5,5 in a stable environment, while other-directed also is characteristic of a 5,5 orientation, but in an environment of abundance with many changing group memberships. In both situations, however, direction is taken from the groups in which memberships are held. In one case it is repetitive, in the other, it is shifting, but the person is equally dependent on the group for his sense of what to do. See Riesman, D., N. Glazer, and R. Denney, op. cit., pp. 17-48. |
| 75 | 28 | How shame relates to 5,5 is discussed in Lynd, H.M. *On Shame and the Search for Identity.* New York: Science Editions, 1961. |
| 75 | 29 | Feelings of inferiority arise in a 5,5-oriented person when he suspects himself of not being in line. Fromm, E., op. cit., p. 181. |
| 76 | 3 | A person with a 5,5 orientation is potentially the victim of deep anxiety. See Fromm, E., op. cit., p. 181. |
| 76 | 15 | This balancing emphasis on production and people is described in Davis, R.C. *The Fundamentals of Top Management.* New York: Harper, 1951, pp. 72-73. |

| Page | Line |  |
|------|------|--|
| 76 | 19 | This kind of 5,5 orientation needs to be compared with involvement, participation, commitment—the 9,9-oriented values. Allen, L.A. *Management and Organization.* New York: McGraw-Hill, 1958, pp. 43-44. Also, Levine, J., and J. Butler. "Lecture Versus Group Decision in Changing Behavior." *Journal of Applied Psychology,* 36, (1952) pp. 29-33; Maier, N.R.F. *Psychology in Industry,* 2nd ed. Boston: Houghton, 1955, pp. 138-139. |
| 76 | 21 | *The Managerial Grid: A Self-Examination of Managerial Styles.* Austin, Tex.: Scientific Methods, Inc., 1962 (Revised 1978). Reproduced by permission. |
| 76 | 40 | Communication as an interaction skill is discussed in many sources. See as examples, Nichols, R., and L.A. Stevens. *Are You Listening?* New York: McGraw-Hill, 1957; Katz, R.L. "Skills of an Effective Administrator." *Harvard Business Review,* 31, (1955) pp. 33-42; Allen, L.A., op. cit.; Tannenbaum, R., and W.H. Schmidt. "How to Choose a Leadership Pattern." *Harvard Business Review,* 36, (1958) pp. 95-101; Rogers, C.R., and R.E. Farson. "Active Listening." In C.R. Anderson, and M.J. Gannon, eds., *Readings in Management.* Boston: Little, Brown and Co., 1977, pp. 284-303. |
| 77 | 6 | This point is in Shull, F.A. "Administrative Perspectives of Human Relations." *Advanced Management,* March (1960) pp. 18-22; Roethlisberger, F.J. "The Foreman: Master and Victim of Double Talk." *Harvard Business Review,* 23, (1945) pp. 283-298. |
| 77 | 19 | This give-and-take approach to production-people dilemmas is given in Pfiffner, J.M., and R.V. Presthus. "The Role of Human Relations." In K. Davis, and W. Scott, eds., *Readings in Human Relations.* New York: McGraw-Hill, 1959, p. 253; Davis, R.C., op. cit. |
| 77 | 33 | Riesman, D., N. Glazer, and R. Denney, op. cit., p. 312. |
| 78 | 5 | The work of Lewin and others with groups of children has led to increased understanding of the orientation of individuals around goals. The "Democratic" leadership described by Lewin et al. embraces a number of 5,5 actions. See Lewin, K., and R. Lippitt. "An Experimental Approach to the Study of Autocracy and Democracy." *Sociometry,* 1, (1938) pp. 292-300; Lewin, K., R. Lippitt, and R.K. White. "Patterns of Aggressive Behavior in Experimentally Created 'Social Climates'." *Journal of Social Psychology,* 10, (1939) pp. 271-299; Lippitt, R. "An Experimental Study of Authoritarian and Democratic Group Atmospheres." Studies in Topological and Vector Psychology. I. *University of Iowa Studies in Child* |

| Page | Line | |
|---|---|---|
| | | *Welfare,* 16, No. 3 (1940) pp. 43-195; Lippitt, R. "Field Theory and Experiment in Social Psychology: Autocratic and Democratic Atmospheres." *American Journal of Sociology,* 45, (1939) pp. 26-49; Lippitt, R., and R.K. White. "The 'Social Climate' of Children's Groups." In R.G. Barker, J.S. Kounin, and H.F. Wright, eds., *Child Behavior and Development.* New York: McGraw-Hill, 1943, pp. 485-508; Lippitt, R., and K. Lewin. "Adventures in the Exploration of Interdependence." *Sociometry Monograph,* 17, (1947) pp. 22-28. |
| 78 | 21 | Sandwich technique in performance appraisal discussed in Planty, E.G., and C.E. Efferson. "Counseling Executives After Merit Rating or Evaluation." *Personnel,* March (1951) pp. 384-396; Koontz, H., and C. O'Donnell. *Principles of Management,* 2nd ed. New York: McGraw-Hill, 1959, p. 352. |
| 78 | 40 | Reliance on tradition for conflict management is a hallmark of a 5,5 orientation. See Merei, F. "Group Leadership and Institutionalization." *Human Relations,* 2, (1949) pp. 23-39; Riesman, D., N. Glazer, and R. Denney, op. cit.; Beach, D.S. "An Organizational Problem—Subordinate-Superior Relations." *Advanced Management,* (1960) pp. 12-15. |
| 79 | 22 | Looking to others for guidance under conditions of ambiguity is basic to a 5,5 orientation. See Festinger, L.A. *Theory of Cognitive Dissonance.* Palo Alto, Cal.: Stanford University, 1957; Thomas, W.I., and F. Znaniecki. "Three Types of Personality." In C.W. Mills, ed., *Images of Man.* New York: George Braziller, 1960, p. 408; Riesman, D., op. cit.; Tannenbaum, R., I.R. Weschler, and F. Massarik. *Leadership and Organization: A Behavioral Science Approach.* New York: McGraw-Hill, 1961, p. 47. |
| | | The depth of influence on individuals from conformity pressures is fully demonstrated in behavioral science research. See Grace, H.A. "Conformance and Performance." *Journal of Social Psychology,* 40, (1954) pp. 333-335; Asch, S.E. "Studies of Independence and Conformity: I. A Minority of One Against a Unanimous Majority." *Psychological Monograph,* 70, No. 9 (1956); Brehm, J., and L. Festinger. "Pressures Toward Uniformity of Performance in Groups." *Human Relations,* 10, (1957) pp. 85-91; Merei, F., op. cit.; Jackson, J.M., and H.D. Saltzstein. "The Effect of Person-Group Relations on Conformity Pressures." *Journal of Abnormal & Social Psychology,* 57, (1958) pp. 17-24; Kiesler, C.A., and S.B. Kiesler. *Conformity.* Reading, Mass.: Addison-Wesley Publishing Co., 1969; Berg, I.A., and B.M. Bass, eds. *Conformity in Deviation.* New York: Harper, 1961. |

| Page | Line | |
|------|------|---|
| 80 | 1 | The 5,5-oriented use of surveys, for example, is discussed in Randall, C.B. *The Folklore of Management.* New York: Mentor, 1961, pp. 52-53. |
| 80 | 9 | For discussion of early and continuing recognition of the role of informal organization, see Barnard, C.I. *The Functions of the Executive.* Cambridge: Harvard University, 1938, pp. 114-123; Koontz, H., and C. O'Donnell, op. cit., pp. 290-292. Others include Gulick, L., and L. Urwick, eds. *Papers on the Science of Administration.* New York: Institute of Public Administration, 1927; Urwick, L. *The Elements of Administration.* New York: Harper, 1944; Mooney, J.D. *The Principles of Organization.* New York: Harper, 1947; Taylor, F.W. *Scientific Management.* New York: Harper, 1948; Fayol, H. *General and Industrial Management.* New York: Pitman, 1949; Holden, P.E., S. Fish, and H.L. Smith. *Top Management Organization and Control.* New York: McGraw-Hill, 1951; Koontz, H., and C. O'Donnell, op. cit., pp. 238-240; Roethlisberger, F.J., and W.J. Dickson. *Management and the Worker.* Cambridge: Harvard University, 1939; Homans, G.C. *The Human Group.* New York: Harcourt, Brace, 1950; Festinger, L., Schachter, S., and K. Back. *Social Pressures in Informal Groups.* New York: Harper, 1950; Festinger, L. "Informal Communications in Small Groups." In H. Guetzkow, ed., *Groups, Leadership and Men: Research in Human Relations.* Pittsburgh: Carnegie, 1951, pp. 28-43; Schachter, S. "Deviation, Rejection and Communication." *Journal of Abnormal & Social Psychology,* 46, (1951) pp. 190-207; Festinger, L., H.B. Gerard, B. Hymovitch, H.H. Kelley, and B. Raven. "The Influence Process in the Presence of Extreme Deviates." *Human Relations,* 5, (1952) pp. 327-346; Seashore, S.E. *Group Cohesiveness in the Industrial Work Group.* Ann Arbor: University of Michigan, 1954; Sherif, M., and C. Sherif. *An Outline of Social Psychology* (rev. ed.). New York: Harper, 1956, pp. 146-177; Marrow, A.J. *Making Management Human.* New York: McGraw-Hill, 1957, pp. 154-170; Zaleznik, A., C.R. Christensen, and F.J. Roethlisberger. *The Motivation, Productivity, and Satisfaction of Workers: A Prediction Study.* Boston: Harvard University, 1958, pp. 121-135; Dalton, M. *Men Who Manage.* New York: Wiley, 1959; Koontz, H., and C. O'Donnell, op. cit., pp. 291-292; Doutt, J.T. "Management Must Manage the Informal Groups Too." *Advanced Management,* 24, (1957) pp. 26-28; Davis, K. "A Method of Studying Communication Patterns in Organizations." *Personnel Psychology,* 6, (1953) pp. 301-312; Whyte, W.F. "An Interaction Approach to |

| Page | Line | |
|------|------|---|

the Theory of Organization." In M. Haire, ed., *Modern Organization Theory.* New York: Wiley, 1959, pp. 155-183; Gray, J.L., and F.A. Starke. *Organization Behavior, Concepts and Applications.* Columbus, Ohio: Charles E. Merrill Publishing Company, 1977, pp. 132-150; Longenecker, J.G. *Essentials of Management.* Columbus, Ohio: Charles E. Merrill Publishing Company, 1977, pp. 140-145; Haimann, T., and R.L. Hilgert. *Supervision: Concepts and Practices of Management,* 2nd ed. Cincinnati: South-Western Publishing Co., 1977, pp. 170-171.

80    16    The experimental and industrial literature provides many examples of group production standards and pressures against "rate busters" and violators who go against group norms and standards. Ways of "beating" the supervisor and rules also are cited. See Blau, P.M. *The Dynamics of Bureaucracy.* Chicago: University of Chicago, 1955, pp. 172-179, 184-188; Blau, P.M. "Cooperation and Competition in a Bureaucracy." *American Journal of Sociology,* 59, (1954) pp. 530-535; Rice, A.K. "The Use of Unrecognized Cultural Mechanisms in an Expanding Machine Shop; With a Contribution to the Theory of Leadership." *Human Relations,* 4, (1951) pp. 143-160; Festinger, L., H.B. Gerard et al., op. cit., pp. 327-346; Roethlisberger, F.J., and W.J. Dickson, op. cit.; Whyte, W.F. *Money and Motivation.* New York: Harper, 1955; Roy, D. "Quota Restrictions and Goldbricking in a Machine Shop." *American Journal of Sociology,* (1952) pp. 427-442; Crutchfield, R. "Conformity and Character." *American Psychologists,* 10, (1955) pp. 191-198; Fromm, E., op. cit., pp. 196-197; Riesman, D., N. Glazer, and R. Denney, op. cit., p. 24; Lynd, H.M., op. cit.; Gellerman, S.W. *Motivation and Productivity.* New York: American Management Association. 1963, pp. 151-159.

81    19    The "groupthink" mentality is discussed and analyzed as it relates to the Bay of Pigs and other decisions. See Janis, I. *Groupthink.* Boston: Houghton Mifflin, 1972.

82    2    Evaluation of compromise to resolve differences is in Simmel, G. *Conflict* and *The Web of Group-Affiliations.* (Trans. by K.H. Wolff and R. Bendix.) Glencoe, Ill.: Free Press, 1955, pp. 114-116.

82    21    Discussions of 5,5-oriented mechanisms such as accommodation and adjustment for relieving tension are presented in Pitts, J.R. "Introduction to Personality and the Social System. Part III." In T. Parsons, E. Shils, K.D. Naegele, and J.R. Pitts, eds., *Theories of Society,* Vol. II. Glencoe, Ill.: Free Press, 1961, p. 711; Allen, L.A., op. cit., p. 327; March, J.G.,

| Page | Line | |
|------|------|---|

and H.A. Simon. *Organizations.* New York: Wiley, 1958, pp. 129-130; Strauss, G., and L.R. Sayles. *Personnel: The Human Problems of Management.* Englewood Cliffs, N.J.: Prentice-Hall, 1960, p. 178; Danielson, L.E., and N.R.F. Maier. "Supervisory Problems in Decision Making." In E.A. Fleishman, ed., *Studies in Personnel and Industrial Psychology.* Homewood, Ill.: Dorsey, 1961, pp. 361-368; Maier, N.R.F., and L.E. Danielson. "An Evaluation of Two Approaches to Discipline in Industry." In E.A. Fleishman, ed., op. cit., pp. 369-375.

**84   6**   For using transfers as a separation device, see Tannenbaum, R., et al., op. cit., 1961, p. 108.

**84   8**   How to redraw organization charts to resolve problems is in Brech, E.F.L. *Organization: The Framework of Management.* London: Pitman, 1956, Ch. 4; Koontz, H., and C. O'Donnell, op. cit., pp. 286, 288.

**85   7**   How status and prestige operate to reinforce 5,5 adjustments is discussed in Mills, C.W. *White Collar.* New York: Oxford, 1953, pp. 254-258; Thibaut, J.W., and H.H. Kelley. *The Social Psychology of Groups.* New York: Wiley, 1959, pp. 222-238; Strauss, G., and L.R. Sayles, op. cit., pp. 68-74; Mausner, B. "Studies in Social Interaction: III. Effect of Variation in One Partner's Prestige on the Interaction of Observer Pairs." *Journal of Applied Psychology,* 37, (1953) pp. 391-393; Cole, D. " 'Rational Argument' and 'Prestige-Suggestion' as Factors Influencing Judgment." *Sociometry,* 17, (1954) pp. 350-354; Sherif, M., and C. Sherif, op. cit., 1956; Koontz, H., and C. O'Donnell, op. cit., p. 323.

**85   21**   The creativity issue is discussed in Mills, C.W., op. cit., 1953, pp. 53-54; Dow, A.B. "An Architect's View on Creativity." In H.H. Anderson, ed., *Creativity and Its Cultivation.* New York: Harper, 1959, pp. 32-33; Stoddard, G.D. "Creativity in Education." In H.H. Anderson, ed., op. cit., p. 181; Hader, J.J. "Role Perception in Management Training for Creativity." *Advanced Management,* 23, (1958) pp. 18-31; Hilgard, E.R. "Creativity and Problem-Solving." In H.H. Anderson, ed., op. cit., pp. 170-171; Bellows, R., T. Gilson, and G.S. Odiorne. *Executive Skills: Their Dynamics and Development.* Englewood Cliffs, N.J.: Prentice-Hall, 1962, pp. 298-299; Osborn, A.F. *Applied Imagination* (rev. ed.). New York: Scribner's, 1957.

**86   15**   Evidence from sociological and anthropological studies indicates that people who get into and conform with the norms of the group in which they hold membership seem to have lower levels of suscep-

| Page | Line | |
|------|------|---|
| | | tibility to disease, particularly when the environment is homogeneous and undemanding. See Hinkle, L.E., Jr., and H.G. Wolff. "An Investigation of the Relation Between Life Experience, Personality Characteristics, and General Susceptibility to Illness." *Psychosomatic Medicine*, 20, (1958) pp. 278-295; Leighton, D.C., et al. *The Character of Danger*, Vol. 3. New York: Basic Books, 1963; Cassel, J.T. "Physical Illness in Response to Stress." In S. Levine and N.A. Scotch, eds., *Social Stress.* Chicago: Aldine, 1970, pp. 189-209. Hinkle, Leighton, and Cassel state that people conforming to culturally-acceptable patterns tend to be mentally and physically more healthy. See also Moss, G.E. *Illness, Immunity, and Social Interaction.* New York: John Wiley & Sons, 1973, p. 155. Moss also suggests that those persons who become alienated from their membership group are more likely to be susceptible to disease than those who hold membership. See pp. 170-172. |
| 86 | 21 | The idea of "inferiority complex" was introduced into psychology by Adler, A. *The Education of Children.* Chicago: Henry Regnery Company, 1970, p. 36. |
| 87 | 2 | The dynamics of the "Who am I?" dilemma are developed quite fully by Wheelis, A., op. cit., pp. 125-138. |
| 87 | 25 | Research reinforcing this point of view has been presented by Moss, G.E., op. cit. |
| 87 | 27 | The role of anxiety in peptic ulcer context is clarified by Mahl, G.F., and R. Karpe. "Emotions and Hydrochloric Acid Secretion During Psychoanalytic Hours." *Psychosomatic Medicine*, 15, (1953) pp. 312. |
| 87 | 33 | Adjustment and fitting in as a value in child rearing is discussed in Kovar, L.C. *Faces of the Adolescent Girl.* Englewood Cliffs, N.J.: Prentice-Hall, 1968, p. 35. |
| 87 | 35 | Fromm affirms that a 5,5 orientation comes from parental guidance that emphasizes to the child the importance of adjusting to the group. Fromm, E., op. cit., p. 140. |
| 88 | 2 | Using the norms and mores of the community in an uncritical way to guide one's own behavior is commented upon by Riesman, D., N. Glazer, and R. Denney, op. cit., pp. 72-74. |
| 88 | 4 | An important distinction is made between socialization, a 5,5 orientation, and social development, a 9,9 characteristic. See Anderson, H.H. "Creativity as Personality Development." In H.H. Anderson, ed., op. cit., pp. 137-138. |
| 88 | 10 | The importance of "other children" as a model for a child's development is depicted in Kovar, L.C., op. cit., pp. 39-41. |

| Page | Line | |
|------|------|---|
| 88 | 14 | Popularity is a motivating factor in 5,5-oriented child rearing, as described in Riesman, D., N. Glazer, and R. Denney, op. cit., pp. 59-62, 91-102; Kovar, L.C., op. cit., pp. 41-47. |
| 88 | 20 | The importance of peers in defining a child's reaction to new situations is described in Kovar, L.C., op. cit., pp. 36-38; Wheelis, A., op. cit., pp. 92, 126. |

This characterization of a 5,5 orientation has been called by Blos "uniformism." It is present whenever a person is emersed in the peer group with acceptance of its norms and standards as infallible and regulatory. Blos points out that this may assist a teenager in moving away from family dependence toward autonomy. However, he also points out that for numerous teenagers, the excessive reliance on peer norms becomes a way of life and forecloses the capacity for self-regulation and independence. Blos, P. *On Adolescence, A Psychoanalytic Interpretation.* New York: Free Press, 1962.

| | | |
|------|------|---|
| 88 | 40 | Using "experts" as a source of guidance for one's parental practices is described by Riesman, D., N. Glazer, and R. Denney, op. cit., pp. 65-66. |
| 90 | 1 | Caution regarding the giving and receiving of advice is described in detail by Sforza, C. *The Living Thoughts of Machiavelli.* New York: Fawcett, 1958. |
| 90 | 3 | Use of flattery, showing interest, and so on in order to gain influence over another is described by Carnegie, D. *How to Win Friends and Influence People.* New York: Simon & Schuster, 1964, p. 27. |
| 90 | 4 | Resistance of workers to management efforts to lift factory morale may stem from the fact that they are given the "glad hand" rather than being genuinely involved. The "glad hand" is a 5,5 facade. Historically it has been practiced by morale engineers, personnel department specialists, and some training directors. See Riesman, D., N. Glazer, and R. Denney, op. cit., pp. 302-303, 311-312. |
| 92 | 5 | These tactics are described in Maccoby, M. *The Gamesman.* New York: Simon and Schuster, 1976, pp. 86-97. |
| 92 | 13 | Commentaries on the human relations swing include, Schoen, D. "Human Relations: Boon or Bogle?" *Harvard Business Review*, March-April (1957) p. 15; Ohmann, O.A. "Search for a Managerial Philosophy." *Harvard Business Review*, 35, (1957) pp. 41-51; Lachman, M.S. "The Supervisor Hasn't Had a Chance." *Advanced Management*, 23, (1958) pp. 17-18; McGregor, D. *The Human Side of Enterprise.* New York: McGraw-Hill, 1960, p. 34. |
| 92 | 33 | Whyte, W.H., op. cit. |

| **Page** | **Line** | |
|------|------|---|
| 93 | 19 | When red tape determines decisions, not problem solving, a bureaucracy is operating in a 5,5 way. See Blau, P.M., op. cit., pp. 172-179, 184-188; Jennings, E.M. *An Anatomy of Leadership.* New York: Harper, 1960, p. 27; Mills, C.W., op. cit., pp. 80-81; Herzberg, F., B. Mausner, and B.B. Snyderman. *The Motivation to Work.* New York: Wiley, 1959, p. 125; Jennings, E.M. *The Executive: Autocrat, Bureaucrat, Democrat.* New York: Harper & Row, 1962, p. 90. |
| 93 | 35 | Penn Central as a 5,5-oriented organization that was not able to grapple with its problems and ending up in bankruptcy is reported by Binxen, P., and J. Daughen. *Wreck of the Penn Central.* Boston: Little, Brown & Co., 1971. |

### Chapter 7

| 95 | 1 | 9,9-oriented concepts of involvement, participation, commitment, conflict resolution, etc. were brought to early definition by Simmel in 1908. See Simmel, G. *Conflict* (Trans. by K.H. Wolff). Glencoe, Ill.: Free Press, 1955; Metcalf, H.C., and L. Urwick. *Dynamic Administration: The Collected Papers of Mary Parker Follett.* New York: Harper, 1940, pp. 31-32. The theory and concepts of 9,9 management find expression in the research of Lewin and associates in the 1930s, particularly the concepts of *participation, goal-setting, involvement* and *commitment, interpersonal relations*, and strategies for individual and organizational *change.* See Lewin, K. *Field Theory in Social Science.* New York: Harper, 1951. See also Lewin K. "Forces Behind Food Habits and Methods of Change." *Bulletin of National Research Council,* 108, (1943) pp. 35-65; Lewin, K. "Frontiers in Group Dynamics: Concept, Method and Reality in Social Science: Social Equilibria and Social Change." In T.M. Newcomb, and E.L. Hartley, eds., *Readings in Social Psychology.* New York: Holt, 1947, pp. 330-344; Lewin, K. "Frontiers in Group Dynamics: II. Channels of Group Life: Social Planning and Action Research." *Human Relations,* 1, (1947) pp. 143-153; Lewin, K. *Resolving Social Conflicts: Selected Papers on Group Dynamics.* New York: Harper, 1948; and Lewin, K. "Behavior and Development as a Function of the Total Situation." In L. Carmichael, ed., *Manual of Child Psychology.* New York: Wiley, 1946, pp. 791-844. For a discussion of and additional relevant references to Lewin's work, see Deutsch, M. "Field Theory in Social Psychology." In G. Lindzey, ed., *Handbook of* |

| Page | Line | |
|------|------|---|
| | | *Social Psychology*, Vol. I. Reading, Mass.: Addison-Wesley, 1954, pp. 181-222. |
| | | Extensive documentation as to how various experts in different fields have dealt with issues related to 9,9 in comparison with other Grid styles are shown in the Appendix of this book. |
| 95 | 2 | Argyris and McGregor have crystallized and put into perspective what are thought to be the more mature needs of individuals in the work situation. See Argyris, C. *Personality and Organization*. New York: Harper & Bros., 1957, pp. 20-53; McGregor, D. *The Human Side of Enterprise*. New York: McGraw-Hill, 1960, pp. 45-58. See also Borgatta, E.F., A.S. Couch, and R.F. Bales. "Some Findings Relevant to the Great Man Theory of Leadership." In A.P. Hare, E.F. Borgatta, and R.F. Bales, eds., *Small Groups: Studies in Social Interaction*. New York: Knopf, 1955, pp. 568-574; Haythorn, W. "The Influence of Individual Members on the Characteristics of Small Groups." *Journal of Abnormal & Social Psychology*, 48, (1953) pp. 276-284. |
| 95 | 5 | The "productive orientation" is close in meaning to "concern for production," coupled with "concern for people," as in the 9,9 orientation. See Fromm, E. *The Sane Society*. Greenwich, Conn.: Fawcett Publications, 1955, p. 37. |
| 95 | 8 | The motivation to make a contribution of a 9,9 character is explained by Fromm as an act of giving. "This experience of heightened vitality and potency fills me with joy. I experience myself as overflowing, spending, alive, hence, as joyous. Giving is more joyous than receiving, not because it is a deprivation, but because in the act of giving lies the expression of my aliveness." Seen in this light, giving or making a contribution is a manifestation of self-actualization. See Fromm, E. *The Art of Loving*. London: Unwin Books, 1957, p. 26. |
| | | The emotional aspects of a 9,9-oriented relationship are seen as consisting of at least four components: care, responsibility, respect, and knowledge. Fromm, E., op. cit., 1955, p. 38. |
| | | Family and other analogies to the work situation are developed in Wolfe, D.M. "Power and Authority in the Family." In D. Cartwright, ed., *Studies in Social Power*. Ann Arbor: Institute for Social Research, 1959, pp. 100-101; Vroom, V.H. *Some Personality Determinants of the Effects of Participation*. Englewood Cliffs, N.J.: Prentice-Hall, 1960, pp. 1-18. |
| 95 | 12 | Rollo May devotes Chapter 12, 287-325, to the meaning of care, equivalent to the motivational care of a |

| Page | Line | |
|------|------|---|
| | | 9,9 orientation. See May, R. *Love and Will*. New York: Norton, 1969. |
| 95 | 31 | *The Managerial Grid: A Self-Examination of Managerial Styles*. Austin, Tex.: Scientific Methods, Inc., 1962 (Revised 1978). Reproduced by permission. |
| 96 | 24 | Goal-oriented behavior of organization members is reviewed in Blake, R.R., and J.S. Mouton. *Corporate Excellence Through Grid Organization Development*. Houston: Gulf, 1968. |
| 96 | 27 | Several consequences for subordinates of 9,9-oriented leadership are specified: (1) subordinates more explicitly relate individual motivations to organization goals; (2) participation induces greater clarity of identification and awareness of paths to various goals; (3) the opportunity of participants to increase their control over what happens is increased; (4) once participation has clarified steps to be taken, autonomy is increased; (5) when personnel participate, the resultant thinking through of consequences increases their own involvement in bringing successful outcomes about. See Mitchell, T.R. "Motivation and Participation: An Integration." *Academy of Management Journal*, 16, No. 4 (1973) pp. 670-679; Lawler, E.E. *Motivation in Work Organizations*. Monterey, Calif.: Brooks Cole, 1973, pp. 83-84; Zenger, J., and D. Miller. "Building Effective Teams." *Personnel*, 52, No. 2 (March-April 1974) pp. 20-29. |

In examining the literature and experimental work concerned with participation, it is important to distinguish between pseudo and genuine participation. Attempts to make people *think* or *feel* their ideas are important, or manipulation of ego involvement, or artificial status-raising activities are not seen to be *sound* participation. The work of Coch and French and the insights of Levine and Butler make significant contributions to the 9,9 concept of participation. See Coch, L., and J.R.P. French, Jr. "Overcoming Resistance to Change." *Human Relations*, 1, (1948) pp. 512-532; and Levine, J., and J. Butler. "Lecture Versus Group Decision in Changing Behavior." *Journal of Applied Psychology*, 36, (1952) pp. 29-33. For additional representative experimental studies and discussions, see the work of Lewin, previously cited, and, Marrow, A.J., and J.R.P. French, Jr. "Changing a Stereotype in Industry." *Journal of Social Issues*, 1, No. 3 (1945) pp. 33-37; Lewis, H.B., and M. Franklin. "An Experimental Study of the Role of the Ego in Work; II. The Significance of Task Orientation in Work." *Journal of Experimental Psychology*, 34, (1944) pp. 195-215; French, J.R.P., Jr. "Group Productivity." In H. Guetzkow, ed., *Groups, Leadership and*

| Page | Line | |
|------|------|---|
| | | *Men: Research in Human Relations.* Pittsburgh: Carnegie Press, 1951, pp. 44-54; Gerard, H.B. "The Anchorage of Opinions in Face-to-Face Groups." *Human Relations*, 7, (1954) pp. 313-325; Kidd, J.S., and D.T. Campbell. "Conformity to Groups as a Function of Group Success." *Journal of Abnormal & Social Psychology*, 51, (1955) pp. 390-403; Berkowitz, L., and B.I. Levy. "Pride in Group Performance and Group Task Motivation." *Journal of Abnormal & Social Psychology*, 53, (1956) pp. 300-306; Cohen, E. "The Effect of Members' Use of Formal Groups as a Reference Group Upon Group Effectiveness." *Journal of Social Psychology*, 46, (1957) pp. 307-309; Marrow, A.J. *Making Management Human.* New York: McGraw-Hill, 1957, pp. 182-200; Juan, J.M. "Improving the Relationship Between Line and Staff." In K. Davis, and W. Scott, eds., *Readings in Human Relations.* New York: McGraw-Hill, 1959, pp. 238-248; McGregor, D., op. cit., p. 130; Vroom, V.H., op. cit.; French, J.R.P., Jr., I.C. Ross, S. Kirby, J.R. Nelson, and P. Smyth. "Employee Participation in a Program of Industrial Change." In E.A. Fleishman, ed., *Studies in Personnel and Industrial Psychology.* Homewood, Ill.: Dorsey, 1961, pp. 281-295. See also Trow, D.B. "Autonomy and Job Satisfaction in Task-Oriented Groups." *Journal of Abnormal & Social Psychology*, 54, (1957) pp. 204-209; Bradford, L.P., and G.L. Lippitt. "The Individual Counts . . . in Effective Group Relations." In L.P. Bradford, ed., *Group Development.* Washington, D.C.: National Training Laboratories, NEA, 1961, pp. 25-30. |
| 96 | 29 | Guest's work is a description of the managerial actions of a 9,9-oriented manager. See especially "Plant Y," post-1953. Guest, R.H. *Organizational Change: The Effect of Successful Leadership.* Homewood, Ill.: Dorsey, 1962, pp. 40-81. |
| 96 | 30 | This study showed that scores on a locus of control test are correlated with leadership style. Locus of control indicates whether people are internals—believing that what happens to them occurs because of their behavior; or externals—believing that what happens to them does so because of chance. Internals appear to be more satisfied with participatory 9,9-like kinds of leadership, while externals are more satisfied with directive or 9,1 kinds of leadership. Runyon, K.E. "Some Interactions Between Personality Variables and Management Styles." *Journal of Applied Psychology*, 57, (1973) pp. 288-294. |
| 96 | 38 | Importance of self-control for achieving organization purpose is discussed in Goodacre, D.M. "Group Characteristics of Good and Poor Performing Combat |

**Page**        **Line**

Units." *Sociometry,* 16, (1953) pp. 168-178; Maier, N.R.F. *Psychology in Industry.* Boston: Houghton, 1955, pp. 172-173; Stagner, R. "Motivational Aspects of Industrial Morale." *Personnel Psychology,* 11, (1958) pp. 64-70; Barnes, L.B. *Organizational Systems and Engineering Groups.* Boston: Harvard University, 1960, pp. 152-156.

96          40        Greater attention, through education, to the thoughts and feelings of people and the development of capacities for involvement, participation, and commitment are requisites for sounder management than what is being realized today. See Mayo, E. *The Human Problems of an Industrial Civilization.* New York: Macmillan, 1933; Whitehead, T.N. *The Industrial Worker.* Cambridge: Harvard University Press, 1938; Roethlisberger, F.J., and W.J. Dickson. *Management and the Worker.* Cambridge: Harvard University Press, 1939; Coch, L., and J.R.P. French, Jr., op. cit.; Marrow, A.J., op. cit., 1957; Likert, R. *New Patterns of Management.* New York: McGraw-Hill, 1961; Blake, R.R., and J.S. Mouton. *Group Dynamics—Key to Decision Making.* Houston: Gulf, 1961; Blake, R.R., and J.S. Mouton. "The Developing Revolution in Management." *Training Directors Journal,* 16, (1962) pp. 29-52.

For a review of additional experimental studies and investigations in this and related areas, see Wilensky, H.L. "Human Relations in the Workplace: An Appraisal of Some Recent Research." In C.M. Arensberg, ed., *Research in Industrial Human Relations.* New York: Harper, 1957, pp. 25-50; Cartwright, D., and A. Zander, eds., *Group Dynamics—Research and Theory,* 2nd ed. Evanston, Ill.: Row, Peterson, 1960; Hare, A.P., E.F. Borgatta, and R.F. Bales, eds., *Small Groups: Studies in Social Interaction.* New York: Knopf, 1955; Fleishman, E.A., ed., op. cit.; Lindzey, G., ed., op. cit., Vols. I and II; Maccoby, E.E., T.M. Newcomb, and E.L. Hartley, eds., *Readings in Social Psychology* (3rd ed.). New York: Holt, 1958; Bass, B.M. *Leadership Psychology and Organizational Behavior.* New York: Harper, 1960; Stoodley, B.H., ed., *Society and Self.* Glencoe, Ill.: Free Press, 1962; Rosenbaum, M., and M. Berger, eds., *Group Psychotherapy and Group Function.* New York: Basic Books, 1963.

97          11        A similar point is made in Guest, R.H., op. cit., pp. 77-81. See also Opinion Research Corporation's *How to Develop More Profit-Minded Employees.* Princeton: Opinion Research, 1963; Pages, M. "The Sociotherapy of the Enterprise." In W. Bennis, K. Benne, and R. Chin, eds., *The Planning of Change.* New York: Holt, Rinehart & Winston, 1961, p. 179.

| Page | Line | |
|------|------|---|
| 97 | 16 | A point of view emphasizing the importance of the organization as the unit of change appears in Bucklow, M. "A New Role for the Work Group." *Administrative Science Quarterly*, 11, No. 1 (1966) pp. 59-78. |
| 97 | 26 | Various educational alternatives to the lecture method are studied in Maier, N.R.F. "An Experimental Test of the Effect of Training on Discussion Leadership." *Human Relations*, 6, (1953) pp. 161-173; Bradford, L.P., et al., *Explorations in Human Relations Training*. Washington, D.C.: National Training Laboratory in Group Development, 1953; Blake, R.R., and J.S. Mouton, op. cit., 1961; Blake, R.R., and J.S. Mouton. "Improving Organizational Problem Solving Through Increasing the Flow and Utilization of New Ideas." *Training Directors Journal*, 17, No. 9 (1963) pp. 48-57 and No. 10 pp. 38-54; Corsini, R.J., M.E. Shaw, and R.R. Blake. *Roleplaying in Business and Industry*. Glencoe, Ill.: Free Press, 1961. See also Mouton, J.S., and R.R. Blake. *Instrumented Team Learning: A Behavioral Approach to Student-Centered Learning*. Austin, Texas: Scientific Methods, Inc., 1975. |
| 97 | 31 | For descriptions of the Scanlon Plan see Schutz, G.P. "Worker Participation on Production Problems: A Discussion of Experience with the 'Scanlon Plan.'" *Personnel*, 28, (1951) pp. 201-210; Whyte, W.F. *Money and Motivation*. New York: Harper, 1955, pp. 166-188; Lesieur, F.G., ed., *The Scanlon Plan*. New York: Wiley, 1958; McGregor, D., op. cit., pp. 110-123; Strauss, G., and L.R. Sayles. *Personnel: The Human Problems of Management*. Englewood Cliffs, N.J.: Prentice-Hall, 1960, pp. 326, 662, 670-674; Tracy, H. "Scanlon Plans: Leading Edge in Labor-Management Cooperation." *World of Work Report*, 2, No. 3 (1977) pp. 25, 32. |
| 97 | 32 | Team norms/standards not pertinent to problem-solving task requirements can impede performance. Productivity-relevant norms are pertinent for examination and change. See Napier, R., and M. Gershenfeld. *Groups: Theory and Experience*. Boston: Houghton-Mifflin, 1974. |
| 97 | 38 | Case studies related to teamwork development are in Blake, R.R., and J.S. Mouton. *Corporate Excellence Through Grid Organization Development*. Houston: Gulf, 1968, pp. 92-157; Kuriloff, A.H., and S. Atkins. "T Group for a Work Team." *Journal of Applied Behavioral Science*, 2, No. 1 (1966) pp. 63-93; Margulies, N.P., and A.P. Raia. "People in Organizations: A Case for Team Building." *Training and Development Journal*, 22, No. 8 (1968) pp. 2-11; Golembiewski, R.T., S.B. Carrigan, W.R. Mead, R. |

Munzenrider, and A. Blumberg. "Toward Building New Work Relationships: An Action Design for a Critical Intervention." *Journal of Applied Behavioral Science,* 6, No. 2 (1972) pp. 135-148; Gibb, J.R. "TORI Theory: Consultantless Team-Building." *Journal of Contemporary Business,* 1, No. 3 (1972) pp. 33-41; Harvey, J.B., and C.R. Boettger. "Improving Communication within a Managerial Workgroup." *Journal of Applied Behavioral Science,* 7, No. 2 (1971) pp. 164-179; Zand, D.E. "Collateral Organization: A New Change Strategy." *Journal of Applied Behavioral Science,* 10, No. 1 (1974) pp. 63-89; Weisbord, M.R., H. Lamb, and A. Drexler. *Improving Police Department Management through Problem-Solving Task Forces: A Case Study in Organization Development.* Reading, Mass.: Addison-Wesley, 1974; Varney, G.H., and J. Lasher. "Surveys and Feedback as a Means of Organization Diagnosis and Change." In T.H. Patten, Jr., ed., *OD—Emerging Dimensions and Concepts.* Washington, D.C.: American Society for Training and Development, 1973, pp. 75-82; Herman, S.M. "A Gestalt Orientation to OD." In W.W. Burke, ed., *Contemporary Organization Development: Conceptual Orientations and Interventions.* Washington, D.C.: NTL Institute for Applied Behavioral Science, 1972, pp. 69-86; Thomas, A., B. Izmirian, and J. Harris. "Federal Cutbacks: An External Crisis Intervention Model." *Social Change,* 3, No. 2 (1973) pp. 1-3.

98        10    Demonstration of relationships between productivity and satisfaction is reported in Lawler, E.E., op. cit., pp. 83-84.

98        14    Phases that groups pass through as they move toward accomplishment of a task have been measured and characteristic patterns of interactions described. See Parsons, T., R.F. Bales, and E.A. Shils. *Working Papers in the Theory of Action.* Glencoe, Ill.: Free Press, 1953, pp. 111-161; Kelley, H.H., and J.W. Thibaut. "Experimental Studies in Group Problem Solving and Process." In G. Lindzey, ed., op. cit., Vol. II, pp. 735-785; Pepinsky, H.B., and P.N. Pepinsky. "Organization Management Strategy, and Team Productivity." In L. Petrullo, and B.M. Bass, eds., *Leadership and Interpersonal Behavior.* New York: Holt, Rinehart & Winston, 1961, p. 229; and Shepard, H.A., and W.G. Bennis. "A Theory of Training by Group Methods." *Human Relations,* 9, (1956) pp. 403-414.
Productivity is increased when a person participates actively in setting goals over which he has control. See Terborg, J.R. "The Motivational Components of Goal Setting." *Journal of Applied Psychology,* 61, No. 5 (1976) pp. 613-621.

| Page | Line | |
|------|------|---|
| 98 | 17 | A questionnaire approach to follow up on the impact of a 9,9-oriented management-by-objectives program in an organization manufacturing tools demonstrated advantages resulting from it such as better planning, better identification of problem areas, more objective performance measures, and improved communications. Tosi, H., and J. Carrol. "Management Reaction to Management by Objectives." *Academy of Management Journal,* 11, No. 4 (1968) pp. 415-426. |
| 98 | 19 | A 9,9-oriented approach to management-by-objectives results in subordinates reporting, to a statistically significant level, greater goal involvement, and substantially greater agreement between boss and subordinate about the job to be done and ways of improving their current performance. See Huse, E.F., and E. Kay. "Improving Employee Productivity through Work Planning." In J. Blood, ed., *The Personnel Job in the Changing World.* New York: American Management Association, 1964, pp. 301-302. Specifications for setting effective objectives in an MbO program are found in *Industry Week,* June 8, 1970, pp. 40-45. |
| 98 | 24 | Analysis of properties of 9,9-oriented goals are available in Dewey, J. *Democracy and Education.* New York: MacMillan, 1944, pp. 100-110; Sherif, M., and C. Sherif. *An Outline of Social Psychology* (rev. ed.). New York: Harper, 1956, pp. 152-156, 194, 230, 317-330; Sherif, M., O.J. Harvey, B.J. White, W.R. Hood, and C. Sherif. "Intergroup Conflict and Cooperation: The Robbers Cave Experiment." Norman, Okla.: Institute of Group Relations, 1961, pp. 159-197; Krech, D., R.S. Crutchfield, and E.L. Ballachey. *Individual in Society.* New York: McGraw-Hill, 1962, pp. 398-402. A number of texts which describe mechanics of management-by-objectives without particular regard for creating a behavior climate conducive to use such a method include Odiorne, G.S. *Management By Objectives.* New York: Pittman Pub. Corp., 1956; Humble, J. *Improving Business Results.* Maidenhead, Berks.: McGraw-Hill, 1967; Reddin, W.J. *Effective Management By Objectives.* New York: McGraw-Hill, 1971. See also McConkey, D.D. *How to Manage By Results,* 3rd ed. New York: American Management Association, 1977; McConkey, D.D. *MBO for Nonprofit Organizations.* New York: American Management Association, 1975; McConkey, D.D. *Management By Objectives for Staff Managers,* 3rd ed. New York: Vantage Press, Inc., 1977; McConkey, D.D., and R. Vanderweele. *Financial Management By Objectives.* Englewood Cliffs, N.J.: Prentice-Hall, 1976; Morrisey, G.L. *Appraisal and Development Through Objectives and Results.* |

| Page | Line |
|------|------|

Reading, Mass.: Addison-Wesley, 1972; Morrisey, G.L. *Management By Objectives and Results.* Supervisory Series. Reading, Mass.: Addison-Wesley, 1970; Morrisey, G.L. *Management By Objectives and Results in the Public Sector.* Reading, Mass.: Addison-Wesley, 1976; Varney, G.J. *Management By Objectives.* Chicago, Ill.: Dartnell Corporation, 1971. For a review of field research that leads to the conclusion that MbO can be effective when the program is properly designed and implemented, see Ivancevich, J.M. "A Longitudinal Assessment of Management by Objectives." *Administrative Science Quarterly,* 17, No. 1 (1972) pp. 126-138.

98      40      Research pertinent to goal clarity appears in Lewin, K., op. cit., 1951, p. 255; Raven, B.H., and J. Rietsema. "The Effects of Varied Clarity of Group Goal and Group Path Upon the Individual and His Relation to His Group." *Human Relations,* 10, (1957) pp. 29-44; Cohen, A.R. "Situational Structure, Self-Esteem, and Threat-Oriented Reactions to Power." In D. Cartwright, ed., op. cit., pp. 35-52; Gerard, H.B. "Some Effects of Status, Role Clarity, and Group Goal Clarity Upon the Individual's Relations to Group Process." *Journal of Personality,* 25, (1957) pp. 475-488.

99      11      Herzberg, et al., conclude that motivation of a more fundamental and long-lasting character is embedded in the activity of the work itself, *i.e.,* responsibility, achievement, advancement, and other factors that create a sense of significant accomplishment. These are 9,9-oriented aspects of contributing. Factors not directly related to work, *i.e., hygienic,* or 1,9-oriented factors, take on more importance as work becomes less challenging and meaningful. See Herzberg, F., B. Mausner, and B.B. Snyderman. *The Motivation to Work.* New York: Wiley, 1959, pp. 64, 70, 132, 144. Also see White, R.W. "Motivation Reconsidered: The Concept of Competence." *Psychological Review,* 66, (1959) pp. 297-334; Myers, M.S. "The Human Factor in Management Systems." *California Management Review,* XIV, No. 1 (1971) pp. 5-10.

99      13      Assignment to undemanding jobs is reported to be related to reduced managerial success in later years. Berlew, D.E., and D.T. Hall. "The Socialization of Managers: Effects of Expectations on Performance." *Administrative Quarterly,* 11, No. 2 (1966) pp. 207-223.

100      17      Typical demonstration of the role of feedback relative to management-by-objectives is in Walters, R.W. *Job Enrichment for Results: Strategies for Successful Implementation.* Reading, Mass.: Addison-Wesley, 1975, pp. iii-xi, 1, 213-214, 307.

| Page | Line | |
|------|------|---|
| 100 | 22 | This is the Zeigarnik effect as described in Coch, L., and J.R.P. French, Jr., op. cit.; Lewin, K., op. cit., 1951, pp. 229-236; Levine, J., and J. Butler. op. cit.; Horwitz, M. "The Recall of Interrupted Group Tasks: An Experimental Study of Individual Motivation in Relation to Group Goals." *Human Relations*, 7, (1954) pp. 3-38; Bass, B.M. "Conformity, Deviation, and a General Theory of Interpersonal Behavior." In I.A. Berg, and B.M. Bass, eds., *Conformity and Deviation.* New York: Harper, 1961, pp. 48-49; Zeigarnik, B. "Das Bekalten Erledigter Handlungen." *Psychologische Forschung*, 9, (1927) pp. 1-85. See also Cartwright, D., and A. Zander, eds., op. cit., 1960, pp. 370-395; Horwitz, M., and F.J. Lee. "Effects of Decision Making by Group Members on Recall of Finished and Unfinished Tasks." *Journal of Abnormal & Social Psychology*, 49, (1954) pp. 201-210; Smith, A.J., H.E. Madden, and R. Sobol. "Productivity and Recall in Cooperative and Competitive Discussion Groups." *Journal of Psychology*, 43, (1957) pp. 193-204. |
| 100 | 40 | Research on motivation results in a description of a number of strategic leadership characteristics, all of which appear to be 9,9 in their orientation. These include (1) recognizing and/or arousing subordinates' needs for outcomes over which the leader has some control; (2) increasing personal payoffs to subordinates for goal attainment; (3) making the path to those payoffs easier by coaching and direction; (4) helping subordinates clarify expectancies; (5) reducing frustrating barriers; and (6) increasing opportunities for personal satisfaction, contingent on effective performance. Filley, A.C., R.J. House, and S. Kerr. *Managerial Process and Organizational Behavior.* Glenview, Ill.: Scott, Foresman, 1969, p. 254. |
| 101 | 27 | The work of Marrow, Bavelas, and others represents a successful attempt of one management group to apply 9,9 concepts in its organization development effort. See Marrow, A.J., op. cit., 1957, p. 29; Hare, A.P. "Small Group Discussions with Participatory and Supervisory Leadership." *Journal of Abnormal & Social Psychology*, 48, (1953) pp. 273-275. See also Marrow, A.J., A.E. Bowers, and S.E. Seashore. *Management by Participation.* New York: Harper, 1967; and Marrow, A.J., S.E. Seashore, and D.G. Bowers. "Managing Major Change." In A.J. Marrow, ed., *The Failure of Success.* New York: AMACOM, 1972, pp. 103-119. |
| 101 | 32 | Studies of the significance of linking individual effort to organization purpose include French, J.R.P., Jr. "The Disruption and Cohesion of Groups." *Journal of Abnormal & Social Psychology*, 36, (1941) pp. 361-377; |

| Page | Line | |
|------|------|---|

French, J.R.P., Jr. "Group Productivity." In H. Guetzkow, ed., op. cit., pp. 44-54; Marrow, A.J., op. cit., 1957, pp. 108-122. A discussion of organizational objectives is in Drucker, P.F. *The Practice of Management.* New York: Harper, 1954, p. 63.

**101    36**   The conclusion is reached that a conflict-solving, participation-based approach to management by objectives implemented in OD terms can be highly successful. See Byrd, R., and J. Cowan. "MBO: A Behavioral Science Approach." *Personnel,* 51, No. 2 (1974) pp. 42-50.

**101    38**   Goal setting in the context of performance appraisal is described in McGregor, D., op. cit.; Blake, R.R., and J.S. Mouton, op. cit., 1961, pp. 39-49; Blake, R.R., and J.S. Mouton. "Re-examination of Performance Appraisal." *Advanced Management,* 23, No. 7 (1958) pp. 19-20; Blake, R.R., and J.S. Mouton. "Power, People, and Performance Reviews." *Advanced Management,* 10, No. 4 (1961) pp. 13-17. See also Whisler, T.L., and S.F. Harper, eds., *Performance Appraisal.* New York: Holt, Rinehart & Winston, 1962; and Kellogg, M.S. *Closing the Performance Gap.* New York: American Management Association, 1967.

**102    2**   A 9,9 approach to management by objectives is reported to have the following results: produces a shift from a more personal to a more job-centered evaluation of performance; produces a better identification of problem areas; promotes better mutual understanding between supervisors and subordinates; improves communication; increases productivity. See Raia, A. "Goal Setting and Self-Control." *Journal of Management Studies,* 2, No. 1 (1965) pp. 34-58.

**102    11**   Systematic analyses of conflict appear in Simmel, G., op. cit., pp. 38-39; Tannenbaum, R., I.R. Weschler, and F. Massarik. *Leadership and Organization: A Behavioral Science Approach.* New York: McGraw-Hill, 1961, p. 103; Blake, R.R. "Psychology and the Crisis of Statesmanship." *American Psychologist,* 14, (1959) pp. 87-94. Also in Bennis, W.G., K.D. Benne, and R. Chin, eds., op. cit., pp. 466-477; Blake, R.R., and J.S. Mouton. "The Intergroup Dynamics of Win-Lose Conflict and Problem-Solving Collaboration in Union-Management Relations." In M. Sherif, ed., *Intergroup Relations and Leadership.* New York: Wiley, 1962, pp. 94-140; Blake, R.R., H.A. Shepard, and J.S. Mouton. *Managing Intergroup Conflict in Industry.* Houston: Gulf, 1964; Likert, R., and J.G. Likert. *New Ways of Managing Conflict.* New York: McGraw-Hill, 1976; Pelz, D.C. "Motivation of the Engineering and Research Specialist." *American*

**Page**        **Line**

*Management Association, General Management Series*, 186, (1957) pp. 25-46; Fromm, E. "The Creative Attitude." In H.H. Anderson, ed., *Creativity and Its Cultivation.* New York: Harper, 1959, p. 51; Benne, K.D. "Democratic Ethics and Human Engineering." In W.G. Bennis, K.D. Benne, and R. Chin, eds., op. cit., p. 143; Blake, R.R., and L.P. Bradford. "Decisions . . . Decisions . . . Decisions." In L.P. Bradford, ed., op. cit., p. 70; Likert, R., op. cit., 1961, p. 117; Blake, R.R., and J.S. Mouton. "The Fifth Achievement." *Journal of Applied Behavioral Science*, 7, No. 2 (1971) pp. 146-163; Burke, R.J. "Methods of Resolving Interpersonal Conflict." *Personnel Administration*, 32, No. 4 (1969) pp. 48-55; and Filley, A.C. *Interpersonal Conflict Resolution.* Glenview, Ill.: Scott, Foresman, 1975.

A view of conflict as valuable for organization creativity is expressed in Robbins, S. *Managing Organizational Conflict: A Nontraditional Approach.* Englewood Cliffs, N.J.: Prentice-Hall, 1974.

102        22        Task motivation and involvement among research personnel are maximized by high management trust and by freedom from burdensome routine. Friedlander, F., and N. Margulies. "Multiple Impacts of Organizational Climate in Individual Value System Upon Job Satisfaction." *Personnel Psychology*, 22, (1969) pp. 171-283.

Relations between trust and creativity studied by Klimoski, R.J., and B.L. Karol. "The Impact of Trust on Creative Problem Solving Groups." *Journal of Applied Psychology*, 61, No. 5 (1976) pp. 630-633.

102        34        A study designed to measure the disruptive effects of interpersonal competitiveness is reported by Deutsch, who also investigated the facilitative effect of members perceiving themselves to be interdependent in cooperative effort. See Deutsch, M. "An Experimental Study of Effects of Cooperation and Competition upon Group Process." *Human Relations*, 2, (1949) pp. 199-231.

103        4        Communications between two individuals or among several in the group tend to come to a level or equilibrium, i.e., either two individuals each talk a great deal, a moderate amount, or to a small degree. It is less common for one to talk a lot, the other a little. See Homans, G. "Social Behaviors as Exchange." *American Journal of Sociology*, 63, No. 6 (1958) pp. 597-606.

103        6        This equilibrium is discussed in Newcomb, T.M. "The Prediction of Interpersonal Attraction." *American Psychologist*, 11, (1956) pp. 575-586; Gouldner, A.W. "The Norm of Reciprocity: A Preliminary State-

| Page | Line | |
|------|------|---|
| 103 | 25 | Importance of trust for a strong relationship is dealt with in Peterson, O.F. "Leadership and Group Behavior." In G. Lippitt, ed., *Leadership in Action.* Washington, D.C.: National Training Laboratories, National Education Association, 1951, pp. 27-30; Mellinger, G.D. "Interpersonal Trust as a Factor in Communication." *Journal of Abnormal & Social Psychology*, 52, (1956) pp. 304-309; Maier, N.R.F., op. cit., 1955, p. 139; Schein, E.H. "Forces Which Undermine Management Development." *California Management Review*, Summer, (1963) pp. 31-33; Argyris, C. *Interpersonal Competence and Organizational Effectiveness.* Homewood, Ill.: Dorsey, 1962; Thibaut, J.W., and J. Coules. "The Role of Communication in the Reduction of Interpersonal Hostility." *Journal of Abnormal & Social Psychology*, 47, (1952) pp. 770-777. |
| | | An organization development approach to shifting from distrust to trust is in Gibb, J.R. "The TORI Experience as an Organizational Change Intervention." In W.W. Burke, ed., op. cit., pp. 109-126. |
| 104 | 9 | Creativity stimulated by conflict is discussed in Thomas, W.I., and F. Znaniecki. "Three Types of Personality." In C.W. Mills, ed., *Images of Man.* New York: George Braziller, 1960, p. 409; Anderson, H.H. "Creativity in Perspective." In H.H. Anderson, ed., op. cit., pp. 236-267; Solem, A.R. "An Evaluation of Two Attitudinal Approaches to Delegation." *Journal of Applied Psychology*, 42, (1958) pp. 36-39; Hilgard, E.R. "Creativity and Problem-Solving," pp. 170-171; Dow, A.B. "An Architect's View on Creativity," p. 41; Murray, H.A. "Vicissitudes of Creativity," p. 110; all in H.H. Anderson, ed., op. cit.; Bass, B.M., op. cit., 1960, pp. 128-132; Ziller, R.C., R.D. Behringer, and J.D. Goodchilds. "Group Creativity Under Conditions of Success or Failure and Variations in Group Stability." *Journal of Applied Psychology*, 46, (1962) pp. 43-49; Perlmutter, H.V., and G. De Montollin. "Group Learning of Nonsense Syllables." *Journal of Abnormal & Social Psychology*, 47, (1952) pp. 762-769; Hall, E.J., J.S. Mouton, and R.R. Blake. "Group Problem-Solving Effectiveness Under Conditions of Pooling Versus Interaction." *Journal of Social Psychology*, 59, (1963) pp. 147-157. |
| 104 | 21 | A comprehensive study of critique methodologies is in Blake, R.R., and J.S. Mouton. *Making Experience Work: The Grid Approach to Critique.* New York: McGraw-Hill, 1978. |
| 104 | 31 | See Nirenberg, J.S. *Getting Through to People.* Englewood Cliffs, N.J.: Prentice-Hall, Inc., 1963, pp. 81-94. |

| Page | Line | |
|------|------|---|
| 104 | 36 | An extensive study of confrontation for value clarification is contained in Blake, R.R., and J.S. Mouton. *Consultation.* Reading, Mass.: Addison-Wesley, 1976, pp. 224-226.<br><br>Confrontation as an approach to conflict resolution. In Anderson, H.H. "Creativity as Personality Development." In H.H. Anderson, ed., op. cit., pp. 124, 130. This work identifies the essence of 9,9 attitudes toward creativity and conflict. His concept of "social development" (9,9) versus "socialization" (5,5) is penetrating; Blake, R.R., op. cit., 1959, pp. 87-94; Kallejian, V.J., I.R. Weschler, and R. Tannenbaum. "Managers in Transition." *Harvard Business Review,* 33, (1955) pp. 55-64; Guest, R.H., op. cit., pp. 50-58; Read, W.H. "Upward Communication in Industrial Hierarchies." *Human Relations,* 15, (1962) pp. 3-15. See also Bach, G.R., and P. Wyden. *The Intimate Enemy.* New York: William Morrow and Company, Inc., 1969. |
| 105 | 9 | The importance for problem-solving effectiveness between groups solving conflicts through confrontation is analyzed in Blake, R.R., and J.S. Mouton, op. cit., 1964; Walton, R.E., J.M. Dutton, and H.G. Fitch. "A Study of Conflict in the Process, Structure and Attitudes of Lateral Relationships." In A.W. Rubenstein, and C.G. Haberstroh, eds., *Some Theories of Organization,* rev. ed. Homewood, Ill.: Richard D. Irwin and The Dorsey Press, 1966; and Farris, G. "Organizing Your Informal Organization." *Innovation,* 25, (1971) pp. 2-11. |
| 105 | 34 | A high degree of 9,9-oriented cohesion strengthens members' desires for group success. Zander, A., and H. Meadow. "Strength of Group and Desire for Attainable Group Aspirations." *Journal of Personality,* 33, No. 1 (1965) pp. 122-139.<br><br>Cohesion increases when team members can influence selection of colleagues; in turn this benefits productivity. Van Zelst, R.H. "Sociometrically Selected Work Teams Increase Production." *Personnel Psychology,* 5, (1952) pp. 175-185. |
| 106 | 25 | Though it may be desirable to utilize participation, a question arises as to whether leaders possess the skills essential for inducing effective participation. The conclusion drawn is that without such skills, participatory leadership technique has no contribution to make to effectiveness, but such skills can be acquired through training. Maier, N.R.F. *Problem Solving, Discussions and Conferences: Leadership Methods and Skills.* New York: McGraw-Hill, 1963. |
| 106 | 27 | Two approaches to here-and-now applied behavioral science strategies of education are involved. The first |

**Page       Line**

is described in a series of sources, including Shepard, H.A., and W.G. Bennis. "A Theory of Training by Group Methods." *Human Relations*, 9, (1956) pp. 403-414; Weschler, I., and J. Reisel. "Inside a Sensitivity Training Group." *Industrial Relations Monograph*, 4. Los Angeles: Institute of Industrial Relations, University of California, 1959; Tannenbaum, R., et al., op. cit., 1961; Bennis, W.G., K.D. Benne, and R. Chin, eds., op. cit.; Hornstein, H.A., B.B. Bunker, W.W. Burke, M. Gindes, and R.J. Lewicki. *Social Intervention: A Behavioral Science Approach.* New York: The Free Press, 1971; Dyer, W.G. *Modern Theory and Method in Group Training.* New York: Van Nostrand Reinhold Company, 1972; Margulies, N., and A.P. Raia. *Organizational Development: Values, Process, and Technology.* New York: McGraw-Hill, Inc., 1972; Marrow, A.J., ed., op. cit., 1972; Marrow, A.J. *Making Waves in Foggy Bottom.* Washington, D.C.: NTL Institute, 1974; Yalom, I.D. *The Theory and Practice of Group Psychotherapy*, 2nd ed. New York: Basic Books, Inc., 1975; Golembiewski, R.T., and A. Blumberg. *Sensitivity Training and the Laboratory Approach*, 3rd ed. Itasca, Ill.: F.E. Peacock Publishers, Inc., 1977.

The second approach is reflected in instrumented team learning Grid Seminars as described in Mouton, J.S., and R.R. Blake. "University Training in Human Relations Skills." *Group Psychotherapy*, 14, Nos. 3 and 4 (1961) pp. 140-153; Mouton, J.S., and R.R. Blake. *Instrumented Team Learning*, 1975; Blake, R.R., and J.S. Mouton. *Corporate Excellence Through Grid Organization Development*, 1968; Frampton, T.J. "Good Managers Are Made." *Electronic Design*, 17, (1973) pp. 77-79; Blake, R.R., and J.S. Mouton. *Making Experience Work: The Grid Approach to Critique*, 1978.

Examples of methods useful for learning 9,9 team skills include Blake, R.R., and Mouton, J.S. "The Instrumented Training Laboratory." In I. Weschler, and E. Schein, eds., *Issues in Human Relations Training.* Washington, D.C.: National Training Laboratories, National Education Association, 1962, pp. 61-76; "Managers Chart Their Way." *Business Week*, October 20, 1962, p. 192; and Mouton, J.S., and R.R. Blake, op. cit., 1975.

107        28        The overriding importance of removing self-deception as a basis for learning is emphasized in Chapters 1 and 12, this book. See also Blake, R.R., and J.S. Mouton, op. cit., 1968, pp. 51-54.

108        4         Achieving teamwork through team building. See Zenger, J., and D. Miller. "Building Effective Teams." *Personnel*, 52, No. 2 (1974) pp. 20-29.

| Page | Line | |
|------|------|---|
| 108 | 14 | The logic of team building on a within-company basis is provided in the following quote. "A simple answer can be given by analogy to a baseball or a football team. Both of these are organizations in a very real sense, and both are concerned with team action. Ridiculous though it sounds, if the conventional approach of training individuals one-by-one were applied in developing a baseball or a football team, each of the team members would be trained at the hands of specialists, also one-by-one, away from the organization and isolated from the others with whom he must eventually engage in team action. Then, all members would be returned to the organization and thrown together on the assumption that since all had learned individually, they automatically would be able to work together effectively. There would literally be no need for practice, and no one would think to help the team develop a set of common signals, because each person should have learned all that he needed to learn in his own specialized training program in order to become an effective team member. "The absurdity in this can further be seen in the analogy of the football team where each designated individual would gain specialized training in schools, one school concerned with training guards, another with centers, etc. After persons had been trained individually, they would be returned to the football club for the purpose of playing together in the belief that an effective team operation would result after skills of individuals had been perfected. Both of these examples point to the fallacy in logic of a conventional approach to training when the goal of organizational health is successful team action." In Blake, R.R., and J.S. Mouton. "How Executive Team Training Can Help You." *ASTD Journal*, 16, No. 1 (1962) pp. 4-5. |
| 108 | 17 | This point of view is fundamental to the study of psychosomatic factors. See Pelletier, K.R. *Mind as Healer, Mind as Slayer*. New York: Delacorte Press, 1977, pp. 104-105. |
| 108 | 27 | Maslow, A.H. *Motivation and Personality*. New York: Harper, 1970, pp. 156, 159, 161, 166-168. |
| 110 | 6 | Levinson, H. "How Good is Your Mental Health?" *Reader's Digest*, 87, (1965) pp. 54-58. |
| 110 | 20 | Selye, H. *Stress Without Distress*. Philadelphia: J.B. Lippincott Co., 1974, p. 102. |
| 110 | 36 | Selye, H., ibid., p. 74. |
| 111 | 20 | Experimental analysis of autonomy is evaluated in Kovar, L.C. *Faces of the Adolescent Girl*. Englewood Cliffs, N.J.: Prentice-Hall, 1968, pp. 4-5; Riesman, D., N. Glazer, and R. Denney. *The Lonely Crowd*. Garden City, N.J.: Doubleday, 1950, p. 328; and Kunkel, F.M., |

| Page | Line | |
|------|------|---|

and R.E. Dickerson. *How Character Develops: A Psychological Interpretation.* New York: Charles Scribner & Sons, 1946, pp. 125-140, 157-159, 176-178. Autonomy analyzed in Meier, R.L., and E.C. Bandfield. "Review of 'The Lonely Crowd.' " *Ethics,* January, (1952). See Riesman, D. *The Lonely Crowd* for more on autonomy. See also Argyris, C., and D.A. Schön, op. cit., pp. 85-95.

**111 · 23** · Self-direction in the context of social responsibility is discussed in Bell, G.D. *The Achievers.* Chapel Hill, N.C.: Preston-Hill, 1973, pp. 104-105.

**111 · 29** · Research shows that when a child in the one year age range has a secure attachment with its mother, this relationship provides a base from which even strange situations can be explored and strangers met without distress. See Ainsworth, M.D.S., and B.A. Witting. "Attachment and Exploratory Behavior of One-Year-Olds in a Strange Situation." In B.M. Foss, ed., *Determinants of Infant Behavior,* 4, (1969) pp. 111-136.

**111 · 38** · Self-respect as a basic factor in a 9,9 orientation is discussed in Fromm, E., op. cit., 1955, pp. 31-33; Shibutani, T., op. cit., p. 291; Fromm, E., op. cit., 1959, p. 47; Steckle, L.C. *The Man in Management.* New York: Harper, 1958, pp. 70-82; and Branden, N. *The Psychology of Self-Esteem.* New York: Bantam Books, 1969, pp. 109-139.

**112 · 11** · 9,9-oriented child rearing is described as follows. For example, when a child misbehaves, parents are likely to ask why he did so and to help the child see the consequences that happen to other people who behave similarly. Punishment is meted out only when it has been discussed and the reasons for it are well understood. Parents teach the child that he can and should control his own behavior on the basis of an internalized set of standards and norms rather than being controlled based upon parental requirements, peer pressures, or simply getting by. Douvan, E., and J. Adelson. *The Adolescent Experience.* New York: Wiley, 1966.
Limit-setting by parents is discussed in Dreikurs, R., and L. Grey. *Logical Consequences: A New Approach to Discipline.* New York: Meridith Press, 1968, pp. 62-82.

**113 · 2** · The positive effects of parent-child cooperation is discussed in Adler, A. *Social Interest: A Challenge to Mankind.* New York: Capricorn Books, 1964, p. 29. See also Dreikurs, R., R. Corsini, and S. Gould. *How to Stop Fighting with Your Kids.* Chicago: Ace Printing, 1974, pp. 49-56.

**113 · 11** · Evidence that children who are held in esteem by their associates in school come from homes where

| Page | Line | |
|------|------|---|
| | | they enjoy secure and rewarding relationships with parents and brothers and sisters confirms the importance of solid emotional attachments in the home as a precondition for the emergence of a 9,9 orientation. See Campbell, J.D., and M.R. Yarrow. "Perceptual and Behavioral Correlates of Social Effectiveness." *Sociometry*, 24, (1961) pp. 1-20; Maslow, A.H. "Creativity in Self-Actualizing People." In H.H. Anderson, ed., op. cit., pp. 85-86, 88; and Sullivan, H.S. *The Interpersonal Theory of Psychiatry*. New York: Norton, 1953. |
| 113 | 15 | The adverse consequences of affection as a means of control is discussed in Baldwin, A.L. "The Effects of Home Environment on Nursery School Behavior." *Psychological Monograph*, 63, (1949) pp. 1-85; Dinkmeyer, D., and R. Dreikurs. *Encouraging Children to Learn*. Englewood Cliffs, N.J.: Prentice-Hall, 1963; Dreikurs, R. *The Challenge of Child Training*. New York: Hawthorne, 1972, pp. 115-116, 151-152; Moustakas, C. *Personal Growth*. Cambridge: Doyle Publishing Co., 1969, pp. 38-46. |
| 113 | 16 | Generosity is observed to be characteristic of a 9,9 orientation and it has been shown to arise in childhood under conditions where a warm, nurturing adult acts toward children in a generous manner. When children experience such a warm nurturant adult, they demonstrate an increased degree of generosity over what would otherwise be expected. Under experimental conditions the effect has been shown to last for a minimum of two weeks. Yarrow, M.R., P.M. Scott, and C.Z. Waxler. "Learning Concern for Others." *Developmental Psychology*, 8, (1973) pp. 240-260. |
| 113 | 20 | Implications of unconditional love for promoting self-respect are discussed in Kovar, L.C., op. cit., pp. 6-7, 107-111. |
| 113 | 32 | This idea is developed in Dreikurs, R., and L. Grey, op. cit., 1968, pp. 33-43. |
| 113 | 41 | Parents providing a child with a modeling orientation are discussed in Dreikurs, R., op. cit., 1972, pp. 18-21. Demonstrating responsibility in a model way is an important factor in child development. See Dreikurs, R., ibid., pp. 21-26. |
| 115 | 1 | Described in Sforza, C. *The Living Thoughts of Machiavelli*. New York: Fawcett, 1958. |
| 116 | 34 | This point of view is illuminated by Bradford, L.P. "The Case of the Hidden Agenda." In L.P. Bradford, ed., op. cit., pp. 60-68. |
| 117 | 1 | Allusions to this strategy are to be found in March, J.C., and H.A. Simon *Organizations*. New York: |

| Page | Line | |
|------|------|---|
| | | Wiley, 1958, p. 54; and Allen, L.A. *Management and Organization.* New York: McGraw-Hill, 1958, p. 43. |
| 117 | 29 | Corporate evolution is discussed in Blake, R.R., W.E. Avis, and J.S. Mouton. *Corporate Darwinism: An Evolutionary Perspective on Organizing Work in the Dynamic Corporation.* Houston: Gulf, 1966. |
| 117 | 39 | Problem-solving approaches to union-management relations are described in Selekman, B.M. "Conflict and Cooperation in Labor Relations." *Harvard Business Review*, 25, (1949) pp. 318-338; Whyte, W.F., op. cit., pp. 90-94; Blake, R.R., and J.S. Mouton. "Union-Management Relations: From Conflict to Collaboration." *Personnel*, 38, No. 6 (1961) pp. 38-51; Blake, R.R., and J.S. Mouton. "The Intergroup Dynamics of Win-Lose Conflict and Problem-Solving Collaboration in Union-Management Relations." In M. Sherif, ed., op. cit., 1962; Hughes, C.L. *Making Unions Unnecessary.* New York: Executive Enterprises Publications, 1975; "Steinberg's: People Are the Pulse." *Food Topics*, 22, No. 7 (1967) pp. 9-23. |
| 118 | 6 | Showing conditions under which productivity leads to satisfaction and conditions under which satisfaction leads to productivity is reported in Wanous, J.P. "A Causal-Correctional Analysis of the Job Satisfaction and Performance Relationship." *Journal of Applied Psychology*, 59, No. 2 (1974) pp. 139-144. |
| 118 | 5 | Viewed from the perspective below, 9,9-oriented management enables managers to contribute towards excellence throughout an organization by creating a climate and culture in which there is real openness; trust; understanding at every level of corporate goals; understanding at corporate level of difficulties associated with action and implementation that exist "at the coal face" which are so often *not* understood elsewhere. It can perhaps be said that the *ability* and the *willingness* of a 9,9-oriented manager to be consultant and educator, as well as boss, is a key difference between this and all other styles. This provides the purest way of creating managerial, professional, and business acumen in depth throughout an enterprise. The following quote is illuminating. "Those whose work we have studied here [in Australia] are most successful when they spend less than 35 to 40 percent of their time *managing*—via planning, organizing, staffing, directing, controlling—and 65 percent or more consulting and educating. In performing the latter tasks they do not exercise power and authority of knowledge and competence." David-Lloyd Thomas Personal Correspondence dated July 24, 1977. This concept is illustrated in Figure R-2. |

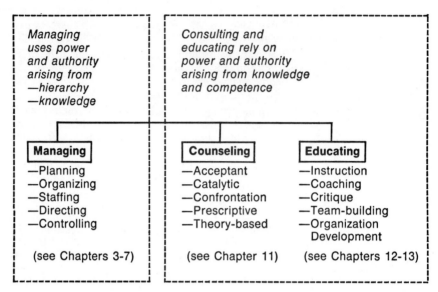

*Figure R-2. Any manager has three jobs, each of which requires a specific set of responsibilities.*

| Page | Line | |
|------|------|---|
| 118 | 40 | 9,9-like behavior in comparison with 9,1-like behavior is strongly related to higher performance quality ratings by subordinates. See Cummins, R.C., "Leader-Member Relations as a Moderator of the Effects of Leader Behavior and Attitude." *Personnel Psychology*, 25, (1972) pp. 655-660. |
| 119 | 1 | A predictive study by Indik, et al., demonstrates that 9,9-oriented behavior is associated with productivity throughout an organization as a whole. A high level of job performance tends to be positively associated with (1) openness of communication between boss and subordinates, (2) subordinates' satisfaction with the supervisors' support, (3) a relatively high degree of mutual understanding of viewpoints and problems among those who work together, and (4) a relatively high degree of local influence and autonomy in work-related issues. Indik, B.P., et al. "Superior-Subordinate Relationships and Performance." *Personnel Psychology*, 14, No. 2 (1961) pp. 357-374. |

A significant positive correlation between high job performance and experience of a positive organizational climate, including such attributes as openness, support, etc., is reported in La Follette, W.R., and H.P. Sims. "Is Satisfaction Redundant with Climate?" *Organizational Behavior and Human Performance*, 13, No. 2 (1975) pp. 257-278.

| Page | Line | |
|---|---|---|
| 119 | 16 | Although confounded with certain aspects of 5,5-oriented behavior, the "Stars" observed and described by Moment and Zaleznik exhibited behavior and actions like that characteristic of a 9,9-oriented manager. See Moment, D., and A. Zaleznik. *Role Development and Interpersonal Competence.* Boston: Harvard University Press, 1963, pp. 120-122; also Bell, G.D., op. cit., pp. 104-124, 181-187 for additional descriptions of 9,9-oriented managerial behavior. |
| 119 | 21 | Initiation as a leadership factor is described by Kipnis, D., and W.P. Lane, op. cit.; see also Fleishman, E.A. "Twenty Years of Consideration and Structure." In E.A. Fleishman, and J.G. Hunt, eds., *Current Developments in the Study of Leadership.* Carbondale: Southern Illinois University Press, 1973, pp. 24-27. |
| 119 | 29 | Fromm affirms the proposition that a 9,9 orientation involves the ability to act on one's convictions based upon full commitment, while simultaneously maintaining openness to reservations and doubts regarding the validity of such convictions. He says, "... to tolerate uncertainty about the most important questions with which life confronts us—and yet to have faith in our thought and feeling, inasmuch as they are truly ours ... " In this way the closeness of faith in one's capacity to reason in a valid manner is coupled with uncertainty as to the validity of results reached. Fromm, E., op. cit., 1955, p. 180; see also Cleveland, S.E., and R.B. Morton. "Group Behavior and Body Image." *Human Relations*, 15, (1962) pp. 77-85; Crutchfield, R. "Conformity and Character." *American Psychologist*, 10, (1955) pp. 191-198; and Anderson, H.H., ed., op. cit., p. 119. |

### Chapter 8

| Page | Line | |
|---|---|---|
| 121 | 7 | The paternalistic role is extensively discussed in Freud, S. *Group Psychology and the Analysis of the Ego.* New York: Liveright, 1949. Use of Freudian thinking for diagnosis of paternalism in business is offered by Levinson, H. *The Exceptional Executive. A Psychological Conception.* New York: Mentor, The New American Library, Inc., 1968, pp. 33-34. |
| 121 | 11 | Another version of paternalism is formulated by Hersey and Blanchard. They correlate behavior with the kind of supervision that would be called for, depending upon where the subordinate is in the life cycle from immature to mature. Paternalism comes through when the immature subordinate is described in terms of the manner in which supervision is employed to give him direction. The idea is that an |

immature subordinate is first told who, what, where, when, and how to do something, and only after the subordinate has demonstrated compliance is he given socio-emotional support in the form of trust and respect such as attention, encouragement, compliments, friendship, etc. for having followed instructions. This is paternalistic management.

As he develops greater skill, he is given less "who, what, where, and how" and more socio-emotional support until he finally becomes self-sufficient. At this point socio-emotional support is reduced to a minimum. Thus, the supervisor creates a relationship of paternalism at the beginning and then reduces it as the subordinate becomes more proficient. What is missing in this formulation is any concept of how boss feedback and boss-subordinate critique can be relied upon to aid the subordinate to take a problem-solving orientation to his own learning, thereby increasing his self-responsibility, not to get socio-emotional rewards, but to be effective. See Hersey, P., and K.H. Blanchard. *Management of Organization Behavior: Utilizing Human Resources*, 2nd ed. Englewood Cliffs, N.J.: Prentice-Hall, 1972, pp. 134-159.

121          12

The following excerpt from Harrington is a vivid example of paternalistic behavior. ". . . The president of a railroad forces his associates to attend meetings, shivering at dawn, in an old circus tent. In another frame of mind, he will suddenly present a browbeaten underling with a new Lincoln Continental or a two-week vacation in Hawaii. . . . The ambition to rise out of his species and attain a higher form of being—not only after death, like most people, but now, today— cuts him off, sometimes intolerably, and when this happens he lunges in the direction of humanity. For him, sudden gifts are the coin of brotherhood. They perform a dual service, at once binding and unsettling to the recipient, and at the same time allowing the imitation-diety an illusion of having reached someone." Harrington, A. *The Immortalist*. Millbrae, Calif.: Celestial Arts, 1977, pp. 120-121.

122          1

For a positive viewpoint on paternalism, see McMurray, R.N. "The Case for Benevolent Autocracy." *Harvard Business Review*, 36, No. 1 (1958) pp. 82-90. See also Heckmann, I.L., Jr., and S.G. Huneryager, eds. *Human Relations in Management*. Cincinnati: South-Western, 1960, p. 106.

123          24

This point of view is developed by Fromm. ". . . In feudal society the lord was supposed to have the divine right to demand services and things from those subject to his domination, but at the same time he

| Page | Line | |
|------|------|---|
| | | was bound by custom and was obligated to be responsible for his subjects, to protect them, and to provide them with at least the minimum—the traditional standard of living." Fromm, E. *The Sane Society.* Greenwich, Conn.: Fawcett Publications, Inc., 1969, pp. 87-88. |
| 123 | 38 | A case study demonstrating wide-arc pendulum effects in organization life is reported by Guest, R.H. *Organizational Change: The Effect of Successful Leadership.* Homewood, Ill.: Dorsey, 1962, pp. 17-38. Another case study that also revealed wide-arc pendulum effects is by Blake, R.R., and J.S. Mouton. *Diary of an OD Man.* Houston: Gulf Publishing Company, 1976. A description of and warning against permitting wide-arc pendulum swings to occur is forwarded by Randall, C.B. *The Folklore of Management.* New York: Mentor, 1962, pp. 66-71. |
| 125 | 9 | The use of employee relations personnel as counselors is discussed in Stagner, R. *Psychology of Industrial Conflict.* New York: Wiley, 1956, pp. 192-193, 316, 390-391. |
| 125 | 13 | The use of counseling to reduce tensions in World War II is described in Zimmerman, C.J. "Management's Role in Mental Health." *Advanced Management,* September (1960) pp. 5-8. |
| 125 | 20 | An example of counter-balancing in industry occurred in the aftermath of the Hawthorne experiment. See Roethlisberger, F.J., and W.J. Dickson. *Management and the Worker.* Cambridge: Harvard University, 1939; Mayo, E. *The Human Problems of An Industrial Civilization.* Boston: Harvard Business School, 1946; Dickson, W.J., and F.J. Roethlisberger. *Counseling in an Organization: A Sequel to the Hawthorne Researches.* Boston: Division of Research, Graduate School of Business Administration, Harvard University, 1966, pp. 269-328. |
| 125 | 34 | An example of counterbalancing is seen in the concept of the Assessment Center. The assessors who make competency judgments for promotion or development of a managerial candidate are not managers or supervisors but, rather, are experts on behavioral assessment. Once selections are made, then managers should be able to supervise such chosen persons. Under this concept, managerial skills related to the judgment of human qualifications are replaced by a cadre of diagnostic experts who make selection judgments. Managers' responsibilities are limited to developing competence in planning, organizing, and directing, but not staffing. See Byham, W.C. "The Use of Assessment Centres in Management Development." In B. Taylor, and G.L. Lippitt, *Management* |

*Development and Training Handbook.* Maidenhead, Berkshire, Eng.: McGraw-Hill Book Company (UK) Limited, 1975, pp. 63-82. See also Byham, W.C. "Assessment Centres: The Place for Picking Management Potential." *European Business*, 35, July-Sept. (1972); Byham, W.C. "Assessment Centres for Spotting Future Managers." *Harvard Business Review*, July-August (1970); and Wiengarten, J. "The Hard Look in Employee Appraisal." *Dun's Review*, 88, September (1966) pp. 41-42+.

127        3    The underlying assumption of a statistical 5,5 orientation is that the means justifies the end. If you have to "9,1" someone and chop him down to move your position forward, you do it. If the best way to get your way is to appeal to a subordinate's 1,9 needs for love and approval to gain his support, you do it. If you can avoid opposition by ignoring someone who should be consulted, but who might block your program, you do that. Appease others if doing so will move you toward your objective. Be paternalistic, manipulative, whatever. Under this view, principles, morality, ethics, whatever might restrict freedom of movement is disregarded, since the means used justify the end to be reached. This approach ignores the possibility that one's self-validated preconception of the "best" action will never be tested and evaluated for soundness against behavioral science principles.

Lippitt makes this point explicit. "Experience and study, therefore, have demonstrated to me that between the two extremes of guesswork and formula there is a middle ground on which most leaders operate. Here they recognize occasions which demand situational leadership—appropriately autocratic or laissez-faire—and other occasions which permit the integration of human resources with conscious renewal processes. Organization renewal can live quite comfortably and effectively in this middle ground." See Lippitt, G.L. *Organization Renewal: Achieving Viability in a Changing World.* New York: Appleton-Century-Crofts, 1969, p. 7.

The same point of view is commended by Reddin. "Even with little ongoing change about them, managers sometimes find they need to have high flex in the apparently unchanging job they have. A manager supervising ten men might easily find that two work best when left alone, two need continuous direction, three need to be motivated by objectives, and three others need a supportive climate. So, in the space of a day an effective manager may well use all four basic styles when dealing with such a variety as a dependent subordinate, an aggressive pair of coworkers, a secretary whose work has deteriorated, and his superior who is interested only in the immediate task at hand. Obviously, to try to use a single basic style in these situations would lead to low effectiveness to say the least. To the extent the organization and technology allow individual treatment, a high-flex and sensitive manager could satisfy the demands of all these different situations and so achieve maximum effectiveness." See Reddin, W.J. *Managerial Effectiveness.* New York: McGraw-Hill, 1970, p. 53.

This point of view also characterizes Jennings. "Although the changing, dynamic administrative scene of today requires flexibility, this does not mean being wishy-washy. The flexible man is firm when the nature of the situation requires firmness or the purposes for which he stands require vigorous action. . . . The flexible man knows when bureaucratic techniques are required and knows how to use them in the service of his administrative responsibility. . . . The flexible executive practices freedom and equality, shares himself on the basis of the mutual interests of the individual and the organization. He is firm, however, when the continued unity and productive cohesiveness of the group are threatened by the power ambitions or compulsive orderliness of others. In short, the ideal executive today blends autocracy, bureaucracy, and democracy into an effective administrative style that can be adapted to meet the evolving needs and problems of his administrative responsibility." See Jennings, E.E. *The Executive: Autocrat, Bureaucrat, Democrat.* New York: Harper & Row, 1962, p. 264.

127        20    Statistical 5,5 strategies may also be used by a subordinate with respect to his relationship with those higher in the organization. See Vance, C.C. *Boss Psychology: Help Your Boss Make You a Success.* New York: McGraw-Hill, 1975.

127        42    An approach to negotiation strategies which is of a statistical 5,5 character is described by Nierenberg, G.I. *The Art of Negotiating.* New York: Hawthorn Books, Inc., 1968.

**Chapter 9**

128        19    The situationalism model of leadership, which leads to the view that management provides followers with the kind of leaders they have come to expect, is most fully developed by Fiedler. This is a "match" theory that implies that 1,9-oriented subordinates should be given a 1,9-oriented supervisor, a 5,5-oriented subordinate a 5,5-oriented supervisor, and so on. This view is based on a static model of the status quo that dis-

regards the possibility that boss-subordinate relationships can be changed in order to improve the situation itself, thereby creating a quality of leadership that can change situations into what they should become rather than adjusting to them as they currently exist. Fiedler, F.E. *A Theory of Leadership Effectiveness.* New York: McGraw-Hill, 1967; and Fiedler, F.E., M.M. Chemers, and L. Mahar. *Improving Leadership Effectiveness: A Leader Match Concept.* New York: John Wiley & Sons, Inc., 1976, pp. 10-12. The Fiedler point of view is also basic to the thinking of other commentators, including Reddin, W.J. *Managerial Effectiveness 3-D.* New York: McGraw-Hill, 1970, pp. 199-201; Lippitt, G.L. *Organization Renewal.* New York: Appleton-Century-Crofts, 1969, p. 7; James, M. *The OK Boss.* Reading, Mass.: Addison-Wesley, 1975, p. 52; Tannenbaum, R., and W.H. Schmidt. "How To Choose a Leadership Pattern." *Harvard Business Review,* 36, (1958) p. 101; Hersey, P., and K.H. Blanchard. *Management of Organization Behavior: Utilizing Human Resources,* 2nd ed. Englewood Cliffs, N.J.: Prentice-Hall, 1972, pp. 121-123, 127-128. See also Hersey, P., and K.H. Blanchard. "Interview." *Group & Organization Studies,* 2, No. 1 (1977) pp. 9-24.

129          6

This view is amply reinforced by Grid research in eight nations. See Mouton, J.S., and R.R. Blake. "Issues in Transnational Organization Development." In B.M. Bass, R. Cooper, and J.A. Haas, *Managing For Accomplishment.* Lexington, Mass.: D.C. Heath and Company, 1970, pp. 208-224. Research conducted at the Institute for Social Research at the University of Michigan affirms the same point of view. See Likert, R., and J.G. Likert. *New Ways of Managing Conflict.* New York: McGraw-Hill, 1976, pp. 51-55.

129          32

How principles undergird behavior can be seen in the following study of problems which managers identify as of highest priority for solution. These are communication and planning. Yet they are symptomatic of deeper problems that are the more basic barriers to effectiveness. See Blake, R.R., and J.S. Mouton. *Corporate Excellence Through Grid Organization Development.* Houston, Tex.: Gulf Publishing Company, 1968, pp. 3-8. This point of view is also in Argyris, C., and D.A. Schön. *Theory in Practice: Increasing Professional Effectiveness.* San Francisco: Jossey-Bass, 1974, especially in his descriptions of Model II, pp. 85-95; Fleishman, E.A. "Twenty Years of Consideration and Structure." In E.A. Fleishman, and J.G. Hunt, eds., *Current Developments in the Study of Leadership.* Carbondale: Southern Illinois

| Page | Line | |
|------|------|---|
| | | University Press, 1973, pp. 1-40, particularly p. 37; McGregor, D. *The Human Side of Enterprise.* New York: McGraw-Hill, 1960, pp. 45-57, 59-176; Herzberg, F., B. Mausner, and B.B. Snyderman. *The Motivation to Work,* 2nd ed. New York: John Wiley & Sons, Inc., 1959; Herzberg, F. *The Managerial Choice.* Homewood, Ill.: Dow Jones-Irwin, 1976, pp. 49-101. |
| 129 | 38 | The basic literature of psychoanalysis and psychotherapy is consistent with this point of view. A formulation is in Dollard, J., and N.E. Miller. *Personality and Psychotherapy.* New York: McGraw-Hill, 1950, pp. 148-154, 432-434. |
| 130 | 12 | Versatility can be characteristic of any Grid style. Depending on the situation, for example, there is a characteristic 9,1 way of being helpful ("Here's how you should do that."), hostile ("Shut up."), compassionate ("I felt sorry for him but he has no one but himself to blame."), or compelling ("Drop what you're doing and complete this."). |

Alternatively a 9,1-oriented person may become angry when his instructions are disregarded. Then he may spank his child, swear at his subordinate, sneer at his wife, or silently resist his boss. Spanking, swearing, sneering, and silent resistance all are *different* from one another, and therefore they demonstrate versatility but reflect a consistent 9,1 style underlying the four different situations.

The study showing some implications of 9,9-oriented versatility is reported by Graen, G., F. Dansereau, Jr., and T. Minami. "Dysfunctional Leadership Styles." In *Organization Behavior and Human Performance,* 7, No. 1 (1972) pp. 216-236.

| Page | Line | |
|------|------|---|
| 132 | 25 | The participative mode of managing is superior regardless of time, technology, or temperament. See research by Miles, R.E. "Leadership Styles and Subordinate Responses." In C.A. Anderson, and M.J. Gannon, *Readings in Management: An Organizational Perspective.* Boston: Little, Brown & Company, 1977, pp. 196-209. |
| 132 | 36 | Free choice contrasted with decision under pressure. See Yukl, G.A., M.P. Malone, B. Hayslip, and T.A. Pamin. "The Effects of Time Pressure and Issue Settlement Order on Integrative Bargaining." *Sociometry,* 39, No. 1 (1976) pp. 277-281. |

One demonstration of the effectiveness of behavior under conditions of free choice is provided by Zipf, who demonstrated in the evolution of languages that most frequently used words are those that call for the least expenditure of energy, i.e., small, one syllable words are the most common in all languages studied. Zipf, G.K. *The Psycho-Biology of Language.* Boston: Houghton Mifflin Company, 1935, pp. 3-19, 22-29.

| Page | Line | |
|---|---|---|
| 133 | 1 | The positive effects on productivity associated with participation were demonstrated experimentally in an early study by Coch and French, who found that participation improved performance when those involved engaged in deciding the conditions of work. Coch, L., and J.R.P. French, Jr. "Overcoming Resistance to Change." *Human Relations*, 1, (1948) pp. 512-532. French, Israel, and Ås repeated this study and further demonstrated that the participation principle holds most strongly when workers feel that their participation is legitimate. French, J.R.P., D. Israel, and D. Ås. "An Experiment on Participation in a Norwegian Factory." *Human Relations*, 13, No. 1 (1960) pp. 3-19. |
| 133 | 5 | Mutual respect as the basis of a sound relationship is discussed in Rogers, C.R. *Client-Centered Therapy.* Boston: Houghton Mifflin, 1951. See also Hall, C.S., and G. Lindzey. *Theories of Personality.* New York: Wiley, 1957, pp. 467-502; Loomis, J.L. "Communication, the Development of Trust and Cooperative Behavior." *Human Relations*, (1959) pp. 305-315; Deutsch, M. "The Effect of Motivational Orientations upon Trust and Suspicion." *Human Relations*, 13, (1960) pp. 123-139; Shibutani, T. *Society and Personality.* Englewood Cliffs, N.J.: Prentice-Hall, 1961, p. 291; Bowers, D.G. "Self-Esteem and the Diffusion of Leadership Style." *Journal of Applied Psychology*, 47, (1963) pp. 135-140. |
| 133 | 7 | Communication network research involving one-way versus two-way communication demonstrates better understanding and greater problem-solving effectiveness under two-way rather than under one-way conditions. Bavelas, A., and D. Barrett. "An Experimental Approach to Organizational Communication." *Personnel*, 27, No. 5 (1951) pp. 366-371. Leavitt, H.J. "Some Effects of Certain Communication Patterns on Group Performance." *Journal of Abnormal and Social Psychology*, 46, (1951) pp. 38-50; and Kelley, H.H. "Communication in Experimentally Created Hierarchies." *Human Relations*, 4, (1951) pp. 39-56. Examples of "bad" communication include Athanassiades, J. "The Distortion of Upward Communication in Hierarchical Organizations." *Academy of Management Journal*, 16, No. 2 (1973) pp. 207-226; Roberts, K.H., and C. O'Reilly. "Failures in Upward Communications: Three Possible Culprits." *Academy of Management Journal*, 17, (1974) pp. 205-215. |
| 133 | 10 | See Frankl, V. *Man's Search for Meaning: An Introduction to Logotherapy.* New York: Washington Square Press, Inc., 1963. Many additional references verifying the same principle are in the Chapter 7 references. |

The literature dealing explicitly with job enrichment verifies this point. See Walker, C., R. Guest, and A. Turner. *The Foreman on the Assembly Line.* Cambridge, Mass.: Harvard University Press, 1956; Herzberg, F., *op. cit.*, pp. 103-200; and Walters, R.W. *Job Enrichment For Results: Strategies for Successful Implementation.* Reading, Mass.: Addison-Wesley, 1975; Ford, R. *Motivation Through the Work Itself.* New York: American Management Association, 1969.

Conflict resolution by confrontation is universally recognized as the most valid basis for resolution of differences and as the one approach with fewest adverse side effects. See Metcalf, H.C., and L. Urwick. *Dynamic Administration: The Collected Papers of Mary Parker Follett.* New York: Harper, 1940, p. 32. Lawrence and Lorsch conclude the following: Comparison between organizations where 9,1, 1,9 and 9,9-oriented solutions to conflict were compared demonstrated that the two highest performing organizations used 9,9 confrontation to a greater degree than the other four organizations; the next two organizations used confrontation more than the two lowest performing organizations, thus verifying that 9,9 is the best way of relieving conflict. In Lawrence, P., and J. Lorsch, *Organization and Environment: Managing Integration and Differentiation.* Boston: Harvard University School of Business Administration, Division of Research, 1967. Verification is provided by Burke who asked 74 managers to describe the way they and their immediate superiors dealt with conflicts between them. Five different methods of resolution—1,1 withdrawal, 1,9 smoothing, 5,5 compromise, 9,1 forcing, and 9,9 confrontation—were identified. These were then compared to the dependent variables of "constructive use of disagreement" and to planning and evaluating job performance. Comparing extreme scoring subgroups for constructive use of conflict, the most effective managers used the methods in the following order: (1) 9,9 confrontation, (2) 1,9 smoothing, (3) 5,5 compromise, (4) 9,1 suppression, and (5) 1,1 withdrawal. The less effective supervisors used (1) 9,9 confrontation, (2) 9,1 suppression, (3) 1,1 withdrawal, (4) 1,9 smoothing, and (5) 5,5 compromise. He also obtained 53 descriptions of effective conflict resolution and compared them with 53 descriptions of ineffective handling from 57 respondents. Of these, 58.5% of the effective statements were 9,9 confrontation, and 79.2% of the ineffective statements were 9,1 suppression of differences. See Burke, R.J. "Methods of Resolving Superior-Subordinate Conflict: The Constructive Use of Subordinate Differences and Disagreements." *Organiza-*

*tional Behavior and Human Performance,* 5, (1970) pp. 393-411.

133        15        Another demonstration compares active give-and-take participation with laissez-faire and with forced resolution of differences. It demonstrated for several hundred subjects that active participation resulted in participants' feeling most responsible for what they had created and also greater satisfaction with the product. Blake, R.R., and J.S. Mouton. *Group Dynamics—Key to Decision Making.* Houston, Texas: Gulf Publishing Company, 1961, pp. 32-35.

Herzberg shows the impact on subordinates of creating conditions where they accept increased responsibility with the conclusion that increased responsibility promotes greater productivity and effectiveness. Herzberg, F., op. cit., pp. 116-117, 149-153.

133        20        The role of feedback-based critique is central to most approaches to applied human learning and is therefore seen as a key to growth and development. Early recognition of its importance is in Bradford, L.P., J.R. Gibb, and K.D. Benne. *T-Group Theory and Laboratory Methods.* New York: Wiley, 1964; Torbert, W.R. *Learning from Experience, Toward Consciousness.* New York: Columbia University Press, 1972, pp. 8-19; and Blake, R.R., and J.S. Mouton. *Making Experience Work: The Grid Approach to Critique.* New York: McGraw-Hill, 1978.

133        23        A study showing consequences stemming from interactions between two people with the same or different Grid styles engaged in bargaining is reported by Cummings, Harnett, and Stevens. They found that in bargaining situations, two 9,1's pitted against each other produce a stalemate 80% of the time. A 9,1-oriented person against a 1,9-oriented person wins 90% of the time; a 9,1-oriented person against a 9,9-oriented person, the 9,1 wins 50% of the time. A 1,9-oriented person against a 1,9-oriented person results in a stalemate 80% of the time; a 1,9-oriented person against a 9,9-oriented person results in the 9,9-oriented person winning. Quick agreement is reached when a 9,9 is against a 9,9. See Cummings, L.L., D.L. Harnett, and O.J. Stevens. "Risk, Fate, Conciliation and Trust: An International Study of Attitudinal Differences Among Executives." *Academy of Management Journal,* 14, (1971) pp. 285-304.

138        25        The original research on career success is reported in Blake, R.R., and J.S. Mouton. *The Managerial Grid.* Houston, Texas: Gulf Publishing, 1964, pp. 225-246. See also Hall, J. "To Achieve or Not: The Manager's Choice." *California Management Review,* 18, No. 4 (1976).

| Page | Line |
|------|------|
| 139 | 6 |

Descriptions and comparisons of most and least effective leaders demonstrate that 9,9-oriented managers are chosen for the former and 1,1-oriented managers for the latter. See Sank, L. "Effective and Ineffective Managerial Traits Obtained as Naturalistic Descriptions From Executive Members From a Super-Corporation." *Personnel Psychology*, 27, No. 3 (1974) pp. 423-434.

### Chapter 10

| | |
|------|------|
| 140 | 15 |

"We" is a word that characterizes the 9,9 approach to management better than any other. "Confronted with this situation, *we* decided to take this action. Once a goal has been agreed on, *we* coordinate our efforts toward reaching it. The problem was there but no one really understood what it was until *we* got together and swapped notes." "We" is a 9,9 word. It specifies mutuality, jointness, shared responsibilities, coordinated effort—all indicators of a voluntary "joining up."

What words compare with it? "Them" is one, used when subordinates point to bosses who are not "us." *I* is another, and it is used in the context of "you." "I want you to do that . . ."; an unbalanced relationship of direction and compliance.

One of the challenges of management is to get relationships off a "them, I-you" basis, and on to a "we" approach where the several who can contribute to solving problems feel a "we-ness" responsibility for doing so. "We" by no means implies that everything is dealt with by everyone all the time; however, in complex managerial work, "we" may mean something very different, such as each of us works separately, but we're tied together by common objectives.

| | |
|------|------|
| 142 | 31 |

Communication and problem solving networks studied experimentally usually represent one-to-one interpersonal links, rather than one-to-all links as described here. However, in the "chain" of "circular" nets, an individual is able to interact with at least two people in a reciprocal fashion. The actual one-to-all pattern, where every person can interact with all others is usually not considered. See Bavelas, A. "Communication Patterns in Task-Oriented Groups." *Journal of the Acoustical Society of America*, 22, (1950) pp. 725-730. See also Cartwright, D., and A. Zander, eds. *Group Dynamics—Research and Theory*, 2nd ed. Evanston, Ill.: Row, Peterson, 1960; Leavitt, H.J. "Some Effects of Certain Communication Patterns on Group Performance." *Journal of Abnormal & Social Psychology*, 46, (1951) pp. 38-50; Kelley, H.H. "Communication in Experimentally Created

| | | |

Hierarchies." *Human Relations*, 4, (1951) pp. 39-56; Heise, G.A., and G.A. Miller. "Problem Solving by Small Groups Using Various Communication Nets." *Journal of Abnormal & Social Psychology*, 46, (1951) pp. 327-336. See also, Vroom, V.H., and P.W. Yetton. *Leadership and Decision-Making.* Pittsburgh: University of Pittsburgh Press, 1973; Tannenbaum, R., I.R. Weschler, and F. Massarik. *Leadership and Organization: A Behavioral Science Approach.* New York McGraw-Hill, 1961, pp. 98-100.

144   25   The first differentiation as to the pertinence of one-alone, one-to-one, one-to-all in teamwork appears in Blake, R.R., and J.S. Mouton. "Three Strategies for Exercising Authority: One-Alone, One-to-One, One-to-All." *Personnel Administration*, 27, No. 4 (1964) pp. 3-5, 18-21.

144   26   Two basic principles underlie this table. One is decision quality. The other is decision acceptance or implementation.
*Quality.* If a decision of quality can be reached by one person managing alone, then, with only one exception, involvement of others is wasteful because they can add nothing to its quality. The exception is when consultation with one or several others would contribute to their development.
*Acceptance or Implementation.* Implementation of a decision has two aspects. One is understanding of how to do it. The other is readiness of one or several persons to carry it out. If understanding and readiness can be assumed, then a one/alone decision can be made and announced. If not, then others should be involved. See Maier, N.R.F. *Psychology in Industry*, 2nd ed. New York: Houghton Mifflin Company, 1955, pp. 165-171; Blake, R.R., and J.S. Mouton. *The Managerial Grid.* Houston: Gulf Publishing, 1964; Vroom, V.H., and P.W. Yetton. *Leadership and Decision-Making.* Pittsburgh: University of Pittsburgh Press, 1973, pp. 10-58; and Heller, F.A. *Managerial Decision-Making.* London: Tavistock Publications Limited, 1971, pp. 53-55.

148   39   In identifying *generativity* as a significant life stage, Erikson meant what development of subordinates has come to stand for in the 9,9 context. He says, "...Generativity is primarily the interest in establishing and guiding the next generation." See Erikson, E.H. *Childhood and Society.* New York: W.W. Norton & Company, 1950, p. 231.

## Chapter 11

157   28   An inclusive study of strategies of counseling and consultation is contained in Blake, R.R., and J.S.

| Page | Line | |
|------|------|--|
| | | Mouton. *Consultation.* Reading, Mass.: Addison-Wesley, 1976. |
| 157 | 29 | An alternative view of helping relationships is formulated in Kolb, D.A., and R.E. Boyatzis. "On the Dynamics of the Helping Relationship." In D.A. Kolb, I.M. Rubin, and J.M. McIntyre, eds., *Organizational Psychology: A Book of Readings.* Englewood Cliffs, N.J.: Prentice-Hall, Inc., 1971, pp. 339-355. |
| 158 | 35 | Early descriptions of the acceptant approach to industrial counseling come from Roethlisberger, F.J., and W.J. Dickson. *Management and the Worker.* Cambridge: Harvard University Press, 1939. A similar application in the academic setting is described by Rogers, C.R. *Counseling and Psychotherapy.* Boston: Houghton Mifflin, 1942. |
| 159 | 1 | From Consultation Seminar Materials. Austin, Tex.: Scientific Methods, Inc., 1975. Reproduced by permission. |
| 159 | 38 | A description of the catalytic mode of consulting is provided by Schein, E.H. *Process Consultation: Its Role in Organization Development.* Reading, Mass.: Addison-Wesley, 1969. |
| 160 | 3 | From Consultation Seminar Materials, Austin, Tex.: Scientific Methods, Inc., 1975. Reproduced by permission. |
| 161 | 2 | The use of confrontation to clarify value conflicts is described by Ellis, A. *Reason and Emotion in Psychotherapy.* New York: Lyle Stuart, 1962. |
| 161 | 11 | From Consultation Seminar Materials. Austin, Tex.: Scientific Methods, Inc., 1975. Reproduced by permission. |
| 162 | 1 | Prescriptive consultation in the industrial setting is described by Levinson, H., J. Molinari, and A.G. Spohn. *Organization Diagnosis.* Cambridge, Mass.: Harvard University Press, 1972. |
| 162 | 6 | From Consultation Seminar Materials. Austin, Tex.: Scientific Methods, Inc., 1975. Reproduced by permission. |
| 162 | 34 | The theory-based mode of consultation is described in Blake, R.R., and J.S. Mouton. *Consultation.* Reading, Mass.: Addison-Wesley, 1976, pp. 378-385. |
| 163 | 6 | From Consultation Seminar Materials. Austin, Tex.: Scientific Methods, Inc., 1975. Reproduced by permission. |
| 164 | 14 | The contrast of managerial Grid styles with counseling modes pictured here is amplified in Blake, R.R., and J.S. Mouton. *Consultation.* Reading, Mass.: Addison-Wesley, 1976, pp. 441-467. |

| Page | Line | |
|------|------|---|
| | | *Organizational Dynamics,* Spring (1974) pp. 54-65. See also "Steinberg's: People Are the Pulse." *Food Topics,* 22, No. 7 (1967) pp. 9-23; Clasen, E.A. "Blake in the Corporate Bloodstream." *Proceedings:* National American Wholesale Grocers' Association, Executive Conference, September (1966) pp. 37-39; Cooper, B. "Management Training—How to Make it Pay." *Statist,* October (1966) pp. 982-983; Foster, G. "Making Managers—Executives on the Grid." *Management Today,* April (1966) pp. 33-38. Foster, G. "The Managerial Grid in Action at Ward's." *Stores,* 48, (1966) pp. 42-44; Lefton, R.E., and V.R. Buzzota. "Supervisors Can Mix Amity and Authority." *The Modern Hospital,* 107, No. 4 (1966) pp. 129-132; Albers, C.H. "Strengthening the Links in a Hotel Chain." In A.J. Marrow, ed., *The Failure of Success.* New York: AMACOM, 1972, pp. 289-290. |
| 180 | 2 | The concept of the unit of change is discussed in Lippitt, R., J. Watson, and B. Westley. *The Dynamics of Planned Change.* New York: Harcourt, Brace, 1958; Cartwright, D. "Achieving Change in People: Some Applications of Group Dynamics Theory." *Human Relations,* 4, (1951) pp. 381-392; Lewin, K. *Field Theory in Social Science.* New York: Harper, 1951; Lewin, K. "Behavior and Development as a Function of the Total Situation." In L. Carmichael, ed., *Manual of Child Psychology.* New York: Wiley, 1946; Lewin, K. "Frontiers in Social Science." In D. Cartwright, ed., *Group Dynamics.* New York: Harper, 1951. (See Chapter 7 of this book for a more complete discussion and review of Lewin's work.) A comprehensive review of strategies for individual manager development is in Craig, R.L., and L.R. Bittel, eds., *Training and Development Handbook.* New York: McGraw-Hill, Inc., 1967, pp. 363-395. |
| 180 | 14 | Blake, R.R., and J.S. Mouton. *Corporate Excellence Through Grid Organization Development.* Houston: Gulf Publishing Company, 1968, p. 73. For a more extended treatment of the unit of development, see pp. 68-74. |
| 182 | 9 | For a description of the goals and activities of a Grid seminar, see Blake, R.R., and J.S. Mouton, ibid., pp. 34-66. |
| 182 | 13 | A case study of Grid organization development which included wage personnel appears in Blake, R.R., J.S. Mouton, R.L. Sloma, and B.P. Loftin. "A Second Breakthrough in Organization Development." *California Management Review,* 11, No. 1 (1968) pp. 73-78. |
| 182 | 37 | One-week seminars are open to the public. These sessions enable participants to explore Managerial Grid |

concepts in depth. Scientific Methods, Inc., Box 195, Austin, Texas, presents Grid seminars in the United States, Canada, England, The Netherlands, and its associate organizations in Australasia, Austria, Brazil, Colombia, Finland, Germany, Japan, Mexico, Pakistan, South Africa, Switzerland, and Venezuela, conducted in the language of the country.

Prior to the beginning of Phase 1, all organization members study this book and answer training instruments of a quantitative nature. In total, approximately 30 hours of prework are completed.

An examination of the impact of Phase 1 Grid seminars on behavior and performance in an electronics firm is reported by Frampton, T.J. "Good Managers Are Made." *Electronic Design*, August (1973) pp. 77-79. A comparable description in a marketing oriented company is by Pierro, H.P., Jr. "Applying the Managerial Grid to a Real-Life Sales Situation." *Training and Development Journal*, 27, No. 11 (1973) pp. 20-27. See also Clark, G. "Managerial Grid Training: An Application in ICI Pharmaceuticals Division." In M.L. Berger, and P.J. Berger, eds., *Group Training Techniques*. Essex, Eng.: Gower Press (1972) pp. 49-65; and Prindle, J. "The Quest for 9,9." *The Credit Union Executive*, 2, No. 2 (1972) pp. 8-13. Use of the Grid in the training of professional personnel in a mental hospital is described by Kreinik, P.S., and N.J. Colarelli. "Managerial Grid: Human Relations Training for Mental Hospital Personnel." *Human Relations*, 24, No. 1 (1971) pp. 91-104. See also "Stretched on the Grid." *Shell Magazine*, 50, No. 733 (1970) pp. 6-10. Grid organization development in a military context is described in Naval Electronics Laboratory Center, U.S. Navy. "Organization Development at NELC." *Trade Talk*, 3, No. 7 (1969) pp. 3-7, and "OD Continues at NELC, San Diego." *Trade Talk*, 4, No. 2 (1970) pp. 3-4. Quantitative research evaluating the impact of Phases 1 and 2 in a large high-technology company is reported by Hart, H.A. "The Grid Appraised—Phases 1 and 2." *Personnel*, September-October (1974) pp. 44-59; Texas Instruments Corporation. "Grid Objectives Support Achievement of TI Goals." *The TI World*, 25, No. 2 (1968) p. 1; Morrison, H.R.W. "Object: Managerial Perfection." *Board of Trade Journal*, April 1968 pp. 2-5; Davies, R. "The Grid—A Personal Experience." *Industrial Training International*, 5, No. 4 (1970) p. 175; Hart, H.A. "The Grid on a Grand Scale." *Industrial Training International*, 6, No. 12 (1971) p. 364; Bird, J. "Management and the Managerial Grid." *Business Review*, 10, No. 7 (1967) pp. 283-286; Brolly, M. "The

**Page**        **Line**

Managerial Grid." *Occupational Psychology*, 41, (1967) pp. 231-237. Kronborg, R.H. "The Managerial Grid Concept." *Hospital Administration*, 15, No. 2 (1967) pp. 17-20; McCormick, A.D. "Management Development at British-American Tobacco." *Management Today*, June 1967 pp. 126-128; Merck & Company. "The Managerial Grid." *Merck Review*, 28, No. 1 (1967) pp. 16-23; National Foremen's Institute. "The Managerial Grid Goes Into Action." *Employee Relations Bulletin*, 1034, January 25, 1967, pp. 1-6; National Foremen's Institute. "The Managerial Grid." *Executive Bulletin*, 269, January 15, 1967, pp. 1-5. Malouf, L.G. "Managerial Grid Evaluated." *Training and Development Journal*, 20, No. 3 (1966) pp. 6-15; Owen, G. "Bringing Personal Conflicts Into the Open." *Financial Times*, April 28, 1966; "The Principles of Successful Man Management." *Rydge's Management Service*, 1, No. 2 (1966) pp. 1-15; Marsh, A. "An Introduction to the Managerial Grid." *Industrial Welfare*, October 1965 pp. 256-259; Morrison, H. "Towards 9,9." *Keeping Track*, 8, No. 4 (1965) pp. 16-17; Portis, B. "Management Training for Organization Development." *The Business Quarterly*, 30, No. 2 (1965) pp. 44-54; Robertson, W. "The Managerial Grid." *Monetary Times*, 5, No. 8 (1965) pp. 12-20 and No. 9 pp. 39-45; Robertson, B. "A New Way to Develop Management Resources." *Canadian Transportation*, August 1965, pp. 18-23; Young Presidents' Organization. "The Managerial Grid." *YPO Enterprise*, 15, No. 5 (1965) pp. 8-9; Blake, R.R., J.S. Mouton, L.B. Barnes, and L.E. Greiner. "Breakthrough in Organization Development." *Harvard Business Review*, 42, No. 6 (1964) pp. 133-135; Blake, R.R., and J.S. Mouton. "Improving Organizational Problem Solving Through Increasing the Flow and Utilization of New Ideas." *Training Directors Journal*, 17, No. 9 (1963) pp. 48-57 and No. 10 pp. 38-54.

183        21        Blake, R.R., J.S. Mouton, L.B. Barnes, and L.E. Greiner, op. cit.

184        29        For a more detailed examination of the rationale underlying seminar composition and administration and the six phases of OD, see Blake, R.R., and J.S. Mouton. *Corporate Excellence Through Grid Organization Development*, op. cit., pp. 301-308.

186        33        A comparison of alternative strategies of team building is presented in Blake, R.R., and J.S. Mouton. "Group and Organizational Team Building: A Theoretical Model for Intervening." In C.L. Cooper, ed., *Theories of Group Processes*. Chichester, Sussex, England: John Wiley & Sons Ltd., 1975, pp. 103-129. See also Simmonds, G.R. "Organization Develop-

| Page | Line | |
|------|------|---|
| | | ment: A Key to Future Growth." *Personnel Administration,* 30, No. 1 (1967) pp. 19-24; and Blake, R.R., J.S. Mouton, and M.G. Blansfield. "How Executive Team Training Can Help You." *Journal of the American Society of Training Directors,* 16, No. 1 (1962) pp. 3-11. |
| 187 | 5 | An experiment on communication in a three-level hierarchy setting is reported by Blake, R.R., and J.S. Mouton. "Improving Organizational Problem Solving Through Increasing the Flow and Utilization of New Ideas." *Training Directors Journal,* 17, No. 9 (1963) pp. 48-57 and No. 10 pp. 38-54. |
| 188 | 27 | Strategies and case study applications of Phase 3 to relieve intergroup cleavages are presented in Blake, R.R., H.A. Shepard, and J.S. Mouton. *Managing Intergroup Conflict in Industry.* Houston: Gulf, 1964; McGill Industrial Relations Centre. " 'Dialog': A Steinberg Experiment." *McGill Industrial Relations Centre Review,* Fall 1967 p. 3; and Blake, R.R., and J.S. Mouton. "Intergroup Therapy." *International Journal of Social Psychiatry,* 8, No. 3 (1962) pp. 196-198. |
| 195 | 32 | Figure 13-3 from Blake, R.R., and J.S. Mouton. *Corporate Excellence Through Grid Organization Development,* op. cit., p. 75. Conditions favorable for successful organization development are described in more detail, ibid., pp. 67-91. |
| 196 | 2 | Man-based, as contrasted with systematic OD, is an alternate approach to increasing organization effectiveness. See Bennis, W.G. *Organizational Development: Background and Prospects.* Reading, Mass.: Addison-Wesley, 1969; Beckhard, R. *Organizational Development: Strategies and Models.* Reading, Mass.: Addison-Wesley, 1969; Schein, E.H. *Process Consultation in Organizational Development.* Reading, Mass.: Addison-Wesley, 1969; Walton, R. *Interpersonal Peacemaking: Confrontations and Third Party Interventions.* Reading, Mass.: Addison-Wesley, 1969; Lawrence, P., and J.W. Lorsch. *Organizational Intervention.* Reading, Mass.: Addison-Wesley, 1969; and Harrison, R. "Choosing the Depth of Organizational Intervention." *Journal of Applied Behavioral Science,* 6, No. 2 (1970) pp. 181-202. The Likert approach uses survey research and data feedback as the mechanism for shifting perceptions within an organization of how it is performing relative to how it might, were it to be managed in a different way. The Likert approach is close to systematic OD, yet it does not involve managers in learning a comprehensive theory nor a programmed sequence of interventions that evaluate all significant |

variables of organization. See Likert, R., and J.G. Likert. *New Ways of Managing Conflict.* New York: McGraw-Hill, 1976; and Likert, R. *The Human Organization.* New York: McGraw-Hill, 1967. See also Bowers, D.G., and J.L. Franklin. "Survey-Guided Development: Using Human Resources Measurement in Organizational Change." *Journal of Contemporary Business,* 1, No. 33 (1972) pp. 24-26.

Other representative work which describes additional approaches to development include Lippitt, R., J. Watson, and B. Westley. *The Dynamics of Planned Change.* New York: Harcourt, Brace, 1958; Lippitt, G.L. *Organization Renewal.* New York: Appleton-Century-Crofts, 1969; Nadler, L. *Developing Human Resources.* Houston: Gulf Publishing Company, 1970; Miles, M.B., and R.A. Schmuck. "Improving Schools Through Organization Development: An Overview." In R.A. Schmuck, and M.B. Miles, eds., *Organization Development in Schools.* Palo Alto, Calif.: National Press Books, 1971, pp. 1-27; Golden, W.P. "On Becoming a Trainer." In W.G. Dyer, ed., *Modern Theory and Method in Group Training.* New York: Van Nostrand Reinhold, 1972, pp. 3-29; Fordyce, J.K., and R. Weil. *Managing with People: A Manager's Handbook of Organization Development Methods.* Reading, Mass.: Addison-Wesley, 1971; Gibb, J.R. "TORI Theory: Consultantless Team-Building." *Journal of Contemporary Business,* 1, No. 3 (1972) pp. 33-41; Davis, S.A. "An Organic Problem-Solving Method of Organizational Change." *Journal of Applied Behavioral Science,* 3, No. 1 (1967) pp. 3-21; Levinson, H. *The Great Jackass Fallacy.* Boston: Harvard University, 1973; Burke, W.W., ed., *Contemporary Organization Development: Conceptual Orientations and Interventions.* Washington, D.C.: NTL Institute for Applied Behavioral Science, 1972; Crockett, W.J. "Team Building—One Approach to Organizational Development." *Journal of Applied Behavioral Science,* 6, No. 3 (1970) pp. 291-306; French, W. "Organization Development: Objectives, Assumptions, and Strategies." *California Management Review,* 12, No. 2 (1969) p. 26; Berger, M., and P. Berger, eds., *Group Training Techniques.* Epping: Gower Press, 1972; Jaques, E. "Interpretative Group Discussion as a Method of Facilitating Social Change: A Progress Report on the Use of Group Methods in the Investigation and Resolution of Social Problems." *Human Relations,* 1, No. 4 (1948) pp. 533-549; Jones, M. *Social Psychiatry: A Study of Therapeutic Communities.* London: Tavistock, 1952; Bennis, W.G., K.D. Benne, and R. Chin, eds. *The Planning of Change: Readings in the Applied Behavioral Sciences.* New York: Holt,

Rinehart and Winston, 1961; Margulies, N., and A.P. Raia, eds. *Organizational Development: Values, Process, and Technology.* New York: McGraw-Hill, 1972; Argyris, C. *Management and Organization Development: The Path from XA to YB.* New York: McGraw-Hill, 1971; Bradford, L.P., and J.B. Harvey. "Dealing with Dysfunctional Organization Myths." *Training and Development Journal,* 24, No. 9 (1970) p. 2; Enright, J.B. "On the Playing Fields of Synanon." In L. Blank, G.B. Gottsegen, and M.G. Gottsegen, *Confrontation: Encounters in Self and Interpersonal Awareness.* New York: Macmillan, 1971; pp. 147-177; Herman, S.M. "A Gestalt Orientation to O.D." In W.W. Burke, ed., *Contemporary Organization Development: Conceptual Orientations and Interventions.* Washington, D.C.: NTL Institute for Applied Behavioral Science, 1972, pp. 69-86; Marrow, A.J. *Making Waves at Foggy Bottom.* Washington, D.C.: NTL Institute, 1974; Roberts, E.E. "The Technical Change Program." In A.J. Marrow, D.G. Bowers, and S.E. Seashore, eds., *Management by Participation.* New York: Harper & Row, 1967, pp. 76-87; Herzberg, F. *Work and the Nature of Man.* Cleveland: The World Publishing Company, 1966; Myers, M.S. "Who Are Your Motivated Workers?" *Harvard Business Review,* 42, No. 1 (1964) pp. 73-88; Trist, E.L., G.I. Susman, and G.R. Brown. "An Experiment in Autonomous Working in An American Underground Coal Mine." *Human Relations,* 30, No. 3 (1977) pp. 201-236.

196        6          Specialized problems of organization development, such as spinoffs and mergers, use the basic strategy described. See Blansfield, M.G., R.R. Blake, and J.S. Mouton. "The Merger Laboratory: A New Strategy for Bringing One Corporation into Another." *Training and Directors Journal,* 18, No. 5 (1964) pp. 2-10.

**Chapter 14**

203        23         Managerial Grid Seminar Data. Austin, Texas: Scientific Methods, Inc., 1976.

204        19         A demonstration of self-deception in another area involving students and executives in predictions of success in business games is seen in Larwood, L., and W. Whittaker. "Managerial Myopia: Self-Serving Biases in Organizational Planning." *Journal of Applied Psychology,* 62, No. 2 (1977) pp. 194-198.

204        22         A comprehensive study of the relationship between MAQ and Grid style is by Blake, R.R., and J.S. Mouton. *The Managerial Grid.* Gulf Publishing Company, 1964, pp. 225-246. See also Hall, J. "To Achieve or Not: The Manager's Choice." *California Management Review,* 18, No. 4 (1976).

| Page | Line |
|------|------|

## Chapter 15

209    3    A reconstruction of work from preliterate times to the present is contained in Blake, R.R., W.E. Avis, and J.S. Mouton. *Corporate Darwinism.* Houston: Gulf, 1966. Related studies are by Linton, R. *The Science of Man in the World Crisis.* New York: Columbia University Press, 1945; Titiev, M. *The Science of Man.* New York: Henry Holt and Company, 1954; Childe, V.G. *Man Makes Himself.* New York: The New American Library of World Literature, 1951; Heilbroner, R.L. *The Making of Economic Society.* Englewood Cliffs, N.J.: Prentice-Hall, Inc., 1962; Rostow, W.W. *The Stages of Economic Growth.* New York: Cambridge University Press, 1960; Riesman, D., N. Glazer, and R. Denney. *The Lonely Crowd.* Garden City, New York: Doubleday & Company, 1953; Weber, M. "Bureaucracy." In J.A. Litterer, ed., *Organizations: Structure and Behavior.* New York: John Wiley & Sons, Inc., 1963; Weber, M. *The Theory of Social and Economic Organization.* New York: Oxford University Press, 1947; Allen, L.A. "Leaders Who Fail Their Companies." *Business Horizons,* 8, No. 2 (1966) pp. 79-86; and Jennings, E.E. *The Executive: Autocrat, Bureaucrat, Democrat.* New York: Harper & Row, 1962. Most recent efforts to use evolutionary analysis for explaining the unfolding of work in modern society are by Lievegoed, B.C.J. *The Developing Organization.* London: Tavistock, 1973; and Greiner, L. "Patterns of Organizational Change." *Harvard Business Review,* 45, No. 3 (1967) pp. 119-130.

## Appendix

219      Reproduced by permission from Blake, R.R., and J.S. Mouton. "The Grid as a Comprehensive Framework for Analyzing Human Relationships." Austin, Texas: Scientific Methods, Inc., 1977.

231    8    Bales, R.F. *Personality and Interpersonal Behavior.* New York: Holt, Rinehart and Winston, 1970.

231    12    Schutz, W.C. *The Interpersonal Underworld* (originally titled *FIRO: A Three-Dimensional Theory of Interpersonal Behavior*). Palo Alto, Calif.: Science & Behavior Books, 1966.

231    14    Reddin, W.J. *Managerial Effectiveness 3-D.* New York: McGraw-Hill, 1970; and Hersey, P., and K.H. Blanchard. *Management of Organizational Behavior: Utilizing Human Resources,* 2nd ed. Englewood Cliffs, N.J.: Prentice-Hall, 1972.

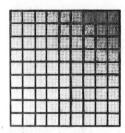

# Author Index

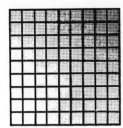

# Subject Index

To avoid confusion with Grid numbers, all page numbers in this index
*are in italics.*

- Achievement oriented management experience
- The capacity to supervise professional staff
- The ability to assess management training needs
- Commitment to high quality continuing management education
- Budget and marketing skills
- New Seminar development skills
- Relevant educational background (i.e. MBA, MPA, or related degrees)

Program Directors will be responsible for the management of an account composed of a diverse array of continuing management education programs, the supervision of support staff, and the development of new seminar offerings.

Interested candidates should send a detailed resume (including salary history and minimum acceptable salary requirement) with work-related references and a brief statement of career objectives to:

Program Manager
Kalmbach Management Center
1735 Washtenaw Avenue
Ann Arbor, Michigan 48109

Applications must be received by October 13, 1978.

A non-discriminatory, affirmative action employer

CENTRAL OFFICE SERVICES

*Jobs*

The
University
of Michigan

THE UNIVERSITY OF MICHIGAN 1817

**Invites application
for the position of
PROGRAM DIRECTOR
(Program Associate II)**

The Division of Management Education at the University of Michigan's Graduate School of Business Administration is currently seeking qualified applicants for responsible management positions in its expanding, non-degree continuing management education program. Candidates should have an interest in both business operations and management training since the job offers a unique blend of both functions.